Baedeker's
Allianz Travel Guide
Rhine

W9-DAO-306

Baedeker's

Allianz 🏛 Travel Guide

Rhine

BAEDEKER STUTTGART

Imprint

151 illustrations
23 town plans, 22 graphic representations, 6 ground plans, 2 special plans, 2 special maps, 1 large panoramic map

Text:
Monika I. Baumgarten, Stuttgart

Editorial work:
Baedeker's editorial staff

English translation:
James Hogarth, Edinburgh

Layout:
Creativ GmbH, Ulrich Kolb, Stuttgart

General direction:
Dr. Peter H. Baumgarten, Baedeker Stuttgart

Cartography:
Ingenieurbüro für Kartographie Huber & Oberländer, Munich

Following the tradition established by Karl Baedeker in 1844, sights of particular interest as well as hotels and restaurants of particular quality are distinguished by ❖ one or ❖❖ two asterisks.

Only a selection of hotels and restaurants can be given; no reflection is implied, therefore, on establishments not included.

In a time of rapid change it is difficult to ensure that all the information given is entirely accurate and up to date; the possibility of error can never be totally eliminated. Although the publishers can accept no responsibility for inaccuracies and omissions, they are always grateful for corrections and suggestions for improvement (please write to: Baedeker, Kemnat, Marco-Polo-Zentrum, D-73760 Ostfildern; Germany).

2nd edition 1994

Copyright:
Karl Baedeker GmbH, Ostfildern (near Stuttgart)

Licensed user:
Mairs Geographischer Verlag GmbH & Co., Ostfildern (near Stuttgart)

Reproductions:
Gölz Repro-Service GmbH & Co. KG, Ludwigsburg

Printed by Mairs Graphische Betriebe GmbH & Co. KG., Ostfildern (near Stuttgart)

Bound by H. Wennberg GmbH, Vaihingen/Enz

Contents

Source of photographs:
Alsfasser (1), Ars Liturgica (1), Landesbildstelle Baden (1), Kurverwaltung Bad Säckingen (1), Baedeker-Archiv (15), H. Baedeker (1), Baier (1), Verkehrsverein Basel (3), Baumgarten (11), Benz (1), Stadt Bingen (1), Stadt Bonn (2), Brugger (2), Claus (1), Corzelius (3), Stadt Duisburg (1), Stadt Düsseldorf (3), Eith (1), Stadt Emmerich (1), Gauls (1), Groote (1), Hachette (1), Hinterwälder (1), Historia-Photo (11), Stadt Ingelheim (2), Stadtbibliothek Karlsruhe (1), Verkehrsverein Karlsruhe (1), Stadt Kehl (1), Stadt Koblenz (1), Köln-Düsseldorfer (37), Krupp (1), Liechtensteinische Fremdenverkehrszentrale (2), Verkehrsamt Linz (1), Mainauverwaltung (1), Gutenberg-Museum Mainz (1), Stadt Mainz (1), Verkehrsverein Mannheim (1), Mayer (1), Kur- und Verkehrsverwaltung Meersburg (1), Mühlbauer (2), Nahm (2), Stadt Neuss (1), Niederländisches Büro für Tourismus (3), Verkehrsverein Nierstein (1), Nohr (6), Stadt Remagen (1), Schädlich (1), Schneiders (1), Schweizerische Käseunion (1), Sperber (1), Stadt Speyer (1), Verkehrsverein Stein am Rhein (1), Rheinisches Landesmuseum Trier (1), Stadt Wesel (2), Stadt Wiesbaden (1), Stadt Worms (4), afx Xanten (1), Zettl (1).

Preface

This travel guide to the Rhine is one of the new generation of Baedeker guides.

Produced by Baedeker in association with the Allianz Versicherungs-AG, whose help has made the new conception possible, these pocket-sized guides, illustrated throughout in colour, are designed to meet the needs of the modern traveller: they are quick and easy to consult, with practical details set out in the margin alongside the main description.

This guide to the Rhine is the official guide of the KD German Rhine Line (Köln-Düsseldorfer Deutsche Rheinschiffahrt AG), which has long operated on the river with its fleet of cruise ships and comfortable passenger vessels. The link between Baedeker and the KD Line has a historical basis; for the year 1827, in which Karl Baedeker (1801–1859) opened his publishing house in Koblenz, was also the year in which the Prussian Rhine Steamship Line (Preussisch-Rheinische Dampfschiffahrts-Gesellschaft), founded in Cologne in 1826 and now known as the 'Köln-Düsseldorfer', or 'KD' for short, introduced its first regular passenger and express freight service on the Middle Rhine between Cologne and Mainz. In 1832 Karl Baedeker, in association with the Koblenz publishing house of Fr. Röhling, took over Professor J. A. Klein's "Handbook for Travellers: the Rhine from Mainz to Cologne", which had first appeared in 1828; and thereafter "Baedeker's Rhine" became a staple element in the firm's activities. Much altered and enlarged over the years, it went through 34 editions down to 1931; the first English edition was published in 1861, the 18th and last one in 1926.

The present guide is divided into four main parts: The first part gives a general account of the Rhine, its geographical, economic, political and historical significance, famous personalities associated with the river, and so on. The second part describes its course, going downstream from its sources to its mouths, devoting particular attention to the river between Basle and Rotterdam. The third part presents information about the towns and other places along the river, indicating their features of interest. The fourth part is devoted to practical information. Both the sights and the practical information are listed in alphabetical order.

Baedeker's Allianz travel guides are noted for their concentration on essentials and their convenience of use. They contain numerous specially drawn plans and coloured illustrations; and an integral part of this guide to the Rhine is a large panoramic map of the river.

We wish all users of this guide a profitable exploration of the Rhine and a pleasant cruise on the ships of the KD German Rhine Line!

Baedeker

Facts and Figures

General

Overall view

The Rhine is Europe's most important waterway and scenically its most attractive. It originates in the S.E. Swiss canton of Grisons, where the Vorderrhein and the Hinterrhein unite to form the Alpine Rhine (Alpenrhein). It then flows through Lake Constance (Bodensee), forms the Rhine Falls at Schaffhausen and continues on its way to Basle as the High Rhine (Hochrhein). At Basle it turns north and flows as the Upper Rhine (Oberrhein) through the Upper Rhine plain (Oberrheinische Tiefebene). Between Mainz and Bingen it follows a westerly course and then bears north-west through the Rhenish Uplands (Rheinisches Schiefergebirge) as the Middle Rhine (Mittelrhein), flanked by numerous old castles. Below Bonn it is known as the Lower Rhine (Niederrhein). Within the flat territory of the Netherlands it divides into a number of delta arms (notably the Lek and the Waal), which finally flow into the North Sea.

Length and catchment area

The river has a total length of some 1320 km and a catchment area of over 250,000 sq. km. Along with Lake Constance it forms a reservoir of drinking-water for a population of some 30 million.

European river

The Rhine can truly be described as an international river, since it traverses or borders no fewer than six countries: the Swiss Confederation, the Principality of Liechtenstein, the Republic of Austria, the Federal Republic of Germany, the French Republic and the Kingdom of the Netherlands.

Names

The origin of the name Rhine (German 'Rhein', originally also 'Rein') has not been definitely established; it is believed, however, to have been derived at an early period from a Germanic word cognate with the English 'run' (in the sense of 'flow'). To the Celts the river was known as 'Renos', to the Romans as 'Rhenus'; in Romansh it is 'Rein' or (as in Italian) 'Reno', in French 'Rhin', in Dutch 'Rijn'. It is familiarly referred to in German as 'Vater Rhein' ('Father Rhine').

Headstreams: Vorderrhein and Hinterrhein

The principal headstreams of the Rhine are the Vorderrhein (Romansh Rein Anteriur; length 68 km), which flows out of the little Lake Toma (Lai da Tuma; alt. 2345 m), at the foot of Mt Badus (2928 m) some 3 km south of the Oberalp Pass, and the Hinterrhein (Romansh Rein Posteriur; length 65 km), which rises some 35 km to the south-east in the névé between the Rheinquellhorn (3200 m) and the Rheinwaldhorn (Mt Adula; 3402 m), some 8 km west of the San Bernardino Pass (now bypassed by a tunnel). Both of these rivers are soon reinforced by numerous mountain streams and flows of melt-water from glaciers.
The main tributaries of the Vorderrhein, all coming from the south, are the Medelser Rhein (Rein de Medel), Somvixer Rhein

◀ *Loreley Rock: famous defile on the Middle Rhine*

General

(Rein de Sumvitg), Glogn (with its tributary stream the Valser Rhein) and Rabiusa, of the Hinterrhein the Averser Rhein (from south-east; drawing most of its water from the Reno di Lei and Madriser Rhein) and Albula (from east). Some 10 km above Chur (Cuera/Cuoira), capital of the canton of Grisons, at Reichenau/Tamins, the Vorderrhein and Hinterrhein join to form the Rhine proper, which from this point to Lake Constance is also known as the Alpine Rhine (Alpenrhein).

Alpine Rhine
(Alpenrhein)

The Alpine Rhine (length 100 km) at first flows north-west past Chur, where it is joined by the Plessur (from south-east), and then turns north into a wide valley filled with glacial deposits. At Landquart it is joined by the river Landquart, coming from the east, and at Bad Ragaz by the Tamina, coming from the south-west. Near Sargans (canton of St Gallen) the frontiers of Switzerland, Austria and the little principality of Liechtenstein meet on the Rhine, which thereafter marks the whole of the principality's western boundary. Beyond this the Alpine Rhine forms the frontier between Switzerland and Austria, with the exception of a short stretch round Diepoldsau. A short distance downstream from the northern tip of Liechtenstein the Ill flows into the Rhine from the south-east. At the frontier town of St Margarethen the Old Rhine, still marking the frontier, turns north-west and flows into Lake Constance at Altenrhein, within the town of Rorschach. Much of its water, however, is carried northward into the lake by a canal cut through Austrian territory at the turn of the 19th century which flows into the Fussacher Bucht, 6 km west of Bregenz, capital of the province of Vorarlberg.

Lake Constance
(Bodensee)

Lake Constance (known in German as the Bodensee) lies under the northern edge of the Alps, bounded by Germany, Switzerland and Austria, though the actual frontier lines remain largely un-demarcated. With an area of 545 sq. km and a maximum length of 76 km it is by far the largest German lake; it is the third largest lake in Central Europe, coming after Lake Balaton in Hungary and Lake Geneva, and the second largest of the lakes fringing the Alps.

From south-east to north-west Lake Constance is divided into the Obersee, extending from Bregenz Bay to Eichhorn (Konstanz), and the much narrower, shorter and shallower Überlinger See (between the Bodanrück and Linzgau) and Untersee, which is separated from the main lake by a strip of land traversed at Konstanz by the Rhine. At its northern end the Untersee is split into two 'fingers', the Gnadensee (between the island of Reichenau and the Bodanrück) and the Zeller See (in Radolfzell Bay between the Höri and Mettnau peninsulas).

In each of the three parts of the lake there is an island of some size. Near the east end of the Obersee is the island town of Lindau, at the south end of the Überlinger See the island of flowers, Mainau, and in the Untersee the larger vegetable-growing island of Reichenau with its historic and artistic treasures.

The very variable flow of the Alpine Rhine and the many other rivers flowing into Lake Constance lead to considerable variations in the level of the lake. Every year the Obersee receives some 4 million cubic metres of river-borne deposits, mainly contributed by the Rhine.

The Rhine carries the largest inflow into Lake Constance and the largest outflow from the lake. As the Alpine Rhine it flows into the lake in a long projecting delta at its south-east end, pursues its course along the Obersee, traverses the town of Konstanz as the Lake Rhine (Seerhein; 4 km long, 200–500 m wide) and flows out of the Untersee on Swiss territory at Stein am Rhein as the High Rhine (Hochrhein). The official measurement of distances on the Rhine begins at Konstanz (km 0 = middle of the bridge over the river).

Lake Rhine (Seerhein)

After leaving Lake Constance the High Rhine follows a westerly course, with considerable windings, to Basle, a distance of 140 km. Apart from three short stretches (below Stein am Rhein, within the town of Schaffhausen and between the mouth of the Thur and Eglisau) it marks the frontier between Switzerland (south bank) and the German Federal Republic (north bank).

High Rhine (Hochrhein)

Some 20 km downstream from the west end of Lake Constance and 3 km south-west of the cantonal capital of Schaffhausen, at the town of Neuhausen, the Rhine surges over a ledge of Jurassic limestone 150 m across and between 15 and 25 m high, with two higher rocks rising up from it in the middle of the river. These are the mightiest falls in Central Europe.

Rhine Falls (Rheinfall)

The valley of the High Rhine, bounded on the north by the hills of the Black Forest and on the south by the outliers of the Swiss Jura, offers a tract of very agreeable scenery. With its irregular gradient the river flows relatively fast, harnessed by a number of hydroelectric stations to provide power. The river is navigable only from Rheinfelden (km 149 from Konstanz).

The main left-bank tributaries of the High Rhine are the Thur, Töss, Glatt, Aare (with its tributary streams the Limmat and the Reuss), Ergolz and Birs; the major tributaries on the right bank are the Biber, Durach, Wutach (with its tributary stream the Schlücht), Alb, Murg and Wehra.

Tributaries of the High Rhine

During its course from the sources to Basle (km 165–169) the Rhine drains some two-thirds of the territory of Switzerland,

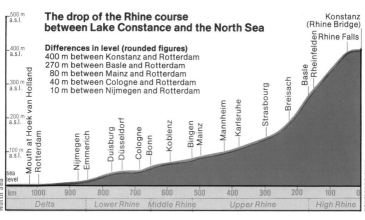

The drop of the Rhine course between Lake Constance and the North Sea

Differences in level (rounded figures)
400 m between Konstanz and Rotterdam
270 m between Basle and Rotterdam
80 m between Mainz and Rotterdam
40 m between Cologne and Rotterdam
10 m between Nijmegen and Rotterdam

General

High Rhine
(continued)

including over 500 sq. km of glaciers. At Basle an average of over 1000 cu. m of Rhine water per second flows northward out of Switzerland.

Upper Rhine
(Oberrhein)

At Basle the Rhine turns north and, now known as the Upper Rhine (358 km), flows sluggishly through the Upper Rhine Plain, canalised for considerable sections of its course. Between Basle and Lauterbourg it forms the frontier between France and Germany.

The Upper Rhine Plain, a rift valley between 30 and 40 km wide which came into being in the Oligocene, is bounded on the east by the Black Forest, Kraichgau and Odenwald, on the west by the Vosges, the Haardt range and the hills of the northern Palatinate. The rocks which emerge along the borders of the valley are overlaid in the plain by deposits dating from the latest period in the earth's development; and the loess beds of the Pleistocene have favoured the development of fertile fruit- and wine-growing areas (Markgräflerland, Alsace, Ortenau, Deutsche Weinstrasse, Bergstrasse, Rheinhessen).

The regulation of the Upper Rhine which was begun by J.G. Tulla in 1817 has reduced the danger of flooding, made the low-lying land bordering the river productive and fertile, and facilitated the movement of shipping; but, on the negative side, it has lowered the water table and largely destroyed the old natural water meadows.

Grand Canal d'Alsace
(Rheinseitenkanal)

Between Basle and Strasbourg the larger vessels sailing on the Rhine use the Grand Canal d'Alsace (Rheinseitenkanal), which has a link with the Rhine-Rhône Canal (Canal du Rhône au Rhin). In the southern section between Village-Neuf and Breisach (53 km; wholly canalised) there are four dams with hydroelectic stations, at Kembs, Ottmarsheim, Fessenheim and Vogelgrün; and between Breisach and Strasbourg there are four other dams and power stations, at Marckolsheim, Rhinau, Gerstheim and Strasbourg, each bypassed by a navigation canal. Farther downstream there are two further dams and power stations, at Gambsheim and Iffezheim.

The main port in the southern part of the Upper Rhine, apart from Basle, is Strasbourg, situated at the end of the Rhine-Marne Canal (Canal de la Marne au Rhin).

Tributaries of the
Upper Rhine

The Upper Rhine has two large tributaries on the right bank, the Neckar and the Main (Rhine-Main-Danube Canal in course of construction); other right-bank tributaries are the Wiese, Kander, Elz (Leopoldskanal), Kinzig, Rench and Murg.
The principal left-bank tributaries are the Ill, Moder, Sauer and Lauter.

Rhine-Neckar area

The main economic centres of the German Upper Rhine are Karlsruhe, the twin towns of Mannheim and Ludwigshafen at the junction of the Rhine and the Neckar, and, near the junction of the Rhine and the Main, the towns of Mainz and Wiesbaden,

Rhine-Main area

at the western end of the important Rhine-Main economic region.

Rheingau

At Mainz the Rhine takes a sharp turn westward and flows through the most northerly part of the Upper Rhine Plain to

Burg Rheinstein, above Trechtingshausen

Burg Stahleck, above Bacharach

Burg Rheinfels, above Sankt Goar

Burg Stolzenfels, near Koblenz

General

Rheingau (continued)

Bingen. To the north, sheltered by the outliers of the Taunus, are the vineyards of the Rheingau, while along the south bank of the river is the Mainz basin, a Tertiary depression bordered

Rheinhessen

by the uplands of Rheinhessen. How far the water of the Rhine reached in prehistoric times is shown by the fossiliferous beds to be seen in sand and marl pits at Gau-Algesheim, Sprendlingen and Weinheim (Alzey).

Middle Rhine
(Mittelrhein)

The Rhine, having turned west at Mainz when faced with the barrier of the Rheingau hills, changes direction again at Bingen and, as the Middle Rhine (128 km), flows north-west through the Rhenish Uplands in a narrow gorge-like valley. Here it has carved its course against the grain of the hard quartzite rocks, separating the Hunsrück on the left bank from the Taunus on the right bank. The mountains were thrust upwards from the Middle Tertiary onwards, while the Rhine cut its way in stages into an existing trough, creating a terraced landscape; gravel resulting from this process can accordingly be found at various different levels.

Between Bingen and St Goar the relatively steep gradient and the narrowness of the river present particular difficulties for shipping. Some stretches which in earlier times were very dangerous – the passage through the Binger Loch ('Bingen Hole'), past the famed Loreley Rock near St Goarshausen and at St Goar – have been made easier by blasting away various projecting rocks, dredging out rock detritus and creating new shipping channels which are in effect canals within the river; and at certain blind spots traffic is regulated by warning signs.

Romantic Rhine

In the more open stretches of the valley between the narrower passages there is room for human settlement, vineyards and fruit-growing. Combined with the numerous castles and castle ruins picturesquely crowning the steep hillsides and with the succession of islands in the river, this produces a constantly changing scenic pattern. Along both banks of the Middle Rhine run very busy railway lines and roads, much used by tourists and holidaymakers: on the left bank B 9, here known as the 'Rheingoldstrasse' (alluding to the story of the Nibelungs); on the right bank B 42, here known as the 'Loreley-Burgenstrasse' ('road of the Loreley and the castles').

Neuwied Basin

Beyond Koblenz, where the Mosel (Moselle) flows into the Rhine at the Deutsches Eck ('German Corner'), the valley opens up into the small Neuwied Basin (Neuwieder Becken), a Tertiary rift in the slates of the Rhenish Uplands which has been filled with fluvial deposits and volcanic ejecta. Along the Rhine busy industrial towns have grown up, while the hinterland of the left bank and the Maifeld uplands, an area of transition to the volcanic Eifel, are predominantly agricultural.

Siebengebirge

Shortly before the river enters the Lower Rhine Plain there rises on the right bank an outlier of the Westerwald, the group of hills, consisting mainly of volcanic detritus, known as the Siebengebirge (alt. up to 460 m), which is believed to take its name from German 'siefen' (= water-bearing valleys). With its rich variety of form this range of hills (the best known peaks being the Drachenfels, Petersberg and Grosser Ölberg) forms a magnificent conclusion to the middle section of the Rhine; it marks, too, the northern limit of wine-growing on the Rhine.

View of the Siebengebirge (on the left the Drachenfels)

The left-bank tributaries of the Middle Rhine are the Nahe, Mosel (Moselle) and Ahr, the valleys of which are noted for their wines. On the right bank there are the Wisper, Lahn and Wied.

Tributaries of the Middle Rhine

Below Bonn the Rhine enters the Cologne Lowlands (Kölner Bucht), the southern part of the extensive Lower Rhine Plain. The result of a rift in a mountain range, this is an area of gently rolling country; only to the south-west of Cologne, in the so-called Vorgebirge, is there a more marked pattern of relief. The seams of brown coal laid down here in the Middle Tertiary, covered only with a thin layer of earth and worked by opencast methods, are the thickest (over 100 m) known in the world.

Lower Rhine (Niederrhein)

On the Lower Rhine (203 km long) a series of important cities have developed over the centuries, playing an important part in the cultural and economic life of Germany: Bonn, capital of the German Federal Republic and birthplace of Beethoven; the Roman foundation and cathedral city of Cologne (Köln); Düsseldorf, capital of the 'Land' of North Rhineland – Westphalia (Nordrhein-Westfalen); the textile city of Krefeld and the industrial centre of Duisburg (with the world's largest inland port at the junction of the river Ruhr with the Rhine), at the western edge of the massive industrial concentration of the Ruhr (Rhineland-Westphalian industrial region).

Beyond this point the wide river basin is covered with fertile fenland. The towns are now smaller, but nonetheless are places which have much history behind them – Wesel, Xanten, Kleve (Cleves), Emmerich. At the foot of the Eltenberg (83 m) the Rhine passes from Germany into the Netherlands (km 857.7 from Konstanz).

Dutch windmills near Kinderdijk

Tributaries of the Lower Rhine

Within Germany the Lower Rhine has the Erft as a left-bank tributary and the Sieg, Wupper, Ruhr, Emscher and Lippe on the right bank. There are also two important canals, the Rhine-Herne Canal and the Wesel-Datteln Canal, linking the Rhine with the Mittelland Canal by way of the Dortmund-Ems Canal.

Rhine-Maas Delta

The hydrographic pattern of the Rhine and the various arms which convey its water to the sea is highly complex, the more so because it is bound up with the course of the Maas and its ramifications.

Bovenrijn

At the German-Dutch frontier, which for the first 8 km runs along the middle of the Rhine, the river takes the name of Bovenrijn (Upper Rhine). 2 km farther on it splits into a northern and a southern arm.

Pannerdens Kanaal

Nederrijn

The northern arm is known as Pannerdens Kanaal as far as Arnhem, where the Gelderse IJssel branches off to flow into the IJsselmeer. From Arnhem to Wijk bij Duurstede it is known as the Nederrijn (Lower Rhine).

Kromme Rijn

Oude Rijn

Shortly before Wijk bij Duurstede the Kromme Rijn ('Curving Rhine') branches off and runs north-west towards Utrecht. Beyond Utrecht the Oude Rijn (Old Rhine) pursues a winding course by way of Alphen aan den Rijn, the old university town of Leyden (Leiden) and Katwijk aan den Rijn to the bathing resort of Katwijk aan Zee, where it flows into the North Sea.

Soon after Wijk bij Duurstede the Nederrijn crosses the Amster-dam-Rhine Canal, which provides a link with the Waal; and from this point to its junction with the Noord (linking it with the Merwede) it is known as the Lek.

Within the city and port area of Rotterdam the river successively bears the names of Nieuwe Maas (New Maas; at IJsselmonde, junction with Hollandse IJssel), Het Scheur and the Nieuwe Waterweg (New Waterway). Between the oil port of Europoort and the ferry port of Hoek van Holland (Hook of Holland) the Nieuwe Waterweg flows into the North Sea (km 1035.5 from Konstanz).

The southern arm of the Rhine, known as the Waal, flows past Nijmegen and continues broadly parallel to the Maas, a short distance to the south (connected by two canals; the Maas continues as the Bergse Maas and the Amer and after its junction with the Nieuwe Merwede flows into the Hollands Diep). At Tiel the Waal is joined by the Amsterdam-Rhine Canal, which provides a connection with the Lek.

From the old outflow of the Maas into the Waal near Gorinchem the southern arm of the Rhine is known as the Merwede. At Dordrecht (where the Nieuwe Merwede flows into the Hollands Diep) the Merwede divides into the Noord (connection with the Lek) and the Oude Maas (Old Maas). The Oude Maas flows south past Rotterdam and joins the Nieuwe Maas (Het Scheur) opposite Vlaardingen.

Under the long-term Delta Plan, which provides for a drastic reduction in the length of the Dutch coastline on the North Sea, the various mouths of the Rhine, Maas and Schelde – with the exception of the Nieuwe Waterweg and the Westerschelde – are being successively closed off by dykes.

Selected towns on the Rhine	Approximate breadth	
Chur	80 m	Breadth of river
Konstanz (Lake Rhine)	150 m	
Basle	200 m	
Strasbourg	280 m	
Karlsruhe	240 m	
Ludwigshafen/Mannheim	280 m	
Mainz	500 m	
Loreley	120 m	
Koblenz	300 m	
Cologne	350 m	
Düsseldorf	400 m	
Emmerich	550 m	
Nijmegen (Waal)	400 m	
Rotterdam (Nieuwe Maas)	400 m	
Hoek van Holland (Nieuwe Waterweg)	1000 m	

The Rhine is by far the most abundantly flowing river in Central Europe, with a relatively regular flow over the year.

The average rate of flow at Basle is about 1030 cu. m per second, at Karlsruhe about 1200 cu. m per second, at Kaub about 1530 cu. m per second and at Wesel about 2460 cu. m per second.

General

Volume of water (continued)

The pattern of flow is determined by two main factors. On the one hand melt-water from the névé and glaciers in the Alps gives rise to a summer maximum on the Alpine, High and Upper Rhine (at Basle June/July); on the other, melt-water from the hills farther down the Rhine produces a spring maximum to the north of the Rhenish Uplands. In this latter area too there may be dangerous spates during the winter following a sudden in-flow of warm air with heavy rain (highest levels recorded during this century: Kaub, 27 February 1970, 793 cm; Wesel, 3 January 1926, 1231 cm). The volume of water is at its lowest at Basle in the months of December, January and February, at Wesel in September and October (lowest levels this century: Kaub, 3 November 1947, 42 cm; Wesel, 19 October 1959, 129 cm).

Freezing of the Rhine

Because of the temperate climate and not least as a result of the effluence of cooling water warmed up by industrial plants and nuclear power stations, nowadays the danger of freezing-over of the Rhine is small (last drifting ice with floes up to 30 sq.m in size blocking the shipping traffic 16.1.–22.2.1963).

Measurement of distances

Throughout the entire length of the Rhine from Konstanz to the Dutch North Sea coast distances from Konstanz in kilometres are marked on the banks of the river.

The measurement begins at the middle of the bridge over the Rhine at Konstanz (km 0) and ends at Hoek van Holland, where the Nieuwe Waterweg flows into the North Sea (km 1035.5).

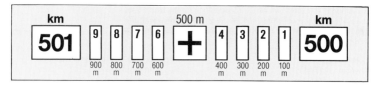

In Switzerland, Germany and France distances are shown on large boards set up on the banks, in black figures on a white ground. Full kilometres are given in large figures; half kilometres (500 m) are indicated by a cross, and intermediate distances of 100 m (from 1 to 4 and 6 to 9) by small figures or vertical lines on narrower boards.

In the Netherlands only full kilometres are shown, in white figures on a black ground.

Use of water

The water of the Rhine is used to supply drinking water (particularly in the Netherlands, which get some three-quarters of their drinking water from the river) and water required by indus-try; it is harnessed to provide electric power (eleven dams and hydroelectric stations on the High Rhine, ten on the Upper Rhine and Grand Canal d'Alsace); and the river is a major waterway for shipping (→Shipping on the Rhine).

Bridges, ferries

The bridges and ferries crossing the river are shown on the large Rhine map at the end of the book.

Climate

Since the Rhine, between its sources in the Swiss Alps and its outflow into the North Sea, flows through regions of very varying altitude and latitude it has a corresponding variety of climates in the different sections of its course.

Alpine Rhine

In the Rhine's catchment area in the Grisons a northern continental climate prevails. The town of Chur, however, which lies at a short distance from the Rhine on the river Plessur, has a favoured situation (average January temperature −1.5 °C), so that fruit and vines grow well here, and at sheltered spots even sweet chestnuts and figs.

In the Alps and the pre-Alpine region a periodic rise in temperature is brought about by the wind known as the föhn. This occurs during a period of low pressure north of the Alps, when air is sucked up from the south to the summit ridge, accompanied by the formation of clouds and heavy rain, and then falls down into the valleys as a warm dry wind, raising the temperature by about 1 °C for every 100 m of altitude; the föhn is popularly said to 'eat up' the snow. The föhn usually brings clear air and good distant vision, but it may cause a certain physical discomfort, particularly to those who are sensitive to changes in the weather. In the past it was dreaded as the cause of fires which sometimes destroyed whole villages.

Lake Constance

The Rhine flows into Lake Constance between Bregenz and Rorschach, forming a delta which projects into the lake. In virtue of its relatively low and southerly situation and its temperate lake climate Lake Constance enjoys milder weather than the rest of the Alpine foreland region, with an early spring and a late autumn. Fruit, vegetables and vines yield good harvests, and on the island of Mainau even subtropical plants flourish.

The water of the lake stores up the warmth of summer until late autumn. January is the coldest month, with average air temperatures only just under freezing point (mean annual minimum −14 °C). The warmest, and also the sunniest, month is July, with average temperatures of fully 18 °C. Every few years the Untersee is covered with ice, but the Obersee very rarely freezes over.

At constant altitude rainfall increases sharply from west to east, going towards the mountains. In the longitude of Romanshorn and Friedrichshafen the annual level of precipitations is 900 mm, at Bregenz almost 1500 mm. The rainiest month is June. As soon as the air temperature approaches thawing point (i.e. when the relative humidity of the air reaches 100 per cent) mist or fog begins to form. This phenomenon – which is frequent mainly in the transitional seasons – occurs when warm air passes over cold ground, but also when humid air cools down, for example as a result of heat loss during the night. Mist or fog is of course a particular hindrance to the movement of shipping.

The wind normally blows off the lake during the day and off the land at night, but this pattern may be varied by the occurrence of thunderstorms or the arrival of the föhn, coming down from the Alpine Rhine.

High Rhine

The High Rhine – the stretch of the river between Stein am Rhein and Basle – also enjoys a mild climate (average January

Climate

temperature 0 ° to −2 °C, July 14–18 °C). While to the south of the High Rhine annual precipitations range between 1000 and 1500 mm, on the north bank (i.e. on the south side of the Black Forest) they go no higher than 1000 mm.

The city of Basle is also climatically favoured in virtue of its situation on the Rhine (average January temperature 1.2 °C, July 18.5 °C, annual average 10.1 °C). Precipitations are relatively low (815 mm annually), since the clouds discharge their rain on the hills of the Jura.

Upper Rhine

Sheltered from wind and rain by the Vosges, the western part (Alsace) of the Upper Rhine valley is a privileged climatic region, with warm summers and mild winters. The average annual temperature at Strasbourg is around 10 °C (January average 1.5 °C, July 19 °C); annual precipitations are 696 mm. The vine-growing piedmont area round Colmar is an island of low rainfall, with barely more than 400 mm annually. Rain-bringing west winds make their way into the Upper Rhine valley through the Belfort gap.

Similarly favourable climatic conditions prevail in Baden, on the German side of the Upper Rhine plain, and in the zone to the north (the Bergstrasse area) which is bounded on the east by the Odenwald and on the west by the Pfälzer Wald (Palatinate Forest). The plain of the Upper Rhine has the mildest climate of any region in Germany, with an average annual temperature (10.3 °C) which is 1.2 °C above the figure for the rest of Germany. There are a number of reasons for this. Lying lower than the surrounding country, this region is sheltered from harsh winds; its orientation from north to south gives it plenty of sun; and rainfall is low (Karlsruhe 672 mm, Mainz 515 mm), thanks to the hills which border the plain on the west.

Particularly favoured is the Kaiserstuhl, between Freiburg and Colmar, where the high summer temperatures and the low rainfall provide the right conditions for viticulture.

Of the larger cities in the Federal Republic of Germany Ludwigshafen and Mainz, in the Upper Rhine valley, have the highest annual and July temperatures (January averge 1.7 °C, July 19 °C, annual 10.5 ° and 10 °C respectively).

A good criterion for judging the warmth of the climate in a particular area is the date when apple-blossom begins to appear, marking the coming of spring. The first apple blossom comes out in the Upper Rhine valley, between Basle and Freiburg, between 10 and 20 April, while in the central Black Forest it does not appear until between 20 and 31 May. Almond and peach trees come into blossom in April, with cherries and plums following on their heels; and by the beginning of June the first cherries are ripe. In Rheinhessen (Rhineland-Hesse), which has the lowest rainfall in Germany (under 500 mm annually), the area round the great bend in the Rhine between Worms, Mainz and Bingen produces the wines for which this region is famed.

Middle Rhine

In the region enclosed by the hills of the Hunsrück, Taunus, Eifel, Westerwald and Siebengebirge the Rhine valley has a markedly low rainfall, for it lies mainly in the lee of the hills and is exposed only in a limited degree to the rain-bringing west winds. At Koblenz the annual rainfall is around 580 mm. The climate of the Middle Rhine is also predominantly mild, in contrast to that of the surrounding hills: Koblenz has an average annual temperature of 11 °C (January 1.8 °C, July 18.5 °C).

The Bonn and Cologne areas have the temperate climate characteristic of Central Europe, moderated by the influence of the Gulf Stream. This means that in general winter temperatures are not unduly low, nor summer temperatures intolerably high (Cologne: January average 2.5 °C, July 18 °C, annual 10.2 °C). In Bonn, however, which is relatively enclosed, it can sometimes be unpleasantly sultry in summer.

Lower Rhine

The Netherlands, where the Rhine splits into a number of arms, has an oceanic climate with relatively cool summers and mild winters (Rotterdam: January average 2.8 °C, July 18.2 °C, annual 10 °C). The prevalent west and south-west winds reinforce the maritime influence. The average rainfall on the Lower Rhine ranges between 650 and 750 mm.

On Lake Constance and the High Rhine, extending approximately to Mulhouse, the average annual number of hours of sunshine ranges between 1500 and 1700; north of this, as far as Mannheim, it is between 1700 and 1900. To the north of Mannheim is the sunniest region in the Federal Republic, with just under 2000 hours of sunshine in the year. By Koblenz, however, the figure has fallen to between 1500 and 1700 hours, and farther down the Rhine it is lower still, at between 1300 and 1500 hours of sunshine in the year.

Sunshine on the Rhine

→Facts and Figures, General

Volume of water of the Rhine

Nature and Ecology

The Rhine was already an important trade route and means of communication between north and south in pre-Roman times. To the Romans it was also a natural frontier and barrier against the incursion of Germanic tribes, as well as a strategic waterway. The abundant flow of water throughout the year and the fact that it was rarely frozen over facilitated the movement of shipping from the earliest times, and during the Middle Ages the Rhine became the most important inland waterway in Central Europe – although even in those days complaints were voiced about the pollution of the water.

Early use of the Rhine

The great importance of the Rhine valley as a traffic artery, still further increased when railways were built on both banks of the river, led to a rapid growth of industry from the 19th century onwards. The old customs stations, trading and market centres expanded to become factory towns. The old-established traditional crafts attracted new industries, and in the course of a hundred years or so considerable stretches of the river developed into continuous industrial and economic zones – the Rhine-Neckar area, the Rhine-Main region, the Neuwied Basin, the Rhineland-Westphalian industrial region. After the second world war traffic on the Rhine received a further stimulus when the old east-west movement of trade and communications altered its course to run north-south.

Development of transport and industry

Today the Rhine is the main axis of the inland waterway network of Central Europe, and accordingly the busiest, most populous and most intensively industrialised waterway in Europe, and the one most affected by the problems of modern civilisation.

21

Ludwigshafen: chemical works

Duisburg: heavy industry

Ecological situation

The harm which man has done to the natural landscape and ecological pattern of the Rhine cannot yet be fully measured but may prove to be irreparable. The rehabilitation of this much misused river – the 'largest sewer in Europe', as it has been called – which must supply a population of some 30 million with drinking water and is also used, particularly in the Netherlands, for the watering of agricultural and horticultural crops, has become a burning multi-national environmental problem.

Years of thoughtlessly discharging untreated domestic, industrial and shipping effluents have done grave damage to the river's ecological equilibrium. Natural water, and particularly running water, has a certain capacity for self-purification; but if this capacity is overtaxed by excessive pollution it 'gives up' and ceases to operate. The water can then support life only to a very limited extent, or perhaps not all. In this sense the Rhine had in many respects 'given up' during the period of unrestrained industrial development after the second world war.
As a result of the catastrophic reduction and poisoning of the fish stock the traditional river fisheries were destroyed.
Bathing in the river was then prohibited on hygienic grounds.

Oxygen content

Oxygen is indispensable for the maintenance of plant and animal life in water. Healthy running water contains approximately 10 milligrammes of oxygen per litre; but this oxygen content is lowered by an over-abundance of plant life due to overuse of fertilisers and by the introduction of excessive quantities of organic waste and the consequent pollution. Moreover the oxygen content is also much reduced by an increase in the temperature of the water. After falling steadily for many years the oxygen content of Rhine water had by the 1970s reached a highly critical low at only 5 milligrammes per litre. Since then the vigorous efforts devoted to the provision of purification plants have led to an improvement in the situation, and one of the essential pre-conditions for the existence of a natural symbiosis of plant and animal life has thus been re-established.

Another danger on some stretches of the Rhine is still the concentration of inorganic substances which do not readily decompose, like mercury, cadmium, chromium, lead, copper and zinc, and which cannot be completely removed in the purification plants. Substances of this kind are regularly discharged into the Rhine at Basle (chemical and pharmaceutical industries), Karlsruhe (Maxau; papermaking), Ludwigshafen (chemical industry) and Mainz (also by way of the Main) and, in large quantities, in the Rhineland-Westphalian industrial region (iron- and steelworks, chemical industry). Some of this material is lost by sedimentation, presenting an incalculable hazard for the future.

Noxious substances

A particular problem for Germany and the Netherlands is the increasing salinity of the Rhine. In addition to the natural salt content of the water some 56,000 tonnes of salt are released daily into the river. Roughly half of this comes from the potash mines of Alsace, where adequate attention has not yet been given to alternative methods of disposal or treatment of the great quantities of salts in the overburden; late in 1983, however, the French government undertook to take remedial measures. Apart from the fact that water with an unduly high salt content is not suitable for the watering of flower and vegetable

Salinity

Biblis: one of the world's biggest nuclear power stations

Nature and Ecology

Salinity (continued)

crops (of particular importance in the Netherlands), there are possible health hazards for the population if their drinking water has an excessive sodium chloride content.

Nuclear power stations

Another problem not yet solved results from the discharge of possible radioactive substances and waste heat by nuclear power stations (Leibstadt, Fessenheim, Philippsburg, Biblis, etc.).

Water control

Overall, however, the efforts devoted during the past ten years to improving the water of the Rhine have borne fruit, and the noxious discharges into the river have been significantly reduced. The Rhine is now one of the best monitored rivers in Europe. At fifteen gauging stations regular water samples are taken and changes in the water quality recorded, enabling sources of pollution to be rapidly traced.

The improvement in the quality of Rhine water has also been promoted by the economic recession and by the increased flow of water in the years since 1976.

Fish life

One consequence of the improvement in the oxygen content of the water has been a marked increase in the stocks of fish. This has been achieved mainly by artificial stocking; for as a result of the busy movement of shipping and the artificial hard bottom of the river-bed, particularly in the upper part of its course, there are few suitable spawning grounds for fish. Among the species now to be found in the Rhine are perch, barbel and roach; less common are eel, pike, gudgeon, ruffe, tench and pike-perch. Trout, catfish and the formerly much-prized Rhine salmon also occasionally occur. The salmon have to be artificially released into the river, for they are unable to get through the 'chemical barrier' between the sea and the spawning grounds.

At many points along the river banks freshwater mussels, water snails, crayfish, leeches, freshwater sponges and flatworms have now been able to re-establish themselves.

At some points, too, bathing in the river is again possible, though perhaps not to be wholeheartedly indulged in.

River landscape

Industrialisation has altered, and sometimes destroyed, not only the quality of the water but also the natural landscape along the banks of the Rhine. This is less true of the Alpine Rhine, Lake Constance, High Rhine and Upper Rhine, where more than a third of the riparian zones remain in their natural state. On the Middle Rhine, however, only some 5% and on the Lower Rhine no more than 0.4% of the banks have preserved their natural character.

On the High Rhine straightenings of the river-bed and other measures for the protection and control of the water have led to marked changes in the landscape along the river.

Consequences of the regulation of the Rhine

A major interference with the landscape of the Upper Rhine Plain was involved in the regulation of the river's course which was begun by J.G. Tulla in the early 19th century. The main objects were to facilitate the movement of shipping, provide protection from flooding and reclaim areas of marshland in the interests of epidemic control; but the work was undertaken in total unawareness of the ecological consequences. Before this straightening the Rhine had followed a sluggish and unpredictable course through the wide meadowlands of its valley in a labyrinth of side-arms, ramifications and meanders. On the spacious flood plain with its warm, moist climate the luxuriant growth of woodland and meadow harboured a rich flora and fauna unique in Central Europe.

Tulla's straightening of the Rhine reduced its course by more than 80 km. This considerably increased the speed of flow, and with it the rate of erosion, so that the river has gouged out its bed to an additional depth of some 5 metres. As a result the level of groundwater has fallen and large stretches of the formerly well watered areas along the banks have been reduced to a steppe-like grassland.

Tulla Stone on the Rhine near Maxau (Karlsruhe)

The problems have been aggravated in recent years by the uncontrolled use of pesticides to exterminate insects (particularly midges and mosquitoes), which has alarmingly weakened the food chain in its lowest link. Thus for certain species with a specialised way of life survival has become difficult in a changed and contaminated environment with a reduced food supply.

Many species of birds once to be seen on the Upper Rhine in large numbers, nesting, wintering or resting on their passage south, have now become rare or have disappeared altogether. The most striking example of this is the stork, the characteristic bird of Alsace, once common and much loved everywhere, which now has to be artificially re-established.

Another casualty of Tulla's regulation of the Rhine was the gold-washing once actively practised on the Upper Rhine. The solid matter carried in suspension in the water now travelled too rapidly downstream, no longer depositing sufficient quantities of the gold-bearing sands ('Rheingold' = 'gold from the Rhine').

In order to counteract the still more rapid flow of water after the construction of the Grand Canal d'Alsace additional weirs were built on the main course of the Rhine between Basle and Strasbourg. The stretch of the river between Basle and Breisach is now for all practical purposes merely an overflow channel for periods of high water and an outfall for the Basle area.

In recent years the importance of preserving a healthy environment has increasingly been recognised, and efforts are being made to alleviate the damage done by modern civilisation and at the same time to provide recreation areas for large cities and conurbations by the establishment of nature reserves and protected areas.

Protection of nature

A broad belt of land extending round much of Lake Constance is now scheduled as a nature reserve, together with an even larger reserve round the Wollmatinger Ried, Untersee and Gnadensee, a dried-up area of 767 hectares which is flooded at periods of high water and is noted for its rich bird and plant life.

The largest continuous areas of riverine woodland on the Upper Rhine are at Kühkopf-Knoblochsaue (between Gernsheim and Oppenheim; 2378 hectares) and Taubergiessen (near Rust; 1600 hectares). Here and in smaller surviving areas of riverine woodland like the Rastatter Rheinaue (845 hectares), Hördter Rheinaue (818 hectares), Lampertheimer Altrhein (516 hect-

Nature and Ecology

Riverine woodland in the Kühkopf-Knoblochsaue nature reserve

Protection of nature
(continued)

ares), Ketscher Rheininsel (490 hectares), Mariannenaue, Fulderaue, Illmenaue and Rüdesheimer Aue (together 470 hectares), Flotzgrün (south of Speyer; 204 hectares), Reissinsel and Kuckucksinsel (Mannheim district; together 92 hectares), Neuhofener Altrhein (50 hectares), Rheinwald Neuenburg (34 hectares), Altrhein-Königssee (Karlsruhe district; 11 hectares) and Tieflachgraben near Au am Rhein (Rastatt district; 10 hectares) there are still largely intact plant communities of oak (Quercus robur), ash (Fraxinus excelsior), smooth-leaved elm (Ulmus carpinifolia), white poplar (Populus alba) and white willow (Salix alba), entwined by traveller's joy (Clematis vitalba). This dense primeval forest is the haunt of nesting, migratory and wintering birds, including such species, now rare, as the cormorant, kingfisher, oriole, great crested grebe, tawny owl, coot, nuthatch and great reed warbler. Even the tree frog is relatively common here.

Abandoned loops of the river, now dried up, are often covered with fenny grassland (e.g. Eich-Gimbsheimer Altrhein, 162 hectares; Hinterer Roxheimer Altrhein, 43 hectares; Sauscholle, Lahr district; 57 hectares; Laubheimer Ried, 15 hectares).

On gravel soils in the Upper Rhine valley there are still occurrences in considerable numbers of orchids and pasque flowers. Occasionally, too, the hand of man (quarries, gravel pits, reservoirs) has created flourishing new biotopes (e.g. in the Altrhein basin at the Wyhlen hydroelectric station on the High Rhine, 24 hectares).

On the Middle and Lower Rhine the only typical remnants of riverine woodland, with alders (Alnus), oaks (Quercus), hornbeams (Carpinus) and beeches (Betula), are the Eller Forst

26

(Düsseldorf district; 60 hectares), the Waldwinkel nature reserve (Kempen-Krefeld district; 17 hectares) and the Urmitzer Werth at Neuwied (4 hectares). On the forbidding rocky slopes of the Erpeler Ley (opposite Remagen; 7 hectares) and on the Langenbergskopf (Neuwied district; 2 hectares) a flora of Pontic-Mediterranean type has been preserved, providing a home for large numbers of songbirds and birds of prey.

Protection of nature (continued)

The largest areas of unspoiled marshland and flood plain on the Lower Rhine are the Rheinaue Walsum (345 hectares), the Rheinaue Friemersheim (181 hectares), the Alter Rhein (Old Rhine) at Bienen-Praest (Rees district; 340 hectares), with the largest occurrence of the fringed water-lily (Nymphoides peltata) in Europe, and the bird sanctuaries at the Xantener Altrhein (223 hectares) and the Milliger and Hurler Meer (Rees district; together 67 hectares).

A distinctive topographical feature, which probably came into being only in the late medieval period, is presented by the dunes at Wissel (Kleve district; 80 hectares), on the left bank of the Lower Rhine, where flood water from the river has enabled many representatives of the flora of the Rhine valley to establish themselves.

The protection of nature, desirable though it is, is unfortunately hampered by a variety of circumstances. The obstacles it has to contend with include rights of ownership and exploitation, administrative delays and political constraints; and some of the worst damage is done, too, by those seeking recreation in the country – the very people for whose benefit the protection of nature is intended – out of mere thoughtlessness and negligence.

Wine

The Rhine owes its world fame not only to its importance as a means of communication and a source of power and to its scenic beauties, but also to its wine.

Rhine wine

The wild grape was probably established north of the Alps in prehistoric times, but the drinking of wine is believed to have been first brought to Central Europe by Greek traders. By the beginning of the 7th century B.C. Phocaeans from northern Greece had settled at Massalia (Marseille), and from there they took the culture of the vine westward into the Iberian peninsula and northward into what is now France.

Beginnings

Following the conquest of Gaul by the Romans towards the end of the lst century B.C. wine advanced into Burgundy and Alsace and to the Rhine and Moselle and became a popular drink. In the 3rd century A.D. the Emperor Probus abolished the monopoly which had confined the growing of wine to the Italian peninsula, and thereafter it was permitted in the provinces. After the withdrawal of Roman rule, however, the growing of wine in the former provinces declined.
Little is known about the position of viticulture during the period of the great migrations. There is evidence, however, that

Wine

the Merovingian and Carolingian kings developed it and that churches and religious houses promoted the growing of wine, particularly in the Rhineland. Thereafter wine gradually made its way into Central and even into Northern Europe, reaching the Baltic around 1400.

Decline

When the powerful Hanseatic towns began to import increasing quantities of light, sweet wines from Italy and Spain and, later, the Reformation closed down the monasteries of northern Europe, the local production of wine declined considerably; and the devastation wrought by the Thirty Years War in the first half of the 17th century brought a further setback.

It was only at the beginning of the 19th century that the merits of pure natural wines began to be appreciated.
Then around the middle of the century the vines of the Rhine and its tributaries were decimated by pests brought in from the New World like phylloxera and mildew. It took many years for new, resistant strains to be bred.

Recovery

Wine-growing, particularly in Germany, took on a fresh lease of life in the 1950s as a result of the development of new and highly productive vine stocks and the granting of large state subsidies under the agricultural policy of the European Economic Community.

Vineyards require to be renewed every 20 to 50 years, and the young vines then take three or four years to become productive.

In this section the wine regions flanking the Rhine are considered in turn, travelling down the river from south to north.

Alpine Rhine

To the north of Chur, capital of the canton of Grisons, is the Bündner Herrschaft ('Grisons Lordship'), where the Rhine wines of Switzerland are produced, in close vicinity to the Alps. The wines are mainly rosé and red, the best-known growths being Malanser, Jeninser, Maienfelder and Fläscher.
Farther down the Alpine Rhine there are the wines of Mels and Berneck, in the canton of St Gallen.

Lake Constance

There are considerable areas of vineyards at the western end of Lake Constance.
In Germany (Baden) there are the wines of Meersburg, Hagnau (first wine-growers' cooperative in Baden established 1881), Markdorf, Bermatingen, Überlingen, Espasingen, Bodman, Konstanz, Allensbach, the island of Reichenau, the Höri peninsula and Kressbronn.
In Switzerland wine is grown on the Untersee between Steckborn and Tägerwilen (birthplace of the viticulturist Hermann Müller, 1850–1927, who produced the Müller-Thurgau grape by crossing Riesling and Sylvaner), at Stein am Rhein and on the Ottenberg, above the Thur valley to the north-west of Weinfelden.

Meersburger and Konstanzer are considered the best of the Lake Constance wines. They are rosé wines, of a delicate pink hue, mostly made from the Blauburgunder grape (Weissherbst; fresh, robust, with an agreeable tartness), which go excellently with the fish of Lake Constance.

The Roman wine boat from Neumagen on the Moselle

The red wine of Lake Constance, made from the Rotburgunder grape, is ruby-red and has a fruity bouquet.

Along the High Rhine, between Lake Constance and Basle, the vineyards are mainly in Switzerland. Among the wines produced here are the Hallauer, Osterfinger and Rheinhalder of Schaffhausen, the Neftenbacher and Wiler of the Töss valley, the Villiger Schlossberger and Geissberger of the Aargau and the Riehener Schlipfen produced on the north bank of the Rhine in the Basle area.

High Rhine

The fame of the wines of Alsace dates back to the Middle Ages, when they were the most popular wines in the German-speaking countries. There are now some 50,000 families of wine-growers in a hundred wine-growing communes, on dry lime soils on the sunny eastern foothills of the Vosges, at heights of between 200 and 450 m, and on a strip of land only some 2 km wide flanking the 150 km long 'Route du Vin d'Alsace'.

Alsace

The grapes grown in Alsace are almost exclusively white. The most important varieties are Riesling (lively, elegant), Sylvaner (fresh, fruity), Pinot Blanc (dry, with a flowery bouquet), Muscat d'Alsace (dry, fruity), Tokay d'Alsace (dry, heavy), Gewurz-traminer (dry, full-bodied) and Pinot Noir (dry, aromatic; Rosé d'Alsace), together with Chasselas and Knipperlé, which have less flavour. Zwicker and Edelzwicker are made by blending various good (sometimes noble) growths of wine.

The wines of Lower Alsace, which has more rain, are inferior in taste and bouquet to those of the drier Upper Alsace. The best

Alsatian grapes

Riquewihr: an Alsatian wine town

Alsace (continued)

are those of Riquewihr, Ribeauvillé, Hunawihr, Sigolsheim, Kaysersberg, Ammerschwihr, Turckheim, Katzenthal, Guebwiller and Thann.

In making their wine the vintners of Alsace attach great importance to purity and allow no additives. The wines they produce are full-bodied, dry, absolutely unadulterated. They can frequently be bought direct from the producers, and the 'Route du Vin d'Alsace' is lined with sales points and advertisements.

The wines of Alsace are normally bottled in slender long-necked green bottles ('flûtes d'Alsace') and served from the bottle in a 'winstub'; only the lesser qualities of wine are served from the cask. The wine is drunk young (up to five years old; only the truly 'great' vintages remain good much longer), at a temperature of 10 °C and, properly, in a tulip glass.

Federal Republic of Germany

Although wine-growing in Germany is concentrated in the south-west of the country, the vineyards are among the most northerly in the world. This geographical situation means that, in contrast to more southern lands, the quality of the wine is closely dependent on the weather in a particular year. In favourable conditions, however, the wines of a particular vintage can achieve the balance and harmony which has spread their fame far beyond the bounds of Germany.

White grapes predominate. Red wines account for only some 15% of total production and are little drunk outside the area where they are grown.

Making of German wine

After the wine harvest (October-November) the grapes are pressed, after which the must soon begins to ferment ('Sauser',

'Federweisser'). When the yeast has been deposited and the wine clarifies (middle to end of November) it is drawn off the sediment, sulphurised and run into tanks. In spring the wine is fined and filtered, and in the course of the summer or autumn it is bottled.

In a year of unfavourable weather must from lesser vineyards is improved by the addition of sugar. Well made wines keep for 10 to 20 years, but with increasing age take on a well-seasoned taste which does not appeal to everyone.

The wines of South Germany and the Mosel (Moselle) are bottled in green bottles, Rhine wines in brown ones. In many places the wine-producers themselves serve the previous year's wine direct to consumers before the new harvest, indicating this by displaying wreaths or sprays of pine branches on their houses ('Strausswirtschaften', 'Besenwirtschaften', 'Winzerwirtschaften').

Every year in autumn a German 'Wine Queen' is chosen from among girls who have already been selected as regional Wine Queens.

Wine Queen

Under a law passed in 1971 wines are no longer classified according to vineyard but are graded according to must content (measured on the Öchsle scale). There are now three basic grades – 'Tafelwein' (table wine), 'Qualitätswein' (quality wine) and 'Qualitätswein mit Prädikat' (quality wine with an additional distinction).

German wine law

'Tafelwein' is an ordinary table wine. It is not required to bear any certificate of quality.

'Qualitätswein' must come from a particular region ('Gebiet'), must have a minimum of must weight and must bear a control number.

'Qualitätswein mit Prädikat' is the term applied to the traditional high-quality wines, which must have no added sugar. There is a traditional hierarchy of grades, now exactly defined and indicated by the 'Prädikat', ranging upwards through 'Kabinett', 'Spätlese' (made from grapes gathered when fully ripe, after the main harvest), 'Auslese' (from grapes picked separately, any imperfect ones being discarded), 'Beerenauslese' (from overripe grapes and grapes with 'noble rot', which concentrates the sugar in the grapes), 'Trockenbeerenauslese' (from grapes which have dried on the vine and have been attacked by noble rot) and 'Eiswein' (from grapes which have been turned to ice by frost).

The following main wine-growing regions on the Rhine are distinguished: Baden, Hessische Bergstrasse ('Hessian Mountain Road'), Rheinpfalz (Rhineland-Palatinate), Rheinhessen (Rhineland-Hesse), Rheingau, Nahe, Mosel (-Saar-Ruwer), Mittelrhein (Middle Rhine) and Ahr.

Wine-growing regions

The Baden wine-growing region (in the 'Land' of Baden-Württemberg) includes the western Lake Constance area and part of Franconia (Tauber valley; wine bottled in the round-bellied flagons known as 'Bocksbeutel'), but the main part of the region lies along the east bank of the Upper Rhine between the sharp bend at Basle and the junction with the Neckar.

Baden

The wealth of Baden's wine-list is displayed in its wide range of fine wines and its varied nuances ot taste. It is made up of a

Kaiserstuhl: abounding in vineyards (in the background the Vosges)

Baden (continued)

number of different districts, with varying soils and climates which offer ideal conditions for different types of grape.

The classic grape varieties of Baden are Gutedel, Müller-Thurgau (a cross of Riesling and Silvaner), Silvaner, Ruländer, Weisser Burgunder, Riesling, Traminer, Gewürztraminer, Spätburgunder (Weissherbst and red wine) and Muskateller. Newer varieties are Scheurebe (Silvaner x Riesling), Freisamer (Silvaner x Ruländer), Muskat-Ottonel, Nobling (Silvaner x Gutedel), Bacchus (Silvaner x Riesling x Müller-Thurgau) and Findling.

The 'Badische Weinstrasse' (Baden Wine Road) takes in most of the wine-producing villages of the Upper Rhineland between Lörrach and Baden-Baden.

Markgräflerland

The Markgräflerland extends from Lörrach to Freiburg im Breisgau. The best-known wine communes in this area are Haltingen, Efringen-Kirchen, Schliengen, Auggen, Müllheim, Badenweiler, Hügelheim, Britzingen, Laufen, Ballrechten-Dottingen, Wettelbrunn, Staufen, Ehrenstetten, Kirchhofen, Pfaffenweiler, Ebringen and Wolfenweiler.

The predominant grape in the Markgräflerland is the Gutedel, a variety which was already being grown in ancient Egypt. It produces wines of the higher grades, fine wines, and wines which are light and palatable. The Müller-Thurgau and Gewürztraminer also do well in this southern climate.

Kaiserstuhl/Tuniberg

The Kaiserstuhl and Tuniberg rise directly out of the Rhine plain to the west of Freiburg im Breisgau. The sunny terraced vineyards, with a thick layer of loess soil over volcanic rocks, yield strong fiery wines. The best-known wine villages are

Ihringen, Achkarren, Wasenweiler, Bickensohl, Oberrotweil, Bötzingen and Sasbach.

From 'Bacchus's kitchen', as these unusual vineyards are known, come heavy, fruity Ruländers, mild Silvaners, Traminers and Gewürztraminers with rich bouquets, but also velvety Spätburgunder red wines and the strong Weissherbst made from Spätburgunder, a Baden specialty.

The Breisgau area, between Freiburg and Lahr, produces clean, well made light sweet wines which are extremely palatable. Among the best known wines are those of Ohrenbach in the Glotter valley, Mundingen, Hecklingen, Kenzingen, Herbolzheim, Ettenheim and Sulz.

Breisgau

Between Offenburg and Baden-Baden, in the sunny foreland region under the shelter of the Black Forest, are the magnificent south-facing vineyards of Ortenau, the largest Rieslinggrowing area in Baden, with such well known names as Gengenbach in the Kinzig valley, Ortenberg, Fessenbach, Zell-Weierbach, Rammersweier, Durbach, Oberkirch, Waldulm, Kappelrodeck, Sasbachwalden, Altschweier, Eisental-Affental, Neuweier, Steinbach, Umweg, Varnhalt and Fremersbach. This area also offers excellent conditions for the production of red wine.

Ortenau

The Kraichgau lies north of Karlsruhe, centred particularly on Weingarten and Bruchsal. Beyond it the 'Badische Bergstrasse' runs from Wiesloch via Heidelberg (on the Neckar) and Schriesheim to Weinheim. The natural beauty of this smiling park-like landscape is matched by the charm of its wines.

Kraichgau/
Badische Bergstrasse

The Riesling and Ruländer grapes produce fresh and subtly elegant wines; the wines made from the Weissburgunder grape are full of character. The noble blue Spätburgunder grape yields an excellent red wine.

The northern part of the Bergstrasse falls within the 'Land' of Hesse. The Roman 'strata montana', it follows the Upper Rhine rift valley along the western slopes of the Odenwald to Darmstadt. This region fringing the hills is noted for its mild climate. In spring, which is earlier here than anywhere else in Germany, the countryside turns into a sea of blossom. In addition to fruit (apricots, peaches, figs, etc.), walnuts, sweet chestnuts, almonds and vegetables, the vine flourishes on the loess soils.

Hessische Bergstrasse

The Bergstrasse wines are substantial white wines with a flowery bouquet, made from Riesling, Müller-Thurgau and Silvaner grapes.

In the Rheinpfalz, the most southerly part of the 'Land' of Rheinland-Pfalz, on the left bank of the Rhine, a swathe of vineyards some 80 km long and only 4–6 km wide extends between Alsace in the south and Rheinhessen in the north, sheltered from the wind by the Haardt hills. The wine villages lie along the 'Deutsche Weinstrasse' (German Wine Road), which runs from Schweigen ('Wine Gate' on the Franco-German frontier) by way of Bad Bergzabern, Neustadt an der Weinstrasse and Bad Dürkheim to Bockenheim.

Rheinpfalz
(Rhineland-Palatinate)

Something like a quarter of the area is occupied by Müller-Thurgau grapes, followed by Silvaner, Riesling and Portugieser (which is used to make red wine).

Wine

The area between the borders of Alsace and Neustadt is known as the Oberhaardt. Among well known wines are those of Schweigen, Bad Bergzabern, Edenkoben, Maikammer and Hambach. The grapes are mostly Muskat, Traminer, Tokajer and Silvaner.

In the Mittelhaardt, the area between Neustadt and Dackenheim, the best Palatinate wines (over 30% fine-quality Riesling) are produced at Gimmeldingen, Ruppertsberg, Deidesheim, Forst, Wachenheim, Bad Dürkheim, Ungstein, Kallstadt and Freinsheim.

In the Unterhaardt, the short northernmost section of the area between Kirchheim and Bockenheim, the wines tend to be smooth and mild.

The wines of the northern Palatinate (Alsenztal, Glantal, Zellertal) are fresh and full-bodied.

Rheinhessen
(Rhineland-Hesse)

Rheinhessen, on the left bank of the Rhine, was formerly part of Hesse but is now in the 'Land' of Rheinland-Pfalz. This upland region of Tertiary rocks between the Rhine and the Nahe, broken up by wide valleys, is a fertile vegetable-, fruit- and wine-growing area in which many farms combine these different crops.

The wines of Rheinhessen are produced in the triangle between Worms, Mainz and Bingen, a northward continuation of Rheinpfalz which is bounded on east and north by the Rhine. The variety of soils in this area is reflected in a corresponding variety in the wines. The grapes most grown here are Müller-Thurgau, Silvaner and Riesling.

The 'Liebfrauenmilch' or 'Liebfraumilch' of the Worms area, whose world-famous name has become a general designation for similar mild wines from other parts of Rheinhessen, is to be found on every wine-list. It grows on loess soils, to which large expanses of land in this region owe their fertility.

The districts on the so-called 'Rhine front' (tourist route, the 'Liebfrauenstrasse', between Worms and Mainz) produce the finest Rheinhessen wines (mostly made from the Riesling grape) – Wormser, Bechtheimer, Alsheimer, Guntersblumer. Dienheimer and Oppenheimer flourish on lime soils, Niersteiner and Nackenheimer on sandstones ('Rotliegendes'). To the north are Bodenheimer and Laubenheimer (now a Mainz wine).

The smooth Ingelheimer red wine grows on marls and drift sand; white wine at Ingelheim and Gau-Algesheim on lime soils. Of a very different kind is the fiery Binger Scharlachberg, which, with other good wines like Eisler and Kempter, grows on the weathered slates and quartzites of the Rochusberg.

The interior of Rheinhessen produces renowned wines like those of Alzey, Gau-Bickelheim and the Selz valley. The heavy marl and lime soils of the upland regions yield a spicy country wine, which acquires a particularly fine bouquet on the chalky quartzite porphyries in the south-west.

Mainz –
centre of the wine trade

The principal centre of the wine trade on the Rhine is the ancient city of Mainz, lying opposite the junction of the Main and the Rhine. Wine was grown here in Roman times on the Kästrich slopes, and it is now again being produced within the city in the suburbs of Laubenheim and Ebersheim.

Mainz, which has been capital of the 'Land' of Rheinland-Pfalz since 1950, is the seat of the only government department in Germany specifically concerned with wine-growing (the Ministry of Agriculture, Viticulture and Forestry of Rheinland-Pfalz), a university Institute of Microbiology and Viticulture, the German Wine Institute, the German Wine Information Board, the Wine Stabilisation Fund and the Wine-Growers' Cooperative of Rheinhessen. The "Deutsche Wein-Zeitung" ("German Wine News") was founded in Mainz in 1864.

Mainz has more than a hundred wine firms, a number of Sekt (sparkling wine) establishments and Germany's largest firm specialising in the transport of wine.

The Mainz Wine Market (August–September) is the largest wine fair on the Rhine.

The Rheingau, the hilly region on the south-westerly slopes of the Taunus range (Rheingaugebirge), lies on the right bank of the Rhine between Wiesbaden and the point where the Rhine cuts through the Rhenish Uplands at the Binger Loch ('Bingen Hole'). Since 1945 it has been part of the 'Land' of Hesse. The hillsides, mostly covered with loess soil and favoured by a mild climate, are intensively cultivated for the production of fruit and above all wine. The wine-growing area extends from the south-facing vineyards of Hochheim on the Main to Lorch on the Rhine. In spite of its relatively small extent this is one of the best, and best-known, wine-producing regions on the Rhine. Here the small-berried Riesling grape is predominant.

Most of the celebrated wine villages lie on the tourist route known as the 'Rheingauer Riesling-Route', which runs alongside the Rhine on the valley terrace.

Rheingau

Rheingau: famous for its wine (view of Rüdesheim from the Niederwald)

Wine

The wines of the Rheingau, which flourish on the weathered slates of the older hills (soil with a high potassium content) and on Tertiary marls, are among the most famous white wines in the world. They are full-bodied, fruity and spicy, with a rich bouquet.

The finest growths are Steinberger (at Kloster Eberbach, in the Hattenheim district), Johannisberger, Rüdesheimer, Erbacher, Rauenthaler, Kiedricher, Winkeler and Hochheimer (from which comes the English word 'hock', widely applied to Rhine wines). Other first-class wines come from Walluf, Martinsthal, Eltville, Hattenheim, Hallgarten, Oestrich, Mittelheim, Geisenheim and Lorch.

At Assmannshausen is produced one of the best-known German red wines (Spätburgunder).

The high quality of the wines produced in the Rheingau, surely the best German wine region, depends partly on favourable situation and climate, partly on the painstaking skills of the wine-growers, practised over many centuries, and partly on the high expertise of the monasteries (Eberbach, Johannisberg) and noble estates responsible for making the wine.

Nahe valley

At Bingen ('Land' Rheinland-Pfalz) the Rhine is joined by a tributary coming in from the south, the Nahe, which has vineyards at many points along the slopes flanking its valley. The white wines made here from the Riesling grape have a smoothness, fullness, vigour and flavour astonishing for such a northerly wine-growing region.

The local wine centre is Bad Kreuznach, the best vineyards in the immediate area of which are Kauzenberg and Brückes. Other good Nahe wines come from Rotenfels, near Bad Münster am Stein, and the hillsides round an old copper mine at Schlossböckelheim.

The 'Naheweinstrasse' (Nahe Wine Road) is a tourist circuit which starts (and finishes) at Bad Kreuznach and takes in the wine villages on the Nahe itself and in the area to the northwest.

Middle Rhine

In the hilly terrain of the Middle Rhine ('Land' Rheinland-Pfalz), between the Binger Loch and the junction with the Mosel at Koblenz, wine-growing is possible only in certain wider stretches of the valley and in the small side valleys. Among wines produced in this area, known as the 'Rheinburgengau' (the 'district of the Rhine castles'), are those of Steeg (a short distance west of Bacharach), Kaub, Oberwesel, (Engehöll, below the Schönburg) and Boppard.

Farther north the vineyards of the Rhine valley extend along the right bank by way of Leutesdorf, Hammerstein and Bad Hönningen to the Drachenfels ('Drachenblut' = 'Dragon's Blood').

Mosel (Moselle)

The course of the Mosel (in English the French form Moselle is often used; from Latin 'Mosella', the Little Mosa or Maas) from its source in the Vosges to its junction with the Rhine at Koblenz has been fringed by vineyards since Roman times. In France and Luxembourg, in the upper reaches of the valley, only very light wines are produced. In the middle section of the valley, however, within the German 'Land' of Rheinland-Pfalz, where the Mosel follows a very winding course, the slopes flanking the river – often extremely steep – provide ideal conditions for the Riesling grape.

Respectable wines are also produced in the valleys of the Mosel's tributaries, the Saar and the Ruwer.

Mosel wines, grown on the slatey soil of hillsides which are mostly of considerable steepness, are light, lively and fragrant. In a poor year, however, they tend to acidity and can hardly be used in their natural state ('naturrein'), without added sugar.
The best-known wine villages on the middle Mosel, going downstream, are Klüsserath, Leiwen, Trittenheim, Neumagen-Drohn, Piesport (a particularly full-bodied wine), Minheim, Wintrich, Brauneberg (wines of outstanding quality), Lieser, Bernkastel-Kues (the finest growths), Graach, Wehlen, Zeltingen-Rachtig, Ürzig, Erden, Lösnich, Kinheim, Kröv, Traben-Trarbach, Enkirch and Pünderich.

The 'Moselweinstrasse' (Mosel Wine Road) is a tourist route which follows the river (canalised and regulated by dams in recent times) from Perl at the 'Dreiländereck' (where the frontiers of France, Luxembourg and Germany meet) to the 'Deutsches Eck' at Koblenz.

Between Sinzig and Remagen the river Ahr, coming from the Eifel hills to the west, flows into the Rhine. In the Ahrgau ('Land' Rheinland-Pfalz), the lower and very winding stretch of the valley between Kreuzberg (near Altenahr) and Bad Bodendorf, wine is believed to have been grown since the end of the 3rd century A.D.
The wines of the Ahr valley, which are mainly red, are grown on slatey soils and are noted for their delicate fragrance. The best wines (from Blauburgunder grapes) come from Walporzheim and Ahrweiler, both now within the town of Bad Neuenahr – Ahrweiler.
The 'Ahr-Rotweinstrasse' (Ahr Red Wine Road) runs through the whole of the Ahrgau.

Ahr valley

Sekt (from Italian 'secco' = 'dry') is German sparkling wine; it is said to have been given the name by the actor Ludwig Devrient (1784–1832).

Sekt

Sparkling wine has been made in France for some centuries, but the principal contribution in this field was made by a 17th century monk, Dom Pérignon (1631–1715), cellarer in the abbey of Haut-Villers in Champagne, who is credited with the discovery of champagne and the invention of a stopper capable of resisting the pressure of the wine. The term 'champagne', which can now be applied only to certain carefully defined sparkling wines produced in the French province of Champagne, came into use only during the revolutionary wars (1793–1815), when there were foreign armies in Champagne.

The first attempts to produce German sparkling wine were made only in 1826 at Esslingen on the Neckar, and later at Grünberg in Silesia, Hochheim on the Main and Eltville and Mainz on the Rhine. It was not until the end of the 19th century, however, that the production of sparkling wine in Germany began to develop on any scale.

Unlike still wine, sparkling wine contains a considerable amount of carbon dioxide in solution and a quantity, according to taste, of added sugar dissolved in wine (known as 'liqueur').

Wine, Sekt (continued)

It is the result of a blend ('cuvée') of carefully selected wines in large casks. After some time in cask the wine, with the addition of pure yeast and sugar, is bottled in stout-walled bottles and kept at an even temperature in the cellar for 6–8 weeks, during which the second fermentation and the maturation of the wine take place. Finally the yeast is filtered out or extracted by the process known as 'dégorgement'.

Following a method devised by the famous French champagne firm Veuve Clicquot, the bottles are stacked in racks, neck downwards; then over a period of several weeks each individual bottle is gently shaken and turned round a little every day, so that the yeast sinks on to the cork and can be easily removed. The Sekt so produced can be marketed, without further treatment, as 'nature' or 'brut' (i.e. very dry indeed), or modified by the addition of varying quantities of sugar to produce different degrees of sweetness – 'extra sec' (very 'dry'), 'sec' (slightly sweet), 'demi-sec' (sweet), 'doux' (very sweet). The wine is not, however, actually put on the market until after several months in the cellar.

There are large Sekt establishments at Wiesbaden and Mainz (which has the lion's share), Eltville and Koblenz, Worms, Hochheim on the Main, Gau-Algesheim, Geisenheim, Bingen and Rüdesheim.

Brandy (Weinbrand)

German brandy ('Weinbrand') is distilled from wine, in a process which separates out the constituent alcohols and the substances carrying the bouquet from their associated water. It acquires its characteristic golden yellow to brown colouring and its delicate taste as a result of the many years it spends maturing in the cellar in small casks made of air-permeable wood. High-proof spirits of this kind must be diluted with water before drinking. Brandies of different origins and ages are blended after maturation in the cellar to achieve a product of standard quality and characteristics.

There are large brandy distilleries in Mainz and the surrounding area and in the Rheingau (Rüdesheim).

Shipping on the Rhine

Beginnings

Celts

Archaeological excavations along the Rhine have shown that during the second millennium B.C. the Celts sailed simple types of craft on the river. The wooden boats still to be seen at some places on the Rhine can be traced back to the type of high-sided boat (originally with leather sails) used by the Celts.

Romans

The movement of shipping on the Rhine – at first serving only the purposes of trade – increased considerably when the Roman legions advancing from Gaul reached the banks of the river. The Romans had a substantial Rhine fleet, the 'Classis Germanica', providing communication between the forts flanking the river. The main boatbuilding centres during this period were at Mainz, Vetera (near Xanten) and Cologne.

Great migrations

The great migrations which began around 400 A.D. put an end to this large-scale shipping activity; the port installations fell into a state of dilapidation, the ships rotted away. The Celts, however, now romanised, preserved the craft of boatbuilding, now practised in the service of their Germanic lords.

During the 8th century the Frisians sailed in their flat-bottomed boats from the mouths of the river to the Upper Rhine (Strasbourg).

In the 9th century the Vikings (Normans) appeared on the Rhine with their rakish longships, plundering and pillaging the towns and villages on the Lower Rhine.

During the Middle Ages the Rhine became the principal trade route between the north and south of Central Europe. Mainz, situated at the junction of the Rhine and the Main, became the main trading centre on the Rhine in the 11th and 12th centuries, but was later overtaken by Cologne. At an early stage ships from Strasbourg were sailing down to the Rhine delta, and seagoing vessels travelled up the river to Cologne. A Koblenz customs ordinance of 1209 refers to ships coming from Basle.
The largest boatbuilding yards during the Middle Ages were at Cologne and Dorsten (east of Wesel).

Until the 16th century shipping on the Rhine was in the hands of the towns, monasteries (e.g. Lorsch, Eberbach) and private merchants and fishermen. On account of the numerous danger spots (rocks, sandbanks, shallows, eddies), particularly on the Middle Rhine, it was not yet possible to sail all the way up and down the river.
Considerable obstacles to the movement of traffic were also presented by customs dues (at their highest in the 14th century, with 62 customs posts; in 1848 still 18). The piratical activities of the 'robber knights' were a constant hazard until the formation of the League of Rhenish Cities in 1254.

Between the 15th and the 18th century different types of vessel were developed on different parts of the river.
On the Upper and Middle Rhine the shallowness of the river and the narrowness of the channel at certain points made it necessary to use vessels of shallow draught, and the main traffic was downstream. A variety of types were developed: on the Upper Rhine the 'Lauertanne' (for a single trip downstream) and the 'Schnieke' (the type mainly used by the shipowners of Strasbourg), on the Middle Rhine the 'Oberländer' (Cologne) and the 'Schelch' (Mainz); later the 'Frankenschiff' and the 'Bönder' on the Middle Rhine and the 'Rheinberger' on the Upper Rhine.
The active Dutch shipbuilding industry influenced the types of vessel used on the Lower Rhine and in the Rhine delta. The principal type was the 'Aak', which, in many variant forms, remained in use for centuries.
Towards the end of the 18th century shipping and trading relationships between the Upper and Lower Rhine intensified. As a result the types of vessel used were to a considerable extent unified, with Dutch influences remaining predominant.

Horses towing a Rhine ship (mural painting, 'Gasthof zum Landsknecht' near Sankt Goar)

The 19th century brought revolutionary changes to shipping on the Rhine. The first steamship to sail on the river, in 1816, was the British-built "Prince of Orange", which left Rotterdam on 8 June, reached Cologne on the 12th and from there was towed upstream to Koblenz by horses. The paddle steamer "Caledonia", also British-built, sailed up the Rhine in 1817; in

Shipping on the Rhine

1824 a Dutch steamship, "De Zeeuw", sailed to Kaub, followed in 1825 by another Dutch vessel, "De Rijn", which went up as far as Strasbourg; and in 1832 the "Stadt Frankfurt" sailed all the way up to Basle.

Passenger ships

In 1827 the Prussian Rhine Steamship Company (Preussisch-Rheinische Dampfschiffahrts-Gesellschaft; now the 'Köln-Düsseldorfer', or 'KD' →Practical Information, Köln-Düsseldorfer) began a regular passenger service between Mainz and Cologne in the "Concordia". To counter the rapid development of the railways, which soon put an end to passenger shipping traffic on the Upper Rhine, the 'KD' brought into use new saloon vessels equipped with every amenity.

The KD Line has constantly promoted the improvement of passenger shipping on the Rhine. After developing the paddle steamer from the old wooden vessels by way of the first iron-hulled steamships to the luxurious double-decked saloon steamers of the turn of the century, they have brought into service in more recent times the largest and most modern passenger ships sailing on European inland waters. The first, and indeed the only, hydrofoil on the Rhine sails under the KD flag along with the comfortable cruise ships which have been specially developed to serve as floating hotels on Rhine cruises between Switzerland and the Netherlands.

Barge traffic

After the construction in 1841 of the first iron barge (250 tons) boatbuilding in timber gradually died out. Within some 80 years the length and breadth of barges roughly doubled and their capacity was multiplied tenfold.
The volume of goods traffic soon exceeded the amount of passenger traffic. From 1821 onwards the sailing boats which had been towed upstream by horses gave place to steam tugs. The original paddle tugs were joined in the course of time by screw-driven vessels.
During the 20th century gas engines, steam turbines and above all diesel engines successively displaced the old steam engines of the Rhine tugs, which reached their highest degree of efficiency in the 1930s.

Consequences of the
second world war

After the devastation of the second world war shipping traffic on the Rhine was brought to a complete standstill. The immediate need was to clear the channel of the debris of the bridges which had been blown up along the length of the river, the wrecks of the ships that had been sunk and the unexploded bombs which lay under the water. It was only after the currency reform of 1948 that shipping on the Rhine slowly began to recover; and both shipping traffic and shipbuilding were still subject to authorisation and control by the occupying powers. The surviving tugs were first repaired and made serviceable, and thereafter increasing numbers of new vessels were laid down. The leading German shipbuilding yards on the Rhine are in the Duisburg area (Ruhrort, Meiderich, Walsum) and at Mainz and Germersheim. In 1954 a research institute concerned with the construction of vessels for inland waters was established in Duisburg.

Powered barges

The age of the traditional towed barges, however, was coming to an end, and motor-driven vessels now came to the fore. The first barges equipped with motors appeared on the Rhine at the

The historic Rhine steamship "Concordia"

The modern cruise ship "France" (off Boppard)

Shipping on the Rhine

Powered barges (continued)

end of the 19th century, but it was many years before powered barges became the rule. They were still the exception in the 1940s; then after the second world war their number grew rapidly.

In addition to the normal type of freight-carrying barges there were now increasing numbers of specialised vessels, particularly tankers. The use of tugs declined, partly on grounds of cost, but also because the powered barges were easily manoeuvrable and did not need the assistance of tugs.

Push towing

The 1950s saw the introduction of push towing. Whereas previously tugs had drawn their train of barges behind them, there now came into use push tugs which pushed their barges ahead of them. The first push tug on the Rhine, the "Wasserbüffel" ("Water Buffalo"; a joint German-Dutch development) began to operate in 1957. Thanks to their powerful engines (up to 4400 kW / 6000 HP), push tugs are easily manoeuvrable and can propel a train of up to six barges with a total capacity of up to 16,000 tons.

Coastal motor ships, river- and sea-going vessels

In addition to powered vessels designed for inland waters there are also, particularly on the Lower Rhine, many coastal motor ships and river- and sea-going vessels (mainly carrying crated goods and containers).

Pollution control vessels

In the task of monitoring and controlling pollution an important part is played by bilge-cleaning boats, vessels for the burning of waste chemicals and laboratory ships. The yellow-painted bilge-cleaning boats remove some 10,000 tons of waste oil from vessels sailing on the Rhine every year.

Push tug "Herkules IV" in action

For the sake of completeness mention should also be made of the vessels used by the police and customs authorities.

The Rhine is the main artery of the Central European waterway system. Between Rheinfelden on the High Rhine and its mouths in the Netherlands it is continously navigable by vessels of up to 3000 tons. Its principal tributaries the Neckar, the Main and the Mosel (Moselle) are canalised and regulated by dams, and are navigable by vessels of up to 1500 tons.

A project for improving the navigability of the High Rhine (involving the construction of locks and a canal bypassing the Rhine Falls at Schaffhausen), with the object of bringing the area round Lake Constance into closer economic association with the Upper Rhine, has been shelved on environmental grounds, since it would involve a dangerous encroachment on the natural landscape.

The Rhine's relatively abundant flow of water over the year and the rarity of obstruction by ice facilitate the movement of shipping; and after the removal of the last obstacles in the waterway on the Middle Rhine conditions for water-borne traffic are excellent along all the navigable stretches of the Rhine.

The Rhine is linked with the French canal system by way of the Rhine-Rhône Canal, the Rhine-Marne Canal and the Mosel (Moselle).
The link between the Rhine and the Danube by way of the Main-Danube Canal (the Rhine-Main-Danube Waterway) is not yet complete.
The Rhine-Herne Canal, the Wesel-Datteln Canal and its continuation in the Dortmund-Ems Canal and the Mittelland Canal enable vessels to sail from the Rhine to the North Sea coast and the rivers of central Germany.
In the Netherlands the Amsterdam-Rijnkanaal enables large vessels to sail north to Amsterdam. There is also a great network of waterways in the Rhine-Maas delta, with connections to the inland waterways of Belgium.

There is a busy traffic between many inland ports on the Rhine, especially on the Lower Rhine, and seaports in Germany and other countries.

The water level of the Rhine is regularly measured, and information about water levels – which is, of course, of great importance to shipping – is broadcast several times daily on the radio.
Water levels are related to an officially established low water level, below which the actual level falls on an average of 20 ice-free days in the year. Since the river bed changes from time to time, fresh measurements of the low water level are taken every ten years.

The following measuring points are used: Rheinfelden (on the Upper Rhine: farthest point of navigation on the Rhine), Maxau (Karlsruhe), Speyer, Mannheim, Worms, Mainz, Bingen, Kaub, Koblenz, Andernach, Bonn, Cologne, Düsseldorf, Ruhrort (Duisburg), Wesel, Rees, Emmerich, Lobith (German-Dutch frontier), Pannerdense Kop (branching of Rhine into Pannerdens Kanaal / Nederrijn / Lek and Waal), Nijmegen (on the

Shipping on the Rhine

Old high-water marks at Kaub

Modern gauge at Wesel

Measuring points (continued)	Waal), Tiel (on the Waal), IJsselkop (where the Hollandse IJssel flows into the Nieuwe Maas at Rotterdam).
Shipping channel	Some stretches of the shipping channel are marked for considerable distances by various signs and signals. In the river itself the passage is usually indicated by buoys with coloured markings and sometimes also with beacons or radar reflectors. In addition there are a variety of navigation signs on the banks of the river (on jetties, embankments, etc.) and on bridges.
Navigation signs: see large Rhine map at the end of the book	
	The river and navigation authorities seek to maintain a minimum depth in the channel, ranging between 1.70 m and 2.50 m in different stretches of the river. Any significant variations of depth are announced.
Warning service (Wahrschau)	Where the shipping channel runs under a bridge or through a narrow stretch of the river where only one-way traffic is possible (e.g. in the hilly stretch between Oberwesel and St Goar) arrangements are made to warn shipping traffic and regulate its movement. This service, run by the river and navigation authorities, is known as the 'Wahrschau' service (from the seaman's warning cry "Wahrschau!" = "Watch out!").
Pilots	Although there is no obligation on vessels sailing on any part of the navigable Rhine to take a pilot, experienced pilots are available if required on the Upper Rhine above Mannheim and on the hilly section of the Middle Rhine.
Central Commission on Navigation on the Rhine	The constitution and functions of the Central Commission on Navigation on the Rhine, established in terms of the final act of

the Congress of Vienna (1815), are based on the Mannheim Rhine Navigation Act of 17 October 1868 and the provisions of the treaty of Versailles (28 June 1919), with some amendments under an international agreement of 20 November 1963 and a supplementary agreement of 3 December 1976 on the protection of the Rhine's water.

The Central Commission, which has its headquarters in Strasbourg, is a permanent diplomatic conference with both advisory and directive powers, consisting of representatives of Belgium, the Federal Republic of Germany, France, the United Kingdom, the Netherlands and Switzerland.

The Commission considers all matters concerning navigation on the Rhine. Its responsibilities include monitoring freedom of navigation, the equal treatment of all flags and the removal of technical, administrative, financial and fiscal obstacles to the movement of shipping, drawing up uniform regulations on police and administrative matters and producing an annual report on navigation on the Rhine.

Under the Mannheim Act of 1868 shipping traffic on the Rhine is subject to control by the Ministries of Transport of the riparian states and by subordinate water and navigation authorities and the water protection police.   Responsible authorities
The relevant regulations for the German section of the Rhine and, in the Netherlands, for Pannerdens Kanaal, the Nederrijn, the Lek and the Waal are contained in the Rhine Navigation Police Ordinance (Rheinschiffahrtspolizeiverordnung), as last issued in 1981. There are special provisions applicable to other Dutch waterways in the Rhine-Maas delta.
In Switzerland and France the appropriate national regulations apply. There are also special provisions applying to port traffic (local port regulations) and ferry traffic (Rhine Ferry Regulations).
In all the larger river ports on the Rhine there are customs posts.

The Agreement on Navigation on Lake Constance, between the Federal Republic of Germany, Switzerland and Austria, which came into effect in 1973, regulates traffic on the Obersee and Überlinger See. The surface of the lake is divided into three sections bordering the three riparian countries; this delimitation is not, however, binding.

Pleasure boating on the Rhine is controlled by regulations of 1978 on the use of pleasure craft on inland waterways (Sportbootführerscheinverordnung-Binnen); on Lake Constance it is controlled by the Lake Constance Navigation Regulations (Bodensee-Schiffahrtsordnung) of 1976.   Pleasure boating

The growth of industry in recent times has been accompanied by the development of a very considerable industrial traffic on the Rhine. Originally the main emphasis was on supplying the iron and steel works of the Ruhr with ore and shipping out Ruhr coal, but the Rhine has now become the most important transport route in Central Europe for bulk goods of all kinds. Since the second world war its role has been greatly increased by the diversion of traffic from an east-west to a north-south direction   Freight traffic

45

Shipping on the Rhine

Freight traffic
(continued)

and by the formation and development of the European Economic Community.

The world economic recession of the 1960s and 1970s, however, has led to a reduction in the volume of traffic on the Rhine and a fall in the number of vessels carrying it.

Freight traffic on the navigable Rhine between Rheinfelden and the mouths of the river has at present an annual volume of over 200 million tonnes. The main goods transported are iron ore, building materials, mineral oils, coal and lignite, pig iron, raw steel, rolling-mill products and scrap metal, chemicals, grain, oil-seeds and feeding stuffs.

Freight handled by selected Rhine ports

| Port | Total freight handled | | Length of quays |
	1981	1982	or banks
Rheinfelden	175,000 t	240,000 t	180 m
Basle	8,536,116 t	7,371,192 t	7,000 m
Strasbourg	11,713,329 t	10,491,014 t	37,800 m
Kehl	1,869,690 t	1,765,120 t	12,150 m
Karlsruhe	9,941,579 t	10,488,791 t	16,020 m
Mannheim	8,563,834 t	8,362,656 t	54,500 m
Ludwigshafen	7,987,703 t	7,882,952 t	20,290 m
Mainz	3,564,375 t	3,435,866 t	7,100 m
Wiesbaden	1,188,651 t	1,237,838 t	5,000 m
Koblenz	1,547,375 t	990,031 t	2,700 m
Andernach	2,826,258 t	3,104,000 t	1,065 m
Bonn	431,110 t	391,296 t	900 m
Cologne	11,804,529 t	12,014,091 t	23,400 m
Leverkusen	2,583,689 t	2,131,000 t	960 m
Neuss	4,305,217 t	4,278,793 t	17,500 m
Düsseldorf	2,326,259 t	2,430,685 t	10,470 m
Krefeld	4,249,365 t	3,382,308 t	11,400 m
Duisburg-Ruhrort	20,895,519 t	20,501,000 t	42,400 m
Wesel	592,198 t	625,193 t	805 m
Emmerich	496,008 t	356,604 t	1,200 m
Dordrecht	2,747,000 t	3,700,000 t	12,000 m
Rotterdam (inland traffic)	122,700,000 t	112,776,000 t	36,800 m

Passenger traffic

The Rhine carries the heaviest passenger traffic of all European rivers, mainly consisting of holiday and excursion traffic during the summer. In this field a major role is played by the Köln-Düsseldorfer company (→Practical Information, Köln-Düsseldorfer).

Lake Constance for its part carries a heavier passenger traffic than any other European lake. The principal carriers are the shipping divisions of the German, Swiss and Austrian Railways, together with the Swiss Untersee and Rhine Shipping Company and, in the field of ferry services, the municipal ferry department of Konstanz.

International Rhine fleet

In accordance with a resolution of the Central Commission on Navigation on the Rhine, all vessels sailing on the Rhine have since 1973 been assigned a number. When so numbered, they can obtain a Rhine navigation certificate and are recognised as belonging to the Rhine fleet. The following table gives statistics of the Rhine fleet in 1982:

International Rhine fleet (continued)

Country	Number of vessels	Capacity in tons
Netherlands	5,602	4,364,000
Federal Republic of Germany	3,017	3,207,000
Belgium	1,755	1,381,000
France	928	552,000
Switzerland	418	645,000
Total fleet	11,720	10,149,000
including tankers	1,444	1,699,000

Noted Personalities

German politician and statesman (b. Cologne, d. Rhöndorf / Bad Honnef), trained as a lawyer. Mayor of Cologne from 1917 until his dismissal by the Nazis in 1933. One of the founders of the Christian Democratic Party after the second world war, and first Chancellor of the German Federal Republic (1949 – 1963). His former home at Bad Honnef – Rhöndorf is a memorial museum (foundation 'Bundeskanzler-Adenauer-Haus').

Konrad Adenauer
(5. 1. 1876 – 19. 4. 1967)

Born in Cologne (which had been founded by her grandfather Marcus Vipsanius Agrippa); sister of Caligula and mother of Nero, on whose orders she was murdered. In 48 A.D. she married her uncle Claudius, whom she persuaded in 50 A.D. to grant her the title of Empress and raise Cologne to the status of a Roman colony, thereafter known as 'Colonia Claudia Ara Agrippinensium' (CCAA).

Agrippina the Younger
(6. 11. 15 – 59 A.D.)

German theologian, philosopher and natural scientist (Albert der Grosse – the Great, Count of Bollstädt; b. Lauingen on the Danube, d. Cologne). While a student at Padua became a member of the Dominican order, for which he established a 'Studium Generale' in Cologne in 1248 – 1254. His commentaries on Aristotle and his scientific studies were of seminal importance.

Albertus Magnus
(c. 1200 – 15. 11. 1280)

German-French sculptor, painter and writer (b. Strasbourg, d. Basle). One of the founders of Dadaism. As a creative artist he belonged to the 'concrete' school of abstract art.

Hans Arp
(16. 9. 1887 – 7. 6. 1966)

German bookseller and publisher (originally Bädeker; b. Essen, d. Koblenz). In 1827 he founded in Koblenz the publishing house which produced the famous Baedeker guides.

Karl Baedeker
(3. 11. 1801 – 4. 10. 1859)

German painter, draughtsman and engraver (called Grien; b. Schwäbisch Gmünd in Swabia, d. Strasbourg). A friend and co-worker of Dürer, whose influence can be seen in his work;

Hans Baldung
(1484/85 – September 1545)

47

Noted Personalities

Konrad Adenauer

Karl Baedeker

Ludwig van Beethoven

H. Baldung
(continued)

worked on the Upper Rhine from 1509 onwards. Although rooted in the Late Gothic, he already shows the freedom and sensuous feeling of the Renaissance. His finest picture is the altarpiece in Freiburg Cathedral (1512 – 1516).

August Bebel
(22. 2. 1840 – 13. 8. 1913)

German politician (originally a wood turner; b. Cologne-Deutz, d. Passugg in the Grisons, Switzerland). One of the founders of the German Social Democratic Workers' Party, in the establishment of which he played a decisive part.

Ludwig van Beethoven
(16.?12.1770 – 26. 3. 1827)

German composer (baptised in Bonn 17. 12. 1770, d. Vienna). A pupil of Haydn, he ranks with Haydn and Mozart as one of the three great masters of the Viennese classical school. His works include piano sonatas, symphonies, string quartets, the opera "Fidelio", masses and lieder.

Carl Friedrich Benz
(25. 11. 1844 – 4. 4. 1929)

German engineer and automobile constructor (b. Karlsruhe, d. Ladenburg in Baden). In 1885, independently of Gottlieb Daimler, he developed a three-wheeled motor vehicle driven by a single-cylinder four-stroke engine. His firm (Benz & Cie) founded in 1883, amalgamated in 1926 with the Daimler firm to form the Daimler-Benz company (AG; 'Mercedes'), with headquarters in Stuttgart.

Jakob Bernoulli
(27. 12. 1654 – 16. 8. 1705)
Johann Bernoulli
(27. 7. 1667 – 1. 1. 1748)

Swiss mathematicians (brothers; both b. and d. in Basle). Jakob Bernoulli made a decisive contribution to the introduction and development of the infinitesimal calculus (description of the Bernoulli numbers). After his death Johann Bernoulli, teacher of Leonhard →Euler and the greatest mathematician of his day, continued his work, particularly on the theory of the integral and differential calculus.

Ernst Bloch
(8. 7. 1885 – 4. 8. 1977)

German philosopher (b. Ludwigshafen, d. Tübingen). Developed on the basis of Jewish-Christian eschatology a Marxist philosophy of hope through which nature and society gradually overcome their inadequacy and achieve a Utopian harmony of life.

Arnold Böcklin
(16. 10. 1827 – 16. 1. 1901)

Swiss painter (b. Basle, d. Fiesole, near Florence). A Romantic artist who produced decorative paintings notable for their strong contrasts of light and shade and their brilliance of colour. He painted idealised landscapes peopled by mythic figures.

German writer (b. Cologne), one of the outstanding figures in post-war German literature. Nobel prize for literature 1972.

Heinrich Böll
(b. 21. 12. 1917)

German writer of the High Romantic period (b. Ehrenbreitstein, Koblenz, d. Aschaffenburg); brother of the woman writer Bettina von Arnim. With his friend (later his brother-in-law) Achim von Arnim he published a collection of German folksongs under the title "Des Knaben Wunderhorn". His short stories and fairy tales show great narrative skill. Brentano is regarded as the creator of the figure of the Loreley, immortalised in the poem by Heinrich →Heine, "Ich weiss nicht, was soll es bedeuten …"

Clemens Brentano
(8. 9. 1778 – 28. 7. 1842)

German dramatist and physician (b. Goddelau, near Darmstadt, d. Zurich). Inspired by the ideas of the French Revolution, he established a 'Society of the Rights of Man' in Giessen and published a pamphlet supporting a peasants' revolt in Hesse. His revolutionary dramas "Dantons Tod" ("Danton's Death") and "Woyzeck" opened up new avenues for the theatre.

Georg Büchner
(17. 10. 1813 – 19. 2. 1837)

German composer and poet (Peter Carl August Cornelius; b. and d. Mainz). Under the influence of Liszt and Wagner he composed music of great delicacy and warmth of feeling. His stage works were unsuccessful, but his numerous lieder, settings of his own poems, have retained their place in the repertoire.

Peter Cornelius
(24. 12. 1824 – 26. 10. 1874)

German philosopher (b. Biebrich, near Wiesbaden, d. Seis am Schlern, South Tirol). Founder of a method of systematic interpretation of intellectual, and particularly historical, ideas (hermeneutics).

Wilhelm Dilthey
(19. 11. 1833 – 1. 10. 1911)

German inventor (Karl Friedrich Drais, Freiherr von Sauerbronn; b. and d. Karlsruhe). Developed a light four-wheeled vehicle driven by human muscular power, later used for line inspection on railways. He also invented a two-wheeled 'running machine' with handlebars and a saddle – the forerunner of the bicycle – which became popular, particularly in Britain and France.

Karl Friedrich Drais
(29. 4. 1785 – 10. 12. 1851)

Roman emperor (Nero Claudius Drusus). Between 12 and 9 B.C., from his base at Mainz, he conducted a campaign against the Germanic tribes on the right bank of the Rhine, advancing as far as the Elbe (Albis). On the way back he died as a result of a fall from his horse.

Drusus
(38 – 9 B.C.)

German philologist (b. Bossigt, near Wesel, d. Sonnenberg, near Wiesbaden). His "Complete Orthographical Dictionary of the German Language" (1880) laid the foundations of a uniform German orthography. The "Duden", now published in Mannheim and Leipzig, remains *the* authoritative work of reference on German orthography.

Konrad Duden
(3. 1. 1829 – 1. 8. 1911)

Swiss general (b. Konstanz, d. Contamines, near Geneva), a reformer of the Swiss Confederation and one of the founders of the International Committee of the Red Cross. As head of the Swiss Survey Board he was responsible for the production of

Guillaume Henri Dufour
(15. 9. 1787 – 14. 7. 1875)

Noted Personalities

G. H. Dufour
(continued)

the Topographical Map of Switzerland, known as the 'Dufour Map', a pioneering work notable particularly for its representation of mountains.

Erasmus of Rotterdam
(28. 10. 1466 – 12. 1. 1536)

Dutch philologist and humanist (from 1496 known as Desiderius Erasmus; b. Rotterdam, d. Basle), the leading thinker of his day. His critical and satirical attacks on the secularisation of theology and the church made him a forerunner of the Reformation – from which, however, he always distanced himself.

Leonhard Euler
(15. 4. 1707 – 18. 9. 1783)

Swiss mathematician (b. Basle, d. St Petersburg). A pupil of Johann →Bernoulli, he replaced the geometric and synthetic method then in fashion by the more general analytical method, which he applied to physical problems. In an extensive and many-sided body of work (Euler formulae, wave theory of light, development of differential calculus, etc.) he formulated fundamental ideas in the fields of mathematics, physics and astronomy.

Anne Frank
(12. 6. 1929 – March 1945)

German Jewish girl (b. Frankfurt am Main, d. in Bergen-Belsen concentration camp), who kept a diary recording her family's life in hiding in Amsterdam until their despatch to German concentration camps. A moving document on the Nazi tyranny, it was translated into many languages and became the subject of a film.

Stefan George
(12. 7. 1868 – 4. 12. 1933)

German lyric poet (b. Büdesheim, near Bingen, d. Minusio, near Locarno). Turning deliberately away from naturalism and scientific positivism, he developed an aesthetic and elitist approach to art which combined beauty and intellectuality in a strict and often rigid form. In his vision of a perfect aesthetic world ideas derived from the heroic tales of classical Greece, medieval asceticism and the aristocratic life were combined with a delight in the decorative.

Gershom Ben Jehuda
(c. 960 – 1028 or 1040)

Jewish legal scholar (known as Meor ha-Gola, 'Light of the Diaspora'; b. Metz?, d. Mainz). Founder of Talmudic scholarship in Germany and France.

Curt Goetz
(17. 11. 1888 – 12. 9. 1960)

German writer and actor (originally Kurt Götz; b. Mainz, d. Grabs, E. Switzerland). Wrote mainly comedies, in which he often played the leading role. Some of his plays were made into films.

Gottfried von Strassburg
(12th – 13th c.)

One of the three great poets of the Hohenstaufen period, along with Hartmann von Aue and Wolfram von Eschenbach. Following an Anglo-Norman model, he wrote the epic poem "Tristan" (unfinished), one of the great works of Middle High German love poetry.

Gustaf Gründgens
(22. 12. 1899 – 7. 10. 1963)

German actor, producer and theatre director (b. Düsseldorf, d. Manila, Philippines). Director of the State Theatre in Berlin (1934 – 45), the Municipal Theatres in Düsseldorf (1947 – 55) and the German Theatre in Hamburg (1955 – 63). On the stage and in films he excelled in the representation of powerful and dynamic characters, and as a producer he was responsible for some notable dramatic and operatic productions.

Matthias Grünewald
(c. 1470/74 – August 1528)

German painter (originally Mathis Gothardt, also known as Nithardt; b. Aschaffenburg?, d. Halle an der Saale). Ranks with

Clemens Brentano

Erasmus of Rotterdam

Johannes Gutenberg

Dürer as one of the two great painters of the Late Gothic period in Germany. His extensive output, only a small part of which has survived, reflects a profound and thoughtful devoutness and wide artistic range. Alongside his moving representations of suffering and sorrow are scenes of mystical transfiguration and fantastic dreams. His masterpiece, the Isenheim Altar (in the Unterlinden Museum, Colmar), already shows the influence of Renaissance ideas.

Inventor of printing with movable characters (originally Henne Gänsfleisch zur Laden, scion of a patrician family of Mainz; b. and d. in Mainz). He developed the main tools of the printing trade: the metal mould for type, the hand casting instrument, the printing press and printer's ink. His masterpiece is the 42-line Gutenberg Bible (1452 – 1455), a copy of which can be seen in the Gutenberg Museum in Mainz.

Johannes Gutenberg
(c. 1397 – 3. 2. 1468)

Dutch painter (b. Antwerp?, buried on 1. 9. 1666 in Haarlem). He painted mainly portraits and groups of people in all walks of life. His very personal style, with its sure and vigorous brushwork, anticipates some features of Impressionism.

Frans Hals
(between 1581 and 1585 – 1666)

Swabian dialect poet (b. Basle, d. Schwetzingen), whose "Alemannic Poems" celebrate rural life in his native southern Baden. His prose tales are written in simple language and cheerfully popular in tone.

Johann Peter Hebel
(10. 5. 1760 – 22. 9. 1826)

German poet, writer and publicist (originally Harry Heine; b. Düsseldorf, d. Paris). Author of the popular 'Loreley' song, "Ich weiss nicht, was soll es bedeuten …" ("I cannot divine what it meaneth …" →The Rhine in Poems and Quotations). His polemical attacks on narrow patriotism, petty-bourgeois mentality and political wrongs in Germany brought him into disfavour with the authorities, but, living in exile in France, he gained a considerable reputation for his elegant and witty style, mingling sensibility and mockery, and his critical intelligence.

Heinrich Heine
(13. 12. 1797 – 17. 2. 1856)

Middle High German poet and minnesinger (known as 'Frauenlob' = 'Praise of Women'; b. in or near Meissen in Saxony, d. Mainz). One of the twelve 'masters of the Meistersang'.

Heinrich von Meissen
(c. 1250 – 29. 11. 1318)

Noted Personalities

Hildegard of Bingen
(1098 – 17. 9. 1179)

The first German woman mystic (b. Bermersheim, near Alzey, d. in Rupertsberg convent, near Bingen). A Benedictine nun, foundress of Rupertsberg convent. In addition to her mystical writings she wrote on scientific and medical subjects.

Hans Holbein the Younger
(1497/98 – 1543)

German painter and draughtsman (b. Augsburg, buried in London on 29. 11. 1543). Hans Holbein is the leading representative of the early Renaissance in Germany. Notable particularly for his portraits, which show great fidelity to life and cool objectivity. His friendship with →Erasmus of Rotterdam and his encounter with the ideas of humanism left a strong imprint on his work.

Johan Huizinga
(7. 12. 1872 – 1. 2. 1945)

Dutch historian (b. Groningen, d. De Steeg, near Arnhem). His main interests lay in the cultural and intellectual world of Burgundy and the Low Countries in the late medieval period.

Karl Jaspers
(23. 2. 1883 – 26. 2. 1969)

German philosopher (b. Oldenburg/Oldbg., d. Basle). Founder of a humanistically oriented psychopathology, and the principal representative of existential philosophy in Germany.

Jean-Baptiste Kléber
(9. 3. 1753 – 14. 6. 1800)

French general (b. Strasbourg, murdered in Cairo), who took part in Bonaparte's Egyptian expedition, inflicted several defeats on the Turks and captured Cairo.

Adolf Kolping
(8. 12. 1813 – 4. 12. 1865)

German churchman (b. Kerpen, near Cologne, d. Cologne). Became a Roman Catholic priest in 1845; founder of 'Gesellenvereine' ('associations of companions'; also known as 'Kolping families') for religious, social, professional and cultural education.

Carl von Kügelgen
(6. 2. 1772 – 9. 1. 1832)
Gerhard von Kügelgen
(6. 2. 1772 – 27. 3. 1820)

German painters. Carl (b. Bacharach, d. Friedheim, near Tallinn) worked at the Imperial court in St Petersburg, painting mainly landscapes. His twin brother Gerhard (b. Bacharach, murdered at Loschwitz, near Dresden) painted religious and mythological pictures in neo-classical style, and was also an excellent portrait-painter.

Wilhelm Lehmbruck
(4. 1. 1881 – 25. 3. 1919)

German sculptor (b. Duisburg-Meiderich, committed suicide in Berlin). One of the leading German representatives of Expressionist sculpture, creating elongated slender-limbed figures which won him an international reputation. His principal works are in the Lehmbruck Museum in Duisburg.

Stefan Lochner
(c. 1410 – 1451)

German painter (b. Meersburg?, d. Cologne). The greatest master of the Cologne school of painters, he combined the strict idealised religious tradition of medieval painting with the 'modern' realism of the Low Countries to achieve an unmistakable personal style. His works include such fine paintings as the "Madonna in the Rose-Garden" and the "Madonna with the Violet" as well as the famous altarpiece dedicated to the city's patron saints in Cologne Cathedral (the so-called 'Dombild').

Gerhard Mercator
(5. 3. 1512 – 2. 12. 1594)

Geographer and cosmographer (originally Gerhard Cremer; b. Rupelmonde?, near Antwerp, d. Duisburg). He developed the Mercator projection as a means of representing the curved surface of the earth on a map with a rectangular grid. His atlas of the world was published posthumously in 1595. There is an important Mercator collection in the Lower Rhineland Museum, Duisburg.

Swiss engraver (b. Basle, d. Langenschwalbach). In his 30-volume "Topographia" and his "Theatrum Europaeum" he produced a magnificent series of views and plans of cities and towns all over Europe which are of great historical and cultural interest.

Matthäus Merian the Elder
(22. 9. 1593 – 19. 6. 1650)

Austrian statesman (Klemens Wenzel Nepomuk Lothar, Fürst von Metternich; b. Koblenz, d. Vienna). A student in Mainz and the Netherlands during the French Revolution, he thereafter devoted his efforts to combatting the extension of the revolutionary movement in Europe. He saw the only prospect of preserving political stability in the maintenance of the monarchic system (the 'Metternich system', based on an equilibrium between the powers).

Prince Metternich
(15. 5. 1773 – 11. 6. 1859)

Protestant clergyman (b. Wesel, drowned at sea), who bought Manhattan island from the Algonquin Indians for a few trinkets and founded the settlement of New Amsterdam, later New York City, U.S.A.

Peter Minuit (Minnewit)
(c. 1580 – 1638 or 1641)

German theologian, Hebrew scholar and cosmographer (b. Ingelheim on the Rhine, d. Basle). His principal works were the "Biblia Hebraica" and the "Cosmographia", with descriptions of territories and towns in the German-speaking countries.

Sebastian Münster
(20. 1. 1488 – 26. 5. 1552)

Mathematican, theologian and philosopher (Nicolaus Cusanus, Nikolaus von Kues, born Nikolaus Chryfftz or Krebs; b. Kues an der Mosel, d. Todi, Italy). Intellectually he stood at the point of transition from the Middle Ages to modern times. He sought to reconcile the opposing forces in human life in the concept of the 'coincidentia oppositorum', seeing all earthly things achieving oneness in God.

Nicholas of Cusa
(1401 – 11. 8. 1464)

Architect (b. Troppau in northern Moravia, d. Düsseldorf), one of the most productive exponents of the Jugendstil (Art Nouveau). A founder member of the 'Vienna Sezession' and the 'Deutscher Werkbund' and a member of the 'Darmstädter Künstlerkolonie' (artists' colony).

Josef Maria Olbrich
(22. 12. 1867 – 8. 8. 1908)

German theologian (name also spelt Rhabanus or Hrabanus Maurus, originally Hraban; b. and d. in Mainz), Archbishop of Mainz 847 – 856. His principal work, "De rerum naturis seu de universo" ("On the Nature of Things, or the Universe", 22 volumes), was a compendium of the learning of antiquity and the early Middle Ages.

Rabanus Maurus
(c. 780 – 4. 3. 856)

German social reformer (b. Hamm an der Sieg, d. Neuwied), founder of agricultural cooperatives and social insurance organisations ('Raiffeisenvereine', 'Raiffeisenkassen', 'Raiffeisenversicherungen').

Friedrich Wilhelm Raiffeisen
(30. 3. 1818 – 11. 3. 1888)

The most celebrated and most creative of the Dutch painters (Rembrandt Harmensz van Rijn; b. Leyden, d. Amsterdam). After a period of productive activity in Leyden he moved in 1632 to Amsterdam, and in 1634 married Saskia van Uijlenburgen, a wealthy woman of good family. During the first ten years in Amsterdam he became the most popular portrait-painter of the day, but thereafter his increasing reluctance to paint his sitters as they desired to be seen brought him into ever greater financial difficulties. He died in poverty and social isolation, leaving

Rembrandt
(15. 7. 1606 – 4. 10. 1669)

Noted Personalities

Rembrandt (continued)

an artistic output of incalculable value (562 paintings, 300 etchings, 1600 drawings).

Joseph Victor von Scheffel
(16. 2. 1826 – 9. 4. 1886)

German writer (b. and d. Karlsruhe), the author of popular students' songs (including "Gaudeamus") and of an epic poem, "Der Trompeter von Säckingen" ("The Trumpeter of Säckingen"), and a novel, "Ekkehard", which reflect his romantically patriotic attitude. His manuscripts are in the Museum of Upper Rhineland Writers in Karlsruhe.

René Schickele
(4. 8. 1883 – 31. 1. 1940)

Writer (b. Oberehnheim in Alsace, d. Vence, near Nice). The son of a German father and a French mother, he worked in Berlin, Paris and Strasbourg as a journalist; from 1916 to 1920 he lived in Zurich, publishing the Expressionist and pacifist "Weisse Blätter"; thereafter he lived until 1932 at Badenweiler in the Black Forest, and later in France. In his works he sought to reconcile the tensions between German and French cultural attitudes.

Schinderhannes
(25. 5. 1783 – 21. 11. 1803)

Bandit chief (real name Johannes Wilhelm Bückler; b. Miehlen in the Taunus, executed in Mainz), who operated mainly in what is now the 'Land' of Rhineland-Palatinate, then held by France. In his plundering expeditions he showed himself an enemy of the French and a protector of the poor, and acquired a legendary fame as a kind of German Robin Hood. Condemned to death in a show trial, he was publicly guillotined in Mainz (guillotine still preserved in police headquarters, Mainz).

Martin Schongauer
(between 1425 and
1453 – 2. 2. 1491)

Engraver and painter (b. and d. Colmar), who continued the tradition of the Upper Rhineland but also showed some Dutch influences. Only a few of his paintings have survived ("Virgin in the Rose-Garden", Dominican Church, Colmar). His many fine engravings strongly influenced the work of Albrecht Dürer.

Robert Schumann
(8. 6. 1810 – 29. 7. 1856)

German composer (b. Zwickau, d. Endenich/Bonn). His works, informed by High Romantic sensibility but also reflecting his inner conflicts, influenced Brahms, Chopin, Schubert and other composers. His lieder included sensitive settings of poems by Goethe, Eichendorff, Mörike and Heine. Apart from these his finest works are his cycles of pieces for the piano and orchestral works in which the piano plays a dominant role. In 1840 he married the pianist Clara Wieck (13. 9. 1819 – 20. 5. 1896), who gave performances of his works. In 1850 he became municipal director of music in Düsseldorf. In 1854, mentally deranged, Schumann attempted to commit suicide by jumping into the Rhine.

Carl Schurz
(2. 3. 1829 – 14. 5. 1906)

Politician and publicist (b. Liblar, near Cologne, d. New York). As a student he became involved in the democratic movement of 1848, and was compelled to flee from Germany and emigrate to the United States. There he soon felt entirely at home and became a convinced Republican. Appointed Secretary of the Interior by President Hayes (1877 – 1881), he strove for domestic reforms and a more humane policy towards the Indians. His wife Margarethe Meyer-Schurz founded the first kindergarten in the United States.

Albert Schweitzer
(14. 1. 1876 – 4. 9. 1965)

Protestant theologian, medical missionary, cultural philosopher and musician (b. Kaysersberg in Alsace, d. Lambaréné, Gabon). In 1913 he established at Lambaréné in Gabon a

Heinrich Heine   *Rembrandt*   *Johann Gottfried Tulla*

hospital which was at first financed out of his own income from organ concerts, lectures and publications. As a theologian his main achievement lay in his study of the life of Jesus, as a musician in his interpretation of Bach's organ works. In 1952 he was awarded the Nobel Peace Prize.

German writer (real name Netty Radvanyi, née Reiling; b. Mainz, d. East Berlin). A member of the German Communist Party, she emigrated in 1933 to France and in 1941 to Mexico, returning to East Berlin in 1947. In her writings she fought against social injustice, oppression and inhumanity. Perhaps her best known work is "Das siebte Kreuz" ("The Seventh Cross"), a novel of the German resistance to Hitler written in exile in Mexico, for which she received the Büchner Prize in 1947.

Anna Seghers
(19. 11. 1900 – 1. 6. 1983)

Roman emperor (Marcus Aurelius Severus Alexander). In 234 A.D. he advanced to the Rhine and built a bridge over the river at Mainz in order to prevent the Germanic tribes from crossing the Limes (the Roman frontier line). In March 235 he was murdered, along with his mother Iulia Mammaea, in a Roman camp at the site of Bretzenheim (now a south-western district of Mainz).

Severus Alexander
(208 – 235 A.D.)

German organ-builder (b. Kleinbobritzsch in Saxony, d. Strasbourg). Among the many organs he built are those of St Leonhard's Church in Basle, Strasbourg Cathedral and the Benedictine abbeys of Marmoutier and Ebersmunster in Alsace. After his death his son Johann Andreas Silbermann (26. 6. 1712–11. 2. 1783) carried on his organ-building workshop in Strasbourg.

Andreas Silbermann
(16. 5. 1678 – 16. 3. 1734)

German civil engineer (b. Karlsruhe, d. Paris). In 1817 he established a school of engineering in Karlsruhe which in 1825 became the Polytechnic School, Germany's first technical college ('Technische Hochschule'; so called from 1885; from 1902 known as the 'Fridericiana'; from 1967 a University). From 1817 onwards Tulla directed the work (not completed until 1885) on the straightening, canalisation and concentration of the Upper Rhine, making possible the reclamation of the marshy land flanking the river.

Johann Gottfried Tulla
(20. 3. 1770 – 27. 3. 1828)

Noted Personalities

Friedrich Weinbrenner
(29. 11. 1766 – 1. 3. 1826)

German architect (b. and d. in Karlsruhe), who ranks with Karl Friedrich Schinkel as one of the best known exponents of the classical style in Germany. He left his distinctive mark on the townscape of Karlsruhe, where he was municipal architect from 1800 onwards.

Count Zeppelin
(8. 7. 1838 – 8. 3. 1917)

German airship constructor (Ferdinand Graf von Zeppelin; b. Konstanz, d. Berlin). Built the first rigid dirigible, launched at Manzell on Lake Constance (now part of Friedrichshafen) on 2 July 1900, which had all the structural features of the 129 later zeppelins.

Carl Zuckmayer
(27. 12. 1896 – 18. 1. 1977)

German writer and dramatist (b. Nackenheim, d. Visp, S. W. Switzerland). In his works, full of refreshing naturalness and popular vitality, he directs his attacks, with cryptic humour and delicate satire, against bourgeois narrowness, subservience and militarism. His principal works are "Der fröhliche Weinberg" ("The Merry Vineyard"), "Der Hauptmann von Köpenick" ("The Captain of Köpenick") and "Des Teufels General" ("The Devil's General").

History

During the Stone Age men live in caves, tents or huts, gaining their subsistence by hunting, gathering and fishing; the social unit is the group or horde. Among the oldest finds on German soil giving evidence of human life are the lower jaw of Heidelberg Man (from Mauer, near Heidelberg) and skeletal remains of Neanderthal Man from the Neander valley near Düsseldorf.
From c. 500,000 to 8000 B.C.

Period of transition to the establishment of permanent human settlements; pile dwellings on Lake Constance. Beginnings of farming and stock-rearing, and of trade and traffic.
8000 – 1800

Bronze Age in Central Europe; favoured materials are bronze, amber and gold.
1800 – 750

Beginning of Iron Age.
around 1000

The Celts (Indo-European peoples) occupy parts of Western and Central Europe and Switzerland (Helvetii).
from 600

The Celts establish the La Tène culture (named after the type site of La Tène in western Switzerland); one of their centres is on the Middle Rhine.
5th century

The Romans conquer southern France and establish the province of Gallia Narbonensis (121).
from 125

The Batavi, a Germanic tribe, in the Rhine delta.
1st century

Germanic peoples press forward from the north towards Celtic territory, including the Rhineland.
around 70

Julius Caesar conquers Gaul; beginning of the linguistic and cultural romanisation of what is now France.
As a result of the wars waged by Rome (first account of Germany in Caesar's "De Bello Gallico") the Rhine becomes the north-eastern frontier of Roman territory. Many later towns and settlements grow up on the site or in the vicinity of Roman camps. The northern part of Gaul is inhabited by the Belgae, a Celtic people.
58 – 51

Caesar constructs the first bridge over the Rhine between Koblenz and Andernach; a second bridge is built farther upstream in 53.
55

Roman rule established on Lake Constance (Latin 'Lacus Venetus').
around 50

Forts established at Cologne, Trier, Koblenz, Mainz, etc., to protect the Rhine frontier.
after 40

The Romans decide to subjugate Germany as far as the Elbe.
around 16

Tiberius defeats the Vindelici (a Celtic people) and establishes a military base at Bregenz, on Lake Constance; other Roman foundations on the shores of the lake are Arbon and Konstanz.
16 / 15

History

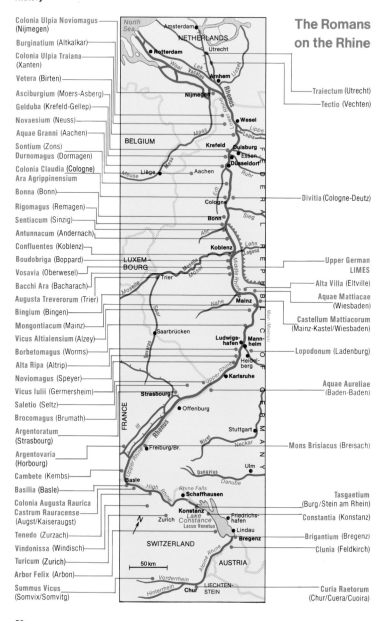

The Romans on the Rhine

Colonia Ulpia Noviomagus (Nijmegen)

Burginatium (Altkalkar)

Colonia Ulpia Traiana (Xanten)

Vetera (Birten)

Asciburgium (Moers-Asberg)

Gelduba (Krefeld-Gellep)

Novaesium (Neuss)

Aquae Granni (Aachen)

Sontium (Zons)
Durnomagus (Dormagen)

Colonia Claudia (Cologne) Ara Agrippinensium

Bonna (Bonn)

Rigomagus (Remagen)

Sentiacum (Sinzig)

Antunnacum (Andernach)

Confluentes (Koblenz)

Boudobriga (Boppard)

Vosavia (Oberwesel)

Bacchi Ara (Bacharach)

Augusta Treverorum (Trier)

Bingium (Bingen)

Mongontiacum (Mainz)

Vicus Altiaiensium (Alzey)

Borbetomagus (Worms)

Alta Ripa (Altrip)

Noviomagus (Speyer)

Vicus Iulii (Germersheim)

Saletio (Seltz)

Brocomagus (Brumath)

Argentoratum (Strasbourg)

Argentovaria (Horbourg)

Cambete (Kembs)

Basilia (Basle)

Colonia Augusta Raurica
Castrum Rauracense (Augst/Kaiseraugst)

Tenedo (Zurzach)

Vindonissa (Windisch)

Turicum (Zurich)

Arbor Felix (Arbon)

Summus Vicus (Somvix/Somvitg)

Traiectum (Utrecht)

Tectio (Vechten)

Divitia (Cologne-Deutz)

Upper German LIMES

Alta Villa (Eltville)

Aquae Mattiacae (Wiesbaden)

Castellum Mattiacorum (Mainz-Kastel/Wiesbaden)

Lopodunum (Ladenburg)

Aquae Aureliae (Baden-Baden)

Mons Brisiacus (Breisach)

Tasgaetium (Burg/Stein am Rhein)

Constantia (Konstanz)

Brigantium (Bregenz)

Clunia (Feldkirch)

Curia Raetorum (Chur/Cuera/Cuoira)

Drusus, stepson of the Emperor Augustus, builds some 50 forts along the left bank of the river to protect the Rhine frontier.	around 15 B. C.
Roman campaigns in western Europe and Germany, sometimes advancing as far as the Elbe.	12. B.C. – 16. A. D.
In a battle in the Teutoburger Wald (Teutoburg Forest) a Roman army commanded by Publius Quinctilius Varus is defeated by the Germans under the leadership of Arminius (Hermann). The Romans are driven back to the Rhine and the Danube.	9 A. D.
The Romans abandon their plan to conquer Germany. The Roman legions are posted at permanent stations on the Rhine – two legions at Vetera (near Xanten), two at Mainz and one each at Neuss, Bonn, Strasbourg and Windisch.	16
The Danube becomes a fortified Roman frontier in south-western Germany; establishment of the province of Raetia.	46
The frontier of the Roman Empire on the Upper Rhine is moved forward to the Black Forest and the sources of the Danube.	69 / 70
Rebellion of the Batavi on the Lower Rhine against Rome.	69 – 71
The Romans conquer the area between the Rhine and the Danube (the Agri Decumates); building of a road from the Rhine to the Danube.	74
Establishment of the provinces of Lower Germany (Germania Inferior), with Cologne as the headquarters of a legate, and Upper Germany (Germania Superior), with Mainz as residence of the governor.	90
In order to prevent incursions by the Germanic peoples the Romans construct the Upper German and Raetian Limes, a system of frontier defences some 550 km long between the Rhine and the Danube. The Upper German Limes begins below Rheinbrohl (between Koblenz and Bonn), reaches the Main at Hanau and continues south through the Neckarland to Lorch. Beyond this the Raetian Limes runs through the Franconian Alb (Fränkische Alb) to the Danube, ending at Eining (west of Kelheim). Forts are established at Wiesbaden, Augsburg, Regensburg, Passau and other sites.	from 90 Limes
Trier becomes capital of the province of Belgica Prima.	117
First Frankish incursion on the Lower Rhine.	239
The Franks and Alemanni conquer territory in Upper Germany and Raetia; the Rhine and Danube again become the frontier of the Roman Empire.	259 / 260
Union of the Roman provinces in western Europe; Cologne and Trier become imperial residences.	259 – 274
Franks, Alemanni and Burgundians cross the Rhine frontier.	286 – 288
Division of the Roman Empire into four (the Tetrarchy); Trier becomes capital of the western section, which is allocated to Constantius.	293

History

334 / 335	Constantius fights the Alemanni in the Lake Constance area.
335	Julian becomes Emperor of the West.
357	Julian defeats the Alemanni at Strasbourg.
around 375	The Huns advance into Europe.
395	The capital of the western Empire is moved from Trier to Milan, the headquarters of civil administration to Arles.
around 400	Beginning of the great migrations.
400 – 402	Roman troops are pulled back from the Rhine and from Raetia.
405	The Alemanni and Franks establish themselves on the Rhine; the Burgundians found a kingdom centred on Worms.
early 5th century	The Burgundians (Nibelungs) are annihilated by the Romans and their allies the Huns.
Nibelungs	The "Nibelungenlied" ("Lay of the Nibelungs"), a Middle High German epic poem written in rhyming four-line stanzas, was composed around 1200, incorporating elements from the heroic legends of various Germanic peoples.

The story of the "Nibelungenlied" is linked with the Rhine. The hero of the poem, Siegfried, traditionally came from Xanten, while the Burgundian kings Gunther, Gernot and Giselher, brothers of Siegfried's beloved Kriemhild, ruled from 413 onwards from their capital at Worms. Hagen of Tronje, King Gunther's faithful follower, came from Tronege (?), thought to have been situated to the west of Worms.

Two different themes are combined in the "Nibelungenlied": Siegfried's wooing of Kriemhild and the fall of the Burgundian kingdom.

Hagen throwing the
Nibelungs' Treasure
into the Rhine
(statue at Worms)

King Gunther promises Siegfried his sister in marriage on condition that he first overcomes Queen Brünhild of Iceland, a woman of fabulous strength, substituting himself for Gunther without her knowledge. Siegfried vanquishes Brünhild with the help of a cloak of darkness; but when the queen later learns of the deception she incites Hagen to murder Siegfried. After Siegfried's death the gold treasure of the Nibelungs, which he had wrested from the dwarf Alberich, passes into the hands of the Burgundian kings, now themselves known as the 'Nibelungs', and is then thrown into the Rhine by Hagen.

Kriemhild, who becomes the wife of Etzel (Attila), king of the Huns, seeks to revenge herself on the Burgundians for Siegfried's death and the loss of the Treasure. During a feast in Hungary to which she has invited her brothers and their retinues an armed conflict develops in which all involved are killed; the last to die are Gunther and Hagen, who refuse to reveal the hiding-place of the Nibelungs' treasure. Finally Kriemhild herself, ruthless in her pursuit of revenge, is killed by Hildebrand, armourer to Dietrich von Berne (Theodoric the Great; Bern = Verona), who is presented as a knightly Christian hero.

This episode reflects an actual historical event – the destruction of the Burgundian kingdom by the Huns at the behest of a Roman general in 436.

The "Nibelungenlied", which is preserved in several manu- scripts dating from the second half of the 13th century, at- tracted renewed interest during the Romantic period, when many German writers were influenced by the literature of the medieval period. Between 1854 and 1874 Richard Wagner (1813 – 1883) wrote his four-part operatic cycle "The Ring of the Nibelung" ("The Rhine Gold", "The Valkyrie", "Siegfried" and "The Twilight of the Gods"), with some alterations of emphasis and the incorporation of various figures from Germanic mythology.

Nibelungs (continued)

The Franks finally gain possession of Roman territories on the left bank of the Rhine.

455

Romulus Augustus, last Roman Emperor of the West, is de- posed by the Germanic military leader Odoacer.

476

Clovis (Chlodwig) I, a Frankish king of the Merovingian dynasty, eliminates the last vestiges of Roman rule in Gaul and founds the Frankish kingdom.

482 – 511

The territory in the Vosges which was occupied by the Aleman- ni during the great migrations and is now ruled by the Franks becomes known as Alsace (German Elsass, from 'Elisaza', "land of the incomers").

around 496

Christianisation of the Germanic peoples, in many places by Irish-Scottish monks.

from 600

Foundation of the great monastery of St Gallen or St Gall (origi- nally the cell of St Gallus).

around 720

Foundation of Reichenau monastery, on the island of that name in Lake Constance.

724

Boniface (672/673 – 754), an English monk, tne 'apostle of Ger- many', becomes titular archbishop of Mainz.

747

Charlemagne, of the Carolingian or Arnulfine house, king of the Franks.

768 – 814

Consolidation of Charlemagne's authority in western Europe by his coronation as Emperor in Rome; revival of the Roman Empire. Division of the Frankish empire into counties; protec- tion of its territory secured by the establishment of 'marches' on the frontiers; imperial strongholds (Aachen, Ingelheim, Worms, Nijmegen, etc.) become economic and cultural centres.

800

War between Charlemagne's three grandsons Ludwig (Louis) the German, Charles the Bald and Lothair I when Lothair claims sole imperial authority.

840

Lothair defeated at Fontenay.

841

Ludwig and Charles confirm their alliance by the Strasbourg Oaths (in Old High German and Old French).

842

Division of the Carolingian empire under the treaty of Verdun. The area west of the Schelde, the west Frankish kingdom (Neustria), falls to Charles the Bald; the east Frankish kingdom

843

History

843 (continued)	(Austrasia) to Ludwig the German (with its western boundary running from the mouth of the Weser by way of the river Ruhr to the Rhine and the Aare); Italy and some territories north of the Alps to Lothair. The districts of Mainz, Speyer and Worms on the left bank of the Rhine are included within Ludwig the German's domain.
843 – 880	The German Empire develops out of the eastern Frankish kingdom.
around 860	The territory extending from the North Sea to the sources of the Maas and the Mosel (Moselle), which formed part of Lothair's kingdom, becomes known as Lotharingia (Lorraine).
870	Under the treaty of Mersen (Meerssen, near Maastricht) Lotharingia is divided between Charles the Bald and Ludwig the German. Alsace falls to the German Empire.
917	Forces of Hungarian cavalry destroy Basle and its Minster.
10th/11th century	Under the Ottonians Romanesque architecture begins to flourish (Mainz and Speyer cathedrals).
1044	Lotharingia is divided into Lower Lotharingia to the north (the present-day Netherlands and Belgium, excluding Flanders) and Upper Lotharingia to the south (the Mosel area).
1079	Under the dynasty of the Hohenstaufens Alsace becomes the heart of the imperial domains; numerous castles are built.
1153	The Hohenstaufen emperor Frederick I Barbarossa commits himself at Konstanz to war with the cities of Lombardy.
1184	Frederick Barbarossa holds a great imperial festival on the Maaraue, near Mainz.
1250 – 1450	Cathedrals in Gothic style built in Freiburg (Breisgau), Strasbourg and Cologne.
1254	Mainz and Worms establish the League of Rhenish Cities (over 70 members) in order to maintain peace and order in the absence of an Emperor.
1338	In the 'Electoral Union of Rhens' ('Kurverein von Rhens'; on the Rhine above Koblenz) the Electors (the territorial rulers who nominate the Emperor) establish the principle that the German king chosen by them is to be recognised as Emperor even without Papal concurrence and coronation in Rome.
1354	The Alsatian towns of Mulhouse (Mülhausen), Colmar, Munster (Münster), Turckheim (Türkheim), Kaysersberg, Sélestat (Schlettstadt), Obernai (Oberehnheim), Rosheim, Haguenau (Hagenau) and Wissembourg (Weissenburg) form the League of Ten Cities, under the authority of an imperial governor.
1356	At Imperial Diets held in Nürnberg and Metz a law known as the 'Golden Bull' is adopted under which the election of the Emperor is finally made the responsibility of the seven Electors (including the archbishops of Mainz, Trier and Cologne and the County Palatine of the Rhine).

In the Appenzell War the League of Cities on Lake Constance supports the abbot of St Gallen against the peasants of Appenzell canton, who are defeated at Bregenz in 1408.	1403 – 1408
The Council of Constance (Konstanz) ends the schism in the church.	1414 – 1418
The Bohemian Reformer Jan Hus is burned at the stake as a heretic in Konstanz.	1415
The Council of Basle, called to bring about reforms in the church, issues various decrees designed to reduce Papal prerogatives.	1431 – 1439
Johannes Gutenberg invents printing with movable type in Mainz.	around 1450
Basle joins the Swiss Confederation.	1501
Konstanz, Zurich and Berne form a League of Cities.	1517
The Rhineland territories of the Palatinate, Nassau and Hesse, the imperial cities of Worms, Speyer, Frankfurt am Main and Wetzlar and parts of the duchies of Cleves (Kleve) and Berg become Protestant.	16th century
Beginning of the Counter-Reformation.	1568
In the conflict over the succession to the duchy of Jülich and Cleves (Kleve) following the extinction of the ducal house claims are put forward by both Catholic and Protestant states.	1609 – 1614
Under the treaty of Xanten Jülich and Berg are assigned to the Catholic Count of Palatinate-Neuburg; Cleves (Kleve), Mark and Ravensberg to the Protestant Elector of Brandenburg.	1614
King Gustavus Adolphus of Sweden captures Mainz.	1631
Under the treaty of Westphalia, which puts an end to the Thirty Years War (1618 – 1648), France receives the Habsburg possessions in Alsace, with the exception of Strasbourg and Mulhouse.	1648
Münster, Palatinate-Neuburg and the Electorates of Cologne and Trier form the Alliance of the Rhine, a regional bloc between France and the Habsburgs.	1654
The Elector of Mainz joins the Alliance.	1655
After the election of Leopold I as Emperor the League of the Rhine, directed against the Habsburgs, is formed at Frankfurt am Main; the members of the League are France and a number of German princes.	1658
Dissolution of the League of the Rhine.	1668
Following decisions by French courts, Louis XIV occupies parts of Alsace and Lorraine.	1678 / 1679
The French annex Strasbourg.	1681

History

1688 – 1697	The war over the succession to the Palatinate, arising out of claims put forward by Louis XIV, leads to grave devastation in the Palatinate (Speyer, Worms; Heidelberg).
1770 / 1771	Goethe studies medicine at Strasbourg University.
1789	During the French Revolution the revolutionary government seeks to incorporate the whole of Alsace in France; Mulhouse becomes French in 1798.
1792	Mainz is declared a republic by members of a revolutionary club under the leadership of Georg Forster.
1795	Peace of Basle between France and Prussia: France remains in possession of the left bank of the Rhine.
1797	Peace of Campo Formio: Austria agrees to the cession to France of the left bank of the Rhine.
1801	Peace of Lunéville between France and Austria: the left bank of the Rhine remains French.
1803	Under the 'Reichsdeputationshauptschluss' (a resolution by a committee of the Imperial Diet meeting at Regensburg) the German ecclesiastical states are abolished.
1806	A number of southern and western German princes are associated in the Confederation of the Rhine under the protection of Napoleon. After the withdrawal of these princes from the Empire the Emperor Francis II resigns the imperial crown.

Blücher crossing the Rhine at Kaub (New Year's night 1814)

Battle of the Nations near Leipzig; end of the Confederation of the Rhine.

During the Wars of Liberation between France and the Allies the Silesian army, under the command of Gebhard Leberecht von Blücher, crosses the Rhine at Kaub and Koblenz on New Year's night.

Congress of Vienna, called to re-establish order in Europe after the Napoleonic wars. The dominant figure is Prince Metternich, an Austrian minister but born in Koblenz. The political principles of the Congress are restoration, legitimacy and solidarity of the princes for the repression of revolutionary and nationalist ideas.
Foundation of the German Confederation (39 states: 35 princes, four free cities), including old Prussian territories (Kleve, Geldern, Moers, etc.) and newly acquired provinces (Kleve-Berg, Lower Rhineland); the Breisgau, hitherto Austrian, passes to Baden and Württemberg.
Establishment of the United Kingdom of the Netherlands (from which Belgium secedes in 1830).
Federal Agreement ('Bundesvertrag'): new Swiss constitution (now 22 cantons).
The final act of the Congress of Vienna calls for the introduction of a code of international law controlling navigation on the Rhine.

Under an agreement reached at the Congress of Vienna Mainz becomes capital of the province of Rheinhessen (Rhine-Hesse). First steamship on the Rhine.

The first steamship on the Rhine (1816)

History

1824	Kleve-Berg and Lower Rhineland are united to form the province of Rhineland.
1827	The Prussian Rhine Steamship Line (Preussisch-Rheinische Dampfschiffahrts-Gesellschaft) introduces its first regular passenger and express freight service on the Middle Rhine between Mainz and Cologne.
1831	In the Rhine Navigation Act adopted in Mainz the states bordering the Rhine − Baden, Bavaria, France, Hesse, Nassau, the Netherlands and Prussia − agree to abolish traditional staple and transshipment rights and the privileges of the old boatmen's guilds and corporations.
1833	Basel-Stadt (Basle City) breaks away from Basel-Land to form an independent half-canton.
1840	Publication of Max Schneckenburger's patriotic poem "Die Wacht am Rhein" ("The Watch on the Rhine").
1868	The Mannheim Rhine Navigation Act comes into force: vessels of all nations entitled to sail on the Rhine. Establishment of the Central Commission on Rhine Navigation, with headquarters in Strasbourg.
1870 / 1871	Franco-German War. Under the peace signed at Versailles (26 February 1871) Alsace (excluding Belfort) and Lorraine (with Metz) are incorporated in the German Empire and become the province of Alsace-Lorraine (Elsass-Lothringen).
1876	Wagner's "Ring of the Nibelung" is performed at the inauguration of the new opera house in Bayreuth.
1914 − 1918	First world war. France seeks to recover the regions of Alsace and Lorraine.
1919	Under the treaty of Versailles Alsace and Lorraine return to France. − Germany cedes possession of the Saar coal-mines to France. − British, French and American forces occupy the Rhineland, which is now controlled by an inter-allied commission.
1925	Locarno Pact: Germany guarantees the inviolability of France's eastern frontier.
1925 − 1930	Phased withdrawal of Allied forces from the Rhineland.
1935	Following a plebiscite, the Saar returns to Germany.
1936	German troops march into the demilitarised Rhineland: no military reaction by the Allied powers.
1939 − 1945	Second world war. German troops occupy Alsace and Lorraine, which now come under the control of the gauleiter of Baden. Practically all the German cities on the Rhine suffer heavy damage by air attack. Rotterdam is devastated by Luftwaffe raids in 1940. Nijmegen and Arnhem suffer devastating damage during the fighting in the closing stages of the war. On 7 March 1945 American forces cross the Rhine on the Remagen bridge (which collapses on 17 March).

After the war Alsace and Lorraine return to France. – German 1945
territory along the Rhine becomes part of the British, French
and American occupation zones, and later of the newly created
'Länder' (provinces) of North Rhineland – Westphalia (Nordrhein-Westfalen), Rhineland-Palatinate (Rheinland-Pfalz), Hesse
(Hessen) and Baden-Württemberg. – Wiesbaden becomes
capital of the 'Land' of Hesse.

Bonn becomes the seat of government of the German Federal 1949
Republic. – Strasbourg is selected as the headquarters of the
Council of Europe, and later as the seat of the European Parlia-
ment.

Mainz becomes capital of the 'Land' of Rhineland-Palatinate 1950
(previously Koblenz).

The 'Länder' of (South) Baden, Württemberg-Baden and South 1952
Württemberg-Hohenzollern are combined to form the 'Land' of
Baden-Württemberg.

Opponents of nuclear power secure a judgment from a 1977
Freiburg court cancelling the provisional authority granted for
the building of a nuclear power station at Wyhl on the Upper
Rhine.

Pope John Paul II visits Cologne on the 100th anniversary of the 1980
completion of the Cathedral.

Mass demonstration by half a million people in Bonn against 1983
the stationing of cruise missiles and new medium-range rock-
ets in the German Federal Republic.
France ratifies the convention on the protection of the Rhine
signed at Bonn in 1976 by the Federal Republic, the Netherlands, Luxembourg, Switzerland and France (which is the last
signatory to ratify the convention); one of the main provisions is
a reduction in the amount of salt to be discharged into the
Rhine from the potash mines of Alsace.

Opening of the Rhein (Rhine)-Main-Donau (Danube)-Channel 1992

The Rhine in Poems and Quotations

Gaius Iulius Caesar
"De Bello Gallico"
("The Gallic War"),
Book IV, Chapter 10
(55 B.C.)

Mosa profluit ex monte Vosego, qui est in finibus Lingonum, et parte quadam ex Rheno recepta, quae appellatur Vacalus, insulam efficit Batavorum neque longius ab Oceano milibus passuum LXXX in Rhenum influit. Rhenus autem oritur ex Lepontiis, qui Alpes incolunt, et longo spatio per fines Nantuatium, Helvetiorum, Sequanorum, Mediomatricorum, Tribocorum, Treverorum citatus fertur et, ubi Oceano adpropinquavit, in plures diffluit partes multis ingentibusque insulis effectis, quarum pars magna a feris barbarisque nationibus incolitur, ex quibus sunt qui piscibus atque ovis avium vivere existimantur, multisque capitibus in Oceanum influit.

The Maas (Meuse) rises in that part of the Vosges mountains which lies in the country of the Lingones, and after being joined by an arm of the Rhine known as the Waal forms the island of the Batavi and flows into the Rhine no more than eighty miles from the Ocean. The Rhine rises in the country of the Lepontii, who live in the Alps, and flows swiftly for a great distance through the territories of the Nantuates, the Helvetii, the Sequani, the Mediomatrici, the Triboci and the Treveri. As it comes near the Ocean it divides into a number of arms, forming many very large islands (many of them inhabited by wild barbarian tribes, some of whom are reputed to live on fish and birds' eggs), and finally flows into the Ocean by several different mouths.

Francesco Petrarca
Letter
(1333)

To Cardinal Colonna in Avignon

I had left Aix-la-Chapelle, having first bathed in the hot springs, like those of Baiae, from which the town is believed to take its name, and came to Cologne, the colony of Agrippina, on the left bank of the Rhine — a place famed for its situation and its river but famed also for its people. Strange how civilised in this land of barbarians are the manners of the citizens, how fair the aspect of the city, how dignified the bearing ot the men, how smart the appearance of the women!

… I had taken up my position on a higher spot of ground from which I could observe what was passing. There was an extraordinary concourse of people with no crush or congestion. Many were garlanded with sweet-smelling herbs and had turned their sleeves above their elbows. They washed their white hands and arms in the rushing stream in cheerful confusion, saying charming things to one another in a foreign-sounding murmur. Scarcely anywhere else have I so clearly understood what Cicero likes to say and what an old proverb says — that all men, when they hear an unknown tongue, are in a sense deaf and dumb. The only consolation for me was that there was no lack of kindly interpreters. For that must surely astonish you, to find that this clime has produced spirits devoted to the Muses. And if Juvenal is surprised that Gaul so eloquently educates the litigious Britons, he must be no less surprised that educated Germany has nurtured sage poets.

... (I was told that) it is an ancient custom of the country, and the women in particular are firmly convinced, that all the misfortunes which the year may hold are washed away by washing in the river on this day, and that afterwards only good fortune will be their lot; and accordingly this purification is carried out annually, and must continue to be carried out, with inexhaustible zeal.

To this I said, smiling: O more than fortunate you are, you dwellers on the Rhine, if your river washes away your distresses; for the Po has not had power to wash away ours, nor yet the Tiber. You send your misfortunes to the people of Britain under the care of Ferryman Rhine, and we would gladly send ours to the Africans and Illyrians; but it is easy to see that we have more sluggish rivers than you ...

... From Mainz I sailed down the Rhine with Ulrike to Koblenz. – Ah, that is a stretch of country like a poet's dream, and the most luxuriant fancy can conceive nothing finer than this valley, which now opens out and now closes in, now is blooming and now desolate, now laughs and now inspires apprehension. Swift as an arrow the Rhine flows on his way from Mainz, as if he could already see his destination, as if nothing must prevent him from getting there, as if he was impatient to reach his goal by the shortest route. Then a vine-clad hill (the Rheingau) bends his stormy course, gently but firmly, as a wife bends the stormy will of her husband, and with quiet steadfastness points out the way which will bring him to the sea. – And he heeds the noble warning and abandons his rash plan. Following the kindly direction he has received, he does not cut his way through the vine-covered hill but turns round it, kissing its beflowered feet as he continues on a gentler course. –

Quiet, broad and majestic, he continues on his way past Bingen: firmly, like a hero going towards victory, and slowly, as if desiring to complete his course. – Then a range of hills (the Hundsrück) throws itself in his way, like a slander cast against unimpeachable virtue. But he breaks through the hills, never faltering, and the rocks give way before him, looking down on him with admiration and astonishment; while he hastens contemptuously past them, but without rejoicing in his triumph, and the only revenge he permits himself is to show their black image in his clear mirror. –

And now, in this valley where the spirit of peace and love speaks to man, where all the beauty and goodness that slumbers in our soul comes to life and all that is base remains silent, where every breath of wind and every wave soothe our passions in their friendly gossipy way and the whole of nature seems to invite man to achieve excellence – how could it happen that this valley became a scene of war? Fields destroyed, vineyards trampled down, whole villages reduced to ashes, strongholds which seemed impregnable cast down into the Rhine – Ah, if one single individual had so many crimes on his conscience he must surely sink down, oppressed by the burden – ...

Heinrich von Kleist
"An Adolfine von Werdeck"
("To Adolfine von Werdeck")
(1801)

"Der Rhein – Teutschlands Strom, aber nicht Teutschlands Gränze" ("The Rhine – Germany's river but not Germany's frontier") is the title of a pamphlet by the poet and political writer Ernst Moritz Arndt (26. 12. 1769 – 29. 1. 1860) published

Ernst Moritz Arndt
(1813)

The Rhine in Poems and Quotations

E. M. Arndt
(continued)

after the Battle of the Nations at Leipzig. It became a popular catch-phrase, and is inscribed on the monument to Arndt in Bonn.

Johann Wolfgang von Goethe
"Sankt Rochus-Fest zu Bingen"
("The Feast of St Roch at Bingen")
(1814)

... A group of close and congenial friends who had been for some weeks taking the cure at Wiesbaden felt a certain restlessness one day, which they sought to assuage by carrying out a long cherished plan. Although it was already past midday, a carriage was at once ordered to take them into the agreeable Rheingau. From the hill above Biebrich there was a view of the wide and beautiful valley of the river with its towns and villages set amid magnificently fertile countryside ...

... We now drove to Schierstein through wide cornfields, decked here and there with nut-trees. Then the fertile land extended towards the Rhine on the left and the hills on the right, which gradually drew nearer the road. The situation of Walluf looked dangerous as well as beautiful, lying under a bosom of the Rhine, as if on a tongue of land. Through the fruit-trees, richly laden with fruit and carefully supported, we saw ships sailing downstream, gaily, doubly favoured.

The eye was drawn to the farther bank, where large and well-built villages could be seen, set amid fertile fields. But soon the glance returned perforce to the nearer bank; for not far away there stood a ruined chapel, rearing its ivied walls from a green meadow, wondrously pure, simple and agreeable. To the right the vine-clad hills now reached right down to the road.

In the little town of Walluf deep peace reigned, though the billeting officer's chalk marks on the doors had not yet been obliterated. Farther on there were vineyards on both sides of the road. Even on level ground with little slope vines alternated with cornfields, and the farther hills to the right were covered with vineyards.

And there, in a open expanse surrounded by hills, with higher summits to the north, was Ellfeld (Eltville), lying close to the Rhine, opposite a large cultivated water meadow. The towers of an old castle and of the church indicated a country town of some size, and the town itself confirmed its status with its old houses of some architectural pretension.

It would be an agreeable occupation to enquire why the first inhabitants of these places chose to settle where they did. Sometimes the reason is to be found in a stream flowing down from the hills towards the Rhine; now it is a situation convenient for landing and discharging a boat, now some other local advantage ...

... Like the other little towns, Erbach was neatly paved, the streets were dry, the ground floors of the houses were inhabited and, as we could see through the open windows, clean and tidy inside. Then followed a palatial country house, its gardens reaching down to the Rhine, with delightful terraces and shady avenues of limes which were a pleasure to the eye.

Here the Rhine took on a different character. It was only a part of itself: the water meadow on its banks constricted it, making it a river of moderate size but one that flowed vigorously and

Gaius Iulius Caesar   *J. W. von Goethe*   *Mark Twain*

powerfully. The vine-covered hills on the right now came right up to the road, borne on stout walls, a recess in which drew our attention. The carriage stopped, and we refreshed ourselves from the abundant flow of water gushing from a pipe. This was the Marktbrunnen (Market Fountain), from which the wine grown on these hills takes its name.

The wall came to an end and the hills lost their steepness; their gentle slopes and ridges were covered with vines. To the left, fruit-trees. Close to the river, concealing it, were thickets of willows.

The road climbed through Hattenheim; on the hill beyond the town the loamy soil was less gravelly. On both sides vineyards, on the left enclosed by walls, on the right embanked. Reichardtshausen, an old monastic property, now belonging to the Duchess of Nassau. The end of the wall, broken down, revealed a house agreeably shaded by acacias.

A lush and gently sloping area on the continuing hills; then the road again drew close to the river, which hitherto had lain some distance away and lower down. Here the plain was given up to agriculture and horticulture, the least eminence to vines. Östrich, on rising ground at some distance from the water, was very prettily situated, with vine-clad hills extending beyond it to the river; and so it continued to Mittelheim, where the Rhine broadened out magnificently. Immediately beyond this was Langenwinkel ('long corner'). The epithet 'long' was well earned, for the place straggled on in a way that tried the traveller's patience, but it presented nothing resembling a corner.

At Geisenheim a flat and low-lying stretch of land extended to the river, which would no doubt flood it in times of spate; it was occupied by gardens and clover meadows. The island in the river and the little town on its banks made an attractive scene. Beyond the town the prospect opened up, with a wide undulating valley reaching between two hill ridges towards the Hunsrück.

As we approached Rüdesheim the low-lying ground on the left became ever more striking, and the idea occurred to me that in

J. W. v. Goethe
(continued)

primeval times, when the mountains at Bingen still formed a barrier, the water dammed up here had levelled this area and eventually, draining away and continuing on its course, had formed the present bed of the Rhine.

And so we arrived in less than three and a half hours at Rüdesheim, where the Crown inn (Gasthof zur Krone), prettily situated near the gate, at once attracted us.

It was built against an old tower, with a view down the Rhine from the front windows and up the river from the rear. Soon, however, we sought the open air. The finest view of the surrounding area was to be had from a projecting stone building. Upstream could be seen the lush green water meadows in all their beauty of perspective. Downstream, on the opposite bank, was Bingen, and farther down, in the river, the Mäuseturm ('Mouse Tower').

Upstream from Bingen, near the river, a hill extended towards the plateau: perhaps a promontory which rose out of the water in the days when it was higher. At its eastern end could be seen a chapel dedicated to St Roch, just restored after suffering war damage. The scaffolding still stood against one side of the building; but in spite of this the saint's feast was to be celebrated on the following day. The local people thought that we had come specially on that account, and promised us a pleasant day ...

George Gordon, Lord Byron
"Childe Harold's Pilgrimage"
(1816)

The castled crag of Drachenfels
Frowns o'er the wide and winding Rhine,
Whose breast of waters broadly swells
Between the banks which bear the vine,
And hills all rich with blossom'd trees,
And fields which promise corn and wine,
And scatter'd cities crowning these,
Whose far white walls along them shine,
Have strew'd a scene, which I should see
With double joy wert *thou* with me.

...

The river nobly foams and flows,
The charm of this enchanted ground,
And all its thousand turns disclose
Some fresher beauty varying round:
The haughtiest breast its wish might bound
Through life to dwell delighted here ...

...

Adieu to thee, fair Rhine! How long delighted
The stranger fain would linger on his way!
This is a scene alike where souls united
Or lonely Contemplation thus might stray;
And could the ceaseless vultures cease to prey
On self-condemning bosoms, it were here,
Where Nature, not too sombre nor too gay,
Wild but not rude, awful yet not austere,
Is to the mellow Earth as Autumn to the year.

The Lorelei

Heinrich Heine
"Loreley-Lied" (1822)
translated by
Mark Twain (S.L. Clemens)
in "A Tramp Abroad"
(1880)

I cannot divine what it meaneth,
This haunting nameless pain:
A tale of the bygone ages
Keeps brooding through my brain:

The faint air cools in the gloaming,
And peaceful flows the Rhine,
The thirsty summits are drinking
The sunset's flooding wine;

Music by Friedrich Silcher
(1837)

The loveliest maiden is sitting
High-throned in yon blue air,
Her golden jewels are shining,
She combs her golden hair;

She combs with a comb that is golden,
And sings a weird refrain
That steeps in a deadly enchantment
The list'ner's ravished brain:

The doomed in his drifting shallop,
Is tranced with the sad sweet tone,
He sees not the yawning breakers,
He sees but the maid alone:

The pitiless billows engulf him! –
So perish sailor and bark;
And this, with her baleful singing,
Is the Lorelei's grewsome work.

Loreley

One of the passengers on one of the first steamships to sail on
the Rhine, the "Concordia", was the correspondent of the
"Morgenblatt für gebildete Stände" or "Morning Gazette for the
Educated Classes", Friedrich von Matthisson, who had already
travelled on the upper course of the Rhine.

Friedrich von Matthisson
"Erinnerungen" ("Memories")
(1827)

On the steamship "Concordia", 16th May 1827

Nothing more elegant or more comfortable than this steamship ... From morning until evening you can enjoy the most
leisurely life for both body and soul ... Everything has been
provided for. There is a small library for the use of the
passengers. The furniture is of a daintiness such as one is
accustomed to see in palaces ... By about noon, in the most
beautiful sunshine, we were at Koblenz, where the wonder ship
stopped for an hour. No sooner was this travelling hotel again
under way than the dinner bell sounded. The meal was such
that I felt that higher powers must have restored to the
Frankfurt "Swan" its ability to float on the water. Even the
liveliest fancy could hardly conceive a more agreeable fashion
of getting about the world than in a steamship like this.

The Rhine in Poems and Quotations

Annette von Droste-Hülshoff
Letter
(1828)

... A steamship of this size is a highly imposing object; indeed, a terrifying one. As you know, it is driven by wheels, which combine with the noise of our rapid movement to create such a hissing sound that it is difficult to hear what people are saying. But that is not the really alarming thing. On the ship there is a tall thick column from which the steam continually pours out in a column of smoke, with immense violence and a noise like that of the flames in a burning building. When the ship is not in motion, or when there is so much steam that it opens the safety valves, the thing begins to roar and howl so fiercely that it seems to be about to take off into the air. In short, it is like an infernal machine — though we are assured that there is no danger ...

Victor Hugo
"Le Rhin" ("The Rhine")
(1838)

... The Rhine combines everything. The Rhine is swift as the Rhône, wide as the Loire, deeply embanked like the Meuse, winding as the Seine, limpid and green as the Somme, historic as the Tiber, royal as the Danube, mysterious as the Nile, spangled with gold like a river of America, covered with fables and phantoms like a river of Asia ...

J.A. Klein / K. Baedeker
"Rheinreise"
("Journey on the Rhine")
(1839)

Plan of journey

The most pleasurable way of seeing the Rhine is undoubtedly on foot. The traveller is free, he can go in any direction he likes, stay where he pleases, climb hills and go up small side valleys. And in doing so he need not go without his creature comforts. In all the towns and even in the villages on the Rhine there are good hotels or inns.

A man who looks around him with a clear eye and lively faculties will discover in the course of his walk all the many beauties which the blessed valley of the Rhine has to offer and will be able to delight in them with all his heart.

Now that the steamship authorities allow the traveller to get out at any stopping-place and to continue his journey on a later ship with the same ticket, and particularly now that the ships travel upstream and downstream several times daily, it is possible to combine the advantages of travelling by steamship with the pleasures of going on foot by leaving the vessel at a place where there are hills offering particularly attractive views or a town with special features of interest, pursuing one's particular interests and then travelling on with the next ship belonging to the same company.

For those travelling in this way any kind of luggage is a great inconvenience; and indeed travellers will soon make the observation that the handling and care of luggage on steamships is a most troublesome matter, involves them in a variety of expenditures and brings them in contact with people who are calculated to reduce very greatly the pleasure of a journey. Those who intend to leave the steamship on a number of occasions will do well to send their luggage on in advance to Cologne, Koblenz or Mainz. Where the number of items is small the freight charges amount to less than the cost of paying a porter each time for carrying luggage from the ship to a hotel.

Most travellers think they have seen the beauties of the Rhine when they have undertaken a quick journey up- and downstream by steamship. It cannot be often enough repeated that no view can be more erroneous than this. However pretty the scenery may appear from the river, its finest charms are displayed only on the hills. Accordingly a stay should be made at Rüdesheim or Bingen, St Goar, Koblenz and Godesberg, whose surroundings offer the greatest variety; and excursions can be undertaken from there on to the hills and into the side valleys.

The Rhine is far the finest
Of the rivers of the earth;
Woe 'tide the man who cannot
Appreciate its worth.

Peter Cornelius
Song
(1840)

And Mainz, the golden city,
Is the river's greatest pride;
Well called, indeed, the golden,
As it shines out far and wide.

It is not only the upper stretches of the Rhine above Cologne that should be visited; and young Germans in particular should not imitate the travelling John Bulls who languish in their cabins from Rotterdam to Cologne and only then go up on deck, because their "Panorama of the Rhine from Cologne to Mainz" or "Guide for Travellers on the Rhine" begins there. The young of Germany should choose as their place of pilgrimage some less frequented place like Xanten, home of the hero Siegfried.

Friedrich Engels
"Siegfrieds Heimat"
("Siegfried's Home")
(1840)

For king-like rolls the Rhine,
And the scenery's divine,
And the victuals and the wine
Rather good.

C.S. Calverley
"Dover to Munich"
(1862)

Felix Krull's Home

Thomas Mann
"Bekenntnisse des
Hochstaplers Felix Krull"
("Confessions of
Felix Krull, Confidence Man")
(1922)

The Rheingau bore me – that favoured tract of land, surely one of the most delightful spots in the inhabited world, mild and without roughness in terms of both weather and soil, richly provided with towns and village and cheerfully populated. Here, sheltered from rude winds by the hills of the Rheingau and fortunately exposed to the midday sun, there flourish those famous towns at the sound of whose names the drinker's heart laughs; here are Rauenthal, Johannisberg and Rüdesheim, and here too is the venerable little town in which, some few years after the glorious foundation of the German Empire, I first saw the light. Situated a little to the west of the bend which the Rhine describes at Mainz, and famed for its sparkling wine, it is one of the principal ports of call of the steamers hurrying up and down the river, and numbers some four thousand inhabitants.

Vive l'Alsace

René Schickele
"Blick auf die Vogesen"
("View of the Vosges")
(1927)

He got out at Rheinweiler and walked slowly over the pontoon bridge.
The Rhine and the narrow bridge lay there under a high spring morning ...
The Rhine, the Rhine!
Claus stopped again and then again, stretched himself, breathing deeply, extended his bare hands, threw back his head and then dropped it again, smiling. His heart beat,

The Rhine in Poems and Quotations

R. Schickele
(continued)

balanced between Germany and France, half way across the Rhine, that sacred river, and drove the blood blithely through his body; and it seemed to him as if a faint glimmer of his blood hovered outside his body, far beyond the reach of his arms, stretched out horizontally to east and west – from one range of hills on the horizon to the other!

Kurt Tucholsky
"Denkmal am
Deutschen Eck"
("Monument at the
Deutsches Eck")
(1930)

... I did not know Koblenz. The first thing that struck me was a large and noisy crowd of bourgeois visitors in an extraordinary state of excitement. Just as black-haired women on a visit to Paris fall victim to the magic of the word 'Paris' and behave as they would never behave at home, so these blonde ladies were quite beside themselves here; the Rhine, Father Rhine, the German Rhine tinkled in the glasses, and it was a fairly hideous sight to watch. The second thing that struck me was the word 'shame' *(Schmach)*. We pronounced the word with a double *ch, Schmachch,* and in saying it we had in mind the French, who were responsible for the 'black shame' (the presence of black troops) of which we had seen so much in our cinemas. Now it was only a white shame, and we did not like it: not because we do not like the French, but because we do not like the military ...

... And so we were walking along the Rhine, but once again I had not learned my geography and had to have things explained to me by Jakopp. There was the fortress of Ehrenbreitstein, on which, for the delight of the youths of the Rhineland, there burned a French flag. The flag, high on its flagstaff, really did burn, died down and then flared up again ... The military do not interest me, and I do not know what sort of a game they were playing with fire. And it is a matter of indifference to me – as indifferent as everything else – what these uniformed fellows do. And there was the Rhine, surrounded by a chatter of false sentiment; and there, just as Goethe tells us, were large ships in process of sailing on this river ... And suddenly I suffered the greatest shock I have experienced on this journey. It is still very clearly in my mind:

We were walking along the broad, tree-lined avenue. In front of us, at the corner, was a photographer's booth; they had put some photographs on display, now as brown as old daguerrotypes. Then the trees came to an end and we found ourselves in an open square. I looked up – and almost collapsed.
There – wham! – stood a gigantic statue of the Emperor William I: a body-blow in stone. It quite took my breath away.

If you looked closer you discovered that it was a magnificent, a Wilhelmine, an artistic work of art. The thing looked like the top of some enormous cake. It represented Germany, the Germany that has been to blame for wars ...
... "Yes," said Jakopp: "that is the Emperor William Monument on the Deutsches Eck." ...

Heinrich Böll
"Undines gewaltiger Vater"
("Undine's Powerful Father")
(1960)

I am ready to believe anything of the Rhine; but I have never been able to believe in its summer serenity. I have looked for this serenity but never found it; perhaps it is an eye defect or a defect in my nature that has prevented me from discovering it. My Rhine is dark and melancholy; it is too much a river of tradesmanlike cunning for me to believe in its summer-like young man's face ...

(An account of a journey up the Rhine in 1933)

Patrick Leigh Fermor
"A Time of Gifts"
(1977)

During the first three days I was never far from a towpath, but so many and confused are the waterways that unconsciously I changed rivers three times: the Noorwede was the first of them, the Merwede followed, then came the Waal; and at Gorinchem the Waal was joined by the Maas. In the morning I could see the great stream of the Maas winding across the plain towards this rendezvous; it had risen in France under the more famous name of Meuse and then flowed across the whole of Belgium; a river only less imposing than the Waal itself, to whose banks I clung for the remainder of my Dutch journey. The Waal is tremendous; no wonder, for it is really the Rhine. 'The Rijn', in Holland, Rembrandt's native stream, is a minor northern branch of the main flow, and it subdivides again and again, loses itself in the delta and finally enters the North Sea through a drainage-canal; while the Waal, gorged with Alpine snows and the waters of Lake Constance and the Black Forest and the tribute of a thousand Rhenish streams, rolls sea-ward in usurped and stately magnificence. Between this tangle of rivers, meanwhile – whose defections and reunions enclosed islands as big as English shires – the geometric despotism of canal and polder and windmill held firm; those turning sails were for drainage, not grinding corn ...

...Coblenz and its great fortress dropped behind and the mountains took another pace forward. Serried vineyards now covered the banks of the river, climbing as high as they could find a foothold. Carefully buttressed with masonry, shelf rose on shelf in fluid and looping sweeps. Pruned to the bone, the dark vine-shoots stuck out of the snow in rows of skeleton fists which shrank to quincunxes of black commas along the snow-covered contour-lines of the vineyards as they climbed, until the steep waves of salients and re-entrants faltered at last and expired overhead among the wild bare rocks. On the mountains that overhung these flowing ledges, scarcely a peak had been left without a castle. At Stolzenfels, where I stopped for something to eat, a neo-Gothic keep climbed into the sky on a staircase of vineyards, and another castle echoed it from Oberlahnstein on the other shore. Then another rose up, and yet another: ruin on ruin, and vineyard on vineyard ... They seemed to revolve as they moved downstream, and then to impend. Finally a loop of the river would carry them away until the dimness of the evening blurred them all and the lights of the shore began to twinkle among their darkening reflections ...

When the cliffs above were too steep for snow, spinneys frilled the ledges of shale, and fans of brushwood split the sunbeams into an infinity of threads. Higher still, the gap-toothed and unfailing towers – choked with trees and lashed together with ivy – thrust angles into the air which followed up the impulse of the crags on which they were perched; and, most fittingly, their names all ended in the German word for 'angle' or 'rock' or 'crag' or 'keep': Hoheneck, Reichenstein, Stolzenfels, Falkenburg ... Each turn of the river brought into view a new set of stage wings and sometimes a troop of islands which the perpetual rush of the river had worn thin and moulded into the swerve of the current. They seemed to float there under a tangle of bare twigs and a load of monastic or secular ruins. A few of these eyots were sockets for towers which could bar the river

The Rhine in Poems and Quotations

P. L. Fermor (continued)

by slinging chains to either bank and holding up ships for toll or loot or ransom ...

Bernard Levin
"Enthusiasms"
(1983)

... From Wiesbaden to Bonn the old road follows the Rhine like a faithful dog, unwilling to let its master out of its sight for a moment. At times we seemed to be hanging right over the bank, and the countryside looked as it must have done five hundred years before. Conversation in the car was still brisk when we joined the river, but it died out in all three of us soon afterwards; for the Frenchman and the Englishwoman this territory was familiar, and to me it was unknown, but we were all three ravished by what we saw, and felt, without discussing it, that words could add nothing to what lay before us, so that we need do nothing but feast upon it with our eyes, our feelings and our souls.

The road wound as the river did; at every bend there was a change of view. The fields were golden, the villages, each with its whitewashed church, many of them onion-spired, slept in the sun as though determined not to awaken until Barbarossa's return; the castles, looking more like the sets for a production of "Tannhäuser" than any stage designer would dare to provide, were perched high on scraps of crag that would have given the very eagles vertigo; valleys and hills so gentle that between them they constituted little more than ripples in the earth undulated on either bank; terraced vineyards stepped gingerly down to the water's edge, as if to try the temperature with a toe. ...

Karl-Geert Malle
"Spektrum der Wissenschaft"
("Science Spectrum")
(August 1983)

The Rhine – a Model of Pollution Control

... Measures for the purification of effluents have made most progress on the Rhine, which undoubtedly ranks among the most thoroughly investigated and most carefully monitored rivers in the world ... Introducers of effluents are largely under a requirement to carry out their own monitoring, subject to checking by government authorities. These authorities carry on continuous monitoring of water quality in land-based stations with the most modern equipment and from survey vessels. The results are collated with those of other riparian states and published ...

Monitoring is also carried on, quite independently, by waterworks which use Rhine water purified by passing through soil bordering the river. These results too are subject to the international checking process. Thus a mass of data is available, making possible critical evaluations of many kinds ...

Oxygen content, salinity, eutrophication, increase in temperature, heavy metal content, residual substances, specific compounds: all these problems are carefully monitored in the densely populated and highly industrialised Rhine catchment area. The efforts of the last ten years have brought about a fundamental improvement, and the Rhine now offers a classic example of responsible pollution control.

Attempts to achieve further improvement must, however, continue; and it is of urgent importance to strengthen international cooperation. A priority for future research must be the investigation of particular compounds; the discovery of any significant new hazard potentials is now scarcely to be expected.

The Rhine from the Sources to Basle

This chapter supplements the main part of the Guide, which is concerned with the Rhine between Basle and Rotterdam, by giving some account of the upper reaches of the river, between its sources and the Upper Rhine plain. The country through which it passes, the towns and villages to be seen on the way, with the particular features of tourist interest which they offer, are briefly described, following the river downstream from its headstreams the Vorderrhein and Hinterrhein by way of the Alpine Rhine and Lake Constance to the High Rhine.

On the geography of these regions see under → Facts and Figures, General.

Headstreams: Vorderrhein and Hinterrhein

Vorderrhein

Emerging from a small mountain lake a little to the south of the Oberalp pass, the Vorderrhein (in Romansh Rein Anteriur) flows through the picturesque Tavetsch (Tujetsch) valley, passing the hamlets of Tschamut, Selva, Rueras and Camischolas and the chief place in the valley, Sedrun (church of St Vigilius, with a carved altar of 1491), to the altitude and winter sports resort of Disentis or Mustér (large Benedictine abbey), where the Medelser Rhein joins it from the south and the Lukmanier-strasse comes down from the Lukmanier pass.

Valley of the Vorderrhein

Vorderrhein
(continued)

The Vorderrhein then flows through the Surselva region in the mountains of the Grisons, passing Somvix (Sumvitg; from Latin 'summus vicus', = 'highest village'), Rabius, Trun (Truns; Surselva Museum), Tavanasa, Waltensburg (Vuorz, 3 km N, higher up, with fine 14th and 15th c. frescoes in the church) and Strada, to Ilanz (Glion), the 'first town on the Rhine' (first recorded in 765 A.D.) and the market centre of the Surselva. Here the Valser Rhein comes in from the south, accompanied by the beautiful Valser Hochtalstrasse (High Valley Road).

Farther downstream, high above the valley to the north, are the well-known tourist resorts of Laax and Flims (Flem; on Crap Sogn Gion the large winter sports area known as the 'Weisse Arena' or White Arena).

Below Tamins, at Reichenau, the Vorderrhein joins up with the Hinterrhein.

Hinterrhein

The Hinterrhein (Rein Posteriur) emerges from the Zapport glacier in the Rheinwald (Adula) range a little way east of the San Bernadino pass (vehicular tunnel) and flows through the magnificent Rheinwald high valley, with the villages of Hinterrhein, Nufenen and Medels, to Splügen, where the Splügenstrasse comes down from the Splügen pass.

Farther downstream the Hinterrhein is dammed at Sufers to form the Sufnersee. Later it is joined by the Averser Rhein, coming from the south-east, and then cuts its way through the rocky Rofla Gorge (Roflaschlucht) into a wider stretch of the valley, the Schams (Sassám) basin, the chief

Valley of the Hinterrhein

place in which is Andeer (parish church of 1673, stone-built houses with sgraffito decoration), once an entrepot on a medieval trade route, now an altitude and health resort and a winter sports centre.

Some 4 km north of Andeer is the Early Romanesque church of Zillis (Ziran/Ciraun), with a 12th century painted coffered ceiling which is a unique example of very early figural painting.
The Hinterrhein then surges through the famous and once much dreaded Via Mala, a wildly romantic gorge enclosed by 500 m high limestone walls, and comes to the little market town of Thusis (Tusaun), ringed by the ruins of medieval castles, where a road comes in from Tiefencastel by way of the Schin Gorge (Schinschlucht).

"Christ before Pilate"
Panel No. 143 of the painted coffered ceiling in
St Martin's Church at Zillis

Farther down the valley opens out. To the west are the steep slopes of the Heinzenberg; the valley bottom and the lower and gentler slopes to the east form the Domleschg (Tumliasca) area, at the beginning of which the Albula flows into the Hinterrhein from the south-east. The chief places in the Domleschg, a region of many churches and castles, are Cazis, Fürstenau, Rodels, Paspels and Rothenbrunn; at its northern end are Rhäzüns (castle, originally dating from the 13th c.) and Bonaduz.

At Reichenau the Hinterrhein joins with the Vorderrhein to form the Alpine Rhine (Alpenrhein).

Alpine Rhine (from Chur to Lake Constance)

Chur (in Romansh Cuera or Cuoira; probably from Celtic 'kora' = clan), capital of the Swiss canton of Grisons, with a population of 34,000, is situated on a detrital cone deposited by the Plessur, which flows into the Alpine Rhine from the south-east. The town is surrounded by mountains rising to over 2000 m, and in spite of its altitude (c. 600 m) enjoys an unusually mild climate in which fruit and vines flourish abundantly.

Chur claims to be the oldest town in Switzerland (earliest evidence of settlement c. 3000 B.C.; Roman fort, 'Curia Raetorum'; recorded in 452 A.D. as the see of a bishop), and thanks to its excellent strategic situation at the end of major pass roads is an important commercial town and the economic, cultural and intellectual centre of Eastern Switzerland.
Chur is the terminus of the main railway line and the starting-point of the Rhaetian Railway (Rhätische Bahn; narrow-gauge) to Arosa and the Engadine (St Moritz) and the Furka-Oberalp Railway ('Glacier Express') into the Rhône valley (Brig).

The main features of interest are the Cathedral (12th–13th c.; tomb of the Swiss patriot Jürg Jenatsch, 1596–1639, murdered at Chur), with the Cathedral Museum (Dommuseum), containing the Cathedral treasury; the large Bishop's Palace; the old monastic church of St Luzi (12th c.; circular crypt of 8th c.); the Town Hall (1465); the Rhaetian Museum; the Natural History Museum of the Grisons; and the Art Gallery (Kunsthaus).
An interesting walk can be had through the well preserved old town.

Bishop's Palace at Chur

Zizers	The market village of Zizers (Zizras) has a parish church first recorded in 955 and two 17th century mansions which belonged to the Salis family, the Unteres and Oberes Schloss.
Landquart	At the busy road and rail junction of Landquart the river of that name flows into the Rhine from the east, coming down from the well known winter sports resort of Klosters through the Prättigau valley, the mouth of which is commanded by Schloss Marschlins (13th and 17th c.), with its four towers.
Bündner Herrschaft	North-west of Landquart, above the right bank of the Alpine Rhine, is the Bündner Herrschaft ('Grisons Lordship'), its hill slopes covered with orchards and vineyards. The principal wine villages (red and rosé wines) are Malans (many wooden houses), Jenins, Maienfeld (two castles, handsome patrician houses; in the cemetery the grave of the Swiss writer John Knittel, 1891–1970) and Fläsch.
Bad Ragaz	Prettily situated in the valley of the Alpine Rhine at the mouth of the Tamina Gorge (Taminaschlucht), Bad Ragaz (canton of St Gallen) is one of Switzerland's leading spas, using water from hot radioactive springs (37 °C) in the romantic Tamina Gorge which was first piped to Bad Ragaz in 1840.
Sargans	The ancient little mining town of Sargans, an important rail and road junction (Walensee road from Zurich), is surrounded by orchards and vineyards. Above the town is Schloss Sargans (originally 12th c.), which was from 1483 to 1798 the seat of the federal governors responsible for the whole of the Rhine valley from Landquart to Lake Constance.

The Principality of Liechtenstein is an independent mini-state (democratic constitutional monarchy; area 160 sq. km; pop. 26,000) lying between Austria and Switzerland, with the Alpine Rhine forming its western frontier. Its territory extends from the western slopes of the Rätikon range to the Rhine. The most populous part of the country is the Rhine plain, where arable farming is practised; the mountain slopes are forest-covered, and in the high valleys Alpine pasturage and meadowland predominate.

The County of Vaduz, established in 1342, was acquired in 1712 by Prince Hans Adam of Liechtenstein and combined with the lordship of Schellenberg. From 1852 until after the first world war Liechtenstein was joined with Austria in a currency union, but in 1924 it formed an economic union with Switzerland (represented by Switzerland in its relations with other countries, but with its own embassy in Berne; Swiss currency and Swiss customs and postal administration, but with its own stamps).

Its favourable tax laws have made it the headquarters of numerous holding companies. In proportion to its size Liechtenstein is the most highly industrialised nation in the world, and its per-capita income is also one of the highest in the world.

The official language is German, but the normal spoken language is an Alemannic dialect.

The capital and seat of government of the principality is the little town of Vaduz (pop. 5000), which lies near the right bank of the Rhine, dominated by Schloss Vaduz, residence of the ruling Prince of Liechtenstein. The town's principal sights are

Liechtenstein: the Alpine Rhine ...

... and Schloss Vaduz

Alpine Rhine

Liechtenstein
(continued)

the Art Gallery, the Landesmuseum, the Postal Museum and the Art Centre.

The little towns and villages on the hills (the highest of which is the Kühgrat, 2124 m, in the Three Sisters range) and in the upper Samina valley are popular both with summer visitors and with winter sports enthusiasts (Triesenberg, Gaflei, Steg, Malbun).

In the lower-lying part of the country the chief places apart from Vaduz are Balzers, Triesen, Schaan and Nendeln.

Buchs

Buchs, chief town of a district in the canton of St Gallen, is a busy traffic junction point (many haulage firms) and a frontier crossing into Austria (Feldkirch-Innsbruck-Vienna).
At the junction with the road from the Toggenburg district is the imposing Schloss Werdenberg (13th and 16th/17th c.), once the seat of the Counts of Werdenberg.

Hoher Kasten

To the west of the road, on the boundary between the Swiss cantons of St Gallen and Appenzell (half-canton of Innerrhoden), the Hoher Kasten (1295 m; fine views; cableway from Brülisau) rears above the Rhine.

Feldkirch

This old district capital (pop. 24,000) in the Austrian province of Vorarlberg lies at a road and rail junction on the route from Lake Constance to the Arlberg up the valley of the Ill, which here carves a way through a rocky gorge from the Walgau into the broad valley of the Vorderrhein.
Feldkirch is an important educational centre, with many schools (including the Jesuit Stella Matutina College, founded 1855), and since 1968 has been the see of a Roman Catholic bishop.
The old-world little town still preserves part of its circuit of walls. The main features of interest are the Cathedral (completed 1478), the Town Hall, the Museum of Sacred Art in the former church of St Johann and the Schattenburg (12th c.; local museum).

Götzis

Above the little market town of Götzis (Vorarlberg) on the right bank of the Rhine rears the ruined castle of Neu-Montfort, burned down in 1405.

Altstätten

The ancient little Swiss town of Altstätten (canton of St Gallen) lies at the western edge of the Rhine plain, here some 10 km wide. Features of interest are the arcaded houses in the Marktgasse with the type of gable characteristic of Appenzell, the Engelplatz, with the Untertor (Lower Gate), and the modern Church of the Good Shepherd (Gut-Hirt-Kirche).

Hohenems

Almost opposite Altstätten, on the eastern edge of the plain, is the busy little Austrian market town of Hohenems (Vorarlberg). In Schloss Hohenems (built 1560), seat of the Counts of Waldburg-Zeil, two manuscripts of the "Nibelungenlied" were found in 1755 and 1778.

Dornbirn

Dornbirn (pop. 38,000), the largest town in the Austrian province of Vorarlberg, is spaciously laid out at the foot of the Bregenzer Wald. It is a busy industrial town (engineering, textiles; Federal Textile College).

Within easy reach of the town are the Rappenloch Gorge (Rappenlochschlucht), traversed by the turbulent Dornbirner Ach (a right-bank tributary of the Alpine Rhine); the Alploch Gorge (Alplochschlucht) with a 120 m high waterfall; and the Bödele, a rounded hill covered with Alpine meadows and surrounded by pine forests which attracts many visitors with its mountain air and good skiing. From the Bödele there are magnificent views of Lake Constance.

The Vorarlberg industrial town of Lustenau (mainly embroidery production) lies a little way south of the point where the Alpine Rhine divides into the Alter Rhein (Old Rhine), flowing north-west, and the canal (cut at the end of the 19th c.) which runs north into Lake Constance.

Lustenau

The Swiss town of St Margrethen, situated on the left bank of the Old Rhine, surrounded by fruit-orchards, is an important frontier crossing point for road and rail traffic between Switzerland and Austria.
It is a town of warehouses and chemical plants, with many haulage firms, but also has mineral springs (chalybeate, carbonated).
The cemetery church of St Margaretha (1090) has frescoes and Late Baroque altars. In the immediate surroundings are Schloss Bergstein and Schloss Vorburg.

St Margrethen

The trim Swiss frontier town of Rheineck lies on the idyllic Old Rhine. Features of interest are the arcaded streets, an old town gate, the Town Hall (1555), two imposing burghers' houses, the Löwenhof and the Custerhof, the Late Gothic and Baroque church and a ruined castle (view).

Rheineck

The river port of Fussach (Vorarlberg) lies on the left bank of the canalised Rhine just above its outflow into Fussach Bay in Lake Constance. It has a boatyard.

Fussach

Between the Rohrspitz and the Rheinspitz, the two points bounding the Rhine delta with its abundance of fish, is the Rheinau peninsula, with a 1 km wide girdle of reeds round Wetterwinkel Bay which forms an almost completely unspoiled nature reserve, the haunt of numerous species of birds.

Rheinau

Lake Constance (Bodensee)

Lake Constance (in German the Bodensee) is a majestically beautiful expanse of water fringed by old lakeside towns and friendly villages and bounded on the south by wooded hills, beyond which, in the distance, is the chain of the Appenzell Alps, with Mt Säntis (2504 m). Farther east, beyond the wide Rhine valley, are the Vorarlberg Alps, with the Rätikon ridge and Schesaplana (2964 m) rearing above them, and to the east of the lake the Bregenzer Wald (Bregenz Forest), with Mt Pfänder (1064 m), and the Allgäu Alps. The Upper Swabian foreland to the north of the lake and the Linzgau to the west are upland regions traversed by numerous rivers, rising to a height of 837 m (Mt Höchsten) and forming a patchwork of woodland, fields, orchards and scattered villages.

Topography

Lake Constance

The shores of the Obersee, the large eastern section of Lake Constance, are mostly flat, with many large bays and inlets, particularly at the delta-mouths of the Alpine Rhine, Dornbirner Ach and Bregenzer Ach. The long-settled land round the western end of the lake, patterned by the Bodanrück, the Mettnau and Höri peninsulas and the fjord-like Überlinger See, continues westward without any interruption in the Hegau, which with its boldly shaped hills ranks among the most attractive volcanic landscapes in Germany.

Bregenz

Bregenz (originally the stronghold of a Celtic tribe, the Brigantii; later the Roman military post and way-station of 'Brigantium'), capital of Austria's most westerly province, Vorarlberg, lies in Bregenz Bay, at the east end of Lake Constance, the main base of the Austrian Federal Railways' fleet of vessels on the lake. This well known festival city (pop. 27,000), with its range of cultural facilities and institutions, is the only town on Lake Constance situated on the immediate fringe of the Alps.

The spaciously laid out town lies under the commanding peak of Mt Pfänder (1064 m; cableway; motorway tunnel), the main buttress of the Bregenzer Wald with its much frequented holiday places (some still enviably quiet and peaceful) and winter sports centres, and extends southward to the Bregenzer Ach.

The old town of Bregenz has preserved its old-world character, while the newer districts on the lake are modern and well equipped with tourist facilities (casino).
In the Kornmarkt is the richly stocked Vorarlberg Provincial Museum. The Festspielhaus (used for congresses as well as the Bregenz Festival), with its floating opera stage, is at the southwest end of the beautiful lakeside gardens.

Lindau

Lindau (first recorded in 882) is the largest town (pop. 25,000) on the Bavarian shores of Lake Constance. It consists of the garden city of Lindau, spaciously laid out amid orchards on the morainic slopes of the mainland, and the picturesque old town on an island in the lake, with the harbour used by vessels plying on Lake Constance; the two parts are linked by the Seebrücke ('Lake Bridge') and a causeway carrying the railway. During the summer Lindau is a popular holiday resort (casino), and it is also an important venue for congresses and conferences.

The little spa of Bad Schachen, which forms part of Lindau, lies on the shores of the lake amid beautiful gardens.

Wasserburg

The Bavarian health resort of Wasserburg has its picturesque old town centre on a former island, joined with the mainland since 1720, between Nonnenhorn Bay (best viewpoint the Malerwinkel) to the west and the Wasserburg Bay to the east.

Friedrichshafen

Friedrichshafen (originally called Buchhorn; pop. 53,000), in the German 'Land' of Baden-Württemberg, is the largest town on Lake Constance after Konstanz, with a ferry service to Romanshorn on the Swiss shore of the lake.
The town played a prominent part in the early development of aircraft construction (Zeppelin Museum in the Town Hall). It now has a number of engineering works.
The international Lake Constance Trade Fair and Boat Show is held annually in Friedrichshafen.

Lindau on Lake Constance: the Lake Harbour

In the town's industrial district of Manzell Count Ferdinand von Zeppelin (1838–1917) built an airship hangar on the lake in 1899, and the first zeppelin, "LZ 1", took off from here on 2 July 1900. Here too in 1914 Claudius Dornier (1884–1969) established a yard for the construction of flying boats.

Friedrichshafen (continued)

The attractive little town of Meersburg, charmingly situated on the steeply sloping vine-covered slopes of Lake Constance at the point where the Obersee merges into the Überlinger See, has preserved its medieval aspect and is one of the most interesting places on the lake. There is a regular car ferry service between Meersburg and Konstanz.

Meersburg

The Altes Schloss (Old Castle) or Meersburg, originally dating from the 7th century, is the oldest inhabited castle in Germany. The poetess Annette von Droste-Hülshoff (1797–1848) lived in the castle and died there; her room is shown to visitors.

The Marktplatz in the upper town, with its half-timbered houses and the Obertor (Upper Gate), is one of the best-known examples of an old German townscape.
The Neues Schloss was built by the great Baroque architect Balthasar Neumann in 1741–1750 as the residence of the bishops of Konstanz.

In the little lakeside town of Unteruhldingen (commune of Uhldingen-Mühlhofen), which has a popular yacht harbour, is the interesting Open-Air Museum of German Prehistory (Freilichtmuseum Deutscher Vorzeit), with reconstructed pile-dwellings, a Stone Age village and a Bronze Age village.

Unteruhldingen

Meersburg: Old Castle

Konstanz: Mainau – Island of Flowers

Birnau

Birnau, which is also in the commune of Uhldingen-Mühlhofen, has a Baroque pilgrimage church (by Peter Thumb, 1747–1750), beautifully situated amid vineyards above the Überlinger See. The interior is charming, with its curving lines and the harmony of colours in its ceiling frescoes, ornaments and altars in the purest Rococo style.

Überlingen

Überlingen, chief town of the Linzgau, is a very popular holiday resort and spa (Kneipp treatment) situated on the steeply sloping shores of the Überlinger See, The town was founded by the Emperor Frederick Barbarossa in 1180, and has preserved from its five centuries (14th c. to 1802) as an imperial city considerable remains of its old fortifications (walls, towers, moat) and many historic old buildings.

Above the Town Hall, in the Hofstatt, is the Gothic Minster of St Nikolaus, begun in the 14th century and completed in 1586.

To the west of the old town lies the sloping municipal park (laid out 1875), with its rich subtropical vegetation, and farther south along the shore of the lake spreads the extensive spa area. Überlingen has an active cultural and artistic life.

Mainau

The Mainau, a small island (45 hectares) in the Überlinger See with rich subtropical and tropical vegetation, is known as the 'island of flowers', and its beautiful parks and gardens make it one of the most popular tourist resorts in the whole of South Germany. It lies within the commune of Konstanz and is owned by a Swedish foundation of which Count Lennart Bernadotte af Wisborg is director.

Konstanz, chief town of a district in the 'Land' of Baden-Württemberg, situated between the Obersee (Konstanz Bay) and the Untersee, which are linked by the Lake Rhine (See-rhein), is the largest town on Lake Constance (pop. 78,000) and the base of the German Federal Railways' fleet of vessels on the lake (regular car ferry service to Meersburg). It is an important regional cultural centre, with a University (founded 1966), a College of Engineering, two limnological institutes, a weather station, an active theatrical and musical life, a College of Art and several museums and art galleries. It is also a favourite congress and conference centre. The main elements in its economy are commerce, the service trades (tourism; casino), craft production, wine-growing and a variety of industry. There are also a number of printing and publishing houses.

Konstanz

The town developed out of a Celtic fishing settlement which was given the name of 'Constantia' in later Roman times.

At the Council of Constance (1414–1418), the 16th oecumenical council and the largest assembly of the medieval period (50,000 participants, in a town which had a population of only 6000), Martin V was elected Pope and the great schism in the church was brought to an end. The council also condemned the Czech reformer Jan Hus (c. 1370–1415) to death at the stake.

The picturesque old town with its medieval buildings lies between the Rhine (the starting-point of the measurement of distances on the Rhine is under the Rhine bridge, which is km 0) and the Swiss frontier (Kreuzlingen). The spaciously laid out newer part of the town clings to the gentle slopes of the Bodanrück, the eastern part of which, along with the 'flower island' of Mainau, lies within the city boundaries.

Notable among the town's many features of interest are the Minster (originally 11th c., with much later alteration), the Rosgarten Museum (art and culture of the Lake Constance area), the Wessenberg Gallery (pictures, drawings) and the Council Building (Konzilgebäude), originally built in 1388 as a warehouse, in which the only Papal election to be held on German soil took place on 8 November 1417 (now a concert and congress hall).

Reichenau is the largest island in Lake Constance (5 km long, 1.5 km wide, area 428 hectares). Its mild climate and fertile soil, with artificial irrigation, favour the production of large crops of vegetables, replacing the vineyards which formerly predominated. Fish-farming also makes a contribution to the island's economy.

Reichenau

The churches belonging to the once world-famed abbey founded by St Pirmin in the reign of Charles Martel (724) are among the finest examples of Early Romanesque art in Germany, both for their architecture and their magnificent frescoes; they are to be seen in the villages of Oberzell, Mittelzell and Unterzell.

The town of Radolfzell (pop. 24,000), founded in 826 as the monastery of Cella Ratoldi, lies on the Zeller See, a northern arm of the Untersee. The old part of the town has narrow winding streets with handsome noble mansions and patrician houses.

Radolfzell

Lake Constance

The spa and recreation facilities on the Mettnau peninsula make Radolfzell a popular health resort (Kneipp treatment) and holiday centre.

Swiss shore of
Lake Constance
(from east to west)

Altenrhein (a district of the town of Rorschach) lies in the delta of the Old Rhine (Alter Rhein), part of which is a nature reserve. It is the home of the FFA aircraft and automobile factory (Flug- und Fahrzeugwerke Altenrhein; formerly the Dornier works). The well known Dornier flying boats of the 1920s took off from here.

Rorschach, which was granted the right to hold a market in 947, was formerly the port for St Gallen and is now an industrial town (pop. 25,000). It lies at the foot of the Rorschacher Berg in Rorschach Bay.

Arbon (pop. 14,000), situated on a peninsula in the Swiss canton of Thurgau, is a port and a busy industrial town. It occupies the site of the Celtic 'Arbona' and the Roman 'Arbor Felix'.

The small lakeside villages of Uttwil and Kesswil have trim half-timbered houses. On the lake are prehistoric pile-dwellings.

Romanshorn (pop. 9000) is the busiest traffic centre on the Swiss shore of Lake Constance, a port (base of the Swiss shipping fleet on Lake Constance; shipyard belonging to Swiss Federal Railways) and a popular bathing resort. Ferry service to Friedrichshafen on the German side of the lake.
In the Seepark (Lake Park) is the very beautiful Old Church (Romanesque and Gothic).

Münsterlingen, a village and holiday resort on a small peninsula, has a church with a fine Baroque interior. Since 1963, when the lake last froze, it has housed a 16th century bust of John the Baptist, which traditionally transfers between Münsterlingen and Hagnau (SE of Meersburg) whenever the lake freezes.
A number of prehistoric pile-dwellings were found on the lakeside near the village.

Kreuzlingen is a Swiss town (considerable industry) separated from Konstanz only by the frontier. On the lakeside to the north is the carefully tended Seeburg park.

Gottlieben (commune of Tägerwilen), on the Untersee, was the birthplace of Hermann Müller (1850–1927), a vine-grower who produced the Müller-Thurgau grape by crossing Riesling and Sylvaner. It has a castle originally built in 1251 as a subsidiary residence of the bishops of Konstanz (rebuilt in neo-Gothic style in 1837/38) and several fine old half-timbered houses.
A local specialty is the pastry called 'Gottlieber Hüppen'.

Ermatingen is a fishing village and holiday resort on the Staad peninsula (pile dwellings), with fine half-timbered houses. Above the town is the 16th century Schloss Wolfsberg, from which there are fine views.

Mannenbach is finely situated opposite the island of Reichenau (2 km; ferry), with a number of castles looming over the village. Immediately above the village is Burg Salenstein (originally 11th c., rebuilt 1842). On a terrace to the east is Schloss Arenenberg (Napoleonic Museum), built 1540–1546, later rebuilt, which from 1830 to 1837 was the residence of Queen Hortense de Beauharnais (1783–1837), stepdaughter of Napoleon I, whose son Louis Napoléon (1808–1873), later the Emperor Napoleon III, spent a happy childhood here.

Above Mannenbach to the west is the ruined Schloss Sandegg, and a short distance south of this Schloss Eugensberg, built in 1820 for Eugène de Beauharnais, Napoleon's stepson and brother of Queen Hortense.

Steckborn is an ancient little town on a peninsula projecting into the Untersee, with picturesque half-timbered houses, the Turmhof (a small castle built about 1320) and the Town Hall (1667; collection of arms and armour). At the south-west end of the town is the Bernina sewing-machine factory, with a Sewing-Machine Museum.

All round Lake Constance visitors will find examples of art and architecture of all the main periods. The following is a brief selection.

Art and architecture round Lake Constance

The finest examples of Romanesque work are to be found on the island of Reichenau (Minster, Mittelzell; St Georg, Oberzell; SS. Peter and Paul, Niederzell) and at Konstanz (Minster), Lindau (St Peter), Arbon (chapel of St Gallus) and Schienen (St Genesius).

There is much more Gothic work, both religious and secular: Konstanz (St Stephan; Mauritiusrotunde, Minster; Council Building); Meersburg (Grethgebäude); Überlingen (Minster); Lindau (Diebsturm or Thieves' Tower); Bregenz (St Gallus; Martinsturm in upper town); Eriskirch (parish church); Radolfzell (Minster); Markdorf (St Nikolaus; Stadtschloss); Salem (monastic church); Ravensburg (St Jodok; Town Hall; Weigh-House).

Imposing Renaissance buildings are Schloss Heiligenberg, Schloss Wolfegg and the town halls of Lindau and Konstanz.

The Early Baroque period is represented by the Altes Schloss at Meersburg, the Schlosskirche in Friedrichshafen and the Ritterschaftshaus (Knights' House) in Radolfzell.

The most notable buildings of the High Baroque and Rococo periods are the Weingarten abbey church and the pilgrimage church of Birnau. Other fine examples are the Neues Schloss at Meersburg, the Imperial Hall in the former monastery of Salem, the Neues Schloss at Tettnang, the former monastic church of Weissenau (near Ravensburg), the churches of St Martin in Langenargen and St Marie in Lindau, the Schloss and Schlosskirche on the island of Mainau and – last but not least – the Cathedral and monastery library of St Gallen.

Good examples of neo-classical architecture are Schloss Arenenberg (near Mannenbach) and the market square of Heiden.

Modern architecture of the postwar period is represented by two notable building complexes, the School of Economic and Social Sciences at St Gallen and the new University of Konstanz.

There are art museums of particular interest at Konstanz (Rosgarten Museum) and Bregenz (Vorarlberg Provincial Museum).

Art museums

The best preserved examples of old townscapes are to be seen at Meersburg, Lindau and Überlingen; at Stein am Rhein; at

Townscapes

Stein am Rhein (High Rhine)

Townscapes round
Lake Constance (continued)

Ravensburg and Wangen in the Allgäu; and in the lower town of
Konstanz and the upper town of Bregenz.

High Rhine (from Lake Constance to Basle)

Stein am Rhein

The little town of Stein am Rhein, in the Swiss canton of Schaffhausen, lies at the end of the Untersee, the arm of Lake Constance by which the Rhine leaves the lake, under the name of
the High Rhine (Hochrhein). With its frescoed and oriel-win-
dowed houses it is one of the best preserved little medieval
towns in Switzerland. Of particular interest are the Town Hall
(1538), with the town's historical collections; the old house
known as the Weisser Adler (White Eagle) in the Hauptstrasse
(No. 14); the Untertor (Lower Gate) and Obertor (Upper Gate);
and St George's Abbey Museum (Klostermuseum St Georgen).

On a wooded hill to the north of the town, the Klingenberg
(539 m), is the well preserved 12th century Burg Hohenklingen
(view), once the home of the minnesinger Walther von Klingen
(c. 1350).

On the left bank of the Rhine, in the district of Burg, is a hill
(view) with the remains of the Roman fort of 'Tasgaetium' (294
A.D.). Within the area of the fort is the parish church of St
Johann (originally 5th c.; frescoes of c. 1400 in choir).
In the district of Wagenhausen is a Romanesque pillared basili-
ca (1083–1087), all that is left of a small Benedictine house.

The old-world little Swiss frontier town of Diessenhofen was a free imperial city in the Middle Ages. It has well preserved old streets, handsome burghers' houses, old fortifications (Siegel-turm), a church of 1602 and conventual buildings of 1571.
On the opposite bank of the Rhine (old covered wooden bridge; frontier crossing) is the little German town of Gailingen.

Diessenhofen

On the north bank, between Diessenhofen and Schaffhausen, is the German enclave of Büsingen (Swiss currency and customs area).

Büsingen

Schaffhausen (pop. 34,000) capital of the Swiss canton of that name, which lies almost entirely on the north side of the Rhine, enclosed on three sides by Germany, is an important hub of communications and a busy industrial town.
In addition to the charming old town the principal features of interest are the Minster (1087–1150), the well stocked All Saints Museum (Museum zu Allerheiligen; a former Benedictine ab-bey, founded c. 1050) and Kastell Munot, a circular structure, built between 1564 and 1585 in accordance with Dürer's princi-ples of fortification, which stands on a vine-clad hill to the east of the town (fine views).
Schaffhausen is the headquarters of the Swiss Untersee and Rhine Shipping Line, whose vessels ply several times daily dur-ing the summer between Schaffhausen and Kreuzlingen.

Schaffhausen

From Schaffhausen to the Rhine Falls the Rhine forms the boundary between the Swiss cantons of Schaffhausen and Zurich.

The Rhine Falls (Rheinfall) at Schaffhausen are the mightiest falls in Central Europe. Some 4 km south-west of Schaffhausen, at Neuhausen, the water of the High Rhine surges over a ledge of Jurassic limestone 150 m across and 22 m high, with two higher rocks emerging from the river. The flow of water is at its greatest in June and July, after the melting of snow in the Alps. A good view of the falls can be had from the south bank of the Rhine at Schloss Laufen (terraces and gangways leading close

Rhine Falls

Rhine Falls (continued)

to the falls), but the best general view is from Schloss Wörth on the right bank (boat across the river, and boat trip – perfectly safe – to the rock in the middle of the falls).

Rheinau

The picturesque little Swiss frontier town of Rheinau (canton of Zurich) is almost completely encircled by a loop in the river (bridge; frontier crossing; hydroelectric station). The twin-to-wered Baroque church (1704–1711) belonged to a Benedictine abbey (founded in the 9th c., dissolved in 1862) on an island in the river.

Ellikon

A short distance south of the fishing village of Ellikon on the left bank of the Rhine (handsome half-timbered houses; passenger ferry to the German bank of the river) the river Thur flows into the Rhine from the east.

Eglisau

Eglisau, on the right bank, is an old-world little town (canton of Zurich) at a bridge over the Rhine. To the north extends the Rafzer Feld, an area bounded on three sides by German terri-tory. In Rafz is a fine 18th century inn, the 'Goldenes Kreuz'.

Glattfelden

Glattfelden (canton of Zurich), on the river Glatt, which flows into the Rhine a little way downstream, was the home town of the Swiss writer Gottfried Keller (1817–1890) and is frequently referred to in his novel "Der grüne Heinrich"; Gottfried Keller Centre under construction.

Kaiserstuhl

The old frontier town of Kaiserstuhl, picturesquely situated above the south bank of the Rhine, has a massive tower of the 12th/13th century and a Gothic church (remodelled in Baroque style in the early 17th c.).
A bridge (frontier crossing) spans the Rhine to the German town of Hohentengen, with Schloss Rötteln.
At Weiach, a little way upstream, and Rümikon, downstream, are the remains of Roman watch-towers.

Zurzach

Zurzach (canton of Zurich) was the Roman 'Tenedo' (Roman fort and remains of a 5th c. church on the Kirchlibuck). Former-ly a river port noted for its fairs, it is now a well known spa. The swimming pool (hot spring 40 °C) and other spa facilities are to the west of the town centre.
Notable features of the town are the handsome old burghers' houses and the 10th century church (14th c. tower over choir; sarcophagus of St Verena in crypt; rich treasury).
On the right bank of the Rhine (bridge, frontier crossing) is the German village of Rheinheim.

Koblenz

The Swiss town of Koblenz, situated near the confluence of the Aare and the Rhine (hence its name, from Latin 'Confluentes'), is an important road junction which was already a place of some consequence in Roman times. The remains of the Roman watch-tower of Kleiner Laufen date from the 4th century A.D. 4 km W is the Leibstadt nuclear power station.

Waldshut-Tiengen

On the north bank of the Rhine (bridge, frontier crossing) is Waldshut, part of the German double town of Waldshut-Tiengen. Just upstream the river Wutach, coming from the north-east through the Klettgau, flows into the Rhine.

Albbruck

The German village of Albbruck lies on the right bank at the mouth of the rocky Alb valley.

On the south bank (no bridge) is the Swiss village of Schwader-loch, with the remains of two Roman watch-towers (Oberes and Unteres Bürgli).

The little Swiss town of Laufenburg (from 'Laufen' = rapids), in the canton of Aargau, is linked with the German town of the same name on the north bank by a stone bridge (frontier crossing). This is one of the most beautiful spots on the High Rhine, with the wooded hills flanking the river forming an attractive backcloth to the two little towns facing each other across the Rhine.

Laufenburg

The German village of Murg, on the right bank, lies at the mouth of the Murg valley, which joins the Rhine from the north-west, coming from the Hotzenwald, on the southern slopes of the Black Forest.

Murg

The ancient little Baden town of Säckingen (pop. 15,000) has been officially known since 1978 as Bad Säckingen, indicating its status as a spa (saline hot springs, 32 and 28.5°C; treatment and bathing establishment).
On the outside wall of the choir of the Minster (St Fridolin) is the tombstone of Werner Kirchhofer (d. 1690) and his wife Maria Ursula von Schönau, who gave Joseph Victor von Scheffel (1826–1886) the idea for his romantic verse epic "Der Trompeter von Säckingen" ("The Trumpeter of Säckingen"). In a park on the banks of the Rhine is Schloss Schönau (17th and 18th c.; Museum of the High Rhine, collection of trumpets).
The German and Swiss banks of the Rhine are linked by Europe's longest covered wooden bridge (borne on stone

Bad Säckingen

Bad Säckingen: Rhine Bridge (Europe's longest covered wooden bridge)

Bad Säckingen (continued)

piers), over 400 years old, between Bad Säckingen and the Swiss village of Stein (canton of Aargau).

Rheinfelden

On either side of the Rhine, which is navigable from this point (km 149 from Konstanz), is a town called Rheinfelden. The German Rheinfelden on the north bank is an industrial town (pop. 28,000). Its Swiss counterpart is an old-world little town of 7000 inhabitants, its walls and towers rising above the swiftly flowing river; it is also a spa, with strongly saline springs. Notable features are the Town Hall (16th–18th c.), St Martin's church (15th c.; Baroque interior) and the Fricktaler Museum (local history) in the 'Haus zur Sonne' (Marktgasse 12).

On the Swiss bank, in the wide bend between Rheinfelden and Mumpf, are the remains of five Roman watch-towers of the 4th century A.D.

Augst

The Swiss town of Augst lies on the left bank of the Ergolz, which flows into the Rhine from the south, forming the boundary between the cantons of Aargau and Basel-Land. On the bridge over the Ergolz is a Late Gothic inn of 1540.

A little way south of Augst, between the Ergolz and its tributary the Violenbach, is the site of the Roman 'Colonia Augusta Raurica' (founded 44 B.C.), with a large theatre and the remains of several temples.

At the near end of the site are a reconstruction of a Roman house (1953–1957), a museum and the restored Roman theatre of 120–150 A.D. (performances given in summer). Beyond, to the east, are a temple, the principal forum and a basilica. On a hill to the west of the theatre is the large Schönbühl temple; to the south of the theatre are houses and baths.

An amphitheatre was discovered in 1959 to the south-west of the site.

Between Augst and the German town of Grenzach-Wyhlen, in the river, is the Augst-Wyhlen hydroelectric station (1907–1912), with a dam 212 m long.

Kaiseraugst

1 km north-east of Augst, attractively situated on the banks of the Rhine and the right bank of the Ergolz, is Kaiseraugst (canton of Aargau), with remains of the Roman fort of 'Castrum Rauracense'.

Grenzacher Horn

The Grenzacher Horn, a limestone crag on the right bank of the Rhine (km 163 from Konstanz), marks the frontier (road crossing point) between the German Federal Republic ('Land' of Baden-Württemberg) and the Swiss Confederation (cantons of Basel-Stadt and Basel-Land).

On the south (Swiss) bank is Birsfelden (hydroelectric station, river harbour), situated at the junction of the Birs and the Rhine, on the eastern outskirts of Gross-Basel (→ Towns and Places of Interest, Basle).

Sights
along the Rhine
between Basle and Rotterdam

This section presents the main part of the Rhine's course between Basle and Rotterdam – the stretch covered by the cruises of the Köln-Düsseldorfer (KD German Rhine Line).

N.B.

To make it easy for users of this Guide to locate the places they will see during their journey up or down the Rhine, the course of the river is displayed in schematic form in a series of sections, each covering a double-page spread; the actual course of the Rhine can be followed on the large map at the end of the book.

Particular places can be pinpointed with the help of the kilometre figures in the blue strip representing the river, which show distances from Konstanz (see Measurement of distances, p. 18).

When travelling downstream the pages should be read from the bottom upwards, when travelling upstream from the top downwards.

Basle: view over the Rhine to the Minster

Basle ⇌ Chalampé

Chalampé (pop. 1000) is an industrial village; customs post on the frontier with Germany. Nearby a golf-course.

km 199,6

Mulhouse
→Towns and Places of Interest from A to Z

km 196,0

Ottmarsheim (pop. 2000), a small port and industrial town (potash mining), with a *church (consecrated 1049) which originally belonged to a convent of Benedictine nuns. Modelled on the Carolingian Palatine Chapel in Aachen Cathedral, it is an octagonal structure with galleries borne on eight pairs of columns running round the interior.

km 194,5

Ottmarsheim Locks (completed 1952), on the Grand Canal d'Alsace; there are a double lock (185 m × 24 m and 12 m; lift 14.70 m) and a hydroelectric station.

km 193,7

Niffer, a village just north of the branching off of a 16 km long canal, completed 1967, linking the Grand Canal d'Alsace with the Rhine-Rhône Canal.

km 186,2

Kembs (pop. 2000), a little town which occupies the site of the Roman 'Cambete', situated at a bridge over the Rhine.
4 km S is Kembs-Loechle, at the Kembs dam and locks on the Grand Canal d'Alsace, with the first French hydroelectric station on the Upper Rhine (c. 900 million kWh), built in 1928–32 and rebuilt after wartime destruction (1942/43 and 1945).

km 183,6

Kembs Locks (completed 1932), the first and oldest of such installations along the Grand Canal d'Alsace, bypasses the Isteiner Schwelle, formerly a danger to shipping. The complex consists of a double lock (185 m and 95 m × 24 m; lift 13.20 m) and a hydroelectric station. The control bridge was designed by the architect Le Corbusier.

km 179,2

Grand Canal d'Alsace, a ship canal running down the left bank of the Rhine between Basle and Strasbourg, constructed to bypass a stretch of the river which was formerly difficult and dangerous at many points. The section between Basle and Vogelgrun, the oldest part, is a separate canal running parallel to the river, but lower down it follows the main river bed for most of the way, with the necessary dams and locks on short loop canals.

km 173,5

Huningue (pop. 7000), a small French industrial town and port on the Rhine, in Alsace. It was fortified by Louis XIV; subsequently it was several times besieged by Austrian forces, and in 1815 was finally taken and its defences slighted.

km 170,0

Basle (Basel; Gross-Basel)
(Starting and finishing point of the KD Rhine cruises)
→Towns and Places of Interest from A to Z

km 167,5

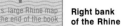

km 208,0

Staufen im Breisgau
→Towns and Places of Interest from A to Z

km 199,3

Neuenburg am Rhein (pop. 8000), a little frontier town built in the 12th c. by the Counts of Zähringen (Margraves of Baden) at an old Rhine crossing. In the 13th c. it was briefly a free Imperial city. The town was devastated in the Thirty Years War and in the Dutch War (1672–1679) and totally destroyed during the War of the Spanish Succession. It was again severely damaged during the second world war. Over the centuries Neuenburg also suffered from the frequent flooding of the Rhine, and in 1525 the floods carried away the 14th c. Gothic Liebfrauenmünster.
There is a road bridge here crossing the Rhine into France.

km 189,4

Bad Bellingen (pop. 3000), a rising little spa town, with the Markusquelle (St Mark's Spring, 38.4 °C), recommended for the treatment of rheumatic complaints and cardiac and circulatory disorders. Magnificent show of tulips in the Kurpark in spring. Roman fountain in the outlying district of Hertingen.

km 186,5

Rheinweiler, a modest village with a mansion (Schloss) which belonged to the Rotberg family and is now an old people's home.

km 180,5

Isteiner Klotz, a limestone crag dating from the Jurassic and Tertiary periods which formerly projected far into the Rhine but has largely been quarried away by man (cement works). In the caves in the rocks, which have now almost completely disappeared, numerous implements of the Mesolithic and Neolithic periods were found, many of them made from the jasper which outcrops here.
The commanding situation of the Isteiner Klotz above the Basle embayment and at the entrance to the Burgundian Gate meant that it was always of military importance and secured by strong fortifications. There are scanty remains of the first castle built here around 1300 (demolished 1409–11). The fortifications of the first and second world wars were blown up at the end of each war.

km 171,0

Weil am Rhein (pop. 26,000), in the 'Dreiländereck' (meeting-place of three countries), lies below the southern Black Forest at a 'step' or sill in the bed of the Rhine, the Isteiner Schwelle. The town first appears in the records in 786, under the name of 'Willa', as a possession of the monastery of St Gallen. It is now an important traffic junction point, with a harbour and some industry. It has an interesting old building, the Staffelhaus (1607).

km 169,9

Kleinhüningen, Basle's port on the Rhine, with a shipping exhibition, "Our Way to the Sea". On the 55 m high grain elevator is a viewing terrace.

− 169,0
km 165,0

Basle (Basel; Klein-Basel)
→Towns and Places of Interest from A to Z

Marckolsheim Locks (completed 1961), on the Grand Canal d'Alsace; there are a double lock (185 m × 24 m and 12 m; lift 13.80 m) and a hydroelectric station (up to 920 million kWh). A pontoon bridge (frontier crossing) leads across the Rhine to the German village of Sasbach am Kaiserstuhl.

■ km 240,0

5 km W of the dam is the little town of **Marckolsheim,** rebuilt after destruction during heavy fighting in 1940. It lies on the French 'Route Fleurie' ('Flower Road'). There is a monument commemorating the Maginot Line, and in Casemate 35/3 a War Museum (conducted tours on application).

Precise manœuvre in a lock

Neuf-Brisach (pop. 2500), a town built by Louis XIV in 1699–1703 as a fortress. With its octagonal plan within star-shaped outer defences, its four gates and its square Place d'Armes in the centre it is a typical example of Vauban's fortification techniques. Vauban Museum in the Porte de Belfort. The town has preserved a number of 17th c. burghers' houses.

km 225,6

Vogelgrun Locks (completed 1959), on the Grand Canal d'Alsace; there are a double lock (185 m × 24 m and 12 m; lift 11.80 m) and a hydroelectric station (820 million kWh).

■ km 224,6

Fessenheim (pop. 2000), village at the **Locks** (completed 1958) of that name on the Grand Canal d'Alsace; there are a double lock (185 m × 24 m and 12 m; lift 15.10 m) and a hydroelectric station (1020 million kWh). The Fessenheim nuclear power station (6 billion kWh annually) came into operation in 1977.

■ km 210,5

s. large Rhine map
the end of the book

km 244,0

Wyhl am Kaiserstuhl, the site of an atomic power station which gave rise to violent controversy. Construction was suspended in 1975 following a court decision.

km 240,2

Sasbach, a village at the NW corner of the Kaiserstuhl range. Until 1850 the Rhine flowed just past the village and was crossed here by the 'royal road' of the Ottonian Emperors. The river is now spanned by a pontoon bridge (frontier crossing) leading to the French town of Marckolsheim. Sasbach has a parish church (St Martin's) which was originally Romanesque but was rebuilt in 1741, and a monument to the French Marshal Turenne, who was killed in an engagement here in 1675.
1.5 km NW, directly above the Rhine, is a ruined castle, the **Limburg** (269 m), in which Rudolf of Habsburg is said to have been born in 1218.

km 234,8

Burkheim, an outlying district of Vogtsburg in the Kaiserstuhl range (218 m; pop. 5000), lies on a hill spur above the Upper Rhine plain. It has a ruined Renaissance castle (16th c.), a picturesque Town Hall (1604), handsome burghers' houses of the 16th and 17th c. and remains of the old town walls, with one town gate.
3 km NW are the ruins of **Burg Sponeck,** a 13th c. castle (private property).

km 232,0

*__Kaiserstuhl__ ('Emperor's Chair'), a small range of volcanic hills (area 16 km × 12 km) between Freiburg (Black Forest) and Colmar (Vosges) which rise sharply out of the Upper Rhine plain to heights of 557 m in the Totenkopf and 555 m in the Neunlindenbuck. Almost everywhere the tuffs and eruptive rocks of a relatively recent volcanic period are covered with a layer of loess between 10 and 20 m thick in which running water has carved out deep channels. These volcanic soils, with high levels of summer sunshine, produce wines of outstanding quality (Achkarren, Bickensohl, Ihringen, Oberrotweil, etc.). This very characteristic area with its rich flora and fauna (butterflies, bees) is well worth a visit.

km 226,5

Breisach am Rhein
→Towns and Places of Interest from A to Z

km 221,0

Freiburg im Breisgau
→Towns and Places of Interest from A to Z

km 210,5

Bad Krozingen (pop. 9000), a spa (hot springs, 40.2 ° and 37 °C) recommended for the treatment of cardiac conditions, circulatory disorders and rheumatism, situated amid vineyards under the hills of the southern Black Forest. In the town is a mansion (Schloss; private property) built in 1579 as the residence of the provost of St Blasien. In the Glöcklehof in Staufener Strasse is St Ulrich's Chapel, with 9th c. wall paintings.
The spa establishment is in the NW of the town.

Sessenheim (German 'Sesenheim'; pop. 1500), a village known to fame as the home of Friederike Brion, the pastor's daughter with whom Goethe fell in love during his student days in Strasbourg (1770–71). In the Protestant church (rebuilt in 1912) is the old pulpit from which Goethe listened to 'a rather dry sermon' but, seated at Friederike's side, 'did not find it too long'. On the outside wall of the church are the tombstones of Friederike's parents. Beside the church is the Auberge du Bœuf (good wine), with a Goethe museum. In the old guard-house to the left of the Town Hall is a Goethe memorial.

km 325,0

Gambsheim Locks (completed 1974), on the Grand Canal d'Alsace; there are a double lock (each 270 m × 24 m; lift 10.35 m) and a hydroelectric station.

km 309,0

Strasbourg
(KD cruise ships call here)
→Towns and Places of Interest from A to Z

km 295,0

Europabrücke (Europe Bridge), a 248 m long bridge over the Rhine between Kehl and Strasbourg (frontier crossing).

km 293,5

Strasbourg Locks (completed 1970), on the Grand Canal d'Alsace; there are a double lock (190 m × 24 m and 12 m; lift 10.80 m) and a hydroelectric station.

km 287,5

Gerstheim Locks (completed 1967), on the Grand Canal d'Alsace; there are a double lock (190 m × 24 m and 12 m; lift 11 m) and a hydroelectric station.

km 272,3

Rhinau, a village on the Grand Canal d'Alsace, at the **Locks** of that name (completed 1964); there are a double lock (185 m × 24 m and 12 m; lift 12.30 m), and, 4 km S, a hydroelectric station (940 million kWh).

km 256,2

Europe Bridge between Kehl and Strasbourg

km 308,9

Freistett, a district of the town of Rheinau, with a notable Early Romanesque church, the Heidenkirchlein (10th c.).

km 293,6

Kehl (pop. 30,000), a frontier town and river port. Originally a fishing village, at a point where there was a medieval crossing of the Rhine, it was developed during the 17th c. into a strongly fortified bridgehead for the free Imperial city of Strasbourg. After an eventful history, reflecting its important strategic situation, Kehl suffered severe damage during the second world war and was rebuilt after the war. – From the banks of the Rhine there is a fine view of Strasbourg. – To the E of the town is a memorial cemetery for those who died in the second world war.

km 293,5

Europabrücke: see opposite page

km 274,4

Meissenheim, a village with a fine 18th c. parish church (Protestant) which has a Silbermann organ. On the outside of the church is the tombstone of Friederike Brion of Sesenheim, Goethe's youthful love, who died here in 1813; there is a memorial room in the Riedhof.

km 266,0

Lahr (Schwarzwald)
→Towns and Places of Interest from A to Z

km 255,0

*Taubergiessen,** an area of rough and marshy water meadows and woodland round the junction of the river Elz (Leopold Canal) with the Rhine. It is now a nature reserve with many rare plants, including the wild vines from which the modern cultivated vines have been developed. To the east lies the village of **Rust**, with a holiday park ('Europa-Park').

km 249,0

Weisweil, a village with a very fine parish church (Protestant), originally Gothic but rebuilt and enlarged in the 18th century.

km 247,0

Kenzingen (pop. 7000), a little country town which has preserved its medieval aspect. The town was founded in 1259 on an oval island in the river Elz. Following the model of other foundations by the Dukes of Zähringen (e. g. Freiburg), it was laid out on a regular plan with the main streets crossing at right angles and a square for the principal church. The Gothic parish church (St Lawrence's) dates from the 13th c. (with much later alteration), the Town Hall from the 16th century. Many of the houses have attractive Gothic and Renaissance details.

Fort Louis ⇄ Altrip

Left bank
of the Rhine

Altrip (pop. 6000), situated on the left bank of the Rhine opposite the old confluence of the Neckar with the Rhine, occupies the site of a Roman fort, 'Alta Ripa' ('high bank'). The mid 18th c. parish church (Protestant) has Roman and medieval fragments built into its structure.

Motorway bridge (A 61), a striking suspension bridge (456 m long), with a 96 m high tower.

Speyer
(KD cruise ships call here)
→Towns and Places of Interest from A to Z

Speyer on the Rhine

Germersheim
→Towns and Places of Interest from A to Z

Neuburg am Rhein (pop. 2500), an old village originally on the right bank of the Rhine, which has frequently changed its course in this area.

Old mouth of the river Lauter. – The storks which used to nest round the mouth of the river in large numbers have now completely disappeared.

Lauterbourg (pop. 2500), situated at the junction of the river Lauter with the Rhine, has been since 1815 a frontier town between the Palatinate (Germany) and Alsace (France). It has a 15th c. church. On the right bank of the Lauter, extending to Wissembourg, are remains of the 18th c. Wissembourg Lines.

Seltz (pop. 2500), the Roman 'Saletio'. Here in 987 the Empress Adelheid, wife of the Emperor Otto I, founded a Benedictine abbey. The modern church preserves the 15th c. Gothic choir of the abbey church.
It is said that until the middle of the 19th c. high-quality gold ('Rheingold') was still being washed out of the sand of the Rhine here, and also at Germersheim.

Iffezheim Locks (completed 1977), on the Grand Canal d'Alsace; the double lock (each 270 m × 23 m; lift 10.30 m) occupies the position of the old Iffezheim yacht harbour.

Fort Louis, on an island in the Rhine. Built by Sébastien le Prestre de Vauban in 1686, it was taken and blown up by Austrian forces in 1793.

Bridges and ferries
crossing the Rhine

km 414,4

km 403,2

km 400,0

km 384,0

km 354,6

km 352,1

km 349,5

km 340,2

km 334,0

km 326,8

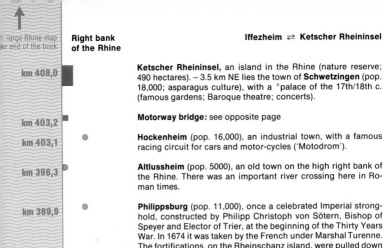

km 408,0

Ketscher Rheininsel, an island in the Rhine (nature reserve; 490 hectares). – 3.5 km NE lies the town of **Schwetzingen** (pop. 18,000; asparagus culture), with a *palace of the 17th/18th c. (famous gardens; Baroque theatre; concerts).

km 403,2

Motorway bridge: see opposite page

km 403,1

Hockenheim (pop. 16,000), an industrial town, with a famous racing circuit for cars and motor-cycles ('Motodrom').

km 396,3

Altlussheim (pop. 5000), an old town on the high right bank of the Rhine. There was an important river crossing here in Roman times.

km 389,9

Philippsburg (pop. 11,000), once a celebrated Imperial stronghold, constructed by Philipp Christoph von Sötern, Bishop of Speyer and Elector of Trier, at the beginning of the Thirty Years War. In 1674 it was taken by the French under Marshal Turenne. The fortifications, on the Rheinschanz island, were pulled down at the beginning of the 19th century.

km 389,2

Nuclear power station (two cooling towers).

km 360,9

Tullastein (Tulla stone), commemorating the regulation of the Rhine by Johann Gottfried Tulla (1770–1828).

km 360,0

Karlsruhe
→Towns and Places of Interest from A to Z

km 354,5

Neuburgweier, a customs port and control post on the Franco-German frontier.

km 344,3

Steinmauern, once the main port for the floating of rafts of timber from the Black Forest.

km 336,0

Rastatt
→Towns and Places of Interest from A to Z

km 333,2

Iffezheim (pop. 4000), on the site of a Roman settlement at a crossing of the Rhine, a few kilometres NW of the spa of **Baden-Baden.** The Roman Catholic parish church, dedicated to St Brigitta of Sweden, dates from the 15th c. but was remodelled in the 19th century. The Iffezheim race-course (international race meetings annually in spring and summer) was laid out in 1858 by the founder of the Baden-Baden casino.

Nackenheim (pop. 3500), an old wine village, birthplace of the dramatist and poet Carl Zuckmayer (1896–1977), who made this the setting of his comedy "Der fröhliche Weinberg" ("The Merry Vineyard"). There is a handsome Town Hall (1751).

km 486,5

Nierstein
→Towns and Places of Interest from A to Z

km 481,8

Near the bank of the river is the site of Roman **Sirona** (named after a Celtic/Roman goddess), discovered in the 19th c., with sulphur springs already in use in the 1st–3rd c. A.D.

km 480,6

Oppenheim
→Towns and Places of Interest from A to Z

km 480,4

Liebfrauenkirche, near Worms

Nibelungenbrücke, the first prestressed concrete bridge, cantilevered outwards, to be built over the Rhine. Of the previous bridge only the 48 m high tower is left.

km 443,3

Worms
→Towns and Places of Interest from A to Z

km 443,2

Frankenthal (Pfalz)
→Towns and Places of Interest from A to Z

km 432,6

Ludwigshafen am Rhein
→Towns and Places of Interest from A to Z

km 424,7

km 496,6

km 494,0

km 488,0

km 472,5

km 463,0

km 462,0

km 459,9

km 443,3

km 437,0

km 428,2

km 424,7

Mouth of the river Main

Ginsheim-Gustavsburg, a double town situated in the angle between the Main and the Rhine at their confluence. Gustavsburg was originally a Swedish fortress founded in 1632.

Trebur (pop. 11,000), first recorded in 829 as a royal stronghold of the Carolingians, and during the medieval period the meeting-place of many Imperial Diets. The Emperor Charles the Fat abdicated here in 887, and here in 1076 was held the Imperial Diet called to settle the investiture conflict (the dispute between the Emperor and the Pope over the right to invest bishops). The Protestant church of St Lawrence is thought to stand on the site of the old Carolingian stronghold.
It is believed that within historical times the Neckar and the Main flowed into the Rhine together here.

* **Kühkopf,** a nature reserve lying within a 16 km long arm of the Old Rhine, which until the river broke through into its present course in the 19th c. was an island lying off the left bank. This watery area, covered with a dense growth of oaks and elms, provides ideal conditions for many rare species of waterfowl. Immediately N, also on the right bank of the river, is the **Knoblochsaue** nature reserve. In this area, close to the river at the northern end of the break-through channel, is the Schwedensäule (Swedes' Column), an obelisk topped by a marble lion, erected by the Swedish military engineer Matthäus Stand to commemorate Gustavus Adolphus's crossing of the Rhine on 7 December 1631. Legend has it that the Swedish king made the crossing not in a boat but on a barn-door. This is the area in which, according to the "Nibelungenlied", the treasure of the Nibelungs was buried under the waters of the Rhine.

On the river bank are remains of a Roman quay.

Gernsheim
(KD cruise ships call here)
→Towns and Places of Interest from A to Z

Biblis (pop. 8000), once a country village (fruit and vegetable growing), now an industrial town, with one of the largest atomic power stations in the world (Unit A, 1145 MW; Unit B, 1240 MW; Unit C, 1228 MW, under construction).

Nibelungenbrücke: see opposite page

Lampertheim
→Towns and Places of Interest from A to Z

Mouth of the river Neckar

Mannheim
(KD cruise ships call here)
→Towns and Places of Interest from A to Z

Heidenfahrt, from which in Roman times there was a ferry to
Erbach on the right bank of the Rhine.

Mainz Cathedral (east side)

Mainz
(KD excursion ships call here)
→Towns and Places of Interest from A to Z

km 513,0

km 511,0

km 508,1

km 505,5

km 503,0

km 502,5

km 498,5

km 497,5

Erbach, now part of Eltville, is first recorded in 980. Features of interest are the parish church of St Mark (R. C.; 15th–16th c.), the Late Gothic Town Hall and the half-timbered houses (with the façades now mostly plastered over) of the 16th–18th century. At the W end of the village is Schloss **Reinhartshausen** (now a hotel), which still belongs to the house of Hohenzollern. Between Erbach and Hattenheim, close to the road, is the Marko-Brunnen (Marko Fountain). The well-known Markobrunner wine produced in this area is mentioned in the records as early as 1104.

Eltville am Rhein
(KD excursion ships call here)
→Towns and Places of Interest from A to Z

Niederwalluf, a village first recorded in 770 which is now incorporated in the town of Walluf (pop. 5000), situated at the entrance to the Rheingau. The little Gothic parish church of St John the Baptist (R. C.) was remodelled in the 18th century. Some 4 km NW is the village of **Rauenthal,** which is noted for its wine. – 6 km up the valley of the Wallufbach, in a beautiful setting, is the little spa of **Schlangenbad.** The name ('Schlange' = 'snake') comes from the harmless Aesculapian snakes which are occasionally found here.

Schierstein, an old wine village surrounded by vineyards and orchards which was incorporated in Wiesbaden in 1926, with a river harbour and Sekt-making establishments. In the Rhine is the island of Rettbergsaue, with recreation facilities.

Wiesbaden
→Towns and Places of Interest from A to Z

Biebrich, a suburb of Wiesbaden since 1926, is first recorded in 874 as the Imperial stronghold of Biburk, situated at a ferry over the Rhine. At the beginning of the 18th c., when the Counts of Nassau made Biebrich their principal residence and the Rhine harbour was constructed, the place enjoyed a rapid development. It is now a considerable industrial town (plastics, chemicals, cement and building materials; Sekt-making establishments).
Near the bank of the Rhine is the **Palace* with its long Baroque façade (1699–1745), which now houses leading companies and institutions of the German film industry, including its voluntary control board. In the upper part of the large park is the Moosburg, a mock castle erected in 1806 which is said to occupy the site of the original medieval castle. – Downstream is a villa on the Rhine in which Richard Wagner composed part of his opera "The Mastersingers of Nuremberg".
KD excursion ships call here.

Kastel, once the Roman bridgehead fort of 'Castellum Mattiacorum'. Formerly a suburb of Mainz, it is now incorporated in Wiesbaden. It has a considerable amount of industry.

Maaraue, an island at the mouth of the Main on which the Emperor Frederick Barbarossa held a brilliant Imperial festival in 1184. It is now a recreation area.

Mouth of the river Nahe

Bingen am Rhein
(KD excursion ships call here)
→Towns and Places of Interest from A to Z

Fulderaue, an island in the Rhine, with a wind wheel.

Ingelheim am Rhein
→Towns and Places of Interest from A to Z

Ober-Ingelheim: part of the old fortifications

km 525,5

Rüdesheim am Rhein
(KD cruise ships and excursion ships call here)
→Towns and Places of Interest from A to Z

km 523,3

Geisenheim
→Towns and Places of Interest from A to Z

km 521,5

Fulderaue: see opposite page

km 520,0

Winkel, an old wine village which has preserved its characteristic *aspect, now part of Oestrich-Winkel. It has many half-timbered houses of the 16th–18th c. (the façades now often plastered over). At the W end of the village is the Brentanohaus (1751), with mementoes of Goethe and other writers of the Romantic period. Near the banks of the Rhine is the Graues Haus (Grey House), said to be the oldest stone-built dwelling-house in Germany (re-using elements of 9th c. masonry); rebuilt in 1964 after a fire, it is now a restaurant.

km 519,0

Mittelheim, another old wine village which is now incorporated in the town of Oestrich-Winkel. Features of interest are the Romanesque church of St Giles (St. Ägidienkirche, 1138; R. C.) and the picturesque houses of the 16th–18th c. There is a ferry from Mittelheim to Ingelheim-Nord (Frei-Weinheim).

km 518,0

Oestrich, a little town situated in the heart of the Rheingau and formerly its economic centre, now part of the joint town of Oestrich-Winkel (pop. 11,000). The Roman Catholic parish church of St Martin (originally 12th c., rebuilt in 1508) is the oldest church in the Rheingau; in the churchyard is a Crucifixion group of the 16th–17th century. The town has many half-timbered houses of the 16th–18th c. (façades now mostly plastered over); particularly picturesque is the *riverside front of the town. Here too is the old wooden *crane (16th c., altered in 17th c.) which is Oestrich's distinctive landmark.
4 km N is the old wine village of **Hallgarten**, now also incorporated in Oestrich-Winkel.

km 516,5

Reichardshausen, an estate surrounded by vineyards on which Eberbach Abbey had wine storage cellars from the 12th century. The present buildings date from 1742.

km 515,8

Hattenheim, an old wine village which is now incorporated in Eltville. Features of interest are the Roman Catholic parish church of St Vincent, built over a Carolingian chapel (much altered, particularly in the 18th c.); the castle of the Barons Langwerth von Simmern (beginning of 12th c.), of which a tower containing living quarters survives; and handsome aristocratic mansions of the 15th–18th centuries.
Some 4 km N is the former Cistercian abbey of *Eberbach (now a State-owned wine-growing estate), with a church of 1186 and well preserved conventual buildings of the 12th–14th century.
A hill on the estate, the **Steinberg**, produces one of the most celebrated wines of the Rheingau.

111

Trechtingshausen (pop. 1000), an old wine village, from which the castles of Reichenstein and Rheinstein can be visited.

km 535,4

*Reichenstein** (in the 19th c. also known as the Falkenburg; now a hotel), a castle built in the 11th c. to protect the properties of Cornelimünster Abbey near Aachen, destroyed by Rudolf of Habsburg in 1282 because of its depredations on travellers, later refortified, again destroyed in 1688 by the French and rebuilt from 1899 onwards. It has a museum (arms and armour, hunting trophies, minerals, etc.).

km 534,5

St Clement's Chapel (Clemenskapelle, 13th c.), on the site of the old village of Trechtingshausen.

km 534,1

*Rheinstein,** a castle perched 80 m above the Rhine, formerly a toll station belonging to the Archbishops of Mainz, when it was known as the Voigtsburg or Vautsberg. It is first recorded in 1279. In 1825–1829 it was rebuilt by Prince Friedrich of Prussia, a cousin of the Emperor Wilhelm I, and it is still owned by a branch of the house of Prussia. It contains a large collection of arms and armour and antiquities.

km 533,0

Monument (1832) commemorating the first widening of the Binger Loch (see opposite page).

km 530,7

Mäuseturm (left) and the ruined castle of Ehrenfels (right)

*Mäuseturm** ('Mouse Tower'), an old watch-tower (13th–14th c.) on a rocky islet in the Rhine, an outpost of Burg Ehrenfels. The legend has it that Archbishop Hatto of Mainz was eaten by mice in the tower as a punishment for causing a number of hungry people to be burned to death. In fact the name comes from the word 'Maut' ('toll'), the tower having served as a toll-collecting post.

km 530,2

Bingerbrück, a suburb of Bingen on the left bank of the Nahe at its junction with the Rhine, owes its origin to the construction of the Rhine and Nahe railway lines.

km 529,4

View of Assmannshausen

km 532,3

Assmannshausen, a much frequented *wine village at the foot of the Niederwald hills, noted for its red wine; it is now incorporated in the town of Rüdesheim. The Roman Catholic parish church (dedicated to the Elevation of the Cross – Kreuzerhöhung) dates from the 14th century. The village has numbers of attractive half-timbered houses. There are hot springs (32.5 °C) which were already in use in Roman times. From Assmannshausen Schloss Niederwald, an old hunting lodge, can be reached either by chair-lift or on foot.
KD excursion ships call here.

km 530,7

***Binger Loch** ('Bingen Hole'), a narrow stretch of the Rhine (only 250 m wide), with numerous rocks and shallows, at the point where the river breaks through the quartzite barrier of the Taunus and Hunsrück hills. Until the late medieval period it was impassable by shipping, and between Geisenheim or Rüdesheim and Lorch all goods had to be transported by land on the old 'Merchants' Road'. At the end of the Middle Ages an artificial channel was cut; in the early 19th c. this was enlarged; and in 1974 it was further widened and deepened, and now, with a width of 120 m, allows unrestricted passage.

km 530,4

Ehrenfels, a ruined castle situated half way up the hillside, surrounded by vineyards. The castle was built about 1211 by the Archbishop of Mainz, no doubt to control the narrow stretch of the valley at Bingen. Later it was granted the right to collect tolls from traffic on the river. It was destroyed in 1689.

Mäuseturm: see opposite page

km 530,2

Schloss Biebrich (Wiesbaden)

Ruins of Burg Nollig

Pfalzgrafenstein

Loreley

Burg Katz

Schloss Arenfels

Marksburg

Remagen Bridge

Ehrenbreitstein Fortress (Koblenz)

Rhine front, Oberwesel

Oberwesel
(KD excursion ships call here)
→Towns and Places of Interest from A to Z

km 550,0

***Schönburg,** a ruined castle perched on a steep-sided crag,
probably begun in the 10th c., with huge towers and a massive
curtain wall which is still completely preserved. The castle was
destroyed by the French in 1689. It has now been restored as a
hotel and a 'Kolpinghaus' (communication centre); by the side
of the castle is a youth hostel.

km 549,1

***Stahleck,** a castle perched on a spur of rock which first ap-
pears in the records in 1135. It was held at one time by Konrad
von Hohenstaufen, and was destroyed by the French in 1689. A
youth hostel is now installed in the ruins (magnificent view).

km 543,1

Bacharach
(KD excursion ships call here)
→Towns and Places of Interest from A to Z

km 543,0

Rheindiebach, a village formerly surrounded by walls, with
Burg **Fürstenberg** – a castle built in 1219 to protect the possessions of the Archbishop of Cologne and as a toll-collection
post, destroyed in 1689 by the French – looming over it; the ruin
is now private property.

km 541,0

Niederheimbach, a long straggling village over which looms
the massive tower of the Heimburg, built in 1305, destroyed in
1689 and restored at the end of the 19th c. by the industrialist
Hugo Stinnes.
KD excursion ships call here.

km 539,4

***Sooneck,** a castle situated on the precipitous slopes of the
Soonwald, probably built in the 11th c. to protect the possessions of Cornelimünster Abbey. Like Reichenstein, it was destroyed in the 12th c. by Rudolf of Habsburg; then in 1344 it
passed into the hands of the Archbishop of Mainz and soon
afterwards was rebuilt. In 1689 it was blown up by the French. It
was restored by Friedrich Wilhelm IV of Prussia in the 1840s
and now belongs to the State (open to the public).

km 537,4

km 554,2

** **Loreley** (Lorelei, Lurlei; from Middle High German 'lure' = 'treacherous', and 'lei' = 'rock'), a massive slate crag rising to a height of 132 m above the Rhine, here narrowed to only 113 m (tunnel through the rock). During the Bronze Age there was a fortified settlement on the summit. The Loreley became world-famed as a result of the legend which achieved wide popularity in the early 19th century – the story of the nymph who dwelt on the rock and lured boatmen and fishermen to their destruction with her singing, until she herself was overcome by love and plunged to her death in the river. Bronze statue of the nymph →Sankt Goarshausen.

km 551,0

Die Sieben Jungfrauen (The Seven Maidens), a line of rocks in the river which according to the legend represent seven maidens who were turned into stone by the river god because they resisted his advances.

km 546,5

* **Gutenfels** (alt. 169 m), an imposing castle, probably begun in the 13th c., which withstood a siege by Landgrave Wilhelm of Hesse in 1504: hence its name of Gutenfels ('good rock'). After the Thirty Years War it fell into decay. Since 1976 it has been restored and developed, and is now a castle-hotel.

km 546,3

Kaub
(KD excursion ships call here)
→Towns and Places of Interest from A to Z

km 545,0

** **Pfalzgrafenstein** (open to visitors), popularly known merely as the 'Pfalz bei Kaub', is a small fortress in the middle of the Rhine just off the village of Kaub, built by King Ludwig the Bavarian in 1326 to enforce the collection of tolls from river traffic and enlarged in the 17th century. It is the only existing structure of its type, and with its elongated hexagonal plan, looking like an sturdy little warship, is of highly picturesque effect.

km 542,0

Lorchhausen, an old village at the beginning of the Rheingau, now part of the town of Lorch. Above the neo-Gothic Roman Catholic parish church are remains of the old fortifications.

km 539,8

Lorch
(KD excursion ships call here)
→Towns and Places of Interest from A to Z

Lorch, at the mouth of the Wisper valley

117

Spay (pop. 2000), a little town formed out of the old fishing villages of Oberspay and Niederspay, lying amid fruit plantations in a wide loop in the Rhine, with fine old half-timbered houses. From the end of the town there is a view (to right) of the Marksburg.

km 578,5

Boppard
(KD cruise ships and excursion ships call here)
→Towns and Places of Interest from A to Z

km 570,5

Bad Salzig, an old village surrounded by fruit orchards (particularly cherries) which is now part of the town of Boppard.
To the W is a spa establishment (radioactive weakly saline water) which attracts patients suffering from gout, rheumatism and disorders of the stomach and intestines.
KD excursion ships call here.

km 566,0

Hirzenach, a long straggling old village which is now incorporated in the town of Boppard. It has a simple Romanesque church with an Early Gothic choir (c. 1250).

km 562,5

*Rheinfels, a ruin perched 115 m above the Rhine, was once the mightiest stronghold on the Middle Rhine and one of the strongest castles in the whole length of the Rhine. It was built by Count Diether III von Katzenelnbogen in 1242 and magnificently rebuilt by Landgrave Philipp II of Hesse-Rheinfels in 1568–69; then in 1797 it was blown up by the French, and from 1818 onwards the remains were used in the construction of the citadel of Ehrenbreitstein. The ruins are now looked after by the Hanseatic Order, an old-established association of merchants. Local museum; magnificent views; castle-hotel.

km 556,9

Sankt Goar
(KD excursion ships call here)
→Towns and Places of Interest from A to Z

km 556,1

km 575,2

Osterspai (pop. 1500), with the Roman Catholic parish church of St Martin (originally 12th c.) and a 13th c. moated castle. Above the village is Schloss Liebeneck.

km 571,3

Filsen, a village in the 'Bopparder Hamm', a great loop in the Rhine under the Filsener Ley (229 m; views).

km 567,0

Kamp-Bornhofen (pop. 2000), a double town lying under the 'Enemy Brothers' (Burg Liebenstein and Burg Sterrenberg), surrounded by fruit-orchards.
Bornhofen has a handsome Gothic pilgrimage church (1435) and a Franciscan friary of 1680–84. Kamp has picturesque old half-timbered houses and a Late Gothic church which belonged to a convent of Franciscan nuns.
KD excursion ships call here.

km 566,5

***Liebenstein** and ***Sterrenberg**, twin castles perched on a high rocky ridge, separated from one another only by a wall and a moat. Legend has it that the castles belonged to two brothers who quarrelled with one another, and they are therefore popularly known as the 'Enemy Brothers' ('Feindliche Brüder'). Sterrenberg (State-owned) may have been in existence before 1100 as an Imperial stronghold; in the mid 16th c. it was abandoned and thereafter fell into ruin. Liebenstein (private property) is younger than Sterrenberg.

km 563,3

Kestert, a long straggling village in the middle of fruit plantations.

km 560,0

Ehrental, formerly a priory dependent on Prüm Abbey. Lead used to be mined in the area.

km 558,9

Wellmich, a little medieval town under Burg Maus which is now part of St. Goarshausen. The Roman Catholic parish church of St Martin (14th c.) contains the fine Early Renaissance tombstone (1545) of Coryn von Nassau (d. 1538).

km 558,7

Maus (properly Burg Thurnberg or Deurenburg), built about 1355, under the name of Burg Peterseck, to protect the possessions of the Archbishop of Trier. After falling into a state of dilapidation in the 19th c. it was restored in 1900–06 on the basis of old documents. It is now privately owned, but visitors are admitted.

km 556,1

Sankt Goarshausen
(KD excursion ships call here)
→Towns and Places of Interest from A to Z

km 555,9

Katz (properly Neu-Katzenelnbogen), a castle built by Count Johann III von Katzenelnbogen about 1370 which fell into ruin in the 18th c., was completely destroyed by the French in 1806 and was restored between 1896 and 1898. It is now a holiday home for the staff of the Federal Ministry of Finance.

Stolzenfels (see p. 122)

Rhenser Mineralbrunnen (Rhens Mineral Spring), which has been used to supply table water since 1680.

Rhens
(KD excursion ships call here)
→Towns and Places of Interest from A to Z

Brey, a village with half-timbered houses and a 14th c. Roman Catholic chapel (altered in 1954).

Königsstuhl, above Rhens

km 586,0

km 585,1

km 580,2

km 580,0

km 575,4

Lahnstein (see p. 123)

*Lahneck (164 m), a castle belonging to the Archbishops of Mainz perched on a precipitous crag. It first appears in the records in 1226, and was probably built to protect the nearby silver-mines; it was enlarged in the 15th c. During the Thirty Years War it was occupied by the Swedes, and after their expulsion fell into a state of dilapidation. In 1688 it was completely destroyed by the French. In the 1850s it was restored in English neo-Gothic style. From the castle there are charming views of the confluence of the Lahn with the Rhine, the Allerheiligenberg and Schloss Stolzenfels, on the other bank of the Rhine.

Braubach
(KD cruise ships and excursion ships call here)
→Towns and Places of Interest from A to Z

Marksburg, the only hilltop fortress on the Rhine which has escaped destruction, commandingly situated on a steep conical crag (castle-museum). It is believed to have been built by Eberhard II von Eppstein in the 13th c. on the site of an earlier castle, and was later enlarged. After many vicissitudes the castle has belonged since 1899 to the Deutsche Burgenvereinigung (German Castles Association). The name Marksburg comes from the castle chapel, which was dedicated to St Mark. The castle contains an interesting collection of arms and armour.

Marksburg

1 Drawbridge Gate	5 North Tower	9 Chapel Tower
2 Forecourt	6 Rhine Tract	10 Sharp Corner
3 Big Battery	7 Keep	11 Powder Corner
4 Little Battery	8 Residential Tract	12 Restaurant

Liebeneck, commandingly situated, was formerly the hunting lodge and summer residence of the Liebenstein family. The Baroque castle, originally built about 1700, with a round tower, was altered in the 19th century.

121

Stolzenfels ⇄ Namedy

Left bank
of the Rhine

Namedy, now part of Andernach, with a church of the 13th and 16th c. and a Schloss of the 16th and 18th c., altered in 1896.

km 616,1

Namedyer Werth, a former island in the Rhine, in the past notable for the Namedyer Sprudel, a geyser-like mineral spring (18 °C) which at intervals of 6 to 7½ hours shot up a 60 m high column of water coming from a depth of 343 m. The nearby plant produces carbonic acid.

km 615,0

Andernach
(KD excursion ships call here)
→Towns and Places of Interest from A to Z

km 613,2

Weissenthurm, with the 'white tower' from which it takes its name, a toll-collecting post of about 1350, and breweries.

km 607,0

Kärlich nuclear power station (under construction), with a hydraulic reactor.

km 605,0

Niederwerth: see opposite page

km 595,0

Mouth of the river Mosel (Moselle)

km 592,3

Koblenz
(KD cruise ships and excursion ships call here)
→Towns and Places of Interest from A to Z

km 591,5

Kapellen-Stolzenfels, an old village which was fortified in the 13th c. when the castle of Stolzenfels was built. Along with the castle it is now part of the town of Koblenz.
In the Roman Catholic parish church of St Menas (14th c., rebuilt in 19th c.) is a figure of St Sebastian which is attributed to the school of Tilman Riemenschneider.

km 585,5

*Stolzenfels,** a neo-Gothic castle built for King Friedrich Wilhelm IV of Prussia in 1836–42 by Karl Friedrich Schinkel and other architects. It occupies the site of a 13th c. castle ot the Archbishops of Trier which was built opposite to the mouth of the Lahn and destroyed by the French in 1689, and incorporates some remains of the earlier structure, in particular the old keep (conducted tours daily).

km 585,2

km 615,0

km 614,5

km 606,0

km 600,9

km 599,0

km 595,5

km 595,0

km 592,3

km 586,0

Namedyer Werth: see opposite page

Leutesdorf (pop. 2000), a charming old wine town, with hand-some ancient mansions, half-timbered houses (16th–17th c.) and remains of 16th c. town walls. The Baroque parish church of St Lawrence (R.C.) has a massive Romanesque tower of about 1200 and a Gothic baptismal chapel and contains 13th c. wall paintings.
The 17th c. pilgrimage church of the Holy Cross (Heiligkreuz) has beautiful Baroque altars.

Neuwied
(KD excursion ships call here)
→Towns and Places of Interest from A to Z

Engers, a little town which is now part of Neuwied. There was a settlement here in Roman times. It has a handsome 18th c. palace of the Electors of Trier, now occupied by the 'Heinrichs-haus' orthopaedic clinic. Near this is the mansion of the von Spee family (1770).

Bendorf (pop. 16,000), an industrial town whose boundaries extend over a considerable area. In **Sayn** (2 km E) are the ruins of the Stammburg and Schloss Sayn, residence of the Princes of Sayn-Wittgenstein, situated on the Schlossberg, together with a former Premonstratensian abbey founded in 1202.

Vallendar
→Towns and Places of Interest from A to Z

Niederwerth, an island in the Rhine, with the village of Nieder-werth, which goes back to Merovingian times. St George's Church (15th c.; R. C.) has wall paintings.

***Ehrenbreitstein** (alt. 118 m; chair-lift), a formidable fortress built in 1816–32 on the site of an earlier stronghold of the Elec-tors of Trier. It now houses the Provincial Museum, with the State Collection of Monuments of Technology, as well as the Museum of the Rhine and a youth hostel. From the terraces there are fine views of Koblenz, the Rhine, the mouth of the Moselle at the 'Deutsches Eck', and the Vordereifel hills.

Lahnstein
(KD excursion ships call at Niederlahnstein and Oberlahnstein)
→Towns and Places of Interest from A to Z

Brohl-Lützing ⇄ Haus Ernich

Haus Ernich, the residence of the French ambassador.

Apollinariskirche (St Apollinaris's Church), a four-towered neo-Gothic church built in 1839–43 by Ernst Friedrich Zwirner, architect of Cologne Cathedral, on the site of a much older pilgrimage chapel. The interior has frescoes by the 'Nazarenes'. In the crypt is preserved the head of St Apollinaris of Ravenna, a disciple of the Apostle Peter.

Remagen
(KD excursion ships call here)
→Towns and Places of Interest from A to Z

****Remagen Bridge** (Ludendorff Bridge), built by General Ludendorff in 1916–1918 at a strategically important crossing of the Rhine. After an unsuccessful attempt by the Germans to blow up the bridge US American forces crossed it on 7 March 1945 and established their first bridgehead on the right bank of the Rhine under the Erpeler Ley, thus opening up the road into northern Germany. On 17 March 1945 the bridge unexpectedly collapsed. The towers at either end have been preserved as a memorial; the one on the left bank contains a Peace Museum.

Bad Kripp, a spa situated at the mouth of the Ahr, now part of the town of Remagen. The water of the Marie-Luisen-Quelle (alkaline, saline, ferruginous, containing carbonates) is used in both bathing and drinking cures.

Sinzig (pop. 14,000), an ancient town situated at a little distance from the Rhine in the fertile plain known as the "Golden Mile", above the junction of the river Ahr with the Rhine. Sinzig was probably the Roman 'Sentiacum', and thereafter it was the site of a Frankish and later an Imperial stronghold. It still has remains of its medieval town walls. It has a mineral spring (containing carbonates) which is used in bathing and drinking cures. – On a low hill is the Late Romanesque parish church of St Peter (13th c.). The Schloss (built in 1854–1858 on the foundations of a 14th c. moated castle) contains a local museum.

Bad Breisig
(KD excursion ships call here)
→Towns and Places of Interest from A to Z

Rheineck (alt. 181 m), built in 1832 on the site of an earlier castle; the 20 m high square tower on the S side, the Wartturm, is a remnant of the old castle of the Counts Palatine which was destroyed by the French in 1689.

Brohl-Lützing (pop. 2500), at the mouth of the narrow Brohl valley, with large trass and tuff quarries which were already being worked in Roman times.
Some 4 km up the Brohl valley is the little spa of **Bad Tönisstein,** with mineral springs (containing sodium and lithium; used in the treatment of rheumatism and disorders of the bladder and kidneys) which were also known to the Romans.

Hammersteiner Werth: see opposite page

Bridges and ferries
crossing the Rhine

km 635,5

km 633,5

km 633,0

km 632,8

km 629,7

km 628,2

km 623,7

km 621,9

km 620,2

km 617,0

Erpel (pop. 2000), an old wine town at the foot of the Erpeler Ley, a basalt cliff 191 m high (wide views). The town has attractive half-timbered houses (17th–18th c.), a handsome Town Hall of 1780, the Romanesque parish church of St Severinus (13th c.; enlarged 1751) and remains of 15th c. town walls.

Remagen Bridge: see opposite page

Linzhausen, part of the town of Linz. Above the village, at **Ockenfels**, is a ruined 14th c. castle, the Burg zur Leyen.

Linz am Rhein
(KD excursion ships call here)
→Towns and Places of Interest from A to Z

Leubsdorf, village with the Saalburg, an old fortified house with four towers, and a neo-Gothic church.

Bad Hönningen
(KD excursion ships call here)
→Towns and Places of Interest from A to Z

Rheinbrohl (pop. 4000), a little wine town with half-timbered houses, situated at the point where the Roman LIMES, a defensive line constructed in the 1st c. A. D., reached the Rhine. Some 2 km N is **Arienheller**, with the bottling plant of the Arienheller mineral spring (the 'Dreikönigsquelle', Three Kings' Spring), the water of which comes from a depth of 390 m.

Hammerstein, consisting of Oberhammerstein and Niederhammerstein. In Oberhammerstein are the Romanesque parish church of St George (c. 1200; R. C.) and the 16th c. Burgmannshof. On a greywacke crag above the town are the ruins of Burg Hammerstein (alt. 196 m), in which the Emperor Henry IV took refuge from his son Henry V in 1105.

Hammersteiner Werth, an island (recreation facilities).

km 633,4

km 632,8

km 630,7

km 629,9

km 627,7

km 623,9

km 621,5

km 618,0

km 617,0

125

Oberwinter ⇄ Bad Godesberg

**Left bank
of the Rhine**

Bridges and ferries
crossing the Rhine

km 647,6

Bad Godesberg
(KD excursion
ships call here)
→Towns and Places of Interest from A to Z

Godesburg, above Bonn – Bad Godesberg

Nonnenwerth, an island in the Rhine with a convent of Franciscan nuns (St. Mariä; girls' school), founded in 1122 as a house of Benedictine nuns. Franz Liszt lived on Nonnenwerth in 1840–41.

km 642,0

Rolandswerth, a long straggling village below the Rolandsbogen which is now an outlying district of Remagen. Above Rolandswerth to the W is a nature reserve centred on the treeless volcanic hill of Rodderberg (195 m), an explosion crater which came into being in glacial times, now filled with loess.

km 641,8

Grafenwerth: see opposite page

km 641,0

Rolandseck, finely situated, with a *view of the Siebengebirge, is another outlying district of Remagen, with handsome villas. High above the town (105 m above the Rhine) is the ivy-clad ruin of *Rolandsbogen (Roland's Arch), the last relic of Burg Rulcheseck, a castle built in 1099 and destroyed in 1633, from which there is a magnificent view of the Siebengebirge (especially fine in the evening). The legend that Charlemagne's paladin Roland died here heartbroken after his beloved Hildegunde retired to Nonnenwerth convent is of recent origin.

km 640,0

Oberwinter, a long straggling village which is now incorporated in the town of Remagen, with fine half-timbered houses (16th–18th c.). In the Unkelbach valley is a wayside shrine of 1409.

km 638,5

km 647,6

km 645,3

km 643,7

km 643,0

km 642,0

km 641,3

km 641,0

km 638,6

km 636,6

Niederdollendorf, part of Königswinter, is the starting point for a visit to the Cistercian abbey church of Heisterbach, of which there survives only a picturesque relic, the end of the choir (Early Gothic, 13th c.).

Königswinter
(KD cruise ships and excursion ships call here)
→Towns and Places of Interest from A to Z

Drachenfels
→Towns and Places of Interest from A to Z, Königswinter

*Siebengebirge, a range of hills at the north-western end of the Westerwald which extends along the right bank of the Rhine a short distance upstream from Bonn, with a length of some 7 km and a breadth of 4 km, offering one of the finest stretches of scenery in the whole length of the Rhine (Siebengebirge Nature Park). The salient hills, which come into prominence as one approaches Bonn, are the Drachenfels (ruined castle, 12th c.), Wolkenburg (no remains of the old castle), Lohrberg, Grosser Ölberg (the highest peak, 460 m), Nonnenstromberg, Petersberg (pilgrimage chapel of 12th c., rebuilt in 18th c.; hotel, see under Königswinter) and Löwenburg (remains of walls and keep of castle).

Rhöndorf, district of Bad Honnef at the foot of the Drachenfels, with half-timbered houses round the Marienkapelle (Chapel of Our Lady, 1714) and the 'Haus im Turm' ('House in the Tower', 13th c.). Rhöndorf was the residence of Konrad Adenauer (1876–1967), first Chancellor of the Federal Republic of Germany. There is an Adenauer Memorial in his house.

Nonnenwerth: see opposite page

Bad Honnef
(KD excursion ships call here)
→Towns and Places of Interest from A to Z

Grafenwerth, an island in the Rhine with an open-air swimming pool fed by a mineral spring (temperature 19 °C). From here there are charming views of Rolandseck and the Rolandsbogen.

Rheinbreitbach (pop. 4000), a little town surrounded by fruit plantations and vineyards, with attractive half-timbered houses. In the late medieval Obere Burg ('higher castle') lived and worked the writer Rudolf Herzog (1869–1943). On the Rheinbreitenbacher Hof is a tablet commemorating the Grimm Brothers, who stayed here for some time.

Unkel
(KD excursion ships call here)
→Towns and Places of Interest from A to Z

Neuss
→Towns and Places of Interest from A to Z

km 740,3

*Zons,** a little town which was formerly held by the Elector of
Cologne, on the site of the Roman 'Sontium', now incorporated
in Dormagen. It has the best preserved circuit of medieval walls
in the Rhineland, constructed by Archbishop Friedrich von
Saarwerden between 1373 and 1400, with numerous watch-
towers set at regular intervals. At the SW corner is the Mühlen-
turm (Mill Tower), which was converted into a windmill in the
15th c., at the NE corner the Zollturm (Toll Tower), with the
Rhine Gate. The Judenturm (Jews' Tower, 14th c.), with its Baroque helm roof, belongs to the archiepiscopal residence,
Schloss Friedestrom, the only other considerable parts of
which are the S gate and a gate tower in the courtyard.
From the nearby Rheindamm there is a view of the river.

km 717,5

Dormagen (pop. 56,000), the Roman 'Durnomagus', now an
industrial town, with Bayer's synthetic fibres plant and other
industries.

km 711,5

Rheinkassel, a suburb of Cologne, with the Roman Catholic
parish church of St Amandus (10th–13th c.).

km 703,4

Ford car plant.

km 698,0

Trading and industrial port of **Köln-Niehl I,** where the ships of
the KD lie at anchor during the winter.

km 695,8

Riehl, a northern suburb of Cologne, with the Zoo and the
Botanic Garden.

km 690,3

Cologne (Köln)
(KD cruise ships and excursion ships call here)
→Towns and Places of Interest from A to Z

km 688,0

Wesseling (pop. 29,000), an industrial town (petrochemicals)
and port (mainly handling lignite and oil), on the site of a Roman fort.
KD excursion ships call here.

km 670,0

Bonn
(KD excursion ships call here)
→Towns and Places of Interest from A to Z

km 654,9

km 744,2

Düsseldorf
(KD cruise ships and excursion ships call here)
→Towns and Places of Interest from A to Z

km 722,0

Benrath, a town now incorporated in Düsseldorf, with a sumptuous Rococo *palace (by N. de Pigage, 1755–1773) charmingly
situated on an ornamental lake. The large park extends to the
banks of the Rhine.

km 713,5

Monheim (pop. 40,000), an industrial town (oil refinery, metal
processing, pharmaceuticals).

km 700,0

Leverkusen (pop. 162,000), a young industrial town, with the
Bayer works (chemicals and pharmaceuticals).

km 688,0

Cologne (Köln; Köln-Deutz)
→Towns and Places of Interest from A to Z

km 678,4

Porz, an industrial suburb of Cologne (motor vehicles, glass,
electrical equipment, etc.). In the district of Wahn is a Schloss
which first appears in the records in the 14th c.; the present
building, surrounded by a moat, dates from the mid 18th c. In
the district of Zündorf, in the Turmhof, is the 13th c. Zollturm
(toll-collecting post), which houses a local museum.
KD excursion ships call here.

km 656,2

Schwarz-Rheindorf, part of Bonn; the two-storey *church, built
in the 12th c. as a castle chapel, is one of the most unusual
Romanesque buildings in Germany.
In **Vilich,** E of Schwarz-Rheindorf, is St Peter's Church (originally 11th c., but much altered down to the 18th c.), which
belonged to a convent of Benedictine nuns founded in 987.

km 654,9

Beuel, an industrial suburb of Bonn.

km 650,0

Oberkassel, an industrial suburb of Bonn, with Portland cement works.

129

Krefeld ⇄ Rotterdam

Rotterdam
→Towns and Places of Interest from A to Z

−1013,5
km 992,7

Dordrecht
→Towns and Places of Interest from A to Z

km 975,5

Loevestein Castle, at the outflow of the Afgedamte Maas into the Waal. Here the great Dutch jurist Hugo de Groot (Grotius) was imprisoned in 1619 as an Arminian, but escaped in 1621, concealed in a chest of books. Small museum.

km 951,3

Zaltbommel (pop. 9000), a little town on the left bank of the Waal, which is tidal up to this point. The town was already fortified by the 13th century. Features of interest are St Maartenskerk (Gothic, 1304), which has a fine tall tower; the 16th c. Huis van Maarten van Rossum (museum); and the attractive old 16th and 17th c. houses in and around the market square. Pilot project for cable television.

km 933,5

Nijmegen
(KD cruise ships call here)
→Towns and Places of Interest from A to Z

km 884,0

Kleve (Cleves)
→Towns and Places of Interest from A to Z

km 857,0

Xanten
→Towns and Places of Interest from A to Z

km 824,0

Wesel railway bridge: see opposite page

km 815,3

Borth, with a large salt mine.

km 808,0

Homberg, now incorporated in Duisburg, is an industrial town, with the harbour of Rheinpreussen.

km 780,0

Moers (pop. 100,000), centre of the Lower Rhineland coal-mining and salt-working area. Once the chief town of a county, it preserves from that period a 15th c. Schloss which now houses a local museum (Grafschafter Museum).

km 779,0

Rheinhausen, first recorded about the year 800 and now part of Duisburg, is an industrial town (Krupp ironworks).

km 774,5

Krefeld
→Towns and Places of Interest from A to Z

km 764,5

km 999,5

Rotterdam
(Starting and finishing point of the KD Rhine cruises)
→Towns and Places of Interest from A to Z

km 983,8

Kinderdijk, a village on the right bank of the Noord, with 19
*windmills still in working order.

km 954,7

Gorinchem (pop. 29,000), once an important strong point; it
was one of the first places recovered from the Spaniards by the
Watergeuzen (1572). Gorinchem has preserved old town gates
and handsome gabled houses of the 16th and 17th centuries.
The church (14th–16th c.) has a 15th c. tower (St-Jan-Toren). In
the Huis Bethlehem (1566) is a small local museum.

km 914,7

Tiel (pop. 30,000), a market town in the fruit-growing area of
Betuwe. In medieval times this was the island district of 'Batua',
reclaimed for agriculture by the draining of the marshes.

km 913,4

End of the Amsterdam-Rijnkanaal (about 70 km long; via
Utrecht), with the **Prins Bernhardsluis,** the largest inland lock
in Europe (350 m long, 18 m wide).

km 867,5

Pannerdense Kop, a hill crowned by the ruins of a castle. Here
the Rhine divides into the Waal (to left) and the Pannerdens
Kanaal (to right; beyond Arnhem Nederrijn, subsequently Lek).

km 862,3

Lobith-Tolkamer (pop. 2500), Dutch frontier town. Tolkamer
lies directly on the Rhine, Lobith 2 km away from it.

km 851,9

Emmerich
→Towns and Places of Interest from A to Z

km 837,4

Rees (pop. 17,000), charmingly situated on a low hill above the
Rhine. The town preserves remains of its medieval walls, particularly on the river front.

km 815,3

Remains of the Wesel railway bridge, destroyed during the second world war.

km 814,0

Wesel
→Towns and Places of Interest from A to Z

km 792,5

Walsum, part of Duisburg, with shipyards and extensive port
facilities, port of transshipment for the town of Oberhausen.
Since 1983 the Rheinau Walsum has been a nature reserve.

km 778,0

Duisburg
→Towns and Places of Interest from A to Z

km 755,7

Kaiserswerth, founded in the 7th c., now part of Düsseldorf,
with the remains of a stronghold of the Emperor Frederick Barbarossa and the old conventual church of St Suitbertus (13th
c.; shrine of St Suitbertus).

131

Towns and Places of Interest from A to Z

This section of the Guide covers not only all larger places and various features of tourist interest along the Rhine between Basle and Rotterdam but also the main places of interest which can be seen on excursions organised in connection with the KD German Rhine Line cruises.

N.B.

Features of interest on the Rhine's headstreams the Vorder-rhein and Hinterrhein, the Alpine Rhine, Lake Constance and the High Rhine are covered in the section →The Rhine from the Sources to Basle.

The blue bold letter symbols in the headlines of each chapter stand for the following countries: B = Belgium, CH = Switzerland, D = Federal Republic of Germany, F = France, NL = Netherlands.

Alsace

F

State: France
Région: Alsace
Départements: Haut-Rhin (Upper Rhine) and Bas-Rhin (Lower Rhine)
Capital: Strasbourg

Alsace (German Elsass), a historic region in the SW of the Upper Rhine Plain, extends westward from the left bank of the Rhine to the hills of the Vosges, reaching in the N to the Pfälzer Wald and in the S to the Sundgau and the Jura. Sheltered by the hills, it has a mild climate which makes it a region of great fertility. Vines flourish particularly here, giving much of the countryside its characteristic aspect.

General

Like the rest of the Upper Rhine plain, Alsace has been cultivated by man since a very early period. Around 1000 B.C. the Celts established their influence here. Under the Romans the region enjoyed 500 years of peace and tranquil development. The vine was introduced by the Romans about 300 A.D. The name of Alsace appears for the first time in 443, in the form 'Elisaza', meaning "those who live across the river": i.e. the Alemanni, who had pushed forward into this area from Germany. In 496 the Alemanni were subjugated by the Franks, and Alsace remained part of the Frankish kingdom until it fell to pieces after the death of Charlemagne. Under the treaty of Verdun in 843 Alsace was allotted to the central duchy of Lotharingia under Lothair; then in 925 it became part of the duchy of Swabia.

History

The Reformation came to Alsace from 1520 onwards. Soon afterwards the region was harassed by peasant wars; then in 1568 came the Counter-Reformation. After the end of the Thirty Years War the whole territory gradually passed to France, with the exception of Strasbourg, which was annexed by Louis XIV in 1681, and Mulhouse, which remained within the Swiss Confederation until 1798.

◀ *Keizersgracht in Amsterdam*

Alsace, History
(continued)

The French Revolution bound Alsace still more firmly to France, with the establishment of the départements of Haut-Rhin and Bas-Rhin. After the Franco-Prussian War of 1870/71 Alsace was incorporated in Prussia and in the German Empire; but Prussia was unable to win over the hearts and minds of the people, and after the first world war it was returned to France, thereafter remaining French apart from the period of German occupation during the second world war (1940–1944).

Since the last war, with Strasbourg as the headquarters of the Council of Europe and other European institutions, Alsace has taken a central place in the movement towards a united Europe. – French is the official language, but a considerable proportion of the population speak Alsatian German, which is akin to the German spoken in Baden. In 1976 Alsace became the first of France's regions to achieve a degree of cultural autonomy.

*Route du Vin d'Alsace

An ideal way of getting to know Alsace, with its picturesque little villages and towns, is to follow the 'Route du Vin d'Alsace', which pursues an attractive winding route of some 120 km between Thann (to the W of Mulhouse) and Strasbourg, through some 12,000 hectares of vineyards.

Amsterdam   NL

State: Netherlands
Province: Noord-Holland (North Holland)
Altitude: below sea level
Population: 693,000

KD German Rhine Line

KD landing-stage:
Passagiers Terminal, Oostelijke Handelskade

General

Amsterdam, the capital of the Netherlands (but not the seat of government or the residence of the monarch, both of which are in The Hague), lies in the province of North Holland at the junction of the Amstel with the IJ, an arm of the IJsselmeer. Together with ten surrounding communes Amsterdam reaches a total population of over a million, making it the largest conurbation in the most highly populated and industrialised part of the Netherlands, the area known as 'Randstad Holland'.

With both a Municipal University and a Free University (Reformed Church), the Royal Netherlands Academy of Sciences and numerous other research institutions and academies of music, more than forty museums and the world-famous Concertgebouw orchestra, Amsterdam is the country's major cultural centre. It is also a focal point and cornerstone of the Dutch economy, with the second largest port in the Netherlands and the busy commercial activity associated with it; and it lies in the middle of an enormous industrial zone extending between IJmuiden and Hilversum (petrochemicals, chemicals, shipbuilding, steelworks, engineering, aircraft and automobile construction, textiles, brewing, as well as the diamond-cutting industry which came to Amsterdam after the sack of Antwerp in 1576). The houses of the old town, in a fan-shaped layout of concentric rings, are built on piles driven through the layers of mud and peat into the firm sandy bottom, at depths of up to 18 m. In

Royal Palace in the Dam

Patrician houses on the Herengracht

the canals (grachten), which have a depth of about 2 m, more than 2,000 houseboats are moored. Several hundred bridges give the city a friendly and often very picturesque aspect. The oldest part of the town is ringed by successive extensions of the 16th and 17th c., extending as far as the Singelgracht.

Amsterdam was founded about 1270, and gained a link with the sea through the opening up of the Zuiderzee in the course of the 13th c. In 1368 it became a member of the Hanse. Its great days began with the wars of Dutch independence, which brought it freedom in 1570, and by the beginning of the 17th c. it was the leading commercial town in Europe, in which art and learning flourished. – In the 18th c. Amsterdam lost much of its fleet as a result of Holland's participation in the war of American independence; and Napoleon's continental blockade (1806–1813) completely destroyed its commerce. It is due to the construction of the North Sea Canal in 1875, the Merwede Canal in 1892 and the Amsterdam-Rhine Canal in more recent years that it has been able to recover its position and establish itself as the second largest port in the Netherlands.

History

The hub of traffic in the inner city is the square known as the Dam (National Monument, commemorating those who died in the second world war), on the western edge of the oldest part of the town. On the W side of the square is the classical-style Royal Palace (17th c.), built on 13,659 piles, with a 51 m high tower (carillon). The principal features of the interior are the royal apartments (still in use) and the splendid Burgerzaal. – In the NW corner of the square is the Nieuwe Kerk (15th c.; Reformed), in which the accession of a new monarch is pro-

Features of interest

*Royal Palace

Amsterdam

Jacob Catskade
Kattensloot
van Hallstraat
Willemsstraat
Haarlemerstraat
Haven
gebou
Lindengracht
Noorderkerk
Museum of Architecture
Frederik Hendrik-plantsoen
Craftmen's Centre
Nassaukade
Marnixstraat
Westerstraat
Singel
Anjeliersstraat
Egelandtiersstraat
Prinsen-
Keizers-
Heren-
gracht
Hugo de Grootstraat
Frederik
Hendrikstraat
Anne Frank-huis
Westerkerk
Nieuwe Kerk
Be
Damrak
Nieuwend
Raadhuisstraat
Museum of money-boxes
Royal Palace
Dam
Rozengracht
Rozenstraat
Laurierstraat
Clercqstraat
Da Costa
Nassaukade
Marnixstraat
gracht
Voor-
Spuistraat
Kalverstraat
Rokin
Nes
Tow Hall
Histor. Museum
Huis op de drie gracht
Begijn-hof
Phonogr. Museum
N.Z.
Spui
Univ. Libr.
Allard Piersc Museu
Bilderdijkstraat
Kinkerstraat
Lennepstraat
Singel
gracht
Spul
Munt-toren
de
Kostverloren
Oostelijk Marktkanaal
vaart
Bellamyplein
Kinkerstraat
van
Jacob
Constantin
straat
Leidse-
gracht
Leidsestraat
Kerkstraat
Nieuwe Spiegelstraat
Heren-
gracht
Keizers-
gracht
Rembrand
ple
Museu Fodor
gracht
Wilhelmina Gasthuis
Helmers-
Overtoom
straat
Stadsschouw-burg
Leidse-plein
Kerkstraat
Prinsen-
Vizelstraat
Vizelgr.
gracht
Overtoom
Vondel-
Vossiusstraat
Hooftstraat
Cornelisz
Jan Luykenstraat
Rijks-museum
Nieuwe
Looiersstra
Haarlem
Den Haag
park
Huygensstraat
Pieter
Eeghenstraat
Willemsparkweg
Van Gogh Museum
Stedelijk Museum
Museumstraat
Hobbemakade
Stadhouderskade
straat
Bol-
Quellijnstraat
Gerard Dous
van
Concert-gebouw

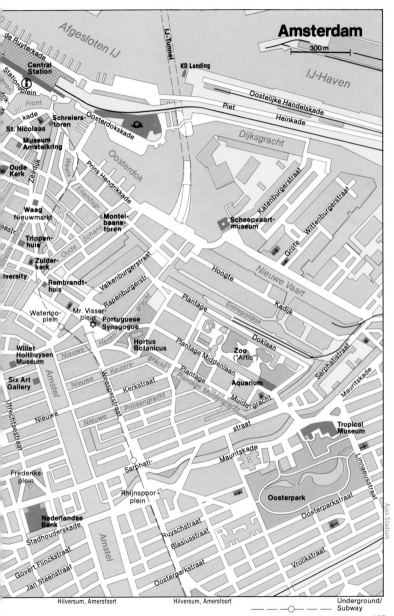

Amsterdam

300 m

Afgesloten IJ

IJ-Tunnel

de Ruyterkade

Central Station

Stationsplein

KD Landing

Oostelijke Handelskade

IJ-Haven

Piet Heinkade

Front

kade

Oosterdokskade

Dijksgracht

Schreiers-toren

St. Nicolaas

Museum Amstelkring

Oude Kerk

Zeedijk

Waals

Prins Hendrikkade

Oosterdok

Katenburgerstraat

Wittenburgerstraat

Eilandsgr.

Scheepvaart-museum

Waag

Nieuwmarkt

Montel-baans-toren

Schans

Oude

Grote

Trippen-huis

Zuider-kerk

Hoogte

Nieuwe Vaart

iversity

Rembrandt-huis

Valkenburgerstr.

Rapenburgerstr.

Plantage

Entrepotdok

Kadijk

Waterloo-plein

Mr. Visser-plein

Portuguese Synagogue

Heren

gracht

Plantage Middenlaan

Doklaan

Sarphatistraat

Willet Holthuysen Museum

Hortus Botanicus

Zoo ("Artis")

Nieuwe

Keizers-

Plantage Muidergracht

Six Art Gallery

Amstel

Nieuwe

Weesperstraat

Kerkstraat

Aquarium

Muidergracht

Mauritskade

Nieuwe

Prinsengracht

straat

Tropical Museum

Utrechtsestraat

Nieuwe

Mauritskade

Linnaeusstraat

Frederiks-plein

Sarphati-

Rhijnspoor-plein

Oosterpark

Oosterparkstraat

Nederlandse Bank

Stadhouderskade

Amstel

Ruyschstraat

Blasiusstraat

Govert Flinckstraat

Jan Steenstraat

Oosterparkstraat

Vrolikstraat

Ajax Stadium

claimed. It contains the tombs of famous naval heroes, including Admiral de Ruyter.

From the Dam a wide street, the Damrak, runs NE to the Central Station, passing on the right the Stock Exchange. On the N side of the station are the landing-stages used by motor launches and ferries. To the W of the station is the 13-storey building housing the harbour offices (restaurant, with fine view). – The harbour was constructed in 1872 at the same time as the North Sea Canal (interesting cruises round the harbour). The entire harbour area was reclaimed from the IJ; the shipping channel was deepened and artificial islands with quays were created. – On the Oosterdok is the Maritime Museum.

From Prins Hendrikkade, near St. Nicolaaskerk, the Zeedijk runs off towards the Nieuwmarkt. This is one of the oldest streets in the city, and one of the most notorious, with a number of overhanging houses. – To the SW, in the picturesque Oudezijde Voorburgwal, is the Amstelkring Museum (religious art). – Farther S is the Oude Kerk (Old Church; 13th c.; Reformed), with a W tower of the 15th–16th c., which has magnificent stained glass of the High Renaissance period (1555).

In the Nieuwmarkt is the St. Anthonieswaag (St Anthony's Weigh-House), built in 1488 as one of the town gates, which now houses the Museum of Jewish History and the Museum of Medical and Pharmaceutical History. To the SW is the Dutch Wine Museum. – To the E of the Nieuwmarkt is another old town gate, the Montelbaanstoren (15th c.). – SW of the Nieuwmarkt is the Town Hall, the old Admiralty House, and to the S of this is the Municipal University (founded in 1632). Diagonally opposite the University is the Driegrachtenhuis (1610). From here the Langebrug leads W to the Rokin, a busy street running from the Dam to the Muntplein; part of the Amstel was filled in to allow it to be built. Parallel to this street on the W is the

narrow Kalverstraat, also running from the Dam to the Muntplein, the city's busiest shopping and commercial street. On its W side is the old Burgerweeshuis (Municipal Orphanage; doorway of 1581), now occupied by the Amsterdam Historical Museum. Close by, to the S, is the Begijnhof (14th–17th c.). – To the S, on the Singel, is the University Library, in which is incorporated the Rosenthal Library (Jewish literature).
In the western part of the inner city are, in Prinsengracht, the Noorderkerk (1622) and, in the Westermarkt, the Westerkerk (1620–31), in which Rembrandt is buried (commemorative stone). At Prinsengracht 263 is the Anne Frank House, in which the Jewish girl whose diary became famous after the second world war lay hidden during the German occupation.

On the S side of the inner city is the Munttoren (Mint Tower, 15th c.), a relic of the town's medieval fortifications. – The Herengracht has preserved the aspect of elegant and fashionable Amsterdam in the 17th and 18th centuries. Near the E end

of this tree-lined canal (Amstel 218) is the Six Picture Gallery, one of the most important private collections in the Netherlands. Farther S, in Keizersgracht, is the Fodor Museum (pictures, mainly of the 19th c.).

The world-famous Rijksmuseum (mainly devoted to the art and culture of the Netherlands) occupies an imposing brick building (1877–85) at Stadhouderskade 42. – SW of the Rijks-museum, at Paulus Potterstraat 7–9, is the Van Gogh Museum, with 200 of his paintings, 500 drawings and 700 letters. In the adjoining building is the Municipal Museum (Dutch and French painting of the 19th and 20th c.). To the S of this museum is the Concertgebouw, home of the famous Concertgebouw Orchestra (founded in 1888). – In the Europaplein is the RAI Congress Centre (area over 45,000 sq.m).

Amsterdam, Features of interest (continued)
*Van Gogh Museum
*Municipal Museum

To the E of the town centre extends the old Jewish quarter, in which the philosopher Spinoza was born in 1632. During the German occupation in the second world war more than 70% of Amsterdam's Jewish inhabitants were deported. At Jodenbree-straat 4 is the Rembrandt House (1606; museum), in which the great painter lived from 1639 to 1658. Nearby, on the N side of the Meijerplein, is the Portuguese Synagogue (1671–75).

*Rembrandt House

To the E of the Jewish quarter, in the Plantage district, are the Botanic Garden and, farther E, the Zoo (aquarium, zoological museum). – To the S, beyond the Singelgracht, is the world-famed Tropical Museum.

*Tropical Museum

A lively diamond trade had already developed in Amsterdam in the 16th c. and quickly expanded. Diamonds discovered in South Africa in 1867 were mostly cut in Amsterdam and the city became the most important diamond centre in the world. The supreme skill of the diamond cutters and polishers of Amsterdam played a decisive role. To an expert, the description 'Amsterdam Cut' is synonymous with perfectly produced work.

Amsterdam – city of the diamonds

The value of a gem diamond depends not only on its cut, but also on its colour, the degree of its purity, as well as the weight of the stone. These four factors determining the value are described after their English initials as the 'four Cs' of a diamond (colour, clarity, cut and carat weight).

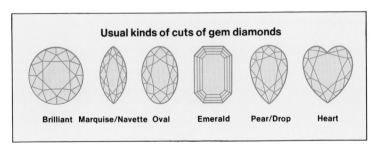

Usual kinds of cuts of gem diamonds

Brilliant Marquise/Navette Oval Emerald Pear/Drop Heart

Andernach   D

State: Federal Republic of Germany
Land: Rheinland-Pfalz (Rhineland-Palatinate)
Altitude: 65 m above sea level
Population: 27,000

KD excursion ships land on the Rhine bank.

KD German Rhine Line

Andernach, General	The old town of Andernach is situated on the edge of the Neuwied basin on the site of the Roman fort of 'Antunnacum'. In the 6th c. it appears in the records as a Frankish royal strong-hold. In later centuries it was a free Imperial city, the possession of which was much disputed.

Features of interest

This old-world little town has preserved its circuit of 14th and 15th c. walls largely intact, with the Koblenz Gate or Burgtor (c. 1450), the Romanesque and Gothic Rhine Gate near the land-ing-stage (with figures of the "Andernach bakers' boys") and the 56 m high Round Tower (1452; view) on the W side of the town. Set in gardens beside the Koblenz Gate are the ruins of a castle of the Electors of Cologne which was destroyed in 1689. – In the market square is the Late Gothic Town Hall (1572), once used as a synagogue; in the courtyard is a 14th c. Jewish bath (shaft 13 m deep, with three bays of vaulting). To the E of the square is the Protestant parish church (14th–15th c.), to the W the Roman Catholic Liebfrauenkirche or Mariendom, a beauti-ful Late Romanesque church (13th c.) with four towers and a fine interior. – At the end of the beautiful gardens flanking the Rhine is the Old Crane (Alter Krahnen), which was erected in 1554–1559 and remained in use (mainly for loading millstones into vessels on the Rhine) until 1911. – In the Leyenscher Hof is a local museum (antiquities).

Old Crane at Andernach

Surroundings of Andernach

From the Kranenberg (216 m), 2 km W, there are charming views (best in the afternoon).

Antwerp (Antwerpen, Anvers)   B

State: Belgium
Province: Antwerpen (Antwerp)
Altitude: 3–9 m above sea level
Population: 490,000

KD German Rhine Line

KD landing-stage:
Tavernierkaai, near Loodswezen Building

General

Antwerp (Flemish Antwerpen, French Anvers), the capital of the Belgian province of that name, is, thanks to its favourable situa-tion on the right bank of the Schelde (Escaut; here up to 500 m wide) 88 km above its outflow into the North Sea, one of the largest seaports in the world and one of the most interesting cities in Belgium. Its harbour has long made it an important commercial city, and banking and insurance developed here at an early stage, together with craft production and industry. Shipbuilding and petrochemicals are now among the city's most important industries, and a special place is occupied by diamond dealing and the diamond industry: within Greater Antwerp there are more than 250 diamond-cutting establish-ments (confer →Amsterdam). The prosperity of earlier cen-turies is reflected not only in the city's fine old buildings but also in the large number of 15th–17th c. pictures it possesses. – Antwerp has the largest community of Orthodox Jews in Europe.

History

Legend has it that the name of Antwerp comes from 'handwer-pen' ('hand-throwing'). In Roman times, it is said, there stood

Cathedral tower and Brabo Fountain   *Steen*

here the castle of a giant named Druon Antigonus who levied tolls on passing seamen and, if they did not pay, cut off one of their hands and threw it into the Schelde. Historical evidence for the existence of the town dates back to the 7th c. In 1031 it appears for the first time in the records as a port, and in 1313 the merchants of the Hanse founded their first settlement here. Under the patronage of the Emperor Charles V developed into the busiest and wealthiest commercial town in Christendom, with a population around 1560 of some 100,000.

The town's prosperity began to decline in the reign of Philip II, and the Duke of Alba's persecution of heretics led thousands of burghers to leave. The Spaniards sacked Antwerp in 1576, when 7,000 people are said to have been killed; and the capture of the town by Alexander Farnese in 1585 was the final blow, its place now being taken by Amsterdam and Rotterdam. By 1790 the population had fallen to only 40,000. – A turn for the better came only at the end of the 18th century. Between 1800 and 1803, on Napoleon's orders, the quays along the Schelde and the old harbour basin were constructed, and thereafter trade and industry developed with remarkable repidity. Under Dutch rule the town's prosperity increased through its trade with the Dutch colonies. – The inner ring of ramparts which had made Antwerp one of the strongest fortresses in Europe was demolished in 1859 and replaced by wide boulevards, but the outer ring was not removed until after the second world war; its line is now marked by the old moat (Vestingwater).

In the centre of the inner city is the Cathedral (Onze Lieve Vrouwekatedraal), the largest Gothic church in Belgium (117 m

Features of interest
*Cathedral

Cathedral (continued)

long, 55 m wide, 40 m high), with a 123 m high N tower (caril-lon). The building of the church began in 1352 and continued into the 16th c. In the S transept are two masterpieces by Ru-bens, the "Raising of the Cross" (1610) and the "Descent from the Cross" (1611–14), and on the high altar is his "Assumption" (1626). – To the W of the Cathedral, in the Grote Markt, is the large Brabo Fountain (1887), showing the Roman governor Sil-vius Brabo in the act of throwing the giant Antigonus's hand into the Schelde. On the W side of th Grote Markt is the Town Hall (1561–65), with a richly decorated interior. The other build-ings in the square are mostly old guild-houses (Gildehuizen) of the 16th and 17th c. The streets behind the Town Hall are very characteristic of old Antwerp.

In Vleeshouwerstraat id the Meat Hall (Vleeshuis, 1501–03), now a museum of applied art and local history. – A little way N, in the Veemarkt, is the former Dominican church of St Paul (1533–71; damaged by fire in 1968). Round the church are many picturesque little corners. – NE of the Cathedral, in Con-scienceplaats, is the former Jesuit church of St Charles Bor-romaeus (1614–21; restored after damage by fire in the 18th–19th c.). – S of the Cathedral, in the busy Groenplaats, is a statue of Rubens (1840). To the SW of the square, in the little

* Plantin-Moretus Museum

Vrijdagmarkt (Friday Market), is the Plantin-Moretus Museum, the house of the famous printer Christopher Plantin, which is one of the finest examples of Flemish Renaissance architecture (16th–17th c.; front part of building 18th c.). The interior, with its work-rooms and business rooms, is a uniquely well pre-served specimen of an old Flemish patrician house.

The commercial heart of the city is in the long street called the Meir, in which are the Royal Palace, originally built as a patri-cian house in 1745, and the Feestzaal (a municipal hall for banquets, receptions, etc.). Down a street on the right between these buildings (Rubensstraat) is the Rubens House (museum), on the site of an earlier house built by Rubens in 1613–17 in which he lived until his death in 1640.

* St. Jacobskerk

To the N of the Feestzaal, in Lange Nieuwstraat, is St. Jacobs-kerk (St James's Church, 15th–16th c.), with a rich Baroque interior. Behind the high altar is the Rubens Chapel, with the painter's tomb. The altarpiece, depicting the Virgin and Child with saints, was painted by Rubens in the last years of his life, and shortly before his death he asked that it should be placed in his burial chapel.

NW of St. Jacobskerk is St Anne's Chapel, begun about 1513. – To the N is the Academy of Art, founded in 1663, which oc-cupies an old Franciscan friary; at Minderbroederstraat 22 is the Museum of Flemish Culture.

* Royal Museum of Fine Art

To the S of the Vrijdagmarkt is St. Andrieskerk (St Andrew's Church, consecrated 1529), which contains a number of fine paintings. In the transept is a small monument to Mary Queen of Scots set up by two of her ladies in waiting. In the large Leopold de Waelplaats is the Royal Museum of Fine Art, a com-prehensive collection of Flemish and Belgian art old and new.

At Lange Gasthuisstraat 19 is the Mayer van den Bergh Mu-seum (furniture, pictures, sculpture). The old chapel of the

Antwerp

300 m

Zandvliet

Rijnkaai
Amsterdamstr.
Londenstr. Noorder-plaats Noorder-laan
Napoleonskaai Ellermanstraat
Bona-parte-dok Willemdok Dambruggestraat
Kon. Stapel-huis
Godefriduskaai
KD Landing Stapelhuis
Oude Leeuwenrui Ankerrui Oranje-steenweg St. Amandus
Waaslandtunnel (vehicles) Tunnelplaats
Ethnogr. Museum St. Antonius St. Jansplein Oude Steenweg Gasistraat
Falconrui
Paar- denmarkt St. Jans- straat Gummarus-straat Diegestraat
St. Paul Klapdorp Vondelstr.
Veemarkt Ned. Kerk Begijnen-hof
Steen Kon. Acad. v. Schone Kunsten
Vleeshuis Minderb.-ru Keizerstraat Prinsstr. Winkelstraat
Folklore Museum Town Hall
Grote Markt Libr. St. Carolus Conservatorium Kon. Atheneum Hl. Hart
St. Jacob
Cathedral Roosevelt-plaats Gemeentestr.
Groenplaats Lange Stock Exchange Nieuwstraat
Toren-gebouw Leysstr. Kon. Opera Koningin Astrid-plein Museum of Nat. Hist.
Plantin-Moretus Museum Meir Meir Feest-zaal De Keyserlei Main Railway Station Dieren-tuin (Zoo)
Lombarden-vest Royal Palace
St. Andries Rubens-huis
Museum Mayer v. d. Bergh Kon. Schouwburg Portuguese Synagogue
Maagdenhuis Paters Jezuïeten Diamond Exchange
Elisabeth Hospital Stads-park R. Gold-muntz Synagogue
St. Joris Quinten Matsijslei Plantin en Moretuslei
Nation. Bank Beth Jitzchok Synagogue
Kronenburgstraat van Eycklei St. Josef
St. Walburgis Boet Kapel Main Synagogue
Marnix-plaats
Museum van Schone Kunsten Gerechts-hof Leemstraat
Amerikalei H. Geestkerk
Museum R. S. van Gelder
Kon. Harmonie

••• Boundary-line of the Jewish Quarter   Koning Albertpark   Pedestrian street

Antwerp, Features of interest (continued)	Maagdenhuis, close by, houses a collection of faience, furniture and pictures. – At the N end of Leopoldstraat is the Royal Theatre (19th c.). To the S is the Botanic Garden.
	The E side of the old town is bounded by wide avenues laid out on that line of the old fortifications of 1540–1543 which were demolished from 1859 onwards. Outside this circuit are the newer districts of the city. – Between the Frankrijklei (one of these avenues), the Zoo and the Koning Albertpark is the old Jewish quarter, home of the largest and most important Jewish community in Europe. In this area, mainly inhabited by strictly orthodox Jews, are many synagogues and one of the Diamond Exchanges.
*National Maritime Museum	The Schelde is tidal for a considerable distance above Antwerp (average tidal movement 4.20 m). Even at low tide it is deep enough to take vessels drawing up to 8 m. Along the banks are 5.5 km of quays 100 m wide (19th c.), at which even large sea-going vessels can moor. The quays are lined by promenades affording wide views. A pedestrian tunnel (572 m long) and the J. F. Kennedy Tunnel (road and rail) run under the river. – In the Steen, a relic of the old castle of Antwerp, is the National Maritime Museum.
*Zandvliet Lock	To the N of the city extend the large northern docks, some of which were constructed by Napoleon. At the northern end is the 10 km long Kanaaldok, with the Frans Tijmanstunnel running under it. It is linked with the Schelde and the new Rhine-Schelde Canal (37 km long) by the Zandvliet Lock, the largest sea-lock in the world.
*Rivierenhof *Nachtegalenpark	Some 3 km E of Antwerp is the suburb of Deurne, with the large recreational park of Rivierenhof. – To the S of the city is the large Nachtegalenpark (Nightingale Park), with the old mansion of Middelheim (open-air museum of sculpture).

Arnhem NL

	State: Netherlands Province: Gelderland Altitude: 20–60 m above sea level Population: 290,000
General	Arnhem, the capital of the Dutch province of Gelderland, lies predominantly on the right bank of the Lower Rhine, some kilometres below the point where the IJssel separates from the Rhine. Part of the city lies in the hills at the edge of the Veluwe, a vast area of woods and moorland.
	Arnhem ist the seat of the Law Courts, of several government agencies and of the Provincial Government of Gelderland, as well as of a number of higher educational institutions such as a School of Drama, a School of Music and a School of Forestry. – Industry plays an important role in the economy of the town. Especially important is the tin-smelting plant founded in 1929, which processes ores from the Dutch Antilles. Apart from this, there are several chemical and engineering plants and other industrial enterprises.

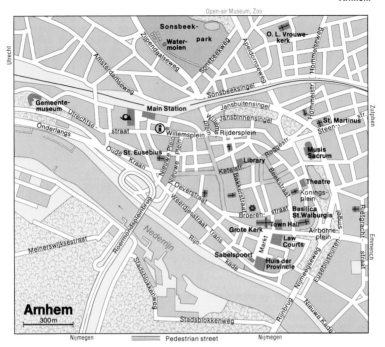

The first mention of Arnhem in chronicles dates from 893, but it is believed that it was built on the site of the Roman settlement 'Arenacum' mentioned by Tacitus. It received its charter in 1233 from Otto III, Count of Geldern. Because of its favourable position on the Rhine, trade flourished throughout the Middle Ages. In the 15th century Arnhem became a member of the Hanse. Emperor Charles V raised the town's status and it became the most important place in Gelderland. In the course of centuries Arnhem fell twice into the hands of the French, who occupied it in 1672–1674 and 1795–1813. In November 1813 the town was conquered by the Prussian troops. Arnhem was heavily damaged in the second world war, especially in the fighting in September 1944, and again when it was taken by the Allies in April 1945, but the town was quickly and skilfully rebuilt.

History

The traffic hub of Arnhem is Willemsplein, not far east from the Central Station. Adjacent, to the south is Nieuwe Plein. South of Nieuwe Plein a line of narrow shopping streets, Rijn-, Vijzel-, Ketel- and Roggestraat lead through the Old City eastwards to Velperplein.

Features of interest

The oldest part of the town can be reached by any one of the side streets going south. Here near the Rhine extends the vast Market Place, at the north end of which stands the Grote Kerk dating from the 15th century (Reformed). From its tower (carillon) there is a beautiful view. In the choir is the fine marble

Arnhem,
Features of interest
(continued)

tomb of the last Duke of Geldern, Charles of Egmond (d. 1538), the rival of Charles V. To the east, opposite the choir of the church, is the old Town Hall, called the Duivelshuis after the three devils above its entrance. It was built c. 1540.

Opposite to the north-east, stand the Law Courts, built in 1958–1963, and the Rijksarchief Gelderland dating from 1880. – On the south side of the square stands the imposing Huis der Provincie, reconstructed in 1954, the seat of the Provincial Government, with a beautiful courtyard. Next to it rises the Sabelspoort, built in the 14th century (the market front dating from 1642), which is a remnant of the city wall.

Further south is the bridge across the Rhine, which was the target of much fighting in the second world war. On the town side stands a monument commemorating the British para-troopers. On the left-hand side is the St. Walburgisbasiliek (Catholic), the oldest church in the town (consecrated in 1422; beautiful pulpit), and the Municipal Theatre. – In the Velper-plein is the Concert Hall 'Musis Sacrum', with exhibition rooms.

West of the Central Station at No. 87 Utrechtseweg, in the grounds of the Reeberg (beautiful view over the Rhine country-side), is the Municipal Museum (Gemeentemuseum), housing a collection of paintings, antiquities and decorative art. Particu-larly interesting is the Chinese and Delft porcelain, as well as a collection of glass. – North from the railway station extends the wooded Municipal Sonsbeek Park, covering 500 hectares (1,236 acres), with a Belvedere, from which there is an exten-sive view over the Betuwe.

Surroundings of Arnhem
*Dutch Open-air Museum

North of the town is the Dutch Open-air Museum (Nederlands Openluchtmuseum, NOM). It can be reached by Zijpendaalse-weg or Apeldoornseweg then by turning respectively left or right into Schelmseweg (4 km). It lies in beautiful wooded coun-tryside and occupies an area of 33 hectares (82 acres). It was founded in 1912 to preserve the Dutch folk art and country way of life, and it offers a unique insight into Dutch peasant handi-crafts and village architecture. The tour takes about 2 hours.

Some 500 m to the west of the Open-air Museum is the Zoo (Burgers Dierenpark), open all year, where a great variety of birds is exhibited. It encloses impressive rocky grounds as well as a Safari Park. – In the suburb of Bronbeek is the Museum of the Dutch-Indian Army (Indisch Legermuseum). It lies between Arnhem and Velp at No. 147 Velperweg.

Bacharach D

State: Federal Republic of Germany
Land: Rheinland-Pfalz (Rhineland-Palatinate)
Altitude: 80 m above sea level
Population: 2,500

KD German Rhine Line

KD excursion ships land on the Rhine bank.

Townscape

Bacharach is a picturesque little town which has long been a noted centre of the trade in Rheingau wines (wine and Sekt cellars). It has preserved its old circuit of walls and towers (14th–16th c.; wall-walk along river front), the best preserved town walls on the Middle Rhine. Above the town are the ruins of Burg Stahleck (see p. 116).

Bacharach (continued)

*Town walls

In the market square are a number of half-timbered houses of the 14th–19th c. and the Late Romanesque church of St Peter (13th c.; Protestant), with a beautiful interior. Within the old Zollhof (Toll Court), which has preserved its enclosing walls, is the Roman Catholic parish church of St Nicholas (17th c.), originally the church of a Capuchin friary.
In the outlying district of Steeg is the Gothic church of St Anne (14th c.; Protestant).

On the footpath up to Burg Stahleck are the ruins, in bright red stone, of the Gothic Wernerkapelle (13th–15th c.), which fell into decay in the early 18th century.

Wernerkapelle

Bad Breisig   D

State: Federal Republic of Germany
Land: Rheinland-Pfalz (Rhineland-Palatinate)
Altitude: 60 m above sea level
Population: 6,500

KD excursion ships land on the Rhine bank.

KD German Rhine Line

Bad Breisig is a much frequented spa with three hot springs (28–33 °C; earthy, alkaline, containing chlorides) which are used in the treatment of heart conditions and disorders of the kidneys and metabolism.

General

In the Kurpark are the Kurhaus, the Ludgerussprudel baths, the Geiersprudel baths and indoor thermal swimming-pool, the Mariensprudel open-air thermal swimming-pool (28 °C) and the Gertrudisquelle open-air mineral baths (15 °C).

Features of interest

In Oberbreisig is the Roman Catholic parish church of St Victor (13th c.), in Niederbreisig the Roman Catholic parish church of the Assumption (Mariä Himmelfahrt, 1718) and numbers of handsome dwelling-houses of the 17th and 18th centuries.

Bad Godesberg (Bonn – Bad Godesberg)   D

State: Federal Republic of Germany
Land: Nordrhein-Westfalen (North Rhine – Westphalia)
Altitude: 60 m above sea level
Population: →Bonn

KD excursion ships land at the Von-Sandt-Ufer (Bastei).

KD German Rhine Line

Bad Godesberg, a spa beautifully situated on the left bank of the Rhine opposite the Siebengebirge (see p. 127), was founded towards the end of the 18th c. by the last Elector of Cologne. After the second world war it became a favourite area with government departments, civil servants and diplomats for

General

**Bad Godesberg,
General (continued)**

both official and residential purposes, and in 1969 it was amalgamated with the Federal capital, →Bonn.

Features of interest

SW of the railway station is the spa district (Kurviertel), with the Stadtpark (Municipal Park), in which are the Stadthalle (Civic Hall), Trinkpavillon (Pump Room) and Neue Kurfürstenquelle (New Elector's Spring; containing sodium and hydrocarbonates), and the Redoutepark, at the W end of which is the Draitschbrunnen, an acidic ferruginous spring used (in the form of both bathing and drinking cures) in the treatment of cardiac and nervous conditions, rheumatism and digestive disorders. In Kurfürstenstrasse, which runs between the two parks, are the classical-style Redoute Kurhaus (1790–92) and the Kurfürstenbad (1964). – On a conical basalt hill above the old town is the Godesburg (alt. 122 m; illustration: see p.127), built in 1210 on the site of a pre-Roman place of sacrifice, destroyed in 1583 and rebuilt as a hotel in 1961. From the keep there are magnificent panoramic views. On the slopes of the hill is the Baroque St Michael's Chapel (1697–99; end of choir Romanesque). From the Von-Sandt-Ufer along the banks of the Rhine there is a fine view of the Siebengebirge.

* **Godesburg**

Bad Honnef   D

State: Federal Republic of Germany
Land: Nordrhein-Westfalen (North Rhine – Westphalia)
Altitude: 78 m above sea level
Population: 21,000

KD German Rhine Line

KD excursion ships land on the Rhine bank.

Townscape

Bad Honnef is an attractive spa at the foot of the Siebengebirge (see p. 127), whose Drachenquelle (Dragon Spring; radioactive, alkaline, acidic) is used in the treatment of digestive problems, heart conditions and circulatory disorders. In this sheltered situation the vegetation is anything up to 14 days earlier than in the rest of the Middle Rhine valley.
In the market square is the Roman Catholic parish church of St John the Baptist, a Late Gothic building (12th and 16th–17th c.), with a tabernacle of 1500 in the N choir. Beside the church is the old sacristan's house. There are several handsome half-timbered houses in the surrounding district.

7 km NE of Honnef, on the Löwenberg (455 m; view), are the ruins of a 13th c. castle, the Löwenburg.

Adenauer House at Rhöndorf

Rhöndorf: see page 127.

Bad Hönningen   D

State: Federal Republic of Germany
Land: Rheinland-Pfalz (Rhineland-Palatinate)
Altitude: 65 m above sea level
Population: 6,000

KD German Rhine Line

KD excursion ships land on the Rhine bank.

The small spa of Bad Hönningen lies on the edge of the Wester-wald and has several hot springs (32 °C; alkaline, containing chlorides) which are used in the manufacture of carbonic acid.

By the railway station is the spa establishment (mineral baths), and on the banks of the Rhine, beautifully situated, are an open-air thermal swimming-pool (30 °C) and an indoor thermal pool.

To the N of Bad Hönningen, in a beautiful park, is Schloss Arenfels (18th c.), built on the site of an earlier 13th c. castle. Here too are fine 18th c. conventual buildings.

Basle (Basel) CH

State: Switzerland
Canton: Basel-Stadt (Basle-Town)
Altitude: 256–282 m above sea level
Population: 182,000

KD ships' landing-stage and agency:
Elsässer Rheinweg, near St.-Johanns-Tor
Starting and finishing point of the KD Rhine cruises

Basle (German Basel), Switzerland's second largest city, lies in the 'Dreiländereck' (meeting-place of three countries) near the German and French frontiers. Since 1833 it has been an inde-pendent half-canton, Basel-Stadt (the other half being Basel-Land). The city is built on both sides of the Rhine, which here takes a sharp turn northward between the Swiss Jura and the Black Forest to enter the Upper Rhine plain. Gross-Basel (Great Basle), the city's commercial and cultural centre, lies on the higher left bank, Klein-Basel (Little Basle), where most of its industry is situated, on the flat right bank.

Situated on the Swiss frontier at an important river crossing, Basle soon developed into an important commercial town. Its heavy commercial traffic is now served by two railway stations and the Rheinhafen (Rhine Harbour) at Kleinhüningen, 3 km N of the city on the right bank of the river. At St-Louis, 9.5 km N in French territory, is the Basle-Mulhouse airport, with a 5 km long access road (customs). The city's main industries are chemicals and pharmaceuticals, engineering and electrical equipment; it also has numerous banks.

'Dreiländereck' at Basle

In the second half of the 1st c. B.C. the hill on which the Minster now stands was occupied by a Celtic settlement, remains of the ramparts of which were found in Rittergasse. The proximity of the town of Augusta Raurica (Augst), founded in 44 B.C., led to the establishment of a Roman military station on the hill in 15 B.C. The name 'Basilia' ('royal fortress') first appears in the records in 374 A.D., and soon after that date there is a reference to Basle as the see of a bishop. In the 10th c. the town belonged to Burgundy, and in 1025 it became part of the German Empire. A long history of conflict with the House of Habsburg ended in 1501 when the town joined the Swiss Confederation. In 1529 it went over to the Reformed faith. The University, founded by Pope Pius II in 1460, became, thanks to the presence of Erasmus from 1521 onwards, a principal centre of humanism, and its fame was maintained by a series of distinguished scholars in later periods: the physician Paracelsus lived in Basle in 1527/28, the mathematicians Jakob and Johann Bernoulli taught in the University in the 17th and 18th c., the cultural and art historian Jakob Burckhardt from 1844 to 1893, the philosopher Friedrich Nietzsche from 1869 to 1879. – Among artists connected with Basle were Hans Holbein the Younger (1497–1543), who spent many years in Basle between 1515 and 1538, and the painter Arnold Böcklin (1827–1901), who was born in Basle and established his fame there.

Features of interest

Gross-Basel (Great Basle), on the left bank of the Rhine, still preserves in its central area some features reminiscent of an old Imperial city, in spite of its many modern buildings and busy commercial activity. – The Marktplatz (Market Square) is dominated by the brightly painted Town Hall (Rathaus, 1504–21) with its arcades, in Late Burgundian Gothic style; the wing on the left and the tall tower on the right are 19th c. additions. The mural paintings in the attractive courtyard are in part the work of Hans Bock (1608–11; restored). The statue (1580) on the outside staircase represents the legendary founder of the town, Munatius Plancus.

SE of the Marktplatz the long Münsterhügel (Minster Hill), with many handsome 18th c. patrician houses, rises above the Rhine. The spacious Münsterplatz, on the site of the Roman fort, is an elegant 18th c. square.

*Minster

The Minster stands on the highest point of the hill, dominating the city with its two slender spires, its walls of red Vosges sandstone and its colourfully patterned roof. The oldest parts of the building date from the 9th–13th c. It was rebuilt in Gothic style after an earthquake in 1356, and had cathedral status until the Reformation. The high altar and much of the furnishings were destroyed by militant Protestants in 1529. The church's greatest treasures were concealed in the vaulting of the sacristy and escaped destruction, but were sold when the canton of Basle was divided into two in 1833 and are now partly in the city's Historical Museum and partly dispersed among other museums throughout the world. – The W front and towers are entirely Gothic, with the exception of the lower part of the N tower (St George's Tower), which dates from the end of the 11th c. The main doorway (c. 1300) is surrounded by rich relief decoration. The St Gallus Doorway in the N transept dates from the 12th c., with numerous Romanesque figures showing an archaic severity of style; it is one of the oldest figured doorways in German-speaking territory. – The nave, with double lateral aisles, is 65 m long by 32.5 m wide. The raised choir, over the crypt, is surrounded by an ambulatory. The columns in the nave and ambulatory have beautiful capitals. In the outer N aisle are numerous tombs and the monument of Erasmus, who died in Basle in 1536. – The crypt has fine Romanesque friezes on the piers and ceiling frescoes. Under the crossing are a collection of lapidary material and the recently excavated walls of a previous church of the early 9th century.

There is a very beautiful double cloister, built in the 15th c. on Romanesque foundations. – Behind the Minster is the Pfalz (the term for a fortified royal residence of the medieval period), a terrace 20 m above the Rhine with fine views of the river and the Black Forest.

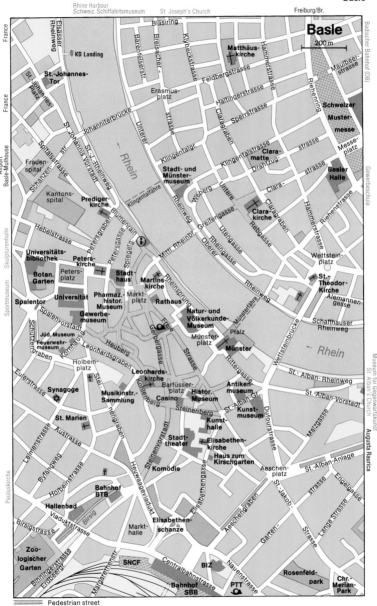

Basle

Rhine Harbour
Schweiz. Schiffahrtsmuseum
St. Joseph's Church
Freiburg/Br.

France
France
Airport
Basle-Mulhouse
Sportmuseum Skulpturenhalle
Pauluskirche

Badischer Bahnhof (DB)
Gewerbeschule
Museum für Gegenwartskunst
St. Alban's Church
Augusta Raurica

Basle

200 m

Blasiring
Bärenfelserstr.
Breisacherstr.
Klybackstrasse
Feldbergstrasse
Hammerstrasse
Maulbeer-strasse

KD Landing
Elsässer
Rheinweg

St.-Johannes-Tor
Johannes-Platz
St.-Johanns-str.
Spitalstrasse
Schanzen-strasse
Frauen-spital
Kantons-spital

Erasmus-platz
Hattingerstrasse
Sperrstrasse
Riehenring
Messe-platz

Schweizer
Muster-messe
Basler
Halle

Predigerkirche
Hebelstrasse
Universitäts-bibliothek
Peters-kirche
Botan. Garten
Peters-platz
Stadt-haus
Spalentor
Universität
Pharmaz. hist. Museum
Gewerbe-museum
Jüd. Museum
Feuerwehr-museum
Synagoge
St. Marien

Johanniterbrücke
Unterer Rheinweg
Rhein
Blumenrain
Petersgraben
Spiegelgasse
Klingentalfähre

Stadt- und Münster-museum
Klingental
Untere
Claramatte
Drahtzug
Clara-strasse
Claragraben
Greifengasse
Utengasse
Rheingasse
Claragraben
Rebgasse
Claragraben
Clarakirche

Wettstein-platz
St.-Theodor-Kirche
Alemannengasse
Schaffhauser Rheinweg

Spalenvorstadt
Schützengraben
Kornhaus
Leonhardsgraben
Holbein-platz
Steinenring
Musikinstr.-Sammlung
Leonhardskirche
Barfüsser-platz
Histor. Museum
Casino
Steinenberg

Martins-kirche
Markt-platz
Rathaus
Natur- und Völkerkunde-Museum
Freie Strasse
Gerbergasse
Münster-platz
Pfalz
Münster
Münsterfähre
Wettsteinbrücke
Rhein
Rheinsprung
Mittl. Rheinbrücke
Oberer Rheinweg

St.-Alban-Rheinweg
Antikenmuseum
St.-Alban-Graben
Kunst-museum
St.-Alban-Vorstadt
Rittergasse
Dufourstrasse
Matzgasse

Euterstrasse
Leimenstrasse
Austrasse
Byfangweg
Holbeinstrasse
Steinengraben
Steinentorstrasse
Heuwaagviadukt
Kunst-halle
Stadt-theater
Elisabethen-kirche
Haus zum Kirschgarten
Komödie
Aeschen-platz
St.-Alban-Anlage
Lange Strasse
Engelgasse

Bahnhof BTB
Hallenbad
Viaduktstrasse
Birsigstrasse
Zoologischer Garten
Binningerstr.
Erdbeergr.
Margarethenstr.
SNCF
Birsig
Markt-halle
Elisabethen-schanze
Elisabethenstrasse
Aeschengraben
Gartenstrasse
Nauenstrasse

BIZ
Bahnhof SBB
PTT
Centralbahnstrasse
Rosenfeld-park
Chr.-Merian-Park

Pedestrian street

151

Town Hall   *Spalentor*

Features of interest
(continued)

NW of the Minster is the richly stocked Museum of Natural History and Ethnography (Natur- und Völkerkundemuseum). – At the W end of the Minster Hill, in a square with a fountain, is St Martin's Church (consecrated 1398), the city's oldest parish church.

**Public Art Collection

SE of the Minster, on St.-Alban-Graben, is the Public Art Collection (Öffentliche Kunstsammlung) or Museum of Art (Kunstmuseum), with the finest collection of pictures in Switzerland, including both old masters and modern art, and also a Print Cabinet. – Diagonally opposite, at St.-Alban-Graben 5, is the Museum of Antiquities (Antikenmuseum), with works of Greek art from 2500 to 100 B.C. and Roman and other Italian art from 1000 B.C. to 300 A.D. – In the busy Barfüsserplatz, housed in the 14th c. Barfüsserkirche (Church of the Barefoot Friars), is the Historical Museum (Historisches Museum), with an important collection on the history of culture and art.

*Historical Museum

To the W of the Marktplatz, reached by a picturesque flight of steps, is the Spalenstadt, a district of the city centred on the tree-shaded Petersplatz. On the E side of this square is St Peter's Church, which was rebuilt at the time of the Council of Basle (1431–87). – On the S side of the square is the University (1938–46), to the W of which is the Spalentor (1370), a fortified gate which marks the end of the old town.

*Spalentor

SW of the old town, in the valley of the Birsig, is the very interesting Zoo, which is world renowned for its success in breeding animals in captivity.

*Zoo

In Klein-Basel (Little Basle) a tree-lined promenade runs along the right bank of the Rhine, affording fine views of the old town.

One of the principal traffic arteries of Klein-Basel is the Riehenring, along which extend the exhibition halls of the Swiss Trade Fair (Schweizer Mustermesse).

Basle, Features of interest (continued)

Gross-Basel and Klein-Basel are linked by six bridges over the Rhine. From the Mittlere Rheinbrücke (Central Rhine Bridge, 1905), on the position of Basle's first bridge, built in 1225, there is a fine view of the Minster. Upstream from this bridge are the Wettsteinbrücke (1879; widened 1937), approached by sloping ramps, the Schwarzwaldbrücke (Black Forest Bridge, 1973), which carries through traffic, and a railway bridge, as well as the dam of the Birsfelden hydroelectric power station. Downstream are the Johanniterbrücke (1882; rebuilt 1966) and the Dreirosenbrücke (1934). There are also three ferries, driven by the current without the use of motors.

Within easy reach of Basle are the remarkable Roman remains at Augst (12 km E; →The Rhine from the Sources to Basle) and – for those interested in anthroposophy – the Goetheanum at Dornach (10 km SE), an overpowering concrete structure built in 1925–1928 to house the headquarters of the Anthroposophical Society founded by Rudolf Steiner (1861–1925).

Surroundings of Basle
*Augusta Raurica

Bingen am Rhein   D

State: Federal Republic of Germany
Land: Rheinland-Pfalz (Rhineland-Palatinate)
Altitude: 77 m above sea level
Population: 24,000

KD excursion ships land at the Rheinanlagen (Rhine bank).

KD German Rhine Line

Bingen is an old town finely situated at the outflow of the river Nahe above the Binger Loch ('Bingen Hole'; see p. 113), where the Rhine cuts a passage through the Rhenish Uplands. Its proximity to this difficult stretch of the river with its rapids and shallows made Bingen an important staging point for traffic on the Rhine from a very early period. The Romans established the fort of 'Bingium' here, close to an earlier settlement, and built a bridge over the Nahe. In 983 Bingen came into the possession of the archbishopric of Mainz, and thereafter was surrounded by walls and protected by the construction of a castle. As a result of numerous fires and much destruction by war (most recently during the second world war) the town has preserved few historic old buildings. – Bingen was the home of St Hildegard of Bingen (1098–1179), but the Benedictine convent of Rupertsberg which she founded on the left bank of the Nahe in 1147 suffered destruction in the 17th c. and was finally demolished in the 19th c. to make way for the railway. The saint is depicted in the background of the Annunciation on the Issenheim Altar (→Colmar). – Nowadays wine-production and the wine trade (brandy distillery, Sekt-making establishment) play a major part in the life and economy of the town. – There are car and passenger ferries between Bingen and →Rüdesheim on the opposite bank of the Rhine.

General

View of Bingen

In the old town, just above the Nahe, is the Late Gothic parish church of St Martin (15th–16th c.; R.C.), which has Carolingian and Romanesque crypts. – The town is dominated by Burg

Features of interest

Bingen (continued)
*Burg Klopp

Klopp (128 m), situated amid beautiful rock gardens on the site of the Roman fort. Built in the 13th c., it was blown up by the French in 1711; the present buildings date mainly from the end of the 19th century. The keep now houses an interesting local museum. From the terrace below the castle there are wide views of the river, taking in the Rheingau, Rüdesheim, the Niederwald, the ruined Burg Ehrenfels half way down the hillside and the Binger Loch with the Mäuseturm (see p. 112).
A railway bridge, a road bridge and the old Drusus Bridge (Early Romanesque), built on Roman foundations, lead across the Nahe to Bingerbrück.

Surroundings of Bingen

Above the town rises the Rochusberg, with the conspicuous St Roch's Chapel (Rochuskapelle; 189 m), founded in 1666 on the occasion of an outbreak of plague and rebuilt in 1889–1894. In a side chapel is a picture presented by Goethe in which he himself is depicted as St Roch.

Bonn   D

State: Federal Republic of Germany
Land: Nordrhein-Westfalen (North Rhine – Westphalia)
Altitude: 64 m above sea level
Population: 286,000

KD German Rhine Line

KD cruise ships' landing-stage and agency →Bad Godesberg
KD excursion ships land opposite the Rheingasse and near the Bundeshaus (Federal Parliament Building).

General

Bonn, the capital of the Federal Republic of Germany, extends over both banks of the Rhine, which here emerges into the Cologne lowlands after its passage through the Rhenish Uplands. The pattern of the city's life is set by its old and famous University, the political activity centred on the government buildings round the Adenauerallee, its busy commercial life and its attractive setting (particularly on the river side, with its view of the nearby Siebengebirge (see p. 127). Since the incorporation of Bad Godesberg, the city possesses a renowned spa resort within its boundaries. – Bonn is famous as the birthplace of Ludwig van Beethoven (1770–1827).

History

Bonn ('Castra Bonnensia') was one of the earliest Roman forts on the Rhine. From 1238 to 1794 it was the residence of the archbishops of Cologne. On 10 May 1949 it was selected as the seat of the government of the Federal Republic of Germany.

Features of interest

In the centre of the old town is the Marktplatz, with the Town Hall (Rathaus, 1737–38). At Rathausgasse 7 is the Municipal Art Collection (20th c. German painting and sculpture). A little way N is the church of St Remigius (13th–14th c.). At Bonngasse 20 is the Beethoven House, the composer's birthplace, now a museum. – SW of the Marktplatz, in Münsterplatz, is the venerable Minster (SS. Cassius and Florentinus), one of the finest Romanesque churches in the Rhineland (11th–13th c.; E crypt 11th c.); on the S side is an attractive 12th c. cloister. – At the near end of Adenauerallee is the Koblenz Gate, in the E wing of the extensive University buildings erected between 1697 and 1725 by Enrico Zuccali and Robert de Cotte as the Electoral Palace;

*Beethoven House

*Minster

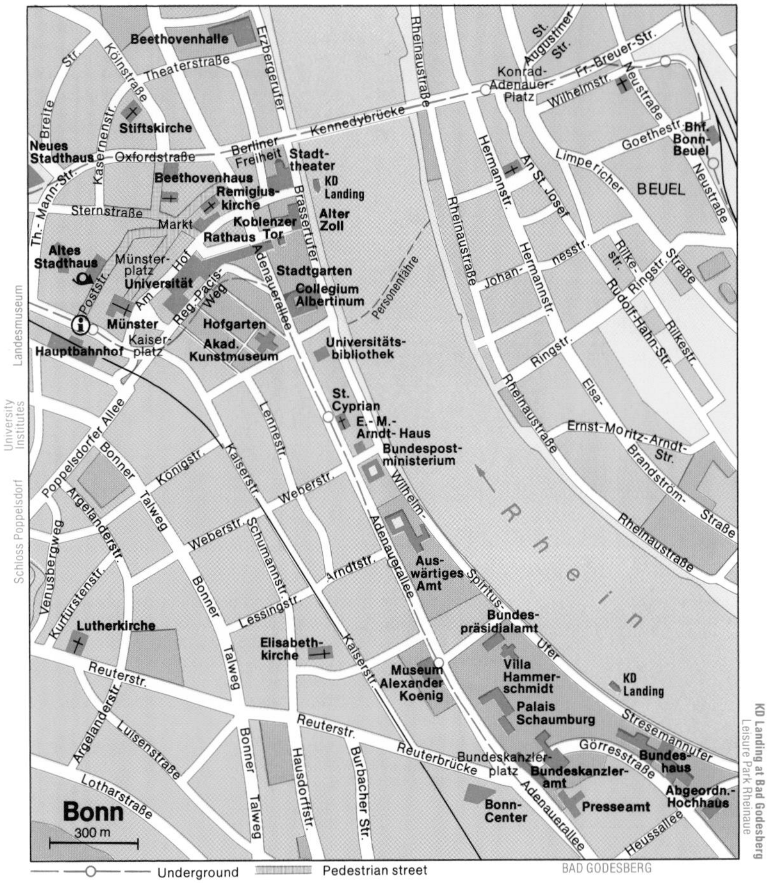

Map legend: —○— Underground ▨▨▨ Pedestrian street

BAD GODESBERG

KD Landing at Bad Godesberg
Leisure Park Rheinaue

beyond it is the Hofgarten. Farther down Adenauerallee are the Villa Hammerschmidt (official residence of the President), the Palais Schaumburg and the Federal Chancellor's Office (Bundeskanzleramt; 1975–77), with a façade 95 m long. On the opposite side of the street is the Alexander König Zoological Museum. In Bundeskanzlerplatz is the Bonn-Center. To the E, in Görresstrasse, is the Federal Parliament Building, the Bundeshaus, with a tower block containing members' offices. Beyond this is the Rheinaue Leisure Park. – To the E of the Koblenz Gate, on the Rhine, are the Stadtgarten (Municipal Park) and the Alter Zoll (Old Custom House), a former bastion with a celebrated view of the Rhine and the Siebengebirge. N of the Alter Zoll, at the bridge over the Rhine, is the Municipal Theatre (1963–65). Beyond the bridge is the Beethovenhalle (1957–59; 1983 restored after damage caused by fire).

Features of interest
(continued)

155

Rhine bank at Bonn

Bonn (continued) Poppelsdorfer Schloss	To the SW of the town, at the end of the Poppelsdorfer Allee, is the Poppelsdorfer Schloss (1715–30), beyond which is the Botanic Garden. Farther SW is the Kreuzberg (125 m), with a Franciscan friary and a conspicuous Baroque church (1627–37; 'Sacred Staircase' on E side by Balthasar Neumann, 1746–51).
* Rhineland Museum	– To the W of the railway station is the Rhineland Museum (Rheinisches Landesmuseum).

Bonn – Beuel: see page 129.
Bonn – Bad Godesberg: see →Bad Godesberg.

Boppard

D

	State: Federal Republic of Germany Land: Rheinland-Pfalz (Rhineland-Palatinate) Altitude: 70 m above sea level Population: 18,000
KD German Rhine Line	KD ships' landing-stage and agency: Rheinallee (Rhine bank).
General	Boppard, once a free Imperial city, lies in the largest loop in the Rhine, known as the 'Bopparder Hamm', which is famous for its wine. The site was occupied originally by a Celtic settlement and later by the Roman fort of 'Boudobriga'. Boppard is a town of picturesque aspect, particularly when seen from the side facing the Rhine, and attracts many passing visitors as well as those who come for the sake of its healthy air and to take the Kneipp cure in the spa establishment.

There are quite considerable remains of the Roman fort (4th c. A.D.) in the Burggraben and Karmeliterstrasse (No. 7 and No. 11, in courtyard). Some stretches of the medieval town walls, complete with gates and towers, have also been preserved. In the market square is the twin-towered church of St Severus (12th–13th c.; R.C.), with Romanesque wall paintings. In Karmeliterstrasse is the Gothic Carmelite Church (14th c.; no tower), with 16th c. choir-stalls and monuments. – On the bank of the Rhine is the tower of a castle belonging to the archbishop of Trier (c. 1340 and 1499), with the Municipal Museum.
Above the town to the S are the conventual buildings (1738) of an Ursuline nunnery (boarding school) which was founded in 1123 as the Marienberg Convent of Benedictine nuns.

Boppard,
Features of interest

From Boppard a chair-lift runs up the Gedeonseck (305 m); from the summit there is a fine view of the loop in the Rhine.

Surroundings of Boppard

Braubach   D

State: Federal Republic of Germany
Land: Rheinland-Pfalz (Rhineland-Palatinate)
Altitude: 71 m above sea level
Population: 3,500

KD ships' landing-stage and agency on the Rhine bank.

KD German Rhine Line

The ancient little town of Braubach (first recorded in 691/92) is situated under the Marksburg (see p. 121). – Most spectacular is the summer festival "The Rhine Aflame" (August) with fireworks and illuminations along the river between Braubach and Koblenz.

General

At the upper end of the town are some remains (wine-cellar) of Schloss Philippsburg, built in 1568. The cemetery chapel of St Martin (c. 1000) has preserved its Romanesque nave. The tower of the former parish church of St Barbara (13th c.) was once part of the town's fortifications. There are a number of handsome old half-timbered houses.

Features of interest

To the E of Braubach in the Zollbach valley are lead and silver works, supplied by mines which go back to pre-Roman times (three conspicuous funnels).

Surroundings

Breisach am Rhein   D

State: Federal Republic of Germany
Land: Baden-Württemberg
Altitude: 191–227 m above sea level
Population: 9,000

Breisach, an old town (large wine- and Sekt-making establishments), restored after suffering severe damage during the last war, is picturesquely situated on a steep-sided basalt crag, rising 35 m above the Rhine valley, which within historical times lay on the left bank of the river. Numerous finds have shown that the site was already occupied in the Bronze Age. On the

General

Breisach: St Stephen's Minster, above the Rhine bank

Breisach, General
(continued)

hill, which they called 'Mons Brisiacus', the Romans established a fort of which only scanty remains have been found. During the Middle Ages Breisach was a major German stronghold. Held by Austria from 1331, it became a bone of contention between Austria and France. In 1742 Maria Theresa ordered the fortifications, which had suffered heavy damage from flooding, to be demolished. Several town gates have survived, including the Rhine Gate (built by Vauban in 1670), which has a magnificent façade.

* Minster

On the Münsterberg (Minster Hill) is St Stephen's Minster (14th c.), with a large carved high altar (1526) by an artist who is known only by the initials H.L. and wall paintings by Martin Schongauer, who died in Breisach in 1491. Also on the Minster Hill stands the historical Radbrunnen-Turm (tower), with an art gallery. – At Münsterbergstrasse 21 is the Breisgau Museum (early history).

To the S of the Münsterberg is the Eckartsberg, another basalt hill.

Breisgau D

State: Federal Republic of Germany
Land: Baden-Württemberg
Capital: Freiburg im Breisgau

Landscape and history

The Breisgau is an old territorial unit on the right bank of the river in the Upper Rhine plain, bounded on the N by the Ortenau district, on the W and S by the Rhine and on the E by the Black Forest. The area first appears in the records in the 8th c. as a county of the Carolingian empire, but was probably an independent lordship from a much earlier period. From the 11th c. it was held by the Counts of Zähringen; at the end of the 14th c. it passed to Austria; in 1801 it was temporarily attached to the duchy of Modena, and in 1805 it fell to Baden.

Breisgau
(continued)

The Breisgau is one of the leading German wine-producing areas (→Facts and Figures, Wine).

Cleves (Kleve)   D

State: Federal Republic of Germany
Land: Nordrhein-Westfalen (North Rhine – Westphalia)
Altitude: 46 m above sea level
Population: 44,000

Cleves (German Kleve), once capital of the Duchy of Cleves and the home of Henry VIII's fourth wife Anne of Cleves, is attractively situated on a hill which formerly bordered the left bank of the Rhine, it is frequented by holiday visitors for the sake of its healthy air. It also has a variety of industry (shoe, margarine and cocoa factories, etc.). The town is linked with the Rhine, which now flows 6 km N, by the 9 km long Spoy Canal, a continuation of the old Kermisdahl arm of the Rhine which was cut in the 11th century. Cleves was laid in ruins in the second world war.

General

On a hill in the centre of the town is the Schwanenburg (15th–17th c.; the name recalls the story of Lohengrin), the old castle of the Dukes of Cleves. In Kavariner Strasse is the former Minorite Church (15th c.; R.C.), with fine carved choir-stalls (1474); in the Haus Koekkoek (Dutch painter B. C. Koekkoek, 1803–62) is the Municipal Museum (art collection). In the small market square is the Stiftskirche (1341–1426), with the tombs of the Dukes of Cleves.

Features of interest

In the range of hills to the W of the town is the attractive Tiergarten (Zoo). At the S end of the range is the Klever Berg (106 m; outlook tower). – The Moritzpark, Forstgarten (with an amphitheatre) and Reichswald (footpaths) are popular recreation areas.

Colmar   F

State: France
Région: Alsace
Département: Haut-Rhin (Upper Rhine)
Altitude: 190 m above sea level
Population: 67,000

Colmar, the chief town of the French département of Haut-Rhin in Upper Alsace and the third largest town in Alsace (after Strasbourg and Mulhouse), lies near the vine-covered foothills of the southern Vosges, in a situation which gives it a very agreeable climate. With its picturesque 16th and 17th c. bur-

General

Colmar, General
(continued)

ghers' houses and its wealth of outstanding works of art it is one of the major tourist attractions of Alsace.

History

The town, first mentioned in the records in 823 as a royal residence under the name of 'Columbarium' (Dovecot), was surrounded by walls in 1120. The Emperor Frederick II granted it the status of a free Imperial city, which soon became the leading market town in Upper Alsace and a centre of art and learning. In 1354 Colmar joined the 'Decapolis', the league of ten free Imperial cities in Alsace. The town was closely involved in the Reformation. It was occupied by the Swedes during the Thirty Years War and by the French in 1673, and thereafter shared the destinies of the region. – Colmar was the birthplace of the painter and engraver Martin Schongauer (c. 1446–1491); and the painter Matthias Grünewald (Mathis Gothardt Neithardt of Würzburg, c. 1470/83–1528), the last and greatest master of the Late Gothic period, also worked here.

Krutenau Quarter

*Unterlinden Museum

Colmar's principal sight is the famous Unterlinden Museum, housed in the former Dominican convent of Unterlinden with its Early Gothic church. The chapel contains fine paintings by early German painters, including Passion scenes by Martin Schongauer and others; its chief treasure, however, is Matthias Grünewald's Issenheim Altar (c. 1515), one of the greatest and most moving masterpieces of German painting. On the first floor of the museum is a rich historical and ethnological collection.

**Issenheim Altar

In the centre of the old town is St Martin's Church (Cathédrale St-Martin; originally Gothic, but remodelled in the 18th c.), with a noble High Gothic choir (1350–66). – In the choir of the Dominican Church (Eglise des Dominicains; Early Gothic, 13th c.) is the famous "Virgin of the Rose-Garden", Martin Schongauer's earliest painting (1473).

*Virgin of the Rose-Garden

*Maison Pfister

In the old town there are many handsome old burghers' houses, notable among them the Maison Pfister (1537), with a wooden gallery, and the Maison des Têtes (1609), now occupied by a famous wine restaurant.

Cologne (Köln)   D

State: Federal Republic of Germany
Land: Nordrhein-Westfalen (North Rhine – Westphalia)
Altitude: 36 m above sea level
Population: 976,000

KD German Rhine Line

Cologne is the place of business and winter harbour of the Köln-Düsseldorfer Deutsche Rheinschiffahrt AG (KD German Rhine Line)
KD ships' landing-stages in Cologne, Frankenwerft (Rheingarten, near Deutz Bridge) and in Cologne-Porz (Rhine bank)
Headquarters:
Frankenwerft 15, D-50667 Köln; tel.: (0221) 20 88-0, 20 88-318 and 319 (information), 20 88-288 (bookings)

General

Cologne (German Köln), the old cathedral city, is also one of the most important traffic junctions and commercial centres in

Cologne: Rhine front

General (continued)

the Federal Republic of Germany, with world-famed trade fairs and a busy shipping traffic (sea-going and on the Rhine). It is the see of an archbishop, with a university, a sports college and the headquarters of the WDR (Westdeutscher Rundfunk) radio and television corporation, and is noted also for sport (Federal Football League matches; Union races and Federal Grand Prix on Weidenpesch race-course) and for the Rhineland Carnival. With its venerable old churches and its Roman remains it is one of the focal points of Western culture. – A characteristic Cologne institution is the 'Kölsche Bierkneipe', a tavern serving 'Kölsch', a light top-fermented beer brewed in the city.

History

Cologne developed out of the Roman colony of 'Colonia Claudia Ara Agrippinensium'. From the end of the 5th c. it was incorporated in the kingdom of the Franks, and was made the seat of an archbishopric by Charlemagne. In the Middle Ages it was one of the leading towns in Germany, and for a time was, along with Lübeck, the most important member of the Hanse. In the 19th c., as part of the province of Rhineland, the town became Prussian. The second world war destroyed most of the inner city, now rebuilt in modern style along with the business district round the Hohe Strasse.

Features of interest
**Cathedral

The landmark and emblem of the city is the mighty Cathedral (Dom), a masterpiece of High Gothic architecture and one of the largest cathedrals in Europe. Begun in 1248, it was the most ambitious building project of the Middle Ages, but work came to a halt at the beginning of the 16th c., and the Cathedral was not completed until 1842–80. Notable features of the interior (area 6,166 sq.m, with 56 piers) are the Reliquary of the Three

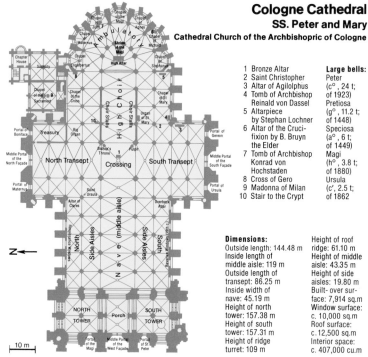

Cologne Cathedral
SS. Peter and Mary
Cathedral Church of the Archbishopric of Cologne

1	Bronze Altar	**Large bells:**
2	Saint Christopher	Peter
3	Altar of Agilolphus	(c°, 24 t;
4	Tomb of Archbishop	of 1923)
	Reinald von Dassel	Pretiosa
5	Altarpiece	(g°, 11.2 t;
	by Stephan Lochner	of 1448)
6	Altar of the Cruci-	Speciosa
	fixion by B. Bruyn	(a°, 6 t;
	the Elder	of 1449)
7	Tomb of Archbishop	Magi
	Konrad von	(h°, 3.8 t;
	Hochstaden	of 1880)
8	Cross of Gero	Ursula
9	Madonna of Milan	(c', 2.5 t;
10	Stair to the Crypt	of 1862)

Dimensions:
Outside length: 144.48 m
Inside length of
middle aisle: 119 m
Outside length of
transept: 86.25 m
Inside width of
nave: 45.19 m
Height of north
tower: 157.38 m
Height of south
tower: 157.31 m
Height of ridge
turret: 109 m

Height of roof
ridge: 61.10 m
Height of middle
aisle: 43.35 m
Height of side
aisles: 19.80 m
Built- over sur-
face: 7,914 sq.m
Window surface:
c. 10,000 sq.m
Roof surface:
c.12,500 sq.m
Interior space:
c. 407,000 cu.m

Cathedral (continued)

Kings (Magi; designed by Nicholas of Verdun; 12th–13th c.) above the high altar; the famous 'Dombild' in the ambulatory, a triptych by Stephan Lochner (Adoration of the Kings, c. 1440); and the fine Early Gothic statuary (14th c.) on the pillars in the choir. In the Chapel of the Cross (Kreuzkapelle) is the famous Gero Cross. The Treasury contains many precious objects. – From the S tower (over 500 steps) there are wide-ranging views.

**Roman-Germanic Museum

On the S side of the Cathedral is the magnificently laid out Roman-Germanic Museum, with the Dionysus mosaic (2nd c. A.D.), the 15 m high tomb of Poblicius (1st c. A.D.) and a rich collection of Roman glass and everyday equipment. Nearby is the Diocesan Museum.

**Wallraf-Richartz Museum
and Ludwig Museum

In Wallrafplatz are the headquarters of WDR (radio and television). Opposite, to the S, are the Wallraf-Richartz Museum and the Ludwig Museum (European painting; move is planned in 1985 to a new terrace building with a concert hall between the Cathedral and the Rheingarten on the Rhine bank). – Farther S is St Columba's Chapel (1949–52).

W of the Cathedral is St Andrew's Church (15th c.; remains of St Albertus Magnus in a Roman sarcophagus in the funerary chapel). Farther W is the Arsenal (Zeughaus), now housing the Municipal Museum. At the end of Zeughausstrasse, on left, is the Roman Tower (Römerturm, 1st c. A.D.), a relic of the Roman town walls.

A little way N is St Gereon's Church, with a long choir (11th c.) and a decagonal domed nave, a structure originally built in Roman times and enlarged in 1227.

* St Gereon

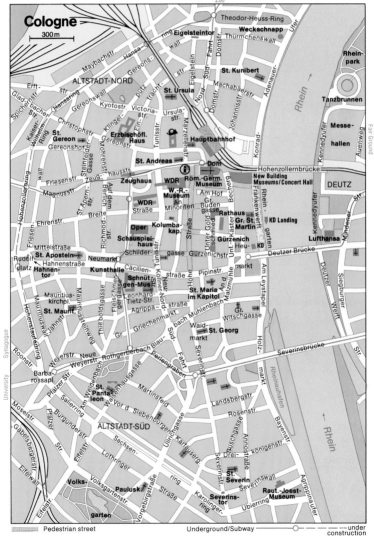

Cologne

300m

Pedestrian street   Underground/Subway ───○── ─ ─ ─ under construction

Cologne

° Praetorium

Severinstor

S of the Cathedral is in the street called Am Hof the Heinzel-männchenbrunnen ('brownies' fountain', 1899) in memory of those zealous little people from a Cologne fairy-tale. Still farther to the S is the Old Town Hall (Altes Rathaus, 15th–16th c.; Hanseatic Chamber). Opposite it is the New Town Hall (1954–57), built on the remains of the Roman Praetorium (museum). To the SW is the Gürzenich, built in 1437–44 as a warehouse and banqueting hall. Farther S is the church of St. Maria im Kapitol (11th–13th c.); inside there are two beautiful carved doors of 1050–65; under the choir is a massive crypt.

In the Neumarkt is the Church of the Holy Apostles (11th–13th c.). To the N is the Municipal Theatre (opera-house 1954–56, theatre 1959–62). At the Glockengasse is the House 4711 (street number dating back to the times of French occupation c. 1800), the house of the makers of famous 'Kölnisch Wasser' (eau-de-Cologne), with a Neo-Gothic façade (carillon).

SE of the Neumarkt, in St Cecilia's Church, is the Schnütgen Museum (ecclesiastical art). Rather less than a kilometre farther S is St Pantaleon's Church (10th–17th c.), with the tomb of the Empress Theophano (d. 991), wife of Otto II.

Between the Rhine bridges Hohenzollernbrücke and Deutzer Brücke stretches along the left Rhine bank the newly laid out Rheingarten (Frankenwerft; vehicular tunnel).

Round the old town runs a semicircular circuit of 'Ring' streets, laid out in front of the former town walls. Of the old fortified town gates there remain the Eigelsteintorburg in the N, the Hahnentorburg in the W and the Severinsburg in the South. A little way N of the Severinstor is the well restored church of St Severinus (11th–15th c.), with an interesting Roman and Frankish cemetery. In the nearby Ubierring is the Rauten-strauch-Joest Museum (ethnography).

In the southern suburb of Marienburg, Bayenthalgürtel No. 9, remains of the Roman Alteburg fort (the ancient headquarters of the Roman Rhine fleet) have been uncovered in 1983.

On the right bank of the Rhine is the district of Deutz, linked with the left bank by the Severinsbrücke (1959; a road bridge, 691 m long), the Deutzer Brücke (1948; road bridge), the Hohenzollernbrücke or Dombrücke (railway and pedestrians) and the Zoobrücke (1966; road bridge), which is crossed at an angle by the Rhine cableway. In Deutz, which occupies the site of the Roman fort of 'Castellum Divitia' (310 A.D.), are trade fair and exhibition halls, a conference centre and the beautiful Rheinpark (Tanzbrunnen or Dancing Fountain; hot mineral baths; chair-lift). – The district of Mülheim, to the N, is reached by way of the Mülheimer Brücke, a suspension bridge with a span of 315 m, rebuilt in the years 1949–1951.

Surroundings of Cologne
° Altenberg Cathedral

° Schloss Augustusburg

Some 20 km NE of Cologne is Altenberg Cathedral (Bergischer Dom), one of the finest examples of Early Gothic architecture in the Rhineland (1255–1379). – 15 km S, at Brühl, is Schloss Augustusburg, built in the 18th c. as the residence of the archbishop of Cologne. Sumptuously decorated and furnished, this

The spires of the Cologne Cathedral, rising behind St Martin's Church ▶

Surroundings of Cologne
(continued)
* Phantasialand

is one of the most charming palaces in the transitional style between late Baroque and Rococo (staircase by Balthasar Neumann; large park). – Near Brühl is the 'Phantasialand' leisure park, the largest of its kind in Germany.

Dordrecht   NL

State: Netherlands
Province: Zuid-Holland (South Holland)
Altitude: 3 m below sea level to 5 m above sea level
Population: 108,000

General and History

* Grote Kerk

Dordrecht is an old town picturesquely situated between the Oude Maas (here navigable by large sea-going vessels), the Merwede and two arms of the Maas, the Noord and the Dordtse Kil, with shipyards, shipping companies, engineering plants and chemical industries; it is also a popular centre of water sports. Thanks to its excellent situation as a port it was once the wealthiest commercial town in the Netherlands, but in the 18th c. it was overtaken by Antwerp and Rotterdam. Today Dordrecht is both a river port and a seaport, with an annual turnover (principally of goods in transit) of some 3.5–4 million tons.

The Ghent Chronicle records that Dordrecht was destroyed by the Norsemen in 937; the first documentary reference to the town, however, is in 1138. When it received its municipal charter in 1220 it was already an important commercial centre trading, through its port, with England, the Rhineland and Flanders. In 1421, however, the area S of the town was covered with water in the so-called 'Elizabeth Flood', the water labyrinth of the 'Brabantse Biesbosch' being a remainder (boat trips).

The attractive principal canal of Dordrecht is the Voorstraats Haven. – The Grote Kerk (Reformed; begun about 1300, rebuilt in the 15th–16th c.) has a massive tower 70 m high (carillon); the interior is notable for a magnificent choir-screen of 1744 and beautiful choir-stalls of 1538–41, the finest of their kind in the Netherlands.

On the Nieuwe Haven is the Museum van Gijn (antiquities), next to it a toy museum. – At Museumstraat is the Dordrecht Museum (paintings of the 17th–19th c.). From the N side of the Groothoofdspoort, an old Gothic town gate which was rebuilt in 1618 (fine relief; domed tower), there is a charming view of the Oude Maas, the Noord and the Merwede.

Duisburg   D

State: Federal Republic of Germany
Land: Nordrhein-Westfalen (North Rhine – Westphalia)
Altitude: 15–83 m above sea level
Population: 560,000

General

Duisburg, an industrial and commercial city on the western edge of the Ruhr, is situated at the confluence of the river Ruhr

Duisburg-Ruhrort: Europe's largest inland port

with the Rhine. It takes first place in Germany in the production of steel, and its harbour on the Rhine is the largest inland port in Europe (20 docks, annual turnover more than 50 million tons). It was a university town in the Middle Ages, and now has a Gesamthochschule (comprehensive higher educational establishment). The opera company it shares with Düsseldorf, the 'Deutsche Oper am Rhein', has an international reputation. The excellent regatta course in the Wedau sports park has made Duisburg a favoured choice for international rowing regattas. – The famous cartographer Gerhard Mercator (1512–1594) lived and taught in Duisburg.

General (continued)

In Frankish times a trading and warehouse centre for the Rhine shipping trade grew up at the end of the Hellweg, the old traffic route between the Rhine and the Weser; and to protect it the Carolingian royal fortress of Thusburg was built in the 8th c. The settlement which grew up round the castle was enclosed by walls (on the line marked by the modern Wallstrassen) around 1100. Under the Hohenstaufens Duisburg became a free Imperial city and a member of the Hanse. An alteration in the course of the Rhine in the 13th c. put an end to a period of high prosperity. It was not until 1831 that Duisburg re-established a link with the Rhine through the construction of its outer harbour. In the latter part of the 19th c. mining and ironworking became established as major industries. The urban area was considerably enlarged by the incorporation of the towns of Ruhrort, Meiderich (both in 1905) and Hamborn (in 1929).

History

In the Burgplatz is the Town Hall (Rathaus, 1897–1902; Mercator Room). In the Salvatorkirche, to the N, can be seen Merca-

Features of interest

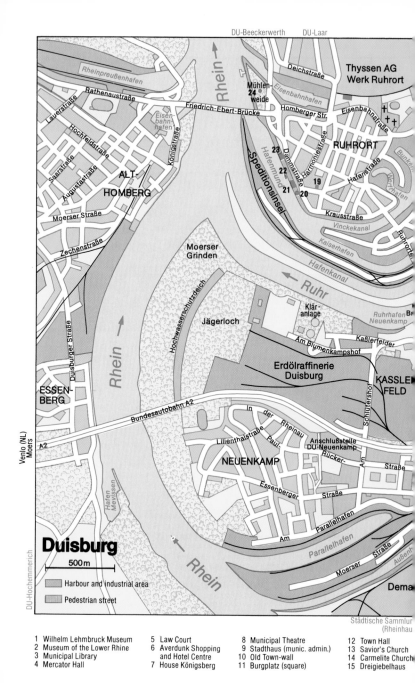

Duisburg

500m

Harbour and industrial area

Pedestrian street

1 Wilhelm Lehmbruck Museum
2 Museum of the Lower Rhine
3 Municipal Library
4 Mercator Hall

5 Law Court
6 Averdunk Shopping and Hotel Centre
7 House Königsberg

8 Municipal Theatre
9 Stadthaus (munic. admin.)
10 Old Town-wall
11 Burgplatz (square)

12 Town Hall
13 Savior's Church
14 Carmelite Church
15 Dreigiebelhaus

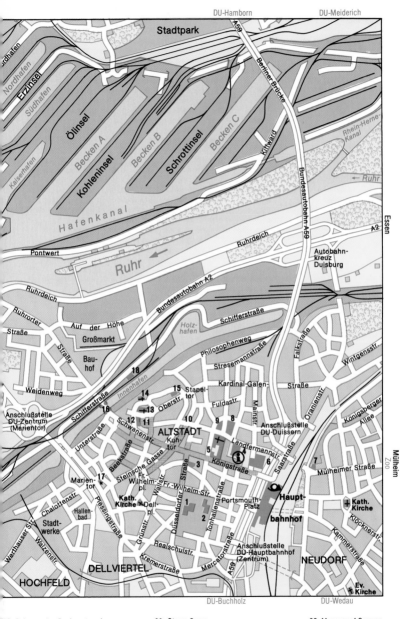

Duisburg, Features of interest (continued)

tor's epitaph. – In Königstrasse, the town's principal street, is the König-Heinrich-Platz, with the Municipal Theatre and the Mercatorhalle (1962; an all-purpose hall for concerts, exhibitions and other events). – In Düsseldorfer Strasse, which runs S off Königstrasse, is the Wilhelm Lehmbruck Museum (1964), which contains the municipal art collection, with many works by the Duisburg-born sculptor Wilhelm Lehmbruck (1881–1919). To the E is the Lower Rhineland Museum (Niederrheinisches Museum; municipal history; collection of maps). – On the wooded Kaiserberg is the Zoo (aquarium; dolphinarium and whalarium, with a white whale).

*Wilhelm Lehmbruck Museum

*Zoo

The Schwanentorbrücke, a bascule bridge, links the town centre with the northern district of Ruhrort, which has grown in size and importance through ironworking and the shipment of Ruhr coal. At the 'Hafenmund' is the Museum of German Inland Navigation (Museum der Deutschen Binnenschiffahrt), with the steam tugboat "Oscar Huber", the dredging bucket power shovel "Minden" and an old steam crane.
The 1,824 m long Berliner Brücke crosses the river Ruhr at the Rhine-Herne Canal to the district of Meiderich. – In the district of Hamborn, farther N, are the large steelworks (Thyssen-Hütte, etc.).

Museum of German Inland Navigation

Wedau

South of the city is the Wedau sports park. A popular recreation area is the Sechs-Seen-Platte (Six Lakes district), with facilities for sailing, swimming and walking.

Düsseldorf   D

State: Federal Republic of Germany
Land: Nordrhein-Westfalen (North Rhine – Westphalia)
Altitude: 38 m above sea level
Population: 595,000

KD German Rhine Line

KD ships land at the Theodor Heuss Bridge, at the Rheinterrassen and at the Rathausufer (excursion ships).
KD agency: Burgplatz (Rathausufer)

General

Düsseldorf, the capital of the Land of North Rhine – Westphalia, situated on the Lower Rhine, here 310 m wide, is the 'office desk of the Ruhr area', the administrative centre of the region's heavy industry. It is a university town, a centre of art and fashion, a city of congresses and trade fairs. This old Electoral capital is a town of wide streets lined with elegant shops and crowded with traffic, of spacious parks and gardens (Federal Garden Show 1987).

The old town with its friendly inns and beer-houses has been called 'the longest bar-counter in Europe'. The opera house ('Deutsche Oper am Rhein') and the theatre are among Europe's leading houses. Other important elements in the city's life are the exhibitions of the Academy of Art, the fashion shows presented by the Fashion College, the brilliant literary and political cabaret "Kom(m)ödchen", the Carnival and the 'Radschläger' (the small boys who turn cartwheels for their own or for visitors' pleasure – and have even had a memorial dedicated to them).

*Königsallee

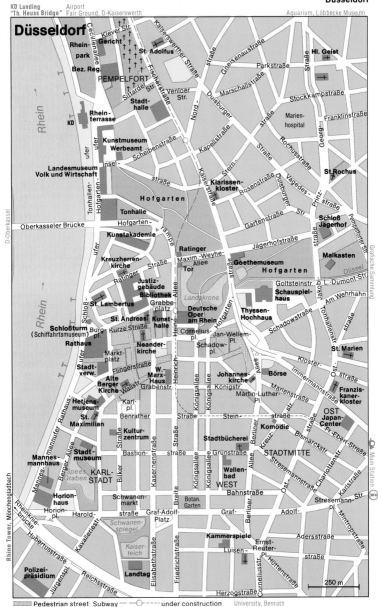

Aquarium, Löbbecke Museum

KD Landing
"Th. Heuss Bridge"

Airport
Fair Ground, D-Kaiserswerth

Düsseldorf

Rhein-
park

Bez. Reg.

Klever Str.

Gericht

St. Adolfus

PEMPELFORT

Sittarder Str.

Rhein-
terrasse

Stadt-
halle

KD

Kaiserswerther Straße

Fischerstraße

Venloer Str.

Nordstraße

Duisburger Straße

Gneisenaustraße

Parkstraße

Marschallstraße

Stockkampstraße

Hl. Geist

Straße

Georg

Franklinstraße

Marien-
hospital

Kunstmuseum
Werbeamt

Landesmuseum
Volk und Wirtschaft

Rhein

Inselstraße

Scheibenstraße

Kapelstraße

Sternstraße

Kaiserstraße

Rochusstraße

Rosenstraße

Duisburger

Klarissen-
kloster

Vagedes-

Str.

St.Rochus

Prinz-straße

Hofgarten

Tonhalle

Oberkasseler Brücke

Tonhallenstraße

Hofgartenstraße

Kunstakademie

Hofgarten-

Gartenstraße

Str.

Schloß
Jägerhof

Pempelforter Str.

D.-Oberkassel

Kreuzherren-
kirche

Ratinger Straße

Tramp

Ratinger
Tor

Maxim.-Weyhe-
Allee

Jägerhofstraße

Goethemuseum

Malkasten

Düssel

Grafische Sammlung

Rhein

Justiz-
gebäude
Bibliothek

Grabbe-
platz

St. Lambertus

Schloßturm
(Schiffahrtsmuseum)

Burg-
pl.

St. Andreas

Kurze Straße

Neander-
kirche

Landskrone

Deutsche
Oper
am Rhein

Kunst-
halle

Heinrichstraße

Cornelius-
pl.

Hofgartenstraße

Schauspiel-
haus

Thyssen-
Hochhaus

L.-Dumont-Str.

Am Wehrhahn

Tonhallenstraße

Jakobistraße

Schadowstraße

St. Marien

Rathaus

Stadt-
verw.

Markt-
platz

Flingerstraße

Alte
Berger
Kirche

Hetjens-
museum

St.
Maximilian

Rheinuferstraße

W.
Marx-
Haus

Wallstr.

Grabenstr.

Karl-
pl.

Benrather

Neustraße

Mühlenstraße

Jan-Wellem-
pl.

Schadow-
pl.

Johannes-
kirche

Königstr.

Martin-Luther-
Pl.

Kreuzstraße

Schadowstraße

Mertensgasse

Marienstraße

Börse

Immermannstraße

Straße

Franzis-
kaner-
kloster

Komödie

OST
Japan-
Center

Bismarckstr.

Fr.-Ebert-Straße

Main Station

Mannesmannufer

Mannes-
mannhaus

Stadt-
museum

Spee's Graben

KARL-
STADT

Berger Allee

Bilkerstraße

Kasernenstraße

Bastionstraße

Stadtbücherei

Grünstraße

Königsallee

Königsallee

Wellen-
bad

WEST

STADTMITTE

Stresemannstraße

Charlottenstraße

Karlstraße

Horion-
haus

Horion-
pl.

Harold-
straße

Schwanen-
markt

Graf-Adolf-
Platz

Breitestraße

Botan.
Garten

Schwanen-
spiegel

Kaiser-
teich

Kavalleriestr.

Elisabethstraße

Friedrichstraße

Kulturzentrum

Bahnstraße

Graf-

Berliner Allee

Adolf-

Ostsraße

Stresemann-
pl.

Mintropstraße

Polizei-
präsidium

Reichsstraße

Haroldstraße

Fürstenwall

Hubertusstraße

Rheinkniebrücke

Rhine Tower, Mönchengladbach

Landtag

Kammerspiele

Luisen-
str.

Ernst-
Reuter-
Pl.

Corneliusstraße

Hüttenstraße

straße

Adersstraße

Herzogstraße

University, Benrath

250 m

Pedestrian street Subway —O---- under construction

Düsseldorf

History

Around the middle of the 12th c. Düsseldorf was still a small fishing village. In 1288 it was granted a charter by Count Adolf von Berg, and in 1386 Duke Wilhelm II made the town his capital. After the Berg family died out (1609) their territory, the Bergisches Land, passed to Palatinate-Neuburg, and Düsseldorf became the capital of the splendour-loving Elector Johann Wilhelm (known as Jan Wellem, 1679–1716), who laid out the new town, drew many artists to his court and established the picture gallery. His brother and successor Karl Philipp, however, moved his capital to Heidelberg in 1716 and Mannheim in 1720. The foundation of the Academy of Art in 1867 made Düsseldorf a centre of artistic life. In recent years the city's economy has prospered, and a Japanese trade centre has been established here.

Features of interest

Düsseldorf's elegant shopping street and promenade is the Königsallee ('Kö'), lined with high class galleries, shops, restaurants and cafés, which runs on both sides of the former town moat from Graf-Adolf-Platz northward to the Hofgarten. – Parallel to the Königsallee on the W are the Breite Strasse, with banks and the offices of large industrial corporations, and the Heinrich-Heine-Allee, in which is the Wilhelm-Marx-Haus (by W. Kreis, 1924–26), the first tower block in Germany. Farther N are the Opera House (to right) and the Kunsthalle (to left). Behind the Kunsthalle is the Baroque St Andrew's Church. Opposite to the Kunsthalle, to the N, in Grabbeplatz, is the Landesgalerie (art gallery).

To the E of the Königsallee is the wide Berliner Allee, with the Chamber of Industry and Commerce and the Rhineland-Westphalia Stock Exchange. In Jan-Wellem-Platz is the 26-storey Thyssen Building, with the Schauspielhaus (theatre; 1970) close by.

* Jägerhof

In the Hofgarten (laid out in 1767) is the Jägerhof (1752–63), a former hunting lodge which now houses the North Rhine – Westphalia art collection. Nearby is the Malkasten ('Paint-Box'), headquarters of the Society of Artists.

To the W, in the old town, is the Markt, with the Town Hall (Rathaus; by H. Tussmann, 1567–73) and an equestrian statue (1711) of Elector Johann Wilhelm II. ('Jan Wellem'). – In the Nesselrode Palace to the S of the Markt is the Hetjens Museum (ceramics of eight millennia) and beyond this, in the Spee Palace, is the Municipal Museum. To the E, in Bilker Strasse, are the Cultural Centre, with a puppet theatre, and the Heinrich Heine Institute. – Still farther S, on the Rhine, is the Mannesmann Building, and S of the Rheinkniebrücke is the 234 m high Rheinturm (television tower; revolving restaurant with fine view); nearby, the 'Landtag am Rhein' (new Diet Building, under construction).

To the N of the Markt are the 13th c. Schlossturm with the Municipal Museum of Navigation (2000 years of shipping on the Rhine) and St Lambert's Church (13th–14th c.), on the banks of the Rhine. – Still farther to the N of the old town, in and around the Hofgarten, are the Academy of Art (Kunstakademie), the Concert Hall (Tonhalle), the Provincial Museum (Landesmuseum Volk und Wirtschaft; social and economic life) and

* Rheinturm

the Museum of Art (Kunstmuseum). – 2.5 km NW are the

Düsseldorf: Rhine front

Trade Fair Grounds, with the Congress Centre and the Rhine Stadium (seating for 68,000). – In the Nordpark is a Japanese garden.

Some 10 km E of Düsseldorf is the Neandertal, with a prehistoric museum and wild life park. – 16 km NE is the 'Minidomm' leisure park, with models of historic and modern German buildings.
Benrath Castle: see page 129.

Eltville am Rhein   D

State: Federal Republic of Germany
Land: Hessen (Hesse)
Altitude: 89 m above sea level
Population: 16,000

KD excursion ships land on the Rhine bank.

Eltville (from Latin 'Alta Villa'), once the chief place in the Rheingau, is picturesquely situated amid vineyards and has large wine- and Sekt-making establishments.

Of the old castle of the archbishops of Mainz there remains only the massive keep (1487); it now houses a memorial to Gutenberg, who may well have stayed in Eltville. The 14th c. Gothic parish church of SS. Peter and Paul has a tabernacle of the late 14th c., a font of 1517 and Renaissance tombs. – Also worth

Eltville, Features of interest
(continued)

seeing are the large complex of the Hof Langwerth von Sim-
mern, with Late Gothic and Renaissance elements, and the
Baroque Hof Eltz, both nowadays wineries.
Off Eltville is the 2 km long island of the Eltviller Aue in the
Rhine.

Kiedrich

3.5 km NW is Kiedrich, famous for its wine, with the Late Gothic
parish church of St Valentine (15th c.; organ c. 1500).

Emmerich D

State: Federal Republic of Germany
Land: Nordrhein-Westfalen (North Rhine – Westphalia)
Altitude: 19 m above sea level
Population: 32,000

General and
Features of interest

Emmerich, an old Imperial and Hanseatic city (status since
1233), the last German town on the Rhine and the customs post
for shipping on the river.

Rhine bank

In the old town, rebuilt after complete destruction during the
second world war, is the Gothic church of St Aldegund (15th
c.), standing near the Rhine, with a notable interior. Downstream is St Martin's Minster (11th–15th and 17th c.), with the
shrine of St Willibrord (10th c.), the oldest example of the
goldsmith's craft on the Lower Rhine; under the choir is an
11th c. crypt. The Town Hall (1939) contains a 15th c. figure of
St Christopher. – At Martinikirchgang No. 2 is the interesting
Rhine Museum (Rheinmuseum) with numerous models of old
Rhine ships, river maps, technical instruments, etc. – Beautiful
Rhine terrace.

Frankenthal (Pfalz) D

State: Federal Republic of Germany
Land: Rheinland-Pfalz (Rhineland-Palatinate)
Altitude: 96 m above sea level
Population: 44,000

Townscape

Frankenthal, an old town which had a famous porcelain manufactory from 1755 to 1800 (collection of its ware in the Town
Hall), is now a considerable industrial town. It suffered severe
destruction during the second world war, but has preserved
reminders of its flourishing past in the substantial ruins of a
Late Romanesque house of Augustinian canons (12th–13th c.)
and two 18th c. town gates, the Speyrer Tor and the Wormser
Tor.

Freiburg im Breisgau D

State: Federal Republic of Germany
Land: Baden-Württemberg
Altitude: 278 m above sea level
Population: 174,000

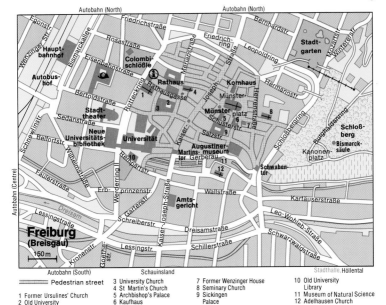

Autobahn (North)   Autobahn (North)

Freiburg (Breisgau)
150 m

Autobahn (South)   Schauinsland   Stadthalle, Höllental

Pedestrian street

1 Former Ursulines' Church
2 Old University

3 University Church
4 St Martin's Church
5 Archbishop's Palace
6 Kaufhaus

7 Former Wenzinger House
8 Seminary Church
9 Sickingen Palace

10 Old University Library
11 Museum of Natural Science
12 Adelhausen Church

General

Freiburg, a commercial and administrative centre, an ancient university town and the see of an archbishop, lies between the Kaiserstuhl and the Black Forest at the point where the Dreisamtal opens into the Upper Rhine plain. It is the gateway to the southern Black Forest. The 1,284 m high Schauinsland, Freiburg's own domestic mountain, lies within the city boundaries, and at its very gates is the wild and romantic Höllental ('Hell's Valley'). Freiburg claims to be 'a city of forests, of Gothic architecture and of wine'. It has what is believed to be Germany's oldest inn, the 'Red Bear' (Zum Roten Bären), the names of its landlords being known as far back as 1311. Characteristic of the town are the charming little streams ('Bächle') flowing along its streets, fed by an abundant supply of water from the hills of the Black Forest.

History

At the end of the 11th c. the Dukes of Zähringen founded below their castle on the Schlossberg a trading and market settlement on the old Black Forest trade route between Swabia and Alsace. The town's favourable situation, its market privileges and the rich deposits of silver in the Black Forest soon gave it a dominant position in the Breisgau. In 1368 the town purchased its freedom from the Counts of Freiburg (who had succeeded the Zähringen family) and submitted itself to the authority of the House of Habsburg. In 1457 Archduke Albrecht founded the University. Later Freiburg acquired importance as a fortress. In 1805, at Napoleon's behest, Freiburg and the Breisgau were ceded by Austria to the newly created Grand Duchy of Baden. In 1827 the town became the see of an archbishop. From 1947 to 1952 it was the seat of the provincial government of Southern

Freiburg, History
(continued)

Baden, but in the latter year was incorporated in the newly established Land of Baden-Württemberg.

Features of interest

The main axis of the city is the Kaiser-Joseph-Strasse, which divides the old part of the town into an eastern half, with the Minster, and a western half, with the Town Hall and the University. Near the S end of the street is the 13th c. Martinstor (St Martin's Gate), which was considerably heightened in 1905.

**Minster

The Minster (13th–16th c.) is one of Germany's greatest masterpieces of Gothic architecture. The high altar, in the choir, has a painting (1512–16) by Hans Baldung Grien, his finest work. In the University Chapel is an altar painting (c. 1521) by Hans Holbein the Younger; and in the aisles are 14th c. stained glass windows. From the platform of the delicately articulated tower (116 m high; begun about 1270) there are magnificent views.

In the Münsterplatz a number of fine old buildings have survived: on the S side (No. 10) the red Merchants' Hall (Kaufhaus, 1532), with an arcade and crow-stepped gables, and (No. 30) the Wenzingerhaus (1761), on the N side the 15th c. Kornhaus.

*Augustinian Museum

In Salzstrasse, housed in an old Augustinian friary, is the Augustinian Museum (Augustinermuseum), with material on the art and culture of Freiburg and the Upper Rhine area. At the end of Salzstrasse is the 13th c. Schwabentor (Swabian Gate).

In the western part of the old town is the Rathausplatz, with the Town Hall (carillon daily at noon), the northern part of which dates from the 16th century. On the NE side of the square is St Martin's Church (Gothic). – In Bertholdstrasse is the Old University (17th/18th c.) and the Roman Catholic University Church (1683–1701). To the W, are the Municipal Theatre (Stadttheater) and the New University Library (1973–78); E of the 'Ring' lie the new university buildings. – In Colombi Park stands the 'Colombischlössle', with the Museum für Ur- und Frühgeschichte (museum of early history).

View of the Minster
from the *Schlossberg

On the Schlossberg (460 m; chair-lift and lift), once occupied by the stronghold of the Zähringen family, are the scanty remains of three castles. From the Kanonenplatz, an old bastion, there is a fine view of the town and the Minster.

Excursions from Freiburg

Attractive excursions from Freiburg are to the summit of Schauinsland (1284 m; cableway), 21 km S; to the Höllental, 20–25 km SE, with the Hirschsprungfelsen (Stag's Leap Crag) and the Ravennaschlucht (Ravenna Gorge); and to the Titisee, 31 km SE.

Geisenheim   D

State: Federal Republic of Germany
Land: Hessen (Hesse)
Altitude: 96 m above sea level
Population: 12,000

Townscape

Geisenheim is an ancient little town and toll collection post for traffic bypassing the rapids at Bingen. It now has a State teaching and experimental institution for viticulture, horticulture and fruit-growing and a number of wine and Sekt establishments. The Roman Catholic parish church (dedicated to the Invention of the Cross – Kreuzauffindung) is known as the 'cathedral of the Rheingau'. Probably founded as early as the 8th c., it was completed in 1518, with two towers of 1638. In front of the Town Hall is a lime-tree (the Gerichtslinde), first mentioned in the records in 1585, under which justice was formerly dispensed (Lime-tree Festival). Geisenheim has a number of handsome aristocratic mansions of the 16th, 17th and 18th centuries. The Longfellow Fountain commemorates a visit by the US-American poet (1807–1882) during his European travels in 1835/36 (see his travel sketches, "Outre-Mer"). – Above the town is the famous Rothenberg vineyard.

Geisenheim (continued)

Conspicuously situated on a vine-clad hill above Geisenheim is Schloss Johannisberg (alt. 185 m), built by Johann Dientzenhofer in 1757–59 on the site of a monastery founded in 1090. It has belonged since 1821 to the Metternich family, who run a famous wine estate here (tasting room; view). The old monastic church, destroyed during an air attack in 1942, was rebuilt after the war. – 1 km N is the ruined castle of Schwarzenstein (fine views).

* Schloss Johannisberg

Germersheim   D

State: Federal Republic of Germany
Land: Rheinland-Pfalz (Rhineland-Palatinate)
Altitude: 105 m above sea level
Population: 13,000

Germersheim, situated at the junction of the river Queich with the Rhine, is the seat of the Department of Applied Linguistics (Interpreters' Institute) of the University of Mainz. It occupies the site of the Roman settlement of 'Vicus Iulii'. The town was re-founded in 1276 by Rudolf I of Habsburg, who died here in 1291 in a castle of which no trace survives. The town's fortifications, rebuilt by Bavaria in 1834, were demolished in 1922/23. Nowadays, Germersheim ranks among the most important shipbuilding places on the Rhine.
The Roman Catholic parish church, originally belonging to a house of the Servite order, dates from the 14th c. but was rebuilt in 1674 after a fire.
Germersheim was also of note, according to an 18th c. antiquary, because "here, as at Seltz, the finest gold is washed out of the sands of the Rhine".

Townscape

Gernsheim   D

State: Federal Republic of Germany
Land: Hessen (Hesse)
Altitude: 90 m above sea level
Population: 8,000

KD cruise land on the Rhine bank (starting and finishing point of the excursions to →Heidelberg)

KD German Rhine Line

Gernsheim, Townscape

Gernsheim is an old boatmen's and fishermen's town on the site of a Roman fort, in the middle of an extensive area devoted to the growing of asparagus. It was the birthplace of Peter Schöffer, who was associated with Gutenberg in the invention of cast metal type; there is a memorial to him (1836) in the market square. The Old Schöffer School houses a local museum. – Not far from Gernsheim is the pilgrims' chapel of Maria Einsiedel (15th c.).

Heidelberg   D

State: Federal Republic of Germany
Land: Baden-Württemberg
Altitude: 110 m above sea level
Population: 134,000

KD German Rhine Line

Excursions to Heidelberg from KD cruise ships' landing-stages at →Speyer or →Gernsheim

General

Heidelberg, the old capital of the Palatinate and an ancient university celebrated in song and poetry, lies at the point where the river Neckar emerges from the hills of the Odenwald into the Rhine plain. Over the old town, caught between the river and the hills, looms its famous castle. The best general view of the town in its beautiful setting is to be had from the Theodor Heuss Bridge or from the Philosophenweg on the other side of the river.

In Heidelberg are the Max Planck Institutes of Nuclear Physics, Medical Research, Astronomy and Foreign Public Law. The products of its industries include printing presses, agricultural machinery, adhesives and sealing materials, and chemical and physical apparatus. Several publishing houses are based in the town.

History

The place first appears in the records in 1196 as a settlement growing up under the protection of a castle. The Counts Palatine made it their residence, and in 1385 Count Ruprecht I founded the University. The present castle was also begun in his time. In 1689 and 1693, during the war over the Palatinate succession, the castle and the town were destroyed, and in 1720 Elector Carl Philipp moved his capital to Mannheim. In 1802 the territory of the Palatinate on the right bank of the Rhine passed to the Margraviate (later Grand Duchy) of Baden. During the second world war Heidelberg escaped damage.

Features of interest

From Bismarckplatz, the Theodor Heuss Bridge (views), the main street (Hauptstrasse; pedestrian zone) runs E for more than 2 km to the Karlstor, a town gate of 1775. In this street is

*Palatinate Museum

the Palatinate Museum (Kurpfälzisches Museum), in the Baroque Palais Morass, with art and historical collections (including the Windsheim Apostles' Altar by Tilman Riemenschneider and a cast of the lower jaw of Heidelberg Man, some 500,000 years old). Farther E are the Church of the Holy Ghost (Heiliggeist-kirche) of 1400–41, formerly the burial-place of the Electors Palatine; the Town Hall (1701–03); the Haus zum Ritter, a fine

Heidelberg, on the Neckar ▶

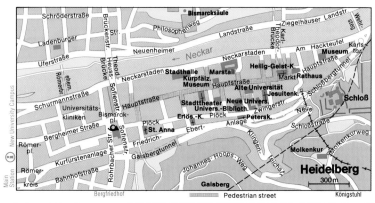

Pedestrian street	

Features of interest
(continued)

Renaissance building of 1592, now a hotel; and the Museum of Ethnography (Völkerkundemuseum), in the Palais Weimar.

To the S of the Hauptstrasse is Universitätsplatz, with the Old University (1711). In the beadle's house on its E side, in Augustinergasse, is the 'Karzer' or student lock-up, used from 1778 to 1914. Adjoining is the New University, built in 1928–31 with American help, and beyond it is the Hexenturm (Witches' Tower), part of the old fortifications. Opposite, in Grabengasse, is

* University Library

the richly stocked University Library (which possesses the 14th c. Manesse Manuscript of medieval songs). The little 15th c. St Peter's Church is now mainly used as the University church. – Farther E, in the Baroque Grand Ducal Palace in Karlsplatz, is the Academy of Sciences. In nearby Pfaffengasse is the birthplace of the first President of Germany, Friedrich Ebert (1871–1925).

Between the Hauptstrasse and the Neckar are the narrow little lanes of the old town. On the Neckarstaden, which runs along the left bank of the river, are the old Hay Barn (Heuscheuer; now lecture-rooms) and the so-called Marstall (now students' Mensa). Downstream is the Congress Centre (formerly Civic

* Old Bridge

Hall), upstream the Karl Theodor Bridge (1786–88) or 'Old Bridge', from which there are fine views.

** Castle

From the Kornmarkt (fine view of the Castle) a funicular (to the Castle, Molkenkur and Königstuhl), the Burgweg (footpath) and the curving Neue Schloss-strasse lead up to the Castle, one of the noblest examples of German Renaissance architecture, built of red sandstone on the terraced hillside (195 m). This once splendid Electoral residence was erected mainly during the reigns of Electors Otto Heinrich (1556–59), Friedrich IV (1583–1610) and Friedrich V (1610–20). Since its destruction by the French (1689 and 1693) it has remained a ruin – in situation, size and picturesque beauty the most magnificent ruin in Germany. On the E side of the E courtyard (performances in summer) is the Ottheinrichsbau (Otto Heinrich Wing), the finest achievement of the early Renaissance period in Germany (1557–66), on the lower floor of which is the German Pharmacy Museum. On the N side of the courtyard are the Gläserner Saalbau (Glass Hall, 1544–49) and the Friedrichsbau, one of the outstanding monuments of the mature Renaissance style in Germany (by Johannes Schoch, 1601–07), with statues of rulers of the Palatinate (originals in the interior). On the W side are the Frauenzimmerbau (Women's Wing, c. 1540), with the Königssaal (concerts), and, set back a little, the Library (c. 1520) and the Gothic Ruprechtsbau (c. 1400). A passage runs under the Friedrichsbau on to the terrace, with fine views. To the left of the Friedrichsbau, lower down, is the Cellar, with the famous Great Tun (Grosses Fass) of 1751, which has a capacity of 2,200 hectolitres; opposite it is a wooden figure of the court fool Perkeo (c. 1728). – From the Great Terrace there is a superb view.

Heidelberg, Castle (continued)

From the Theodor Heuss Bridge the Philosophenweg runs E along the slopes of the Heiligenberg, with a famous view of the town and the castle. Also on the N side of the Neckar are the Zoo and the Botanic Garden.

Attractive excursions from Heidelberg are to the Heiligenberg (443 m), 5.5 km N, with the ruins of St Michael's Church (11th c.); to the Königstuhl (568 m; rack railway), 7 km E, with the 82 m high Television Tower (wide views) and Observatory; to Schloss Schwetzingen, 12 km W, the summer palace of the Electors of the Palatinate in the 18th c., with famous gardens and a Rococo theatre (by Pigage, 1746–52; festival performances); and to Weinheim, 17 km N, with the Schlosspark, a forest of exotic trees and the ruined castles of Windeck and Wachenburg.

Excursions from Heidelberg

*Königstuhl

*Schloss Schwetzingen

Ingelheim am Rhein   D

State: Federal Republic of Germany
Land: Rheinland-Pfalz (Rhineland-Palatinate)
Altitude: 120 m above sea level
Population: 19,000

The town of Ingelheim was formed in 1939 by the amalgamation of the communes of Ober-Ingelheim (Ingelheim-Süd), Nieder-Ingelheim (Ingelheim-Mitte) and Frei-Weinheim (Ingelheim-Nord, with a river harbour). An industrial town (chemicals, pharmaceuticals, etc.) as well as a wine-growing centre, Ingelheim lies in an area of vineyards (famed for their Spätburgunder, a red wine), asparagus fields and orchards. Its best-known son was the theologian, mathematician and cosmographer Sebastian Münster (1488–1552), whose likeness appears on the German 100-mark note.

General and
Features of interest

Model of the Villa Regia

Round the Saalkirche (12th c.) in Nieder-Ingelheim can be seen remains of the Imperial stronghold (Villa Regia) built by Charlemagne and completed by Ludwig (Louis) the Pious. The Roman Catholic parish church of St Remigius, which is mentioned in the records as early as 742, probably belonged to a royal stronghold of the Frankish kings. The early medieval buildings were destroyed by the French in 1689. – Lower down the site of a Merovingian establishment has been identified.

Ober-Ingelheim has preserved its old walls, gates and towers, and has a Romanesque and Gothic church enclosed within a fortified churchyard.

Ingelheim (continued)

In Frei-Weinheim is the town's industrial harbour, with a car ferry across the Rhine to Mittelheim.

Karlsruhe

D

State: Federal Republic of Germany
Land: Baden-Württemberg
Altitude: 116 m above sea level
Population: 272,000

General

Karlsruhe, formerly the residence of the Grand Dukes of Baden, lies near the Rhine in the north-western foothills of the Black Forest, with a characteristic fan-shaped layout centred on the palace. It is the seat of the Federal High Court and Federal Constitutional Court and has a University (College of Technology), an Academy of Art and an Academy of Music, as well as the German Nuclear Research Centre and an Informatics Research Centre. The port on the Rhine, 7 km away, has promoted the establishment of a varied range of industries, including large oil refineries linked with the Marseille-Karlsruhe-Ingolstadt pipeline.

History

Karlsruhe owes its origin to Margrave Karl Wilhelm of Baden-Durlach, who established his new capital here in 1715. It was given its neo-classical stamp by the restrained and elegant buildings, both public and private, erected in the early 19th c. by the architect Friedrich Weinbrenner, who had been trained in Rome. Repeated air raids during the second world war caused heavy destruction, but the damage was made good in a large-scale reconstruction programme. – Karlsruhe was the birthplace in 1785 of Karl von Drais, inventor of a foot-propelled bicycle, and in 1844 of Carl Benz, originator of the petrol engine. He constructed his first petrol-driven vehicle in 1885.

*Schloss

The town's focal point is the Schlossplatz, with the Palace (Schloss), built by Friedrich von Kesslau in 1752–85, partly on the basis of plans by Balthasar Neuman. It now houses the rich Baden Provincial Museum. Behind the palace are the extensive gardens (Schlossgarten). – On the SW side of the Schlossplatz is the State Art Gallery (Staatliche Kunsthalle), with an important collection of pictures. To the N of this is the Federal Constitutional Court (Bundesverfassungsgericht; 1968). – 1 km NE of the Palace is the Wildpark Stadium.

* State Art Gallery

Pyramid

To the S of the Schlossplatz is the Marktplatz, with a 6.50 m high pyramid of red sandstone which has become the emblem of the town; it contains the burial vault of Karlsruhe's founder. On either side of the square, which divides the long Kaiserstrasse into two parts, are the Town Church (Protestant) and the Town Hall, both by Weinbrenner. In the eastern half of the street is the Technical University, founded in 1825. Here Heinrich Hertz discovered electro-magnetic waves in 1885–89.

SW of the Marktplatz, in Friedrichsplatz, is St Stephen's Church (Weinbrenner, 1814). On the S side of the square is the Natural Science Museum (Naturkundemuseum; vivarium), and beyond it, in the Nymphengarten, is the Baden Provincial Library (Badische Landesbibliothek; 1964). To the SW is the old Erb-

Wildpark Stadium

Karlsruhe

Centre

1 State Majolica
  Manufactory Karlsruhe
2 Museum of the Land Baden
3 Orangerie
4 Botanical Garden
5 District Court
6 District Administration
7 District Presidency
8 Youth Centre
9 Industrial Inspection
  of the Land Baden-
  Württemberg (Karlsruhe
  Administration Board)
10 Administration Board
  of the German Federal
  Railways (DB)
11 Surveyor's Office of the Land
12 Main Custom-office
13 Post-office Divisional
  Administration
14 Police Headquarters
15 Concert House
16 Municipal Hall
  (Congress Centre)
17 Nancy Hall
18 Schwarzwald (Black Forest) Hall
19 Garden Hall
20 Vierordtbad (bath)
21 Tullabad (bath)
22 Transportation Museum
23 St John's Church
24 Labour Office
25 St Mary's Church

▨▨▨ Pedestrian street

400 m

grossherzogliches Palais (residence of the heir to the Grand Duchy; 1893–97), now occupied by the Federal High Court. SE of the Marktplatz, near the replanned street intersection at the Ettlinger Tor (Ettlingen Gate), is the Baden State Theatre (1970–75; opera and drama).

Features of interest (continued)

Ettlinger Strasse runs S to the Festplatz, with the Stadthalle (to be converted into a congress and exhibition centre), the Schwarzwaldhalle (Black Forest Hall; 1953/54), an oval glass structure with a boldly contoured roof, and the Nancy Hall

Festplatz

Karlsruhe, Features of interest
(continued)

(1966). – Farther S lies the Stadtgarten (Municipal Park), with the Zoo. – W of the Railway Station is the Europahalle.

Kaub   D

State: Federal Republic of Germany
Land: Rheinland-Pfalz (Rhineland-Palatinate)
Altitude: 79 m above sea level
Population: 1,500

KD German Rhine Line

KD excursion ships land on the Rhine bank.

General and
Features of interest

Statue
of Blücher

Kaub, an old village, formerly a toll-collecting point and traditionally the residence of the Rhine pilots, is still one of the leading wine towns of the Middle Rhine and a centre of the Rhine slate-quarrying trade ('Leien').

Kaub has still well preserved medieval town walls, offering an attractive stroll along the wall-walk. Above the town is Burg Gutenfels (see p. 117). A statue of Marshal Blücher commemorates the crossing of the Rhine by his Silesian army on New Year's Night 1813/14. The pontoon bridge which he threw across the Rhine used the Pfalz as its intermediate point. There is a small Blücher Museum at Metzgergasse No. 6.

Pfalzgrafenstein in the Rhine: see page 117.

Kleve

→Cleves

Koblenz   D

State: Federal Republic of Germany
Land: Rheinland-Pfalz (Rhineland-Palatinate)
Altitude: 60 m above sea level
Population: 114,000

KD German Rhine Line

KD ships land at the Rheinanlagen and Konrad-Adenauer-Ufer.
KD agency: Konrad-Adenauer-Ufer

General

Koblenz, the former residence of the Electors of Trier, is finely situated at the junction of the Mosel (Moselle) with the Rhine. Koblenz is an important traffic junction, the seat of numerous government departments, one of the leading centres of the wine trade on the Rhine and the largest garrison town in the Federal Republic of Germany, with the Federal Agency of Defence Technology and Procurement. The town is dominated by the fortress of Ehrenbreitstein on the right bank of the Rhine. Most spectacular is the summer festival "The Rhine Aflame" (August) with fireworks and illuminations along the river between Koblenz and Braubach.

History

In 9 B.C. the Roman fort of 'Castrum ad Confluentes' was established here to protect the Moselle crossing. In 1018 Koblenz fell into the hands of the archbishops (later Electors) of Trier, who frequently resided here from the 13th to the beginning of the 19th century. The town then became the capital and principal stronghold of the Prussian province of the Rhineland. During the second world war Koblenz suffered considerable destruction. – From 1827 to 1872 the publishing house of Karl Baedeker (1801–1859) was based in Koblenz.

History (continued)

Below the Pfaffendorf Bridge, close to the banks of the Rhine, stands the neo-classical Electoral Palace (Schloss), built by the last Elector of Trier, Clemens Wenceslaus, in 1777–86 (now occupied by government offices; art exhibitions).

Features of interest

Downstream is St Kastor's Church, founded in 836 on a site which was then outside the town; the present building mostly dates from the 12th century. – Beyond this is the 'Deutsches Eck' ('German Corner'), the tongue of land between the Rhine and the Moselle, named after the former House of the Teutonic Order (Deutschherrenhaus; serenades on summer evenings in the 'Blumenhof'). On the point is the Monument to German Unity (fine view, particularly downstream).

*St Kastor

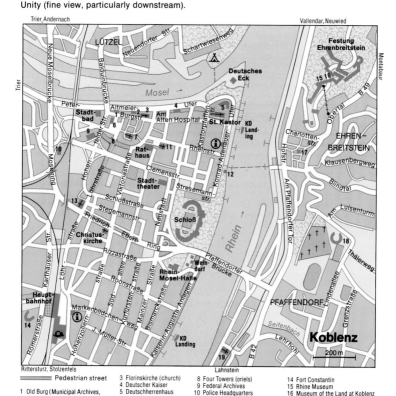

Pedestrian street

1 Old Burg (Municipal Archives, Municipal Library)
2 Museum of the Middle Rhine (Old Kaufhaus, Schöffenhaus)
3 Florinskirche (church)
4 Deutscher Kaiser
5 Deutschherrenhaus with 'Blumenhof'
6 Old Mint
7 St Mary's Church
8 Four Towers (oriels)
9 Federal Archives
10 Police Headquarters
11 Jesuit Church
12 Crane Tower
13 Church of the Heart of Jesus
14 Fort Constantin
15 Rhine Museum
16 Museum of the Land at Koblenz
17 Beethoven Memorial
18 Asterstein Fortress
19 Church of SS. Peter and Paul

Koblenz: junction of the Moselle with the Rhine at the 'Deutsches Eck' (1991)

Features of interest
(continued)

On the highest point of the old town is the Liebfrauenkirche
(Church of Our Lady, 12th–15th c.; R.C.). To the E of this is the
Town Hall (1685–1700). A little way N is the Florinsmarkt, with
the church of St Florinus (12th–14th c.; Protestant) and the
Middle Rhine Museum (Mittelrhein-Museum), in the Altes
Kaufhaus (Old Merchants' House).

On the banks of the Moselle is the old Electoral Castle
(1276–80; Municipal Archives and Library). Close by is the
Balduinbrücke (1343–1420), which crosses the Moselle to the
left-bank suburb of Lützel. Upstream is the New Moselle Bridge
(1954).

From the Electoral Palace the beautiful Rhine Gardens extend
for some 4 km upstream to the island of Oberwerth (bathing
lido, stadium). Above the Pfaffendorf Bridge are the Weindorf
('Wine Village'; built 1925, rebuilt 1951) and the Rhein-Mosel-
Halle.

Surroundings
*Rittersturz

On a steep-sided crag above the Rhine 4.5 km S of Koblenz,
an outlier of the Hunsrück hills, is the Rittersturz viewpoint
(166 m).

Stolzenfels Castle: see page 122.

Köln   D

→Cologne

Königswinter   D

State: Federal Republic of Germany
Land: Nordrhein-Westfalen (North Rhine – Westphalia)
Altitude: 50 m above sea level
Population: 35,000

KD ships' landing-stage and agency: Rheinallee (Rhine bank)   KD German Rhine Line

Königswinter, a popular resort which draws many visitors with   Townscape
its healthy air and its scenic attractions, is delightfully situated
at the foot of the Siebengebirge (see p. 127), and most of
the routes into the hills start from here. From the riverside
promenade there are fine views of Mehlem and the Rodderberg
on the opposite Rhine bank. – Siebengebirge Museum. –
Nibelungs' Hall (Nibelungenhalle), with Dragon's Cave and
Reptile Zoo.
SE of Königswinter is the Drachenfels ('Dragon's Crag'), which
can be ascended on a rack railway (or alternatively on a footpath). This hill, the nearest to the Rhine of the hills of the
Siebengebirge, is closely associated with the legend of Siegfried. The dragon which he killed is said to have lived in a cave

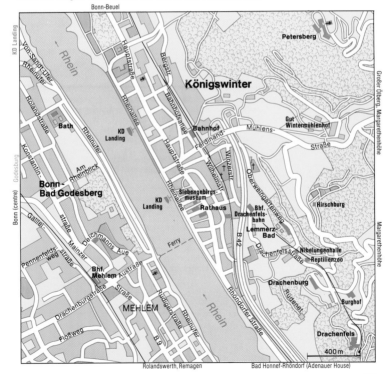

Königswinter (continued)

*Ruins of Burg Drachenfels

on the hill. Less romantically, the trachyte used in the building of Cologne Cathedral was quarried from the slopes of the Drachenfels.

From Königswinter a rack railway 1,520 m long, the first of its kind in Germany when it came into operation in 1883, runs up to the Drachenfels Terrace, with intermediate stations at the magnificent Schloss Drachenburg (19th c.) and the Burghof Hotel and Restaurant, in a hollow below the summit. From the terrace it is a few minutes' walk to the ruins of Burg Drachenfels (321 m), built in 1147 and demolished in 1634. The view from the top is superb, extending as far as Cologne. On the south-western slopes of the hill is the Drachenblut ('Dragon's Blood') vineyard (red wine). – NE of the Drachenfels is the Wolkenburg (324 m). Much of the summit, once crowned by a castle, has been quarried away.

NE of Königswinter rises the wooded Petersberg. The high-lying former Petersberg Hotel served after the second world war as headquarters for the High Commissioners of the West Allies, later on as hotel to lodge state guests. There are plans to convert the building into a guest house of the German Federal Government.

Krefeld D

State: Federal Republic of Germany
Land: Nordrhein-Westfalen (North Rhine – Westphalia)
Altitude: 40 m above sea level
Population: 223,000

General

Krefeld is an industrial town, the main centre of the German velvet and silk industries, which have been established here since the early 18th c.; other major industries are plush manufacture, steel and hardware. There are also a number of agricultural establishments in the town, including the Rhineland College of Agriculture.

Features of interest

The old town, with its regularly planned 18th c. extensions, forms a large rectangle bounded by four wide streets, the Ostwall, Südwall, Westwall and Nordwall.
In the Westwall (Karlsplatz No. 35) is the Kaiser-Wilhelm-Museum (pictures, sculpture, etc.). N of this is the Roman Catholic church of St Dionysius (1754–68), and farther N the Town Hall (Rathaus), in a Schloss of 1795.
In the district of Linn, Andreasmarkt No. 8, is the German Textile Museum (Deutsches Textilmuseum; collection of textiles from all over the world). Also at Linn stands Burg Linn, a 14th c. moated castle, with a 18th c. mansionhouse; nearby a museum (local history, ethnology of the Lower Rhine area, early history).

Lahnstein D

State: Federal Republic of Germany
Land: Rheinland-Pfalz (Rhineland-Palatinate)
Altitude: 70 m about sea level
Population: 19,000

KD excursion ships land at Niederlahnstein and Oberlahnstein.

KD German Rhine Line

Lahnstein, a double town (by consolidation of Oberlahnstein and Niederlahnstein in 1969), is situated on both banks of the river Lahn at its junction with the Rhine.

General

On the left bank, under Burg Lahneck (see p. 121), is Oberlahnstein, with a river harbour and engineering plants. Considerable stretches of the old town walls, with gates and towers, are still preserved. The Old Town Hall (15th c.) is a richly decorated Late Gothic half-timbered building. The Roman Catholic parish church of St Martin (1775) has a 14th c. choir and two Late Romanesque towers. The Mainzer Salhof dates from the 12th c. but was much altered in the 17th century. The Hexenturm ('Witches' Tower') houses the Municipal Museum.

Oberlahnstein

At the SW end of Oberlahnstein is the Martinsschloss, a castle and toll station which belonged to the Elector of Mainz (14th–18th c.). – Above the town to the S is the Liebfrauenkapelle (Chapel of Our Lady) or Wenzelkapelle (Wenceslas Chapel), which was moved to its present site in 1905. In this chapel in August 1400 King Wenzel (Wenceslas) was deposed by the Electors of the Rhineland.

Not far to the E of Oberlahnstein are the 'Kurthermen Rhein-Lahn' (thermal spa, 30 and 36 °C; 'Bad auf der Höhe'); nearby is the 'Naturpark Nassau' (nature reserve).

*Kurthermen

On the right bank of the Lahn, at an important road and rail junction point, is Niederlahnstein. There is evidence of a settle-

Niederlahnstein

Lahnstein: Martinsschloss ...   *... and Burg Lahneck*

Lahnstein, Niederlahnstein
(continued)

ment here in Roman times. Just at the mouth of the Lahn is St John's Church (Johanneskirche), built in the 12th c. on the site of an earlier 9th c. church, burned down in 1794 and restored in the 1850s. Adjoining the church is a Benedictine convent. Nearby are remains of the walls of a 4th c. Roman fort ('burgus') controlling the river.

Three of the town's fine old aristocratic mansions survive – the Heimbachhaus (12th c.), the Arnsteiner Hof (15th c.; now a forestry office) and the Nassauer Hof (16th c.). – At Lahnstrasse 8 is a famous old inn, the 'Wirtshaus an der Lahn', a half-timbered building of 1697 on the site of an earlier 14th c. inn.

To the E of Niederlahnstein, above the right bank of the Lahn, rises the Allerheiligenberg (All Saints' Hill, 157 m), with Stations of the Cross leading up to a monastery and pilgrimage church on the summit of the hill.

Lahr (Schwarzwald)　　　　　　　　　　　　　　　　　　　　D

State: Federal Republic of Germany
Land: Baden-Württemberg
Altitude: 168 m above sea level
Population: 36,000

General

Lahr is a pleasant industrial town on the edge of the Black Forest (Schwarzwald) amid extensive vineyards and tobacco plantations. Since 1801 here is published the popular almanach "Lahrer Hinkender Bote" ("The Lahr Limping Messenger").

Features of interest

Lahr grew up from the mid 13th c. onwards to the N of a castle (burned down in 1677) belonging to the Geroldseck family. The only relic of the castle is the 13th c. Storchenturm (Storks' Tower) which now houses a historical museum. To the E of this is the Early Gothic Abbey Church (13th c.; restored in 19th c.). The Old Town Hall (1608) was remodelled in 1885 in line with the taste of the time. The old part of the town contains a number of handsome houses ranging in date from the 17th to the early 19th century. There is a beautiful municipal park, with a museum of local history. To the W, Dinglinger Hauptstrasse No. 54, a museum of early history.

The Protestant church (12th–15th c.) in the outlying district of Burgheim to the NE has late Gothic wall paintings.

Surroundings

Above the town to the NW, on the Schutterlindenberg (296 m; views), is the so-called 'Constitution Column' (1843).

Lampertheim　　　　　　　　　　　　　　　　　　　　　　　D

State: Federal Republic of Germany
Land: Hessen (Hesse)
Altitude: 92–100 m above sea level
Population: 31,000

Townscape

Lampertheim is first recorded in 832 under the name of 'Langobardenheim' ('Lombard settlement'). Features of interest are the parish church of St Andrew (R.C.; 1770/71), the Town Hall (1738/39) and a number of 18th c. half-timbered houses (Römerstrasse No. 21 a local museum).

Lampertheim, Features of interest

At Neuhaus, 4 km E, is the old hunting lodge of Friedrichsburg, originally built in 1463, destroyed and later rebuilt in the 17th c. and largely demolished in the 18th century. The remains are now incorporated in a chemical factory.

Surroundings of Lampertheim

W of Lampertheim, in an abandoned loop of the Rhine, is the nature reserve and recreation area of Biedensand.

Linz am Rhein   D

State: Federal Republic of Germany
Land: Rheinland-Pfalz (Rhineland-Palatinate)
Altitude: 60 m above sea level
Population: 6,000

KD excursion ships land on the Rhine bank.

KD German Rhine Line

Linz, the 'Colourful Town', a picturesque little town, formerly held by the Electors of Cologne, is situated on the edge of the Westerwald opposite the outflow of the Ahr into the Rhine. The basalt quarried in the surrounding area is shipped from here.

There are many attractive and colourful half-timbered buildings of the 15th–19th c. in the lower town, particularly in the Marktplatz, with the Late Gothic Town Hall (1392), and in the Burgplatz, with Burg Feith (14th c.), once a summer residence of the archbishops of Cologne.

Burgplatz

Of the town's medieval fortifications there survive only some scanty remains of walls and two gate towers (14th-15th c.). Above the town is the Late Romanesque parish church of St Martin (R.C.), which has 13th c. wall paintings and an altarpiece of the Cologne school (1463). From above the church a path runs up the Donatusberg or Kaiserberg (178 m; view).

Some 2 km to the N of Linz is the Burg Ockenfels (hotel).

Lorch am Rhein   D

State: Federal Republic of Germany
Land: Hessen (Hesse)
Altitude: 84 m above sea level
Population: 9,000

KD excursion ships land on the Rhine bank.

KD German Rhine Line

Lorch is an old wine town (wine market referred to in 1274) situated at the mouth of the Wisper valley with its old castles. It occupies the site of a Frankish and Carolingian stronghold, some remains of which are preserved in the courtyard of a house in the market square (No. 1). Until the late medieval period Lorch was the end-point of the 'Merchants' Road' from

General

Lorch, General (continued)	Rüdesheim and Geisenheim which bypassed the rapids in the Binger Loch (Bingen Hole).
Features of interest	The Roman Catholic parish church of St Martin, originally a Romanesque basilican church, has a finely carved high altar (1483). The are a number of old aristocratic mansions, particularly notable being the Hilchenhaus (16th c.). At each end of the bridge over the Wisper (1556) is a round tower; the one at the S end, known as the 'Strunk', was built in 1567 as a prison. The Town Hall (19th c.) houses a little district museum.
Burg Nollig	Above the town, surrounded by vineyards, is Burg Nollig or Nollich (alt. 252 m; private property), a relic of the town's fortifications, of which some other fragments have survived. From the castle there are fine views, particularly of the Lorcher Werth, a long narrow island in the Rhine.
Wisper valley	There is an attractive road up the wooded Wisper valley (31 km), passing the ruined castles of Rheinberg, Kammerburg and Geroldstein, to Bad Schwalbach.

Ludwigshafen am Rhein   D

	State: Federal Republic of Germany Land: Rheinland-Pfalz (Rhineland-Palatinate) Altitude: 85 m above sea level Population: 160,000
General	Ludwigshafen, a modern industrial town, was founded by King Ludwig I of Bavaria in 1843 on the site of an old fortification, the Rheinschanze (1606). It is known throughout the world as the headquarters of BASF (Badische Anilin- und Sodafabrik). Early in 1984 in Ludwigshafen the first cable television project of the Federal Republic of Germany was started.
Features of interest	In the Town Hall Centre is the Municipal Museum (reopened in 1984), in Berliner Strasse (No. 23) the Wilhelm Hack Museum (Municipal Art Collection).
	In the suburb of Oggersheim are the pilgrimage church of the Assumption (Mariä Himmelfahrt, 1774–77) and a house (Schillerstrasse No. 6) in which Schiller lived for some time.

Mainz   D

	State: Federal Republic of Germany Land: Rheinland-Pfalz (Rhineland-Palatinate) Altitude: 82 m above sea level Population: 186,000
KD German Rhine Line (cf. p. 263)	KD excursion ships land at the Adenauerufer (Town Hall).
General	Mainz, the capital of the Land of Rheinland-Pfalz (Rhineland-Palatinate) and a university town, is situated on the left bank of the Rhine opposite the mouth of the Main. It is a historic old town, a former Electoral residence and see of an archbishop

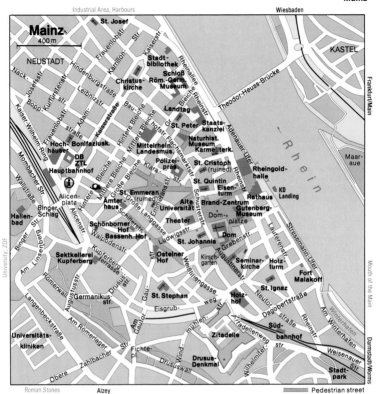

(nowadays of a bishop), and also the city of Gutenberg. It lies in the fertile Mainz basin, the northern part of the Upper Rhine plain, and is the focal point of the western end of the Rhine-Main economic region – a centre of the Rhine wine trade, an important traffic junction and commercial and industrial centre, with the headquarters of radio and television corporations (ZDF, SWF) and publishing houses. It is also one of the great strongholds of the Rhineland Carnival ('Fassenacht').

In 38 B.C. the Romans established the fort of 'Moguntiacum' close to a Celtic settlement, and from about 10 A.D. this was the chief stronghold and headquarters of the military commandant of Upper Germany (Germania Superior).

Since late in the 1st c. A.D. already, a solid bridge crossed the Rhine to the right bank of the river, where the 'Castellum Mattiacorum' (Kastel) protected the bridge-head.

In 742 St Boniface founded the archbishopric, and Mainz became the metropolis of Christianity in Germany. The building of the Cathedral was begun in 1975 under Archbishop Willigis. In

Bridge crossing the Rhine between Mainz and Kastel, depicted on a leaden medaillon found near Lyon in the river Saône (4th c. A.D.; Bibl. Nat., Paris)

Panoramic view of Mainz

1184 the Emperor Frederick Barbarossa held a splendid Imperial festival on the Maaraue. The town – 'Golden Mainz', Aurea
Moguntia – reached its peak of prosperity in the 13th c. as the
chief town of the Rhenish League of Cities, established in 1254.

Around 1450 Johannes Gutenberg, the inventor of printing with
movable type, set up his press in Mainz. The town lost all its
privileges in 1462 as a result of a dispute with the ecclesiastical
authorities. In 1476–77 the University was founded by Archbishop Diether von Isenburg. During the Thirty Years War
Mainz was taken by the Swedes. The heyday of the Electorate of
Mainz was in the 17th and 18th c., when the town took on a
Baroque stamp. In 1792 Mainz was declared a republic, and
Goethe gives an eye-witness account of the devastating bom-
bardment of the town in that year. In 1801 it became chief town
of the French département of Donnersberg, in 1816 capital of
the province of Rheinhessen (Rhine-Hesse). During the second
world war fourfifths of the old town was destroyed. The city
became capital of the Land of Rhineland-Palatinate in 1950.

Features of interest in Mainz
**Cathedral

In the centre of Mainz stands the six-towered Cathedral of SS.
Martin and Stephen (begun 975; mostly 11th–13th c.), which
ranks with the cathedrals of Speyer and Worms as one of the
supreme achievements of Romanesque religious architecture
on the Upper Rhine; it contains some notable bishops' tombs.
In the cloister is the Cathedral and Diocesan Museum. On the N
side of the Cathedral are the Domplätze (Cathedral Squares),
newly laid out in 1975, with a Market Fountain of 1526. At the

**Gutenberg Museum

NE corner is the Gutenberg Museum, a museum of world printing (42-line Gutenberg Bible of 1452–55; reproduction of
Gutenberg's printing-house). Behind it is the 'Brand' shopping
centre (1974), and beyond this, on the banks of the Rhine, the
Town Hall (Rathaus, 1970–73) and the Rheingoldhalle (1968).
During constructional work near here in 1982 eleven Roman
ships were brought to light and preserved. A little way upstream, in the Rheinallee, are two relics of the medieval fortifications, the Eisenturm (Iron Tower, c. 1240) and the Holzturm
(Wooden Tower, 14th; 1802/03 prison of Schinderhannes before his execution).

To the S of the Cathedral, in the old town wiht its narrow
streets and half-timbered houses, are two handsome Baroque
churches, the Seminary Church and St Ignatius's. – In Guten-
bergplatz (latitude 50° N marked on the roadway), opposite the
Theatre, is a statue of Johannes Gutenberg (1398–1468), who

invented the art of printing with movable type about 1440. To the W, in Schillerplatz, are handsome old aristocratic mansions and the Carnival Fountain (1966). – To the S, higher up, is the Gothic St Stephen's Church (14th c.), with windows by Chagall.

Mainz, Features of interest (continued)

*St Stephen

Just below the bridge over the Rhine is the former Electoral Palace (17th–18th c.), with fine state apartments; it now houses the Roman-Germanic Central Museum. Opposite it, to the SE, are the Landtag (parliament of the Land), formerly the House of the Teutonic Order, and the Staatskanzlei (Land government offices). To the N of the palace is the Municipal Library, to the NW the large Christuskirche (Protestant; 1903). – In the street called Grosse Bleiche is the twin-towered St Peter's Church (originally 1752–56). In the former Court Stables (1765–71) is the Middle Rhine Provincial Museum (Mittelrheinisches Landesmuseum; antiquities, pictures). A little way E is the Natural History Museum (Naturhistorisches Museum).

*Roman-Germanic Central Museum

*Middle Rhine Provincial Museum

The Theodor Heuss Bridge (1950) leads over the Rhine to Kastel, formerly a suburb of Mainz, now part of Wiesbaden. – On the plateau W of the city is the campus of the Johannes Gutenberg University, to the SE of which are the Römersteine (Roman Stones; remains of an aqueduct of the Ist c. A.D.).

*Roman Stones

Between the western suburbs of Mombach and Gonsenheim is the Mainzer Sand nature reserve, with interesting steppe flora.

*Mainzer Sand

On the Lerchenberg (205 m), 7 km SW of the city centre, is the Television Centre of the Zweites Deutsches Fernsehen (ZDF; 'Second German Television').

ZDF

Mannheim

D

State: Federal Republic of Germany
Land: Baden-Württemberg
Altitude: 97 m above sea level
Population: 303,000

KD cruise ships land at the Rheinkai (Lindenhof).
KD agency →Speyer

KD German Rhine Line

Mannheim, the former capital of the Elector of the Palatinate, has developed into an important commercial and industrial

General

Schloss

History

city, thanks to its favourable situation on the right bank of the Rhine at the outflow of the canalised Neckar. Here Drais demonstrated his first foot-propelled bicycle in 1817, Benz his first motor vehicle in 1885. Mannheim has one of the largest inland ports in Europe, and at Bonadis Dock ist the world's largest oil-mill.

A notable feature of the central area of the town is its regular grid pattern, in which each block is designated by a letter and a number. Mannheim has numerous educational and cultural institutions, including the University, the Academy of Music and Drama, and several colleges.

The town grew out of the boatmen's and fishermen's village of 'Mannheim' ('Manno's home'), first recorded in 766, which was situated on the high bank of the Rhine where the Electoral Palace now stands. In 1606 Elector Friedrich IV built a Dutch-style fortress on the site of the village and established a trading settlement, which obtained its municipal charter in 1607. During the war over the Palatinate succession the French General Mélac devastated the Palatinate and destroyed Mannheim.

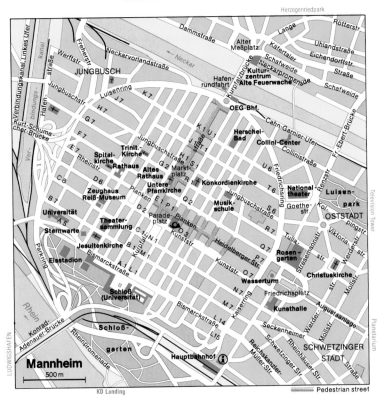

Mannheim

500 m

Thereafter Elector Johann Wilhelm had the town rebuilt in 136 regular blocks; and the town and fortress were now brought together and enclosed within a common circuit of fortifications. In 1720 Elector Karl Philipp moved his principal residence from Heidelberg to Mannheim, and the present palace was built on the site of the old citadel. Karl Philipp and his successor Karl Theodor attracted leading French and Italian architects and artists to their court, and a Palatinate Academy of Sciences was founded in 1763.

This cultural flowering came to an end when Karl Theodor (who had become Elector of Bavaria in 1778) moved his capital to Munich. Under the treaty of Lunéville (1801) the Palatinate territory of the right bank of the Rhine passed to Baden, that on the left bank to France, and Mannheim became a frontier town. At the Congress of Vienna (1815), however, Bavaria recovered the left-bank territory, and King Ludwig I founded Ludwigshafen in that territory in 1843.

The opening up of the Rhine to shipping made Mannheim the terminal point of traffic on the Upper Rhine and set it on the way to further economic progress. The port facilities were developed and improved between 1843 and 1876. During the second world war both the town and the port suffered severe destruction, and post-war rebuilding has given them a very modern aspect.

Near the bank of the Rhine ist the Baroque Electoral Palace (Schloss; 1720–60), one of the largest in Germany. It is now occupied by the University and the District Court. – NW of the Palace is the Jesuit Church (1760), to the N of which are the Theatre Collection and the Arsenal (Zeughaus, 1777–78), now housing the Reiss Museum (archaeology, ethnography, history of the town).

In the spacious Friedrichsplatz (fountains) are the Water Tower (1888), Mannheim's emblem and landmark; the Rosengarten Hall (N side); and the Kunsthalle (Art Gallery; N side), with an excellent collection of paintings and sculpture of the 19th and 20th centuries.

'To the N of Friedrichsplatz, in Friedrichsring, is the National Theatre (rebuilt 1955–57; Grosses Haus and Kleines Haus), originally erected in 1779 N of the Palace and famous for the first performances of Schiller's plays "Die Räuber", "Fiesco", and "Kabale und Liebe" (1782 and 1784).

To the E is the Luisenpark, with a floating stage, animal preserves and a 205 m high Television Tower (1975; revolving restaurant at c. 125 m). At the east end of the Augustaanlage (avenue) is the new Planetarium. – On the opposite bank of the Neckar stretches the Herzogenriedpark, with a modern multi-purpose hall, an open-air bath and a cycle racing track.

Water Tower

The port of Mannheim comprises the Handelshafen (commercial habour; on the 3 km long head-land between Rhine and Neckar), the Industriehafen (industrial harbour; N of the Neckar), the Rheinauhafen (11 km upstream at Rheinau) and the Altrheinhafen (Old Rhine harbour), with the oil harbour (on Friesenheim Island). Harbour tours start at the Kurpfalzbrücke (left Neckar bank).

Mannheim harbours

Maria Laach

* Maria Laach Abbey

State: Federal Republic of Germany
Land: Rheinland-Pfalz (Rhineland-Palatinate)
Altitude: 285 m above sea level

Maria Laach is an abbey ('Sancta Maria ad lacum' = 'St Mary by the lake') on the shores of the Laacher See in the Vordere Eifel (NW of Koblenz). The abbey was founded in 1093 and has been occupied since 1892 by Benedictines from Beuron in Württemberg (Benedictine Academy). The Romanesque basilica (built between 1093 and 1250, consecrated 1156, restored 1956) is one of the finest medieval churches in the Middle Rhine area. In the W choir is the Early Gothic tomb of the founder, Count Palatine Heinrich II (c. 1280).

Laacher See

The beautiful forest-fringed Laacher See is the largest of the many volcanic crater lakes (maars) in the Eifel, with an area of 331 hectares (2.4 km long, 1.8 km wide, up to 53 m deep).

Round the lake are more than forty lava vents and four old volcanoes: to the N the Veitskopf (427 m), to the W the Laacher Kopf (445 m), to the S the Thelenberg (400 m) and to the E the Krufter Ofen (463 m).

Middelburg

State: Netherlands
Province: Zeeland (Zealand)
Altitude: sea level
Population: 38,500

General

Middelburg, the capital of the Dutch province of Zeeland (Zealand), is situated in the middle of the former island of Walcheren on the Veere-Vlissingen Canal and enclosed by a star-shaped moat. It is an important market town and the centre of an extensive farming region. Other major contributions to the economy are made by the tourist and holiday trade and by industry (electrical engineering, chemicals, metal processing, etc.).

History

Middelburg received its municipal charter in 1217 and developed during the Middle Ages into an important commercial town, famed for its cloth industry and as an entrepot for French goods. Towards the end of the 16th c. the silting-up of the river Arne made it increasingly difficult to use the harbour, and thereafter the town declined. The old town was badly hit during the second world war, but almost all the fine old buildings destroyed were rebuilt after the war in their original style.

Features of interest

In the Markt is the 16th c. Town Hall (Stadhuis), once one of the finest Gothic secular buildings in the country. On the façade (1512/13) are 25 figures of Counts and Countesses of Zealand and Holland. To the W of the Town Hall is the Schuttershof (1590), now housing a Museum of Modern Art. Farther S is the Kloveniersdoelen (1607–11), the Hall of the Corporation of Arquebusiers.

NE of the Markt is the oldest part of the town, in the form of a circle. In the Groenmarkt is the Nieuwe Kerk or Abdij, an old abbey church (Reformed), with an 85 m high tower known as 'Lange Jan' (carillon). On the N side of the church is the abbey (Abdij, 13th-16th c.), built round the Abdijplein. In the NW range of buildings is the Zealand Museum.

On the N side of the town, on the Molenwater, is Miniatuur Walcheren, a model of the former island. – Nearby is the Koepoort, the only one of the eight town gates to survive (re-built 1735). – To the SE is the Baroque Oostkerk (1647–67); reformed.

Some 7 km N of Middelburg is the picturesque little town of Veere, which attracts many artists. It was extremely prosperous in the 15th and 16th c., when it had a monopoly of the import of Scottish wool, with a trading post (staple) established by Scottish merchants. From this period of prosperity the town, now shrunk to less than a twentieth of its former population, has preserved a number of handsome burghers' houses, in-cluding in particular the Schotse Huizen or Scottish Houses (museum), the Town Hall (in Flamboyant Gothic style), a large church and a fine draw-well constructed to meet the Scottish merchants' need of clean water for washing their wool.

Middelburg,
Features of interest
(continued)
*Abbey

Surroundings of Middelburg
*Veere

Mulhouse

F

State: France
Région: Alsace
Département: Haut-Rhin (Upper Rhine)
Altitude: 240 m above sea level
Population: 120,000

Mulhouse, situated on the river Ill and the Rhône-Rhine Canal (Canal du Rhône au Rhin), is the largest city in Alsace after Strasbourg, with a port, an industrial zone and a university. After an eventful history the town finally became part of France in 1798.

General

The central feature of the old town is the market square, with the Town Hall (1552), a handsome Renaissance building; the council chamber has 16th and 17th c. stained glass recalling the town's connections with Switzerland. There are several museums and a zoological and botanical garden.

Features of interest

The most unusual of the museums is the National Automobile Museum (Musée National de l'Automobile; 2 km from the town centre in the Avenue de Colmar), founded by the two Swiss brothers Schlumpf and taken over by the workers of their textile factory in 1977, which contains some 600 veteran and vintage cars from many different countries, including more than 1,000 Bugattis. Equally interesting is the French Railway Museum (Musée Français du Chemin de Fer) in the suburb of Dornach, with locomotives and rolling stock from 1844 to the present day. Other museums are devoted to textile printing, art, history (in the Town Hall) and mineralogy. In the Place de l'Europe is the 31-storey Tour de l'Europe (revolving restaurant on top floor).

*Automobile Museum

*Railway Museum

Neuss   D

* St Quirinus

State: Federal Republic of Germany
Land: Nordrhein-Westfalen (North Rhine – Westphalia)
Altitude: 40 m above sea level
Population: 149,000

Neuss, an industrial town and port at the junction of the river
Erft with the Rhine, was once a member of the Hanse. It takes
its name from the Roman legionary fort of 'Novaesium', established at Grimlingshausen in Augustus's time (first record in
16 B.C.).

Near the Marktplatz is the Cathedral of St Quirinus (a Roman
soldier who was converted to Christianity), the finest Late
Romanesque church on the Lower Rhine (begun 1209), with a
central tower and four modern E towers. Below the church, the
interior of which is mostly modern, is a large 12th c. crypt.

On the E side of the Marktplatz is the old Arsenal (Zeughaus),
originally built in 1639 as a conventual church; it was converted
into a concert hall in 1928.

At the S end of the town are the twin-towered Obertor (Upper
Gate; 13th c.); in an annex is the Clemens Sels Museum (1975;
Roman antiquities, town history, fine arts and industrial art).
Not far to the S, on the Nordkanal, is the Stadthalle (Municipal
Hall).

Neuwied   D

State: Federal Republic of Germany
Land: Rheinland-Pfalz (Rhineland-Palatinate)
Altitude: 62 m above sea level
Population: 60,000

KD German Rhine Line

KD excursion ships land on the Rhine bank.

General

Neuwied is an industrial town in the fertile Neuwied basin, on
the site of a Roman fort. It is protected from flooding by large
dykes (water depth gauge).

Neuwied was laid out on a regular plan from 1662 onwards after
its foundation by Count Friedrich von Wied-Neuwied, who
brought in new settlers (including many Protestants and Mora-
vian Brethren) in 1653 to reoccupy the site of the town of
Langendorf which had been destroyed during the Thirty Years
War.

Features of interest

Set in a beautiful park is a palace modelled on Versailles, built
between 1706 and 1756 in place of an earlier 17th c. house.

Other features of interest are the meeting-house of the Mora-
vian Brethren (1783–85) and the Mennonite church (1768).

In the district of Altwied, in a bend of the little river Wied, are the
ruins of Burg Altenwied (12th c.).

Nierstein

D

State: Federal Republic of Germany
Land: Rheinland-Pfalz (Rhineland-Palatinate)
Altitude: 89 m above sea level
Population: 6,000

Nierstein, a little town famous for its wine, is situated on the Rhine in a valley basin which has been continuously inhabited since Neolithic times.

General

The parish church of St Martin (Protestant) dates from the 12th c. but has been much rebuilt and altered following repeated destruction in the 16th-18th century. The Roman Catholic parish church of St Kilian goes back to Carolingian times, but was rebuilt in the 18th century. – In the chapel of a castle which belonged to the Dalberg-Herding family (now a malthouse) are wall and ceiling paintings by Jakob Götzenberger (1839–42) in the Nazarene manner (a style developed by a school of German artists in Rome). In the market square are a handsome Baroque house, the Haxthäuser Hof, and the Old Town Hall, which houses a museum of paleontology.

Features of interest

On a hill to the N of Nierstein is an old watch-tower. – 3 km SW of the town, in the middle of vineyards, is the keep of the Schwabsburg, an old castle which was reduced to its foundations in 1799.

Vineyards at Nierstein

Nijmegen

NL

State: Netherlands
Province: Gelderland
Altitude: 10–25 m above sea level
Population: 147,000

KD cruise ships land at the Waalkade.

KD German Rhine Line

Nijmegen, situated on the left bank of the Waal, the southern arm of the Rhine in the last part of its course to the sea, is, like its neighbour →Arnhem, one of the two gateways of the Netherlands on the Lower Rhine. Above it rise seven hills, the terraced slopes of which look from a distance like the tiers of some gigantic amphitheatre. Nijmegen has a Roman Catholic university and is also a considerable industrial town (metal processing, electrical equipment, textiles, foodstuffs, chemicals). The port of Nijmegen makes it one of the most important points on the inland waterway between the Ruhr and Rotterdam.

General

Nijmegen was a Roman settlement, originally called 'Batavodurum' and later 'Noviomagus'. In the Carolingian period it was an Imperial residence, and later became a free Imperial city and a Hanseatic town. In 1579 it joined the Union of Utrecht. In 1585 it surrendered to the Spaniards, but in 1591 was retaken by Maurice of Nassau. In 1678 the peace treaty between France and the Netherlands was signed here. The town's period of prosperity began only with the development of industry in the latter part of the 19th c., after the demolition of the old fortifica-

History

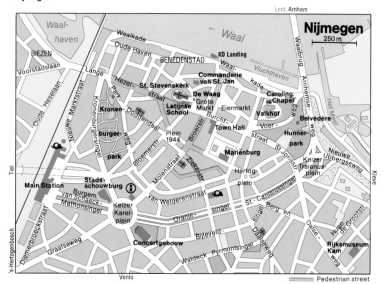

Nijmegen
250 m

Pedestrian street

History (continued)

tions in 1877–84. It suffered heavy damage during the second world war, particulary in the central area, but this was soon made good after the war.

Features of interest

In the centre of the old town is the Grote Markt, with the Waag (Weigh-House, 1612). From here the Kerkboog, a 16th–17th c. arch, leads W to the Grote Kerk or St. Stevenskerk (13th–15th c.; Reformed church), in the choir of which is the tomb of Catherine of Bourbon (d. 1469), wife of Duke Adolf of Guelders. – In the Kerkhof is the old Latin School (1544).

To the N of the Grote Markt is the Commandery of St John (1196; Municipal Museum). – E of the Grote Markt, in the busy Burchtstraat, is the Town Hall (1554, with much later alteration). – Burchtstraat continues E to the Valkhof, an attractive park on a hill above the Waal. This was the site of the Imperial stronghold established by Charlemagne in 768, which was frequently the residence of the court under the Saxon, Frankish and Hohenstaufen emperors. Here the Empress Theophano, wife of Otto II, died in 991, and here Henry VI, son of Frederick Barbarossa and Beatrice of Burgundy, was born in 1165. All that remains of the palace is the Carolingian chapel (consecrated by Pope Leo III in 799) and, to the SE of this, the ruins of a Romanesque choir apse believed to date from the time of Barbarossa (1155). From the chapel there is an attractive view over the Waal plain.

To the E of the Valkhof, at the N end of the Hunnerpark, is the Belvedere, a 16th c. tower. From the Hunnerpark there is an impressive bridge, 700 m long, over the Waal to the suburb of Lent (view of Nijmegen). – At Museum Kamstraat No. 45 is the Rijksmuseum Kam (antiquities from the Nijmegen area).

Grote Markt

Some 4 km SE is the Heilig-Land-Stichting, with faithful reproductions of the Holy Places of the New Testament.
4 km beyond this is the holiday resort of Berg en Dal (Museum
of Africa).

Oberwesel

D

State: Federal Republic of Germany
Land: Rheinland-Pfalz (Rhineland-Palatinate)
Altitude: 80 m above sea level
Population: 4,500

KD excursion ships land on the Rhine bank.

KD German Rhine Line

Oberwesel, the Roman 'Vosavia', was known until the 17th c.
merely as Wesel: an old wine town which extends in a wide arc
along the hillside above the left bank of the Rhine, with the
Schönburg looming over it. With its picturesque old houses
(16th-18th c.) and its beautiful setting it is a town of great
charm.

General

Oberwesel is still surrounded by a circuit of 13th and 14th c.
walls, with 16 of its original 21 towers. At the NE corner is the
massive round tower known as the Ochsenturm (Ox Tower, c.
1400). At the upper entrance to the town is the Roman Catholic
parish church of Our Lady (Liebfrauenkirche; 1308–31), exter-
nally plain but with a sumptuous interior (choir screen of 1350,
high altar of 1331, a fine Baroque organ and other works of art).

Features of interest
*Town walls

*Liebfrauenkirche

View of Oberwesel

Oberwesel,
Features of interest
(continued)

On the town walls on the lower side of the town is the trim little Gothic chapel of St Werner (or Hospital Chapel; c. 1300). On the hill is the Roman Catholic parish church of St Martin (14th c.), with a fortress-like tower.

In the centre of the town are the ruins of a Minorite house founded in the 13th century.

Oppenheim   D

State: Federal Republic of Germany
Land: Rheinland-Pfalz (Rhineland-Palatinate)
Altitude: 84 m above sea level
Population: 5,000

General

Oppenheim is picturesquely situated above the left bank of the Rhine on the slopes of an outlier of the Alzey hills. The Roman settlement of 'Bauconica' and later a free Imperial city, it is now a centre of the wine trade, in an area producing the excellent wines of Rheinhessen, with a State institute of teaching and research in viticulture and fruit-growing.

Features of interest
* St Catherine

Standing on higher ground above the market square is St Catherine's Church (Protestant), with a nave which is one of the finest examples of High Gothic architecture on the Upper Rhine (1330–40). The W towers and the E choir date from the 13th c., the W choir from the 15th. The church has beautiful stained glass (rose window of 1360) and 15th and 16th c. gravestones. On the N side is a charnel-house. – In Wormser Strasse is the interesting German Museum of Viticulture.

Above the church are the ruins of the old Imperial stronghold of Landskrone (alt. 167 m; wide views).

Rastatt   D

State: Federal Republic of Germany
Land: Baden-Württemberg
Altitude: 120 m above sea level
Population: 37,000

General

Rastatt, situated SW of Karlsruhe, a considerable industrial town (furniture, tools, precision engineering, electrical equipment, textiles, etc.) and an important road and rail junction, lies at the point where the Murg valley opens into the Upper Rhine plain. After its destruction by the French in 1689 the town was rebuilt on a symmetrical plan, and from 1705 to 1751 was the residence of the Margraves of Baden.

Features of interest
* Schloss

The Palace (Schloss), in which the treaty of Rastatt ending the War of the Spanish Succession was signed in 1714, was begun in 1697 (architect D. E. Rossi). It is an elegant Baroque structure with a 230 m long garden front, set in a Baroque park which was laid out at the same time as the palace. The interior has ceiling paintings and stucco ornament by Italian masters. It now houses the Wehrgeschichtliches Museum (Army Museum) and a Freedom Museum (Freiheitsmuseum), established in

1974 to commemorate freedom movements throughout German history. In the richly decorated and furnished palace church (by M. L. Rohrer, 1719–23) is the tomb of Margravine Sibylla Augusta, widow of Ludwig Wilhelm of Baden, who acted as guardian of her sons for 19 years.

Opposite the Palace, at Herrenstrasse No. 11, is the Heimatmuseum (local history; Revolution of 1848).

The main axis of the older part of the town is the wide Kaiserstrasse. Half way along this street are St Alexander's Church (R. C.; by J. P. Rohrer, 1756–64) and the Town Hall (1750); between them are two fountains (Alexius-Brunnen and Johannes-Nepomuk-Brunnen).

At Kuppenheim, 4 km SE of Rastatt, is the summer palace (Lustschloss) of Favorite, built for Margravine Sibylla Augusta in 1710–12 by M. L. Rohrer. The interior gives an excellent impression of the way of life of the period. In the park are the Magdalene Chapel (a hermitage chapel dating from 1717) and the Schlosscafé.

Surroundings of Rastatt
*Lustschloss Favorite

At Ötigheim, 6 km N of Raststatt, is an open-air theatre (performances of folk plays).

Remagen

D

State: Federal Republic of Germany
Land: Rheinland-Pfalz (Rhineland-Palatinate)
Altitude: 65 m above sea level
Population: 14,000

KD excursion ships' landing-stage:
Rheinpromenade (Rhine bank)

KD German Rhine Line

Remagen, finely situated a short distance downstream from the outflow of the Ahr into the Rhine, occupies the site of a Celtic settlement and the Roman fort of 'Rigomagus'.

General

At the lower end of the town is the Roman Catholic parish church of SS. Peter and Paul, in neo-Romanesque style, to which the nave of the old Romanesque church (11th c.) serves as a kind of narthex; the choir dates from the 13th c., the W tower from 1674. Below the church terrace and behind the Town Hall can be seen some remains of the Roman fort.

Features of interest

To the E of the choir of the church is the presbytery, with a Romanesque doorway (12th c.; curious carving), and to the right of this is a passage leading to the picturesque little square known as Am Hof and a Gothic chapel which now houses a local museum (closed at present).

From the river front there is a fine view of the Erpeler Ley; wide views also from the Viktoriaberg (alt. 137 m; 2 km SW).

'Remagen Bridge', Apollinariskirche and Rolandseck with Rolandsbogen →Sights along the Rhine between Basle and Rotterdam.

Apollinariskirche

Rhens

D

State: Federal Republic of Germany
Land: Rheinland-Pfalz (Rhineland-Palatinate)
Altitude: 60 m above sea level
Population: 3,000

KD German Rhine Line

KD excursion ships land on the Rhine bank.

General and
Features of interest

Rhens is an old-world little wine town first recorded in the 9th c., with considerable stretches of its old walls and towers, a town hall of the 16th and 17th c. and a number of fine half-timbered houses of the 16th–18th centuries.

Königsstuhl

On a hill to the N of the town is the Königsstuhl ('King's Seat'; picture see p. 120), a stone structure 6 m high resembling a pulpit, affording a fine view. First mentioned in the records in 1308, pulled down by the French in 1803 and re-erected in 1840–42, using some surviving fragments, this stood until 1921 on the banks of the Rhine at the old meeting-place of the Electors of the Rhineland, where preparations were made for the election of a new emperor. Here in 1338 was founded the 'Electoral Union of Rhense' ('Kurverein von Rhense') establishing the principle that the election of an emperor did not require the Pope's approval.

Rotterdam

NL

State: Netherlands
Province: Zuid-Holland (South Holland)
Altitude: sea level
Population: 568,000 (conurbation 1,000,000)

KD German Rhine Line

KD cruise ships land at the Maasboulevard.
Starting and finishing point of the
KD Rhine cruises
KD agency:
Groenendaal 49 a, NL-3011 SN Rotterdam

General

Rotterdam, in the Dutch province of South Holland, is the second largest city in the Netherlands. It lies on both banks of the southern arm of the Rhine known as the Nieuwe Maas (New Maas), which here receives a small tributary, the Rotte. The river is tidal for a long way above the city, with a difference of 1.20 to 2.50 m between high and low tide.

Since its Europoort came into operation in 1966 Rotterdam has been the world's largest port in terms of goods handled. As a consequence of its function as a port the city has developed into a gigantic centre of transit trade and industry, and its potential for growth is still far from exhausted. Its imports include oil, minerals, grain, timber and fats; its main exports are coal and foodstuffs. It is also an important transhipment point for raw tobacco. Its main industries are shipbuilding (with the largest shipyard in Europe), engineering, the manufacture of cars and bicycles, electrical engineering, petrochemicals, foodstuffs, clothing and papermaking. The city owes its rapid de-

*Euromast

Rotterdam harbour scene

velopment to its very favourable situation on a waterway having access to the North Sea throughout the year without any intervening locks. Ships up to 90,000 tons and drawing up to 12 m can enter the seaport; and Rotterdam is also one of the largest inland ports in Europe.

General
(continued)

Rotterdam developed out of a settlement of the early medieval period. The construction of a canal to the river Schie in the 14th c. linked the town with the then important commercial centre of Delft, from whose prosperity it benefited. This flourishing period saw the birth of the town's most famous citizen, the great humanist Erasmus of Rotterdam (b. about 1467, d. 1536). In 1563 most of the town was destroyed by fire. During the 17th c. it enjoyed a fresh period of prosperity, mainly due to its cloth-making and carpet-weaving industries; at this period the port was of less importance, ranking far behind Amsterdam. Its great expansion began after the separation of Belgium from Holland, when the Dutch closed the Schelde (1830–39). The obstacle to the passage of large sea-going vessels by the silting-up of the Maas estuary was removed in 1866 by the construction and later the constant deepening of the Nieuwe Waterweg (New Waterway), and at the point where this entered the North Sea the new suburb of Hoek van Holland (Hook of Holland) grew up. – Rotterdam was almost completely destroyed by German bombing in 1940, and after the war was rebuilt as an entirely modern city.

History

Rotterdam's principal street is the wide Coolsingel, in which stands the Town Hall (Stadhuis, 1914–20), with an imposing tower (carillon). – Beyond the street called the Meent is the

Features of interest

207

Rotterdam

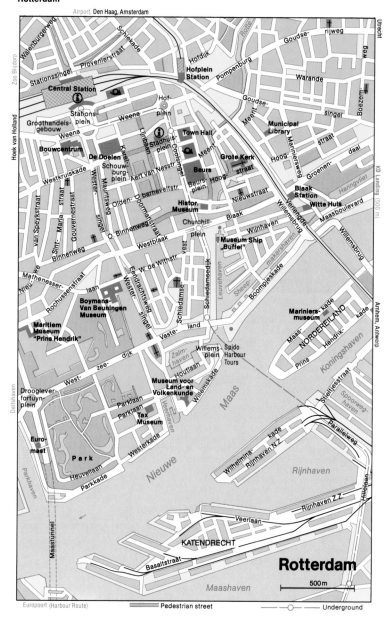

Utrecht

Zoo Blijdorp

Walenburgerweg

Schiekade

Proveniersstraat

Stationssingel

Hofdijk

Route

Goudse-

rijweg

Hofplein
Station

Pompenburg

Warande

Boezem-

Central Station

Stationsplein

Weena

Hofplein

Goudse-

singel

Hoek van Holland

Groothandelsgebouw

Weena

Bouwcentrum

Stations-
plein

De Doelen

Schouwburgplein

Karel

Kruisplein

Westkruiskade

Wester-singel

Mauritsweg

Aert van Nesstraat

Lijnbaan

Stadhuisplein

Town Hall

Coolsingel

Meent

**Municipal
Library**

Marniersweg

Hoog

straat

Groenen-

daal

Grote Kerk

Beurs

Beursplein

Hoog

Nieuwstraat

Blaak

**Blaak
Station**

Witte Huis

Glashaven

Haringvliet

Maasboulevard

KD Landing (500 m)

van Speykstraat

Sint-Maria-straat

Gouvernestraat

Olden-

Doormanstraat

barneveltstraat

**Histor.
Museum**

Churchillplein

Blaak

Wijnhaven

Willemsbrug

Anheim, Antwerp

Mathenesserlaan

Rochussenstraat

Binnenweg

O. Binnenweg

Westblaak

W. de Withstr.

Eendrachtsweg

Wester-singel

Schiedamsedijk

Schiedamse-

land

W. de Withstr.

**Museum Ship
„Buffel"**

Leuvehaven

Sheep-

Boompjeskade

makershaven

Nieuw-

**Boymans-
Van Beuningen
Museum**

Vasteland

**Mariniers-
museum**

Maas-

kade

NOORDEREILAND

Hendrik-

kade

Koningshaven

**Maritiem
Museum
„Prins Hendrik"**

dijk

zee-

Zalm-
haven

Willemsplein

Houtlaan

Willemskade

**Spido
Harbour
Tours**

Prins

Delfshaven

Drooglever-
fortuynplein

West-

Parklaan

Parklaan

Parklaan

Veerhaven

**Museum voor
Land- en
Volkenkunde**

Maas

Staatjesstraat

Spoorweghaven

Parallelweg

Hillelaan

**Tax
Museum**

Westerkade

Wilhelmina-

kade

Rijnhaven N.Z.

**Euro-
mast**

Park

Heuvellaan

Parkkade

Parkkade

Nieuwe

Maashaven

Parkhaven

Maastunnel

Europoort (Harbour Route)

KATENDRECHT

Basaltstraat

Veerlaan

Rijnhaven Z.Z.

Rijnhaven

Rotterdam

500m

▬▬▬ Pedestrian street

——○—— Underground

208

Stock Exchange (Beurs, 1941), and opposite this, to the W, is De Bijenkorf department store (by Marcel Breuer, 1958). In front of this is a 26 m high piece of modern sculpture, Naum Gabo's "Construction" (1957). – Farther S, at the end of the Coolsingel, is the Schielandhuis (17th c.; Historical Museum, closed at present).

Features of interest
(continued)

To the E of the Coolsingel extends one of the oldest parts of the city, which was also one of th areas worst hit in 1940. Here, in the Grote Kerkplein, is the Grote Kerk or St. Laurenskerk (15th c.), with a 64 m high tower (carillon) and a 23 m high organ (1973). – In the Nieuwe Markt is the Municipal Library, which has a valuable collection of works on Erasmus of Rotterdam. – Farther S, in the Blaak, the wide street which runs past the N end of the Leuvehaven, is Ossip Zadkine's monumental work of sculpture, "The Destroyed City" (1953). Nearby is the Witte Huis (White House), a 10-storey office building 46 m high which was Europe's first tower block (1900). – To the SE is the 3 km long Maasboulevard, from the E end of which there is a good view of Rotterdam. The two large bridges over the Maas lead to the port installations in the southern part of the city.

Town Hall

To the S of the Central Station is the Stationsplein, on the W side of which is the massive Groothandelsgebouw (Wholesale Trade Building, 1952–53). Opposite this, to the S, is the Bouwcentrum (Building Centre), an international centre of information and advice on building. – To the S of the Stationsplein is a modern commercial district wiht the Lijnbaan (pedestrian precinct) as its principal shopping street. – To the W, in the Schouwburgsplein, is De Doelen, a concert and conference hall.

1 km S of this is the world-famed Boymans – Van Beuningen Museum (pictures, sculpture, applied art), based on the private collection of F. J. O. Boymans (d. 1847). – To the SW, in Burgmeester's Jacobplein, is the Maritime Museum (history of navigation since the 17th c.; closed at present). A short distance S of this is the entrance to the Maas Tunnel, a road tunnel over 1.5 km long (opened in 1942) which runs under the Maas, here almost 800 m wide, and links the city centre with the southern suburbs. At the northern entrance is the 185 m high Euromast (1960), to the E of which extends a park with beautiful trees and lakes. Beyond the park is the Museum of Geography and Ethnography (Museum voor Land- en Volkenkunde; closed at present). – To the W of the park are a number of smaller docks, beyond which is the old district of Delfshaven, birthplace of the 17th c. naval hero Piet Hein. In the Oude Kerk, on the Voorhaven, are a memorial stone and a bronze tablet commemorating the last service attended by the Pilgrim Fathers before sailing from Delfshaven for America in 1620.

**Boymans –
Van Beuningen Museum

*Maas Tunnel

*Delfshaven

The southern districts of the city on the left bank of the Maas can be reached either by way of the busy Willemsbrug (with a railway bridge running parallel to the road bridge) or the Maas Tunnel. The Willemsbrug crosses the Noordereiland, beyond which is the Koningshaven, the oldest dock on the left bank of the Maas (1873). Beyond this again is the Feijenoord dock area (Binnenhaven and Spoorweghaven). Farther SW are the Rijnhaven and the Maashaven, followed by the smaller Charlois docks.

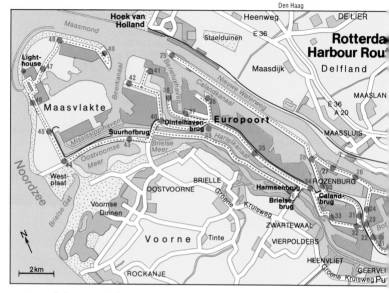

Den Haag

------●----- Harbour route with features of interest

The **Harbour Route of Rotterdam** *(Rotterdamse Havenroute)* marked by the sign reproduced here, is a recommended drive of 90–150 km (56–93 miles) through the extensive harbour area of Rotterdam.

- A **Departure point** (from Spaanse Polder)
- 1 **Europoint** (office block)
- 2 **Oud Delfshaven** (originally the port for the town of Delft, incorporated into Rotterdam in 1886)
- 3 **Coolhaven** (an inland port constructed between the two World Wars) **Maastunnel** (built 1937–1942)
- 4 **Sluisjesdijk** (on a peninsula between Nieuwe Maas and Waalhaven; 1888 the first oil tanks)
- 5 **Waalhaven** / *East Side* (originally constructed in 1907–1930 for bulk cargo: timber, heavy cargo, containers)
- 6 **Waalhaven** / *South Side* (harbour and transport school, container terminal)
- 7 **Prins Johan Frisohaven** (vehicles, including Japanese cars)
- 8 **Heijplaat** (garden city for shipyard employees)

- 9 **Prinses Beatrixhaven** (opened in 1965 as general cargo port; roll-on / roll-off, large banana unloaders)
- 10 **Prinses Margriethaven** (container terminal; large quay cranes)
- 11 **Pernis** (a fishing village on land reclaimed in the 14th c.)
- 12 **1008 km mark on the Rhine** (1008 river kilometres, 625 miles, from the first Rhine bridge at Konstanz on Lake Constance; harbour radar station)
- 13 **Beneluxtunnel** (opened 1967)
- 14 **2nd Petroleumhaven** (Petro-chemical works of Shell and Chevron)
- 15 **Rotterdamse Ster** ('The Star of Rotterdam', access to highway ring road)
- 16 **Petrochemical complex** (Shell, Chevron; start of an oil pipeline to Germany; environmental control complex)
- 17 **Botlekbrug** (bascule bridge with 45 m, 148 feet, clearance) **Botlektunnel** (opened 1980)
- 18 **Geulhaven** (tug and harbour service boats)
- 19 **3rd Petroleumhaven** (Esso Refinery)
- 20 **Chemiehaven** (chemical plants; dischargers for copra and tapioca)
- 21 **Botlek harbours** (grain and ore loading; shipyards)
- 22 **Grain warehouses** (on the Enclosing Dike of the former Brielse Maas now Brielse Meer, built in 1950; elevators, conveyor belts)

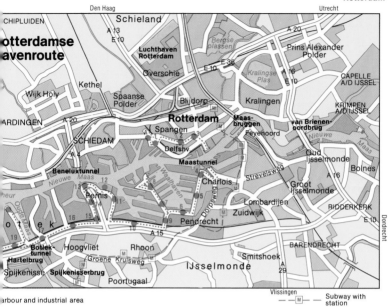

otterdamse avenroute

Harbour and industrial area

— ⓜ — Subway with station

- 23 **St. Laurenshaven** (mineral raw materials)
- 24 **Petrochemical complex** (storage tanks. chemical plants)
- 25 **Shipyards** (Prins-Willem-Alexander Dry Dock; waste disposal area)
- 26 **Rozenburg** (village called 'The Green Heart of Europoort', surrounded by reclaimed industrial areas and dikes)
- 27 **Ferry Rozenburg-Maassluis**
- 28 **Calandkanaal** (canal for seagoing vessels between the Europoort docks and the North Sea)
- 29 **Separation dam** (between Calandkanaal and Nieuwe Waterweg; mooring places for Europoort tugs in Scheurhaven)
- 30 **Calandbrug** (bascule bridge with 50 m. 164 feet, clearance)
  Britanniëhaven (car terminal)
- 31 **Europoort Oost** / *Merseyweg* (plastics factory)
- 32 **Europoort Oost** / *Theemsweg* (chemical plants and cement factory)
- 33 **Rozenburgsesluis** (Rozenburg lock between Hartelkanaal und Calandkanaal; lock size 299 m x 233 m = 981 feet x 764 feet)
- 34 **7th Petroleumhaven** (crude oil transit)
- 35 **"De Beer"** (international Seamen's Centre)

- 36 **4th Petroleumhaven** (Shell, Esso. Chevron, Gulf; mooring station)
  5th Petroleumhaven (Gulf Refinery)
- 37 **Beneluxhaven** (ferry services to Great Britain)
- 38 **Beneluxhaven** (discharge towers, conveyors and silos for grain shipments)
- 39 **Hartelkanaal** (Rhine waterway between the harbour industries of the Maasvlakte and Europoort, and the hinterland)
- 40 **6th Petroleumhaven** (BP Refinery)
- 41 **Europoort** (ore shipment; large discharge towers on the Calandkanaal)
- 42 **Beerkanaal** (pilot station)
- 43 **Oostvoornse Meer** (lake created in the first stage of the Delta plan)
- 44 **Mississippihaven** (natural gas tanks; ore shipments; coal terminal)
- 45 **Maasvlakte power station**
- 46 **Beach** (along the west coast of the Maasvlakte)
  Stone dam (a stone block jetty 4.5 km, 3 miles, long)
- 47 **Port and industrial area** (new lighthouse)
- 48 **Manmade dunes** (imitation oil tank; view of the estuary of the Rhine known as 'Maasmond')
- 49 **8th Petroleumhaven** (Maasvlakte oil terminal for giant tankers)
- E **Terminal point** (between Brielsebrug and Harmsenbrug)

Rotterdam, Features of interest (continued)

To the W of these docks is the Waalhaven, one of the largest man-made harbour basins in the world (area 310 hectares). Beyond the outer district of Pernis, to the W of the Waalhaven at the confluence of the Oude Maas and Nieuwe Maas, where

*Europoort

the Nieuwe Waterweg ('Het Scheur') begins, extend the huge new port installations of the Europoort, in the triangular area between the Nieuwe Waterweg, the Brielse Maas to the S and the North Sea.

*Zoo

In the north-western district of Blijdorp is the Blijdorp Zoo (open enclosures). – To the NE of Rotterdam is the large lagoon of Kralingse Plas (water sports), on the SE shore of which is De Ster, an old snuff and spice mill (restored). – Farther N are two other windmills, the 'Prinsenmolen' (1648) on the Bergse Voor-plas and 'De Vier Winden' (1776) on the banks of the Rotte.

Rüdesheim am Rhein   D

State: Federal Republic of Germany
Land: Hessen (Hesse)
Altitude: 85 m above sea level
Population: 10,000

KD German Rhine Line

KD cruise ships' landing-stage: Rheinanlagen
KD excursion ships' landing-stage and agency:
Rheinpromenade

General

Rüdesheim, am ancient little town, stretches along the right bank of the Rhine under the hills of the Niederwald. The best vineyards, on the Rüdesheimer Berg to the W of the town, are traditionally said to have been planted with Traminer vines by Charlemagne. The excellent local wines and the charming and varied scenery have enabled Rüdesheim to develop since the end of the 19th c. into one of the busiest tourist and holiday centres on the Middle Rhine, with a host of friendly restaurants and wine taverns, particularly along the famous Drosselgasse.

Features of interest

Rüdesheim lay at the end of the 'Merchants' Road' from Lorch which bypassed the rapids on the Rhine – an important strategic situation which was protected by four castles. Near the railway station is the Brömserburg or Niederburg, originally built in the 10th c. and held by the archbishops of Mainz, which now houses the Rheingau and Wine Museum (with a collection of drinking vessels). Beyond this is the Boosenburg or Mittel-burg (rebuilt 1868), which preserves a 10th c. keep. In the centre of the town is a ruined tower, all that is left of the old Vorderburg. Nothing now remains of the fourth castle, the Burg auf der Lach, which stood to the E of the town.

In the market square is the Late Gothic parish church of St James (St. Jacobus, 1390–1400). At the upper end of Rhein-strasse is the Adlerturm (Eagles' Tower), a relic of the town's fortifications. There are numerous old burghers' houses and aristocratic mansions, notable among them the house of the Ritter zu Grünstein family (18th c.), the Bassenheimer Hof (16th c.; enlarged in 19th c.), the Brömserhof (16th–17th c.), housing 'Siegfrieds Mechanisches Musikkabinett' (collection of mechanical musical instruments), and the Klunkhardshof (16th c.).

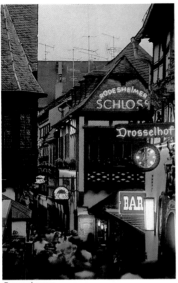

Drosselgasse

Niederwald Memorial

In the Eibingen district is the former Benedictine convent (founded in 1148 as an Augustinian house) of St Hildegard of Bingen, with a church in the Beuron style (17th c., much altered in the 20th c.). – Magnificently situated above Eibingen is the modern Benedictine convent of St Hildegard, founded in 1904. – 3.5 km N of Eibingen is a 14th c. pilgrimage church which originally belonged to a Capuchin friary.

Rüdesheim lies at the foot of the Niederwald (344 m), outlier of the Rheingaugebirge, which along with the hills above Bingen on the other side of the Rhine marks the beginning of the river's passage throught the Rhenish Uplands (Rheinisches Schiefergebirge). On a projecting spur of hill is the conspicuous Niederwald Memorial (Niederwalddenkmal, alt. 308 m; footpath, cableway), a 10.5 m high figure of Germania standing on a 25 m high base which commemorates the establishment of the German Empire in 1871. Designed by Johann Schilling, it was erected in 1877–83. During the unveiling ceremony there was an attempt on the life of the Emperor Wilhelm I and the members of the government who were present, but the attempt was frustrated by a damp fuse. From the foot of the statue there is a superb view of the river and the Rheingau.

From the Niederwald Memorial there is a very rewarding walk on a footpath which runs by way of the mock ruined castle of Rossel, perched high above the Rhine (alt. 265 m) and affording magnificent views, to the old hunting lodge (now a hotel) of Jagdschloss Niederwald (originally 18th c.; beautiful interior), rebuilt and enlarged in 1927–29 after a fire. From here it is possible to continue to Assmannshausen (see p. 113; footpath, chair-lift).

Features of interest (continued)

*Niederwald Memorial

Rossel

Jagdschloss Niederwald

Sankt Goar

D

State: Federal Republic of Germany
Land: Rheinland-Pfalz (Rhineland-Palatinate)
Altitude: 71 m above sea level
Population: 3,500

KD German Rhine Line

KD excursion ships land on the Rhine bank.

General

Sankt Goar, attractively situated under the massive ruin of Burg Rheinfels (see p. 118), owes its origin to the saint of that name, who was active here in the 6th century. In the Middle Ages this was the chief place in the county of Katzenelnbogen and the most strongly fortified town on the Middle Rhine. It was, and still is, the headquarters of the pilotage and warning service (signal station) responsible for helping ships through the narrow passage at the Loreley rock – in the past difficult and dangerous but now much easier as a result of the widening of the shipping channel.

Features of interest

The former conventual church (15th c.; now Protestant) has a Romanesque crypt (1137) in which the remains of St Goar once rested, a stone pulpit of about 1400 and, in a side chapel, the fine marble tombs (16th-17th c.) of Landgrave Philipp II of Hesse (d. 1583) and his wife.

There are some remains of the town's medieval fortifications, including the Hexenturm (Witches' Tower) and the Kanzleiturm (Chancery Tower).

The Rhine at Sankt Goar (right) and Sankt Goarshausen (left)

The path running up to Burg Rheinfels passes the churchyard, against the wall of which is the 'Flammensäule' (Flame Column) or Pfalzfelder Säule, a 1.5 m high Celtic sacrificial stone (copy; original in the Rheinisches Landesmuseum, →Bonn).

Surroundings of Sankt Goar

Sankt Goarshausen   D

State: Federal Republic of Germany
Land: Rheinland-Pfalz (Rhineland-Palatinate)
Altitude: 77 m above sea level
Population: 1,700

KD excursion ships land on the Rhine bank.

KD German Rhine Line

Sankt Goarshausen ('Loreleystadt'), an ancient little town at the foot of Burg Katz (see p. 119), is a long straggling place which has preserved much of its medieval core.

General

At the upper end of the town are two 14th c. watch-towers, relics of its medieval fortifications. The Roman Catholic parish church of St John (1925) has an altarpiece which may be from the school of Lucas Cranach the Elder.

Features of interest

From Sankt Goarshausen the Loreley (see p. 117) can be climbed. On the mole of the winter harbour is a bronze sculpture of the legendary "Loreley" (by Natascha Alexandrovna Princess Jusopov, 1983; picture see p. 114).

**Loreley

Speyer   D

State: Federal Republic of Germany
Land: Rheinland-Pfalz (Rhineland-Palatinate)
Altitude: 104 m above sea level
Population: 44,000

KD cruise ships land on the Rhine bank near the Stadtbad (starting and finishing point of the excursions to →Heidelberg). KD agency:
Albert-Schweitzer-Str. 2,
D-6720 Speyer

KD German Rhine Line

Speyer, a historic old Imperial city, is dominated by its Romanesque Cathedral. It was the see of a bishop from a very early period and the meeting-place of many Imperial Diets. It is an important centre of the wine trade.

General

Speyer was the Roman 'Civitas Nemetum'. The name 'Spira' first appears in the 7th c., and during that century too the town became an episcopal see. From 1294 to 1797 it was a free Imperial city, and the Imperial Diet met frequently in Speyer during that period. It suffered severe destruction in 1689, during the war over the Palatinate succession.

History

The six-towered Cathedral, the largest and most imposing cathedral of the High Romanesque period in Germany, was begun about 1030 by the Salian Emperor Conrad II and conse-

Features of interest
**Cathedral

Speyer

Rhine bank at Speyer by night

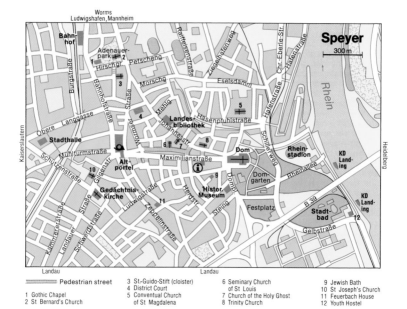

▓▓▓▓ Pedestrian street	3 St-Guido-Stift (cloister)
	4 District Court
1 Gothic Chapel	5 Conventual Church
2 St Bernard's Church	of St Magdalena

6 Seminary Church	9 Jewish Bath
of St Louis	10 St Joseph's Church
7 Church of the Holy Ghost	11 Feuerbach House
8 Trinity Church	12 Youth Hostel

crated in 1061. Between 1082 and 1125, during the reigns of Henry IV and V, a major rebuilding took place. In the W porch are statues of the eight Emperors who are buried in the Cathedral. Notable features of the interior are the raised choir ('Royal Choir'), the crypt (consecrated 1039) and the Imperial burial vault with the remains of the emperors' tombs, some of which were plundered by the French in 1689 (including the tombs of Conrad II, d. 1039; Henry III, d. 1056; Henry IV, d. 1106; Henry V, d. 1125; and Rudolf of Habsburg, d. 1291).

In front of the Cathedral is the Domnapf, a stone basin which was filled with wine for the people of the town at the induction of a new bishop.

A short distance S of the Cathedral are the Historical Museum of the Palatinate (Historisches Museum der Pfalz), the Diocesan Museum and an interesting Wine Museum (Roman wine). At the end of the nearby Judenbadgasse, lying almost 10 m below ground level in a little garden, is the Jews' Bath (Judenbad; c. 1100), belonging to a synagogue which once stood here.

Speyer Cathedral

From the Cathedral the wide Maximilianstrasse runs W to the Altpörtel, a handsome gate-tower of the 13th and 16th centuries.

Some 14 km NW of Speyer, at Hassloch, is the 'Holiday-Park', a large leisure park (350,000 sq.m), with a fairytale park, 'Lilliput', a dolphinarium, a circus and other attractions.

Staufen im Breisgau   D

State: Federal Republic of Germany
Land: Baden-Württemberg
Altitude: 276 m above sea level
Population: 7,000

Staufen is a pretty little old-world town situated at the point where the Münstertal runs into the Upper Rhine plain. A summer holiday resort lying on a popular route into the Belchen area, it also has some medium-sized industrial establishments (brandy distillery, etc.). There is a Goethe Institute in the town.

General

The little town, first recorded in 770, lies on the S side of the vine-clad hill of Staufen (wine known as 'Schlossberg'), with the remains of a castle (earlier than 12th c.; a ruin since 1606) which belonged to the lords of Staufen, who owned the silvermines in the Münstertal (an old mine shaft in the lower part of the valley can be entered).

Townscape

The town has a very picturesque market square, with the Town Hall and a 16th c. fountain; the original Dr Faustus or Faust, a necromancer, is said to have died in the Gasthaus zum Löwen (Lion Inn) between 1536 and 1539.

In St Martin's Church (Late Gothic, 15th c.) is a crucifix which belonged to Sixt von Staufen.

Staufen (continued)

The Unteres Schloss (Lower Castle, 16th and 18th c.) now houses the forestry office.

Excursion from Staufen

Some 8 km E, in the idyllic Upper Münstertal, is the former Benedictine monastery of St Trudpert (originally 10th c.; 18th c. church).

Strasbourg   F

State: France
Région: Alsace
Département: Bas-Rhin (Lower Rhine)
Altitude: 136 m above sea level
Population: 257,000

KD German Rhine Line

KD cruise ships land at the Quai des Belges (Gare Fluviale). KD agency: 31, rue Molière, F-67550 Vendenheim

General

Strasbourg – the capital of Alsace, a university town, the see of a bishop, and as the seat of the Council of Europe, the European Council of Human Rights and the European Science Foundation and the meeting-place of the European Parliament the germ of a future united Europe – lies at the intersection of important traffic routes on the left bank of the Rhine, which at this point is joined by the river Ill, the Rhine-Marne Canal and the Rhine-Rhône Canal.

With its soaring Cathedral and its many burghers' houses of the 16th and 17th c. Strasbourg still retains something of the character of an old free city of the Holy Roman Empire, but is also typically French with its handsome buildings in Louis XV style, dating from the time of the French Cardinal-Bishops of the 18th c., and its numerous mansard roofs.

The city's principal industries are metalworking, the manufacture of building materials and the production of foodstuffs (brewing, pâté de foie gras), followed by papermaking, textiles and tanning. The port of Strasbourg is the largest on the Upper Rhine, and is particularly active in the export trade. – Tourism has now also become an important element in the economy of Strasbourg, which attracts increasing numbers of visitors as the principal tourist centre of Alsace and the venue of numerous congresses and conferences.

History

Around 16 A.D. the Romans established the fortified post of 'Argentoratum' beside an earlier Celtic settlement situated on important traffic routes. In the 4th c. the Alemanni built a new settlement on its ruins, and this appears in the records in the 6th c. under the name of 'Strataburgum' (the 'fortified town on the roads'). Here in 842 Ludwig (Louis) the German and Charles the Bald confirmed their alliance against Lothair I in the 'Strasbourg Oaths', which give important evidence on the Old High German and Old French of the period. – Strasbourg became the see of a bishop in 1003, and rose to considerable prosperity through its shipping and its trade. In 1262, after conflicts with the bishop and the nobility, it achieved independence as a free Imperial city, which for a time was the wealthiest and most brilliant in the Holy Roman Empire. Art and learning flourished in the city. In the 14th c. the Dominican preachers and mystics

Strasbourg: view of 'La Petite France' and the Cathedral

History (continued)

Meister Eckhart and Johannes Tauler lived in Strasbourg, and between 1434 and 1444 Gutenberg developed the art of printing here. After the coming of the Reformation in 1520 Strasbourg numbered among its citizens the Protestant writer and satirist Johannes Fischart (1546–90) and the educationist Johannes Sturm (1507–89), rector of the Protestant grammar school and founder of a theologicial academy which was the forerunner of the University.

In 1681, taking advantage of the weakness of the Empire, Louis XIV occupied Strasbourg, and soon afterwards had it fortified by Vauban. Until 1793, however, the town retained a degree of autonomy, and French cultural influence began to assert itself only in the time of Napoleon.

After the Franco-Prussian War of 1870–71 Strasbourg returned to German sovereignty as capital of the province of Alsace-Lorraine, and remained German until the end of the first world war. The establishment of the Council of Europe in Strasbourg in 1949, together with its history and geographical situation, seemed to make it a predestined future 'capital of Europe'.

Features of interest

The hub of the city's traffic is the Place Kléber, named after General J.-B. Kléber, born in Strasbourg in 1753. In the square is a statue of Kléber, under which is a vault containing his remains. On the N side of the square is the Aubette ('Orderly Room'), built 1765–72 by Blondel, which until 1918 housed the Conservatoire of Music and Guard House.

From the SE corner of Place Kléber the busy Rue des Grandes-Arcades runs S to Place Gutenberg, in the centre of which is a

Strasbourg

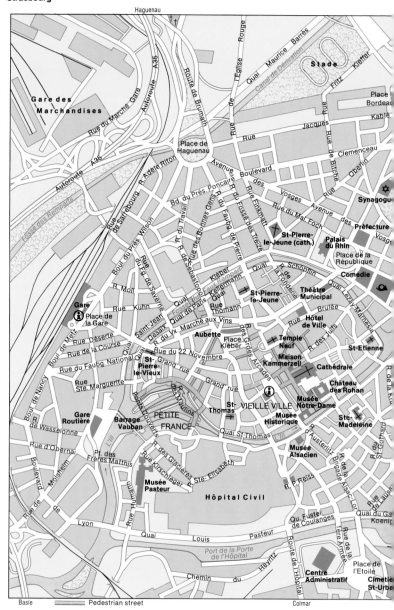

Strasbourg

300 m

Features of interest
(continued)

statue of Gutenberg (1840). On the SW side of the square is the Chamber of Commerce (with tourist information office), the finest Renaissance building in Lower Alsace, erected in 1582–85 as the Town Hall. – From the SE corner of Place Gutenberg Rue Mercière, offering a magnificent view of the W front of the Cathedral, runs into the Place de la Cathédrale.

**Cathedral

The Cathedral of Notre-Dame, built on the foundations of an early Romanesque church begun in 1015, reflects the organic development of architectural styles from Romanesque to Late Gothic (12th–15th c.). The W front was the work of Master Erwin of Steinbach (1277–1318) and his successors; the delicately articulated octagon of the N tower was built by Ulrich von Ensingen of Ulm (1399–1419), the openwork spire, 142 m high, by Johannes Hültz of Cologne (1420–39). In 1793 much ornament and 235 statues fell victim to the fanaticism of the French Revolution. There was even a plan to demolish the spire, since it towered above other buildings and thus offended against the principle of equality; but wiser counsels prevailed, and the spire suffered nothing worse than having a lead Jacobin cap set on its tip. The Cathedral itself became a 'Temple of Reason'. In 1879–89 a Romanesque-style dome was built over the crossing. – On the splendid W front, built of red sandstone from the Vosges, are a large rose window (13.5 m in diameter) and a profusion of sculptural ornament (much of it restored in the 19th c.). – In the tympana of the doorway in the S transept are sculptured representations of the Coronation and the Death of the Virgin (the latter being original), and on either side are two

Rose window

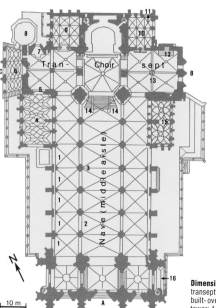

Strasbourg Minster
Cathedral of Our Lady

A Main Portal at the
  West Front (1270–1330);
  above: Rose Window (Ø13.5 m)
B South Portal (c. 1230)
C North Portal (1495–1505)

1 Stained Glass Windows (12th–14th c.)
2 Organ (orig. by A. Silbermann,
  1714–1716; case 1489)
3 Pulpit (by J. Hammer, 1486)
4 St Martin's Chapel (1515–1520)
5 Mount of Olives (15th c.)
6 St Laurence's Chapel (1495–1505)
7 Baptismal Font (by J. Dotzinger, 1453)
8 Sacristy
9 St John's Chapel (c. 1240;
  under the Chapter House)
10 St Andrew's Chapel (12th c.)
11 Exhibition
12 Astronomical Clock
  (orig. 1570–1574)
13 Angels' Pillar (1230–1240)
14 Stair to the Crypt
15 St Catherine's Chapel (1331;
  vault 1563)
16 Stairs to the Platform

Dimensions. – Total length: 118 m; width of the transept:: 58 m; height of the middle aisle: 31.5 m; built-over surface: 4,085 sq.m; total height of the north tower: 142 m; height of the tower platform: 66 m.

masterpieces of sculpture, the famous allegorical figures of the
Church and the Synagogue (c. 1230). – Built on to the N tran-
sept is St Lawrence's Chapel (1495–1505), with a superb Late
Gothic façade.

The interior of the Cathedral (103 m long, as wide as 58 m,
31.5 m high) has beautiful stained glass (12th–15th c.), a Late
Gothic pulpit (1486) and an organ (1714–16) by Andreas Silbermann (d. in Strasbourg 1734). In the S transept are the 'Angels'
Pillar' (Pilier des Anges, 1230–40) and the famous Astronomical
Clock (case, 18 m high, made between 1570 and 1574; works
1838–42). Other notable features are St Catherine's Chapel
(1331 and 1563) in the S aisle and the font (1453) and a
sculptured group of Jesus on the Mount of Olives (15th c.) in
the N transept. Entered from the N transept (but not always
open) is St John's Chapel (c. 1240), with the tomb of Bishop
Konrad von Lichtenberg (d. 1299). There is a three-aisled crypt.
– It is well worth while climbing the tower for the sake of the
magnificient views it affords of the city, the Rhine plain, the
Black Forest and the Vosges.

* Maison Kammerzell

On the N side of the Place de la Cathédrale is the Maison Kammerzell (restaurant), the finest old burghers' house in the city,
with a stone-built lower storey (1467) and a half-timbered
superstructure (1589). At the corner of Rue Mercière is a half-
timbered building of 1567 housing a pharmacy (the Pharmacie
du Cerf) which has occupied this site continuously since 1268.

To the S of the Cathedral is the Place du Château, with the
Château des Rohan (1728–42), which until the Revolution was
the residence of the Cardinal-Bishops of the great house of
Rohan. It contains the Rococo-style apartments occupied by
the bishops, with a library, print room and chapel, as well as the
Archaeological Museum and Museum of Fine Art. In the right-
hand wing is the Museum of Decorative Arts (principally
ceramics and porcelain). – At the SW corner of the Place du
Château is the Maison de l'Œuvre Notre-Dame (14th–16th c.),
which has housed the Œuvre Notre-Dame (the authority responsible for the maintenance of the Cathedral) since 1349. It
contains the Musée de l'Œuvre Notre-Dame, with the originals
of sculpture from the Cathedral and a number of pictures,
mainly by artists of the Upper Rhine region.

* Musée de l'Œuvre
Notre-Dame

To the SW, behind the Maison de l'Œuvre Notre-Dame, is the
picturesque Place du Marché-aux-Cochons-de-Lait (Sucking
Pigs Market). Beyond this is the Grande Boucherie, built
1586–88 as a meat market, which now houses the Municipal
Historical Museum. Across the street to the W is the Ancienne
Douane (Old Custom House), the oldest part of which dates
from 1358; it now contains the Museum of Modern Art (19th and
20th c.). – To the S of the Ancienne Douane, beyond the river Ill,
is the Musée Alsacien (folk art), in a patrician house of 1622.

From Place Gutenberg the Rue des Serruriers (Street of the
Locksmiths) runs SW to St Thomas's Church, the only hall-
church in Alsace, which has a Romanesque W end (1230–50), a
Gothic nave (c. 1330) and an octagonal tower over the crossing
(1348), with a clock which for 400 years has struck the hour four
minutes too soon, in order to make itself heard before the
Cathedral clock strikes. In the apse is the tomb of the French

Strasbourg

marshal Maurice de Saxe (d. 1750), an allegorical marble group by J.-B. Pigalle (1777). The church has a Silbermann organ (1737–40) on which Albert Schweitzer frequently played.

*Quartier des Tanneurs

A short distance NW of St Thomas's Church is the old Tanners' Quarter (Quartier des Tanneurs), with picturesque half-timbered buildings lining its narrow streets. This is the area known as 'Little France' (Petite France). In Rue du Bain-aux-Plantes is the old 'Gerwerstub' ('Tanners' Room'; restaurant). To the SW are the Ponts Couverts – four bridges, formerly roofed, crossing the river Ill, which is here divided into four arms. Here too are four towers, relics of the medieval fortifications. The best view (and also a fine view of the town) can be had from the Grande Ecluse, a dam built by Vauban. – To the N of the Ponts Couverts, on the western edge of the old town, is the church of St-Pierre-le-Vieux (14th–15th c.).

To the E of Place Kléber, in the elongated Place Broglie, is the Old Town Hall, built 1730–36 as the residence of the Landgrave of Hesse and used as a town hall from 1805 to 1976. To the E of this, in gardens, is the Hôtel du Gouvernement Militaire (c. 1760). At the E end of the square is the Opéra du Rhin, the Municipal Theatre (1804–22). On the N side is the Banque de France, on the spot where Rouget de Lisle sang the "Marseillaise" for the first time on 26 April 1792. – NE of the theatre, beyond the old town moat, is the Place de la République, surrounded by public buildings, with a monument commemorating the dead of the first world war.

University

To the E of the old town, beyond the river Ill, is the University (1879–85), with various later buildings housing University institutes, an Observatory and a Botanic Garden. S of this is the Centre Universitaire, with the Ecole Nationale Supérieure des Ingénieurs (College of Technology), the Institute of Chemistry and the Faculty of Letters. – Farther E, towards the river port, is the old Citadel, built 1682–84 as the central element in Vauban's system of fortifications; it is now an attractive park, laid out in 1967. – 1 km W of the University is the large complex of the Hôpital Civil, and some 500 m SE of this is the Administrative Centre of the Strasbourg conurbation, completed in 1976.

A kilometre or so N of the Place de la République is the 110 m high lattice aerial mast of the Maison de la Radio, the Strasbourg headquarters of the French radio and television services. 500 m farther N is the international congress centre known as the Palais de la Musique et des Congrès, a hexagonal building designed to serve a variety of purposes. NE of this are the Exhibition Grounds (Parc des Expositions), with an exhibition hall, an ice-rink and various sports and recreation grounds. –

*Palais de l'Europe

Some 500 m SE, beyond the Ill, is the Palais de l'Europe, built 1972–77 near the older Maison de l'Europe. This is a fortress-like structure of nine storeys (30 m high, 105 m along each side), with an interior courtyard containing the tent-like chamber in which the Council of Europe and the European Parliament (410 members) meet. To the NE is the Palais des Droits de l'Homme, headquarters of the Commission of Human Rights. – To the SE of the Palais de l'Europe extends the beautiful Parc de l'Orangerie, laid out at the beginning of the 19th c., with the Orangery built for the Empress Joséphine, now used for exhibitions and receptions.

To the E and S of the city are the extensive installations of the Port (sightseeing boat trips), with 12 docks and a total area of 1,070 hectares, making it the second largest port on the Rhine (after Duisburg) and France's second largest river port (after Paris). Some 90% of its turnover is concerned with exports (mainly mineral ores, building materials, petroleum products and grain). The old municipal port was considerably enlarged from 1882 onwards, and the port area now extends for more than 100 km along the French bank of the Rhine from Marckolsheim to Lauterbourg.

Strasbourg Rhine harbours (Port Autonome de Strasbourg)

Unkel

D

State: Federal Republic of Germany
Land: Rheinland-Pfalz (Rhineland-Palatinate)
Altitude: 58 m above sea level
Population: 3,500

KD excursion ships land on the Rhine bank.

KD German Rhine Line

Unkel is an old-world little wine town ("Unkeler Funkeler" wine) charmingly situated at the foot of the Leidenberg, which also attracts visitors with its healthy air. It has fine half-timbered houses (in the districts of Heister and Scheuren as well as in the main part of the town), remains of its old walls and an Early Gothic parish church with a richly furnished interior on the Pantaleonsberg. The 19th c. revolutionary poet Ferdinand Freiligrath (1810–1876) stayed for a time in Haus Freiligrath (1760). From the riverside promenade there is a fine view of the Rolandsbogen and the Siebengebirge.

In the district of Heister is Burg Vilszelt, an old moated castle (11th c.) which was rebuilt in the 18th century.

Rhine front

Utrecht

NL

State: Netherlands
Province: Utrecht
Altitude: 5 m above sea level
Population: 235,000

Utrecht, the capital of the province of Utrecht and the fourth largest city in the Netherlands, lies on the Kromme Rijn ('Crooked' or 'Curving Rhine'), which here divides into the Oude Rijn (Old Rhine) and the Vecht, and on the Amsterdam-Rhine Canal, exactly on the geographical divide between the marshland and the sandy areas of the Geest. This situation has promoted the development of the town in the course of history, since the Geest, lying higher, could not be reached by storm tides from the North Sea and was thus an ideal area for human settlement before the technique of dyke-building was devised.

General

Utrecht has long been one of the country's most important political, cultural and economic centres. With a University founded in 1636, it is the seat of a Roman Catholic and an Old Catholic archbishop and of the Oecumenical Council of the

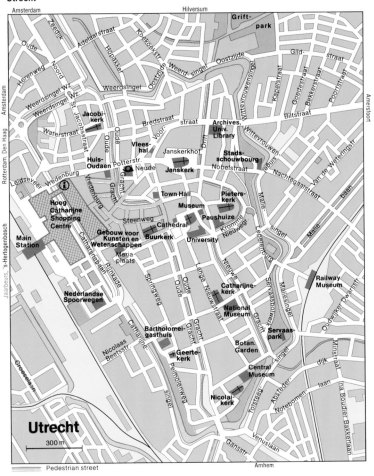

Utrecht

Amsterdam   Hilversum

Grift-
park

Amsterdam

Rotterdam, Den Haag

Jaarbeurs, 's-Hertogenbosch

Amersfoort

Utrecht

300 m

Pedestrian street

Arnhem

General (continued)

Netherlands; it is an important centre of the service trades, commerce and communications; it is a major industrial town (steelworks, rolling mills, engineering, rolling-stock construction, electrical equipment, foodstuffs, petrochemicals, textiles, furniture, etc.); and it is also a great tourist centre, offering the attractions of its picturesque old town with its canals and historic old buildings and of the beautiful surrounding countryside.

History

Utrecht, the Roman 'Traiectum ad Rhenum', later known to the Frisians and the Franks as 'Wiltaburg', is one of the oldest towns in the Netherlands. The Frankish king Dagobert I (628–638) founded the first church in Frisian territory here; the first bishop, in 696, was St Willibrord. The bishops (from 1559 arch-bishops) of Utrecht were powerful and influential prelates, and the town soon became famous for its magnificent churches. It belonged at first to Lotharingia; later it was incorporated in the German Empire, and was frequently the residence of the Emperor. In 1528 Bishop Henry of Bavaria ceded secular authority to the Emperor Charles V, who built the castle of Vredenburg in Utrecht. The Union of Utrecht, a league of the seven Protestant northern provinces which sought separation from the southern Netherlands, was formed here in 1579. In 1672 the town was ravaged and plundered by the French. The treaty of Utrecht, signed in 1713, ended the War of the Spanish Succession.

History (continued)

The old town is surrounded by the Singel, the old moat, along which run attractive promenades. – In the centre of the old town is the Cathedral of St Michael (Dutch Reformed), begun in 1254 on the site of a 10th c. Romanesque church and completed in 1517. The original nave, flanked by double aisles, was destroyed by a storm in 1674, leaving the 112 m high tower standing by itself. The tower (14th c.; carillon) is the tallest in the Netherlands, and provided a model for many other churches. On the S side of the choir is a picturesque cloister (14th–15th c.), which links the Cathedral with the University (founded 1636). Adjoining the choir is the Organ Museum; next to it is the Museum of Contemporary Art (art since 1965). To the SE, in the so-called Pope's House (Paushuize, 1517), are the offices of the provincial government. To the N, on Pieterskerk-hof, is St. Pieterskerk (consecrated 1054), with a Romanesque crypt and a Gothic transept and choir.

Features of interest

*Cathedral

In Nieuwegracht is the House of the Teutonic Order. Nearby are St Catherine's Church (R.C.; from 1524 to 1537 the archiepiscopal cathedral) and, adjoining this on the S, the Catharijne-convent (National Museum).

At Agnietenstraat No. 1 is the Centraal Museum (religious art, antiquities, etc.), in the chapel (1512–16) and refectory of the Agnietenklooster (a house of Augustinian canonesses). – In the southern part of the Oudegracht is a Frisian sacrificial stone ('de gesloten steen'), associated by legend with the Devil.

*Centraal Museum

To the W of the Cathedral, beyond the Maartensbrug, is the old Buurkerk (13th–15th c.). – To the NW is the Hoog Catharijne shopping centre, which is connected with the main railway station. SW of the station are the exhibition halls of the annual trade fair.

N of the Cathedral, in the Janskerkhof, is St. Janskerk (Dutch Reformed), a Romanesque church (c. 1050) with a choir of 1538 and a façade of 1682. To the NE is the University Library (Utrecht Psalter, 11th c.).

To the W of the square called the 'Neude' extends the picturesque Oudegracht, with the Huys Oudaen (14th c.), a castle-like patrician house in which the treaty of Utrecht was signed. Near the N end of the Oudegracht is the St. Jacobikerk (Reformed), founded in 1173 and rebuilt in the form of a Gothic hall-church in the 14th/15th century.
W of the Neude, on the site of a castle destroyed in 1577, is the Vredeburg (Vreeburg), one of the busiest squares in the city.

Patrician houses

Utrecht, Features of interest (continued)	In the newer part of the city is the famous Maliebaan, a 700 m long avenue of lime-trees which was spared by French troops in 1672–73 on the orders of Louis XIV. The old Maliebaan station now houses a Railway Museum.
Surroundings of Utrecht	The pleasant countryside round Utrecht, traversed by the arms of the Rhine and by canals, is a fertile and well cultivated area with many country houses and nice parks.
	Some 25 km SW of Utrecht, at Schoonhoven, is the Dutch Museum of Gold, Silver and Watches.

Vallendar   D

	State: Federal Republic of Germany Land: Rheinland-Pfalz (Rhineland-Palatinate) Altitude: 69 m above sea level Population: 10,000
General	Vallendar is situated on a narrow arm of the Rhine opposite the island of Niederwerth. Many visitors come to the town for the sake of its healty air and its spa treatment facilities (Kneipp cure).
Features of interest	The Roman Catholic parish church of SS. Peter and Marcellus (by Lassaulx, 1837–41) occupies the site of an earlier Late Romanesque church. Vallendar has a number of fine old aristocratic mansions, including in particular the Wiltberger Hof (c. 1700) and the Haus d'Ester or Marienburg (1773), and many attractive 17th c. half-timbered houses.
	In the district of Schönstatt are the ruins of an Augustinian convent (1143) which was destroyed during the Thirty Years War. The new convent (Pallottines) has a modern church (1965–68).

Wesel   D

	State: Federal Republic of Germany Land: Nordrhein-Westfalen (North Rhine – Westphalia) Altitude: 27 m above sea level Population: 57,000
General	The town of Wesel is situated at the junction of the river Lippe with the Rhine and was rebuilt after almost total destruction during the second world war. Peter Minuit (or Minnewit, 1580 to 1638 or 1641), the founder of New York, was a native of Wesel.
	The earliest record of Wesel dates from the 8th c., the municipal chart from 1241. In 1407 it became a member of the Hanse, in 1680 the first fortifications were erected. The port of Wesel is one of the oldest on the Rhine. The road bridge crossing the river between Wesel and Büdingen has a total lenght of 508 m.

A bird's-eye view of Wesel ▶

Wesel,
Features of interest

In the Grosse Markt is the Late Gothic St Willibrord's Cathedral (1501–40; Protestant); its tower dates from 1477/78. The Baroque Berliner Tor (Berlin Gate, 1718–22) in the town's centre remains from the ancient fortifications. In the municipal cultural centre called 'Centrum', in Kornmarkt, is the Municipal Museum (art from the 15th to the 20th c.). The former citadel in the southern part of the town houses a Schill Museum. In the Roman Catholic St Martin's Church (1949) is a finely carved altar of 1510. In the old Fürstenberg Fort is the modern Peace Church (Friedenskirche) or Church of the Holy Angels (1956–58).

On the SE edge of the town is the Schillwiese, with a monument by Schinkel (1835) to eleven officers of Col. Schill's regiment who were shot here by the French in 1809.

Wiesbaden   D

State: Federal Republic of Germany
Land: Hessen (Hesse)
Altitude: 117 m above sea level
Population: 273,000

KD German Rhine Line

KD excursion ships land at Wiesbaden-Biebrich, Rheingaustrasse.

General

Wiesbaden, the capital of the Land Hessen (Hesse), lies at the foot of the wooded Taunus hills with its suburbs reaching down to the Rhine. Its 26 hot springs (46–67 °C), mild climate and beautiful surroundings make it a much frequented health resort; and it is also noted for its theatre and its modern shopping facilities and as the seat of the Federal Criminal Department, the Federal Statistical Office, the Federation of the German Film Industry and well-known publishing houses. There are also several large Sekt-making establishments in the Wiesbaden area.

History

Wiesbaden's healing springs were known to the Romans, who called the place 'Aquae Mattiacorum' (after the local tribe, the Mattiaci, who were a branch of the Chatti). The Roman baths were near the present Kochbrunnen (Boiling Fountain). The name 'Wisibada' ('baths in the meadows') is first recorded by Einhard, Charlemagne's biographer, in 829. In 1236 the Emperor Frederick II celebrated Whitsun at Wiesbaden, now a free Imperial city; but six years later the town was captured and destroyed by the Archbishop of Mainz. Around 1270 it passed to the Counts of Nassau, who made it a subsidiary residence town. In 1744 Count Karl of Nassau-Usingen moved his seat to the newly built palace of Biebrich. In 1816 Wiesbaden became capital of the new Duchy of Nassau and enjoyed a first period of prosperity as a modest Biedermeier-style residence town and spa to which the princes and great ones of Europe came to take the cure. Then in the years before the first world war the town had a further period of splendour as the summer residence of the Emperor and court. In 1945 it became capital of the Land of Hessen (Hesse).

Panoramic view

Features of interest

Wiesbaden's main traffic artery is the wide Wilhelmstrasse, at the N end of which, on the right, is the spa district (Kurbezirk),

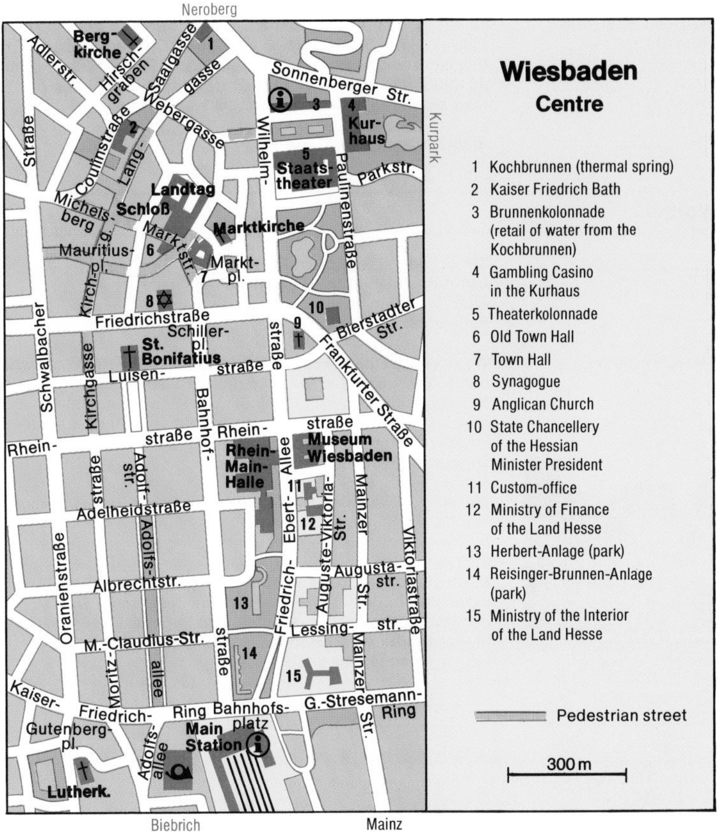

Wiesbaden
Centre

1 Kochbrunnen (thermal spring)
2 Kaiser Friedrich Bath
3 Brunnenkolonnade
  (retail of water from the
  Kochbrunnen)
4 Gambling Casino
  in the Kurhaus
5 Theaterkolonnade
6 Old Town Hall
7 Town Hall
8 Synagogue
9 Anglican Church
10 State Chancellery
   of the Hessian
   Minister President
11 Custom-office
12 Ministry of Finance
   of the Land Hesse
13 Herbert-Anlage (park)
14 Reisinger-Brunnen-Anlage
   (park)
15 Ministry of the Interior
   of the Land Hesse

▭▭▭ Pedestrian street

├─── 300 m ───┤

bounded on the S by the Theatre Colonnade and the Hessian State Theatre (1892–94) and on the N by the Fountain Colonnade. To the E is the Kurhaus (by Friedrich von Thiersch, 1905–09), an imposing building with a massive Ionic portico; in the left wing is the Casino. Behind the Kurhaus extends the well-groomed Kurpark. – To the E, in Aukamm-Allee, are the indoor thermal baths. – To the NW is the Kochbrunnen (15 springs; 60 °C), and nearby, to the SW, the Emperor Frederick Baths (Kaiser-Friedrich-Bad, 1910–13), with the Rheumatism Clinic.

In the Schlossplatz is the Palace (Schloss), built in 1837–41, which now houses the Landtag (parliament of the Land) and government departments. Between the Schlossplatz and the Marktplatz are the Town Hall (Rathaus, 1884–88) and the Market Church (Protestant; 1852–62). – At the S end of the Wilhelmstrasse is the Wiesbaden Museum, with the modern Rhein-Main-Halle opposite it.

Features of interest
(continued)

231

Wiesbaden (continued) *Neroberg	To the N of the town is the wooded Neroberg (245 m; rack railway), with the conspicuous Greek Chapel (Russian Orthodox) and the beautifully situated Opel-Bad (open-air swimming-pool). – In the NW of the town, in Schützenhausweg, is the Fasanerie (animal and plant park).

Biebrich Castle: see page 109.

Worms   D

State: Federal Republic of Germany
Land: Rheinland-Pfalz (Rhineland-Palatinate)
Altitude: 100 m above sea level
Population: 74,000

General and History

Worms is a cathedral city on the left bank of the Rhine and one of the oldest towns in Germany. It is a noted centre of the wine trade and has considerable industry (engineering, chemicals, metal processing). The vineyards round the Gothic Liebfrauenkirche (Church of Our Lady), near the B9 road, produce the famous Liebfrauenmilch (Liebfraumilch).

Worms goes back to an old Celtic settlement ('Borbetomagus') and a later Roman fort ('Civitas Vangionum'). A bishopric was established here in the 4th c., and during the great migrations the town became capital of the Burgundian kingdom which was destroyed by the Huns in 436. The events of this period provided the basis for the story of the Nibelungs. During the medieval period more than a hundred Imperial Diets were held in Worms, the most celebrated being the Diet of 1521 at which Luther defended his doctrines.

Luther Monument

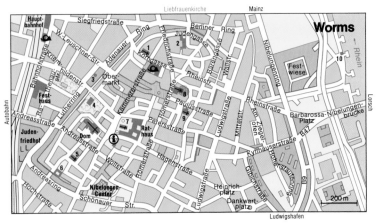

▦▦▦ Pedestrian street	1 Collegiate Church of St Martin
	2 Synagogue, Jews' Gate, Raschi House
▬▬▬ Remains of the	3 Luther Monument
town wall	4 Heylshof Art Gallery

5 Magnuskirche (church)
6 Municipal Museum
(Andreasstift)
7 Trinity Church

8 Friedrichskirche (church)
and Red House
9 Collegiate Church of St Paul
10 Hagen Monument

In the centre of the old town is the Cathedral of SS. Peter and Paul, with six towers, which ranks with the larger cathedrals of Speyer and Mainz as one of the finest achievements of the High Romanesque style (11th and 12th c.). The interior is 110 m long by 21 m wide, rising to a height of 27 m in the nave and 40 m in the domes. In the N aisle are five Late Gothic sandstone reliefs from the demolished Gothic cloister. The choir has beautiful stalls and a Baroque high altar to the design of Balthasar Neumann.

Worms,
Features of interest

To the E of the Cathedral, in the Marktplatz, is the Trinity Church (Dreifaltigkeitskirche, 1709–25), rebuilt in 1954–59 after suffering severe destruction during the second world war. A little way NE is the Romanesque St Paul's Church, with two round towers topped by curious cupolas based on Oriental models.

SW of the Cathedral are the Late Romanesque church of St Magnus (10th–14th c.; Protestant), the town's first church, and the former St Andrew's Church (12th–13th c.; restored 1927–29), which along with the adjoining conventual buildings now houses the richly stocked Municipal Museum.

*Worms Cathedral

NW of these two churches, in the Andreasring, is the oldest and largest Jewish cemetery in Europe, with tombstones dating back to the 11th and 12th centuries.

N of the Cathedral is the Kunsthaus Heylshof, a mansion erected in 1884 on the site of the former Bishop's Palace (painting of the 16th–19th c., sculpture, porcelain, etc.). Still farther N, in Lutherplatz, is the Luther Monument (by Ernst Rietschel, 1868), commemorating Luther's appearance before the Diet of Worms in 1521. To the NE the former conventual St Martin's Church (13th c.)

In the Judengasse (which is protected as a national monument) is the Synagogue (originally 11th c.; ritual bath of 1186), rebuilt in 1961 after its destruction by the Nazis in 1938. Since 1970 the old Jewish quarter of Worms has been the subject of a comprehensive rehabilitation scheme. The old Jewish community house, the Raschi School (named after one of the most celebrated Jewish scholars of the Middle Ages), the area round the Synagogue and various dwelling-houses have already been completed.

Old Jewish Quarter

On the Rhine bank, immediately at the ships' landing-stage, is the statue of Hagen (1906) throwing the treasure of the Nibelungs into the river (picture see p. 60).

Statue of Hagen

Xanten

D

State: Federal Republic of Germany
Land: Nordrhein-Westfalen (North Rhine – Westphalia)
Altitude: 24 m above sea level
Population: 16,500

Xanten, an old cathedral city, claims to be the birthplace of Siegfried, the hero of the "Nibelungenlied". Nowadays it is a friendly town and a cultural centre in the Lower Rhine region

General

Xanten, General
(continued)

with nice leisure facilities ('Nibelungenbad'). There are many relics of its Roman past. The name 'Xanten' comes from the Latin 'ad sanctos' (= 'by the Saints').

History

About 15 B.C. the Roman 'Castra Vetera' was established on the Fürstenberg, S of Xanten (Birten), and it was from here that Varus and his legions set out on the campaign which ended in a disastrous defeat in the Teutoburg Forest. At the beginning of the 2nd c. A.D. Trajan founded his 'Colonia Ulpia Traiana' on the site. By the 8th c. there was a monastic house here, and round it a medieval trading settlement soon grew up. Xanten first appears in the records as a town in 1228, and in 1263 was the laying of the foundation-stone of the Cathedral. In the 16th c. Xanten was reduced to poverty because the Rhine had shifted about two kilometres from the town. – The severe damage suffered by the town during the second world war has been made good (reconstruction reward in 1975).

Features of interest
*Cathedral

The Cathedral of St Victor (originally a monastic church) is, after Cologne Cathedral, the most important Gothic church on the Lower Rhine (1263–1516). The most notable feature of the interior is the large Altar of the Virgin by H. Douvermann (1525). – To the N of the Cathedral are the old conventual buildings (Cathedral Museum); to the S, at Kurfürstenstrasse, is the Regional Museum.
In the NW of the town is the Klever Tor (Cleves Gate, 1393; three holiday apartments). To the NE of the town is the large Archaeological Park (still in course of development), with reconstructed Roman buildings of Colonia Ulpia Traiana (town walls, amphitheatre, harbour temple, etc.); information centre; modern hotel in Roman style.

**Archaeological Park
(Amphitheatre)

Surroundings of Xanten
Kalkar

Some 15 km NW of Xanten lies Kalkar, with the Roman Catholic parish church of St Nicholas (1409–55; important examples of the work of the Kalkar school of woodcarvers).
Near Kalkar a disputed 'fast-breeder' nuclear power station is under construction.

Zierikzee   NL

State: Netherlands
Province: Zeeland (Zealand)
Altitude: below sea level
Population: 10,000

General and Features of interest

Zierikzee, the chief town on the Dutch island of Schouwen-Duiveland in the Rhine-Maas delta, was formed by the amalgamation of six small communes. The main sources of income of the population are the busy holiday and tourist trade and farming on the fertile marshy soil of the island.

The town's main features of interest are three well preserved town gates of the 14th–16th c., the Town Hall (1554; museum) and the tower of St. Lievenskerk, begun in 1454 but left unfinished.

*Zeelandbrug

To the SW of Zierikzee the some 5 km long Zeelandbrug (48 arches) crosses the Oosterschelde.

Zurich (Zürich)

State: Switzerland
Canton: Zürich (Zurich)
Altitude: 410 m above sea level
Population: 380,000

Shuttle bus between Zurich and the KD cruise ships' landing-stage in →Basle

KD German Rhine Line

Zurich (German spelling Zürich), Switzerland's largest city and capital of the canton of Zurich, is also the country's economic and cultural hub; but with all its bustling activity it is still a very attractive city, with carefully cherished traditions and much to interest the visitor. It lies at the north-western end of Lake Zurich astride the river Limmat, which flows out of the lake at this point, between the Uetliberg to the W and the Zürichberg to the E. It has both a University and the Federal College of Technology.

General

Three of the five major Swiss banks have their head offices in the famous Bahnhofstrasse, one of the finest shopping streets in Europe. Zurich is an important industrial centre (mainly textiles, engineering and electrical equipment), and also plays a leading part in stock market business and insurance. In addition it is Switzerland's principal tourist centre, with something like a million visitors a year. A fifth of the country's total national income is earned in Zurich. The city is also Switzerland's most important centre of communications, with its largest airport.

Zurich: city centre on both banks of the river Limmat

Zurich

There was a Roman military post, 'Turicum', on the Lindenhof. The works of Hartmann von Aue and the poems by other medieval minnesingers preserved in the Manesse Manuscript (written in Zurich but now in the University Library, →Heidelberg) are a reminder of the great days of chivalry and courtly literature. The development of Zurich into a city state took a great step forward when the guilds obtained equal rights with the nobility after an assault on the town hall in 1336, and in 1351 it became a member of the Swiss Confederation. In 1523 Ulrich Zwingli (1484–1531) established the Reformation in Switzerland and made Zurich a centre of the Reformed faith, ranking alongside Wittenberg and Geneva. In the 18th c. the town became influential in intellectual life, with such figures as the philosopher Johann Caspar Lavater, the educationalist Heinrich Pestalozzi, the great scholar Johann Jakob Bodmer and the writer Salomon Gessner. In the 19th and 20th c. the town continued to be a centre of liberal thought, with such notable figures as Gottfried Keller, Conrad Ferdinand Meyer, Georg Büchner, August Bebel, Lenin, James Joyce, C.G. Jung, Ludwig Klages and Thomas Mann among its residents. In 1916 the Dadaist school was founded in Zurich.

Features of interest
*Bahnhofstrasse

The pulsating activity of the city centres on the Bahnhofstrasse, which runs from the railway station to the lake, flanked by elegant shops, department stores and banks; granite ashlars pavilion sculpture by Max Bill. In its lower half is the Paradeplatz, with the palatial headquarters of the Schweizerische Kreditanstalt (1876), the Hotel Savoy Baur en Ville (1838) and the well-known Café Sprüngli. In the 18th c. a cattle market was held in the square; later it became a drill ground. – To the W of the Bahnhofstrasse, extending to the Sihlporte, is a district containing many office blocks and the Stock Exchange (Börse). To the E, towards the Limmat, is the Little Town (Kleine Stadt), the western half of the old town.

On the S side of the Main Railway Station (1871) is the Bahnhofplatz (motor traffic only), with a monument to the Swiss statesman Alfred Escher (d. 1882). Under the square is a pedestrian concourse with a modern shopping centre ('Shopville'). – On the N side of the station is the Air Terminal.

**Swiss National Museum

Immediately N of the railway station is the Swiss National Museum (Schweizerisches Landesmuseum), a large castellated building (1893–98) which contains the country's largest collection of material on Swiss history and culture. Of particular interest and importance are the works of religious art, the unique collection of stained glass, the Armoury (with famous murals by Ferdinand Hodler), a series of period rooms of the Gothic to Baroque periods, the collection of antiquities of the early historical period and – a recent acquisition – a celestial globe by Jost Bürgi (1552–1632).

NW of the railway station on the left bank of the river Sihl, at Ausstellungsstrasse 60, is the Museum of Decorative Arts (Kunstgewerbemuseum), which puts on periodic special exhibitions of graphic art, design, architecture and applied art.

Between the Bahnhofstrasse and the Limmat extends the western half of the old town. In this area is the quiet tree-shaded Lindenhof, once the site of the Roman fort. To the south is

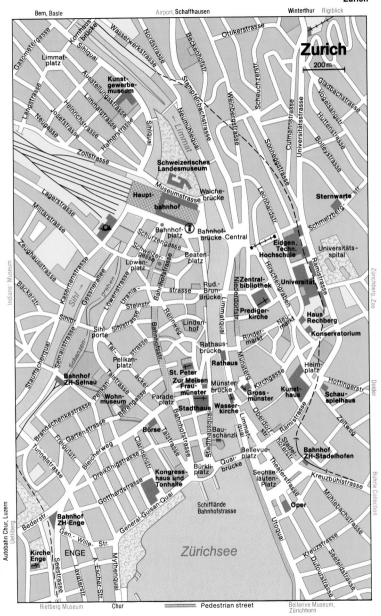

Bern, Basle • Airport, Schaffhausen • Winterthur • Rigiblick

Zurich

200 m

Pedestrian street

Rietberg Museum • Chur • Bellerive Museum, Zürichhorn

St Peter's Church, with a Late Romanesque choir under the tower (early 13th c.) and a Baroque nave (1705). It has the largest clock-faces in Europe (1538), 8.7 m in diameter.

Farther S is the Münsterhof, a charming and historic old square. On the S side is the Fraumünster, an aisled basilica with a Gothic nave (13th–15th c.) and an Early Gothic transept. In the late Romanesque choir are five stained glass windows by Marc Chagall (1970). The undercroft contains remains of the crypt of the abbey church founded by the Emperor Ludwig (Louis) the German in 853. The abbey itself was pulled down in 1898 to make way for the Stadthaus (Town House), but the Romanesque and Gothic cloister still survives.

*Zunfthaus zur Meisen

On the N side of the Münsterhof is the Zunfthaus zur Meisen, a magnificent Baroque guild-house of 1752–57 which now houses the Swiss National Museum's ceramic collection. On the W side of the square is another old guild-house, the Zunfthaus zur Waag (1636).

Along the right bank of the Limmat runs the Limmatquai, a popular shopping street. About half way along, built over the water, is the Town Hall (Rathaus), a massive Late Renaissance building (1694–98) with rich sculptural decoration. Towards the S end of the Limmatquai are a number of elegant guild-houses reflecting the wealth of the guilds which governed the town until 1789: at No. 54 the Haus zur Saffran (1719–23), at No. 42 the Haus zur Rüden (1660), at No. 40 the Haus zur Zimmerleuten (1709). – Immediately S of the Münsterbrücke (Minster Bridge) is the Gothic Wasserkirche ('Water Church', 1479–84), once entirely surrounded by the Limmat. Adjoining the N side of the church is the Helmhaus (1794), with an open fountain-house.

On an open terrace above the river is the Grossmünster (11th–13th c.), which dominates the city with its twin towers (domed tops added in 1782). On the upper part of the S tower, on the side facing the river, is a seated figure of Charlemagne (copy; original in the crypt), who is believed to have founded the house of secular canons to which the church originally belonged. Notable features of the church are the Romanesque capitals, the remains of Gothic wall paintings and the Late Romanesque cloister.

A walk through the eastern part of the old town is full of charm and interest, with many excellent antique shops adding to its attractions. In the Napfgasse is the Brunnenturm (Fountain Tower), headquarters of the Lombard money-changers in the 14th and 15th c. In the Spiegelgasse is a house (No. 17) in which Lenin lived for some time in 1917. In this street too was the cabaret in which Hans Arp and Tristan Tzara launched the Dadaist movement in 1916. In the Neumarkt (No. 27) is the birthplace of the writer Gottfried Keller (1819–90), who was chief clerk of the canton of Zurich from 1861 to 1876. The house in which he died is in the Zeltweg (No. 27).

*Kunsthaus

To the E of the Grossmünster, in Heimplatz, is the Kunsthaus (Art Gallery), with a fine collection of pictures and sculpture from antiquity to the present day. – Facing the Kunsthaus is the Haus zum Pfauen (House of the Peacock, 1888–89), with the

Schauspielhaus (Theatre), one of the most renowned of German-language theatres.

Higher up, to the N, is the University, founded in 1833 and rebuilt in 1911–14; it is the largest of the Swiss universities. – Immediately N is the Federal College of Technology (Eidgenössische Technische Hochschule, ETH), founded in 1855; the buildings (designed by Gottfried Semper) were erected in 1860–64 and enlarged in 1915–25.

At the S end of the Limmatquai is the Bellevueplatz, from which a lakeside promenade affording extensive views runs along the E side of Lake Zurich, under the names of Utoquai and farther on Seefeldquai. 1.5 km from Bellevueplatz is the beautiful Zürichhorn Park.

At the S end of the Bahnhofstrasse is Bürkliplatz, from which General-Guisan-Quai and beyond this Mythenquai run along the W side of the lake. – Near the landing-stage of the motor ships which ply on the lake is the Congress Hall (Kongresshaus), opened in 1939, which is built on to the older Concert Hall (Tonhalle) of 1895. This complex of buildings is one of the major focal points of Zurich's social life with its concerts, conferences and festive occasions of all kinds. – Above the Mythenquai is the Belvoir Park, with old trees, subtropical plants and a restaurant. Higher up, beyond Seestrasse, is the Rieter Park, on the N side of which, in Gablerstrasse, is the Rietberg Museum, in a fine neo-classical villa modelled on the Villa Albani in Rome which was built in 1857 for a German industrialist, Otto Wesendonck.

*Bürkliplatz

To the E of the city is the Zürichberg (679 m), a wooded hill with houses reaching far up its slopes. Here too is the Zoo, one of the finest in Europe. – SW of the city is the Uetliberg (871 m; electric mountain railway). In good weather the view from the top extends to the Valais, Bernese and Glarus Alps; to the N is the Black Forest, to the E Mt Säntis.

*Zürichberg

*Uetliberg

There are a variety of attractive excursions in motor ships on the Lake Zurich (Zürichsee; information: Mythenquai 33).

*Lake Zurich

Practical Information from A to Z

Airports

→ Travel to the Rhine

Bicycle hire

A bicycle is often a good way of seeing the sights at a port of call during a Rhine cruise. At many places there are private bicycle hire agencies, and the German Railway have a hire service at many stations; a list of such stations can be found in a current railway timetable.

Camping

There are numbers of camping sites on both banks of the Rhine. During the main holiday season, however, there is heavy pressure on space, and advance booking is therefore advisable. Camping outside recognised sites is practically impossible in all the countries bordering the Rhine. In any event permission must always be obtained from the owner of the land.

Car hire

Zurich
(CH)

Avis
Gartenhofstr. 17
tel. (01) 2 42 20 40
Zurich Airport
tel. (01) 8 13 00 84

europcar
Josefstr. 53
tel. (01) 2 71 56 56
Zurich Airport
tel. (01) 8 13 20 44

Hertz
Moorgartenstr. 5
tel. (01) 2 42 84 84
Zurich Airport
tel. (01) 8 14 05 11

Basle
(CH)

Avis
Hilton-Hotel, Äschengraben 31
tel. (0 61) 2 71 22 62

Avis: Basle–Mulhouse–Freiburg EuroAirport
tel. (0 61) 3 25 28 40

europcar
Peter-Merian-Str. 58
tel. (0 61) 2 72 85 55
Basle–Mulhouse–Freiburg EuroAirport
tel. (0 61) 3 25 29 03

Hertz
Nauenstr. 33
tel. (0 61) 2 71 58 22
Basle–Mulhouse–Freiburg EuroAirport
tel. (0 61) 3 25 27 80

Avis
Place de la Gare
tel. (88) 32 30 44
Entzheim Airport
tel. (88) 68 82 53

Strasbourg
(F)

Hertz
6, bd. de Metz
tel. (88) 68 93 11
Entzheim Airport
tel. (88) 88 01 99

Avis
Wormser Landstr. 22
tel. (0 62 32) 3 20 68

Speyer
(D)

Avis
Augartenstr. 112–114
tel. (06 21) 44 20 91

Mannheim
(D)

europcar
Neckarauer Str. 50–52
tel. (06 21) 85 20 55

Hertz
Friedrichsring 36
tel. (06 21) 2 29 97

Avis
Andernacher Str. 203
tel. (02 61) 80 03 66

Koblenz
(D)

europcar
Hohenzollernstr. 26
tel. (02 61) 3 30 10

Avis
Clemensstr. 29
tel. (02 21) 23 43 33
Cologne-Bonn Airport
tel. (0 22 03) 40 23 43

Cologne
(D)

europcar
Luxemburger Str. 181
tel. (02 21) 44 10 47

Practical Information

Car hire in Cologne
(continued)

europcar: Neusser Str. 347
tel. (02 21) 76 70 26
Cologne-Bonn Airport
tel. (0 22 03) 5 30 88

Düsseldorf
(D)

Avis
Berliner Allee 32
tel. (02 11) 32 90 50
Düsseldorf Airport
tel. (02 11) 4 21 67 48

europcar
Burgunder Str. 40
tel. (02 11) 5 04 70 41
Höher Weg 49
tel. (02 11) 9 84 04 77
Kölner Landstr. 232
tel. (02 11) 77 10 60
Düsseldorf Airport
tel. (02 11) 4 20 12 66

Hertz
Immermannstr. 65
tel. (02 11) 35 70 25
Düsseldorf Aiport
tel. (02 11) 41 10 83

Rotterdam
(NL)

Avis
Kruisplein 21
tel. (0 10) 4 33 22 33
Rotterdam Airport
tel. (0 10) 4 15 88 24

europcar
Pompenburg 646
tel. (0 10) 4 11 48 60

Hertz
Schrikade 986
tel. (0 10) 4 04 60 88
Rotterdam Airport
tel. (0 10) 4 15 82 39

Amsterdam
(NL)

Avis
Nassaukade 380
tel. (0 20) 6 83 60 61
Schiphol Airport
tel. (0 20) 6 04 13 01

europcar
Overtoom 51–53
tel. (0 20) 6 83 21 23
Schiphol Airport
tel. (0 20) 6 04 15 66

Hertz
Overtoom 333
tel. (0 20) 6 12 24 41
Schiphol Airport
tel. (0 20) 6 01 54 16

Avis
Plantin en Moretuslein 62
tel. (03) 2 18 94 96

Deurne Airport
tel. (03) 2 18 94 96

europcar
Slachthuislaan 27 B
tel. (03) 2 36 29 50

Hertz
Mechelsesteenweg 43
tel. (03) 2 33 29 92

Deurne Airport
tel. (03) 2 30 16 41

Car hire (continued)
Antwerp
(B)

Clothing

In general clothing on KD ships and on excursions from the ship
can range between the comfortable and the casual.
Even at evening functions dress does not need to be unduly
formal.

Consulates

→ Embassies and consulates

Currency

The unit of currency in Switzerland and Liechtenstein is the
Swiss franc (German Schweizer Franken, French franc suisse,
Italian franco svizzero; sfr) of 100 rappen/centimes/centesimi.
There are banknotes for 10, 20, 50, 100, 500 and 1000 francs
and coins in denominations of 1, 2, 5, 10, 20 and 50 rappen and
1, 2 and 5 francs.
There are no restrictions on the import or export of either Swiss
or foreign currency.

Switzerland

The unit of currency in Germany is the mark (Deutsche Mark,
DM) of 100 pfennigs.
There are banknotes for 10, 20, 50, 100, 200, 500, 1000 and 5000
DM and coins in denominations of 1, 2, 5, 10 and 50 pfennigs and
1, 2 and 5 DM.
There are no restrictions on the import or export of either German
or foreign currency.

Germany

The unit of currency in France is the French franc (F) of 100 centimes.
There are banknotes for 20, 50, 100, 200, 500 and 1000 francs
and coins in denominations of 5, 10 and 20 centimes and $1/_2$, 1,
2, 5 and 10 francs.

France

Practical Information

Currency in France (continued)

There are no restrictions on the import or export of either French or foreign currency.

Netherlands

The unit of currency in the Netherlands is the guilder (abbreviated fl. for florin; hfl) of 100 cents.

There are banknotes for 10, 25, 50, 100, 250, 500 and 1000 guilders and coins in denominations of 5, 10 and 25 cents and 1, $2^1/_2$ and 5 guilders.

There are no restrictions on the import or export of either Dutch or foreign currency.

Belgium

The unit of currency in Belgium is the Belgian franc (bfr) of 100 centimes.

There are banknotes for 100, 500, 1000, 5000 and 10 000 francs and coins in denominations of 25 and 50 centimes and 1, 5, 10 and 20 francs.

There are no restrictions on the import or export of either Belgian or foreign currency.

Currency on KD ships

The currency in use on KD ships is the Deutsche Mark (DM).

Eurocheques are accepted up to the value of 400 DM.

The best known Credit cards like Diner's Club, Eurocard, JCB are accepted.

Foreign currency should be changed into DM before boarding the ship.

Currency can be changed on board only in limited amounts.

Customs regulations

General

Of the countries covered in this Guide Germany, France, the Netherlands and Belgium are members of the European Unity (EU).
When crossing frontiers it should be remembered that Switzerland is not a member of the European Unity (EU) and that therefore different customs regulations apply.

Germany, France, Netherlands, Belgium

There are no limits for articles for the private use.

Visitors from other countries: 200 cigarettes or 100 cigarillos or 50 cigars or 250 grammes of tobacco; 2 litres of wine and 1 litre of spirits over 22° Gay-Lussac; goods up to the value of 350 DM.

Switzerland

Visitors may take in, duty-free, personal effects and travel gear, together with 200 cigarettes or 50 cigars or 250 grammes of tobacco, 2 litres of wine and 1 litre of spirits over 22° Gay-Lussac, and other goods up to the value of 100 Swiss francs.

Visitors whose permanent residence is outside Europe may take in, duty-free, 400 cigarettes or 200 cigarillos or 100 cigars or 500 grammes of tobacco.

On passports, etc. →Travel documents

For speed and convenience in dealing with frontier and customs formalities passengers on KD cruises are requested to
deposit their passports or identity cards at the purser's office
on joining the ship. They will be returned at the end of the trip.
All passengers will be issued with a card, written in several
languages, identifying them as passengers on a KD ship; this
card should be carried at all times.

Anyone going ashore on his own, and not on an organised
excursion, should ask at the purser's office for his passport and
take it with him.

Distances between selected ports on the Rhine

see table on page 246

Documents

→Travel documents

Electricity

In all the countries covered by this Guide the voltage is 220;
frequency 50 cycles.
The voltage on KD ships is the same. It should be noted, however, that for safety reasons the use of electric irons in the
cabins is not permitted.

Embassies and consulates

This section lists embassies in each of the countries covered by
this Guide together with consulates in towns on the Rhine.

United Kingdom

Embassy:
Thunstr. 50
CH-3005 Bern
tel. (0 31) 3 52 50 21

in Switzerland

Consulate:
Dufourstr. 56
CH-8008 Zürich
tel. (01) 2 61 15 20 and 2 61 15 23

Embassy:
Friedrich-Ebert-Allee 77
D-53113 Bonn
tel. (02 28) 23 40 61

in Germany

Distances between selected ports on the Rhine

Distances by water in km	Basle	Breisach	Strasbourg	Karlsruhe	Mannheim	Mainz	St. Goar	Koblenz	Remagen	Cologne	Düsseldorf	Duisburg	Wesel	Emmerich	Dordrecht	Rotterdam
Basle	●	58	127	193	258	323	389	424	466	521	577	613	643	685	809	833
Breisach	58	●	69	135	200	274	331	366	408	463	519	555	589	627	751	775
Strasbourg	127	69	●	66	131	205	262	297	339	394	450	486	520	558	682	706
Karlsruhe	193	135	66	●	65	139	157	231	273	328	384	420	454	492	616	640
Mannheim	258	200	131	65	●	74	131	166	208	263	319	355	389	427	551	575
Mainz	323	274	205	139	74	●	57	92	134	189	245	281	315	353	477	501
St. Goar	389	331	262	157	131	57	●	35	77	132	188	224	258	296	420	444
Koblenz	424	366	297	231	166	92	35	●	42	87	153	189	223	261	385	409
Remagen	466	408	339	273	208	134	77	42	●	55	111	147	181	219	343	367
Cologne	521	463	394	328	263	189	132	87	55	●	56	92	126	164	288	312
Düsseldorf	577	519	450	384	319	245	188	153	111	56	●	36	70	108	232	256
Duisburg	613	555	486	420	355	281	224	189	147	92	36	●	34	72	196	220
Wesel	643	589	520	454	389	315	258	223	181	126	70	34	●	38	162	186
Emmerich	685	627	558	492	427	353	296	261	219	164	108	72	38	●	124	148
Dordrecht	809	751	682	616	551	477	420	385	343	288	232	196	162	124	●	24
Rotterdam	833	775	706	640	575	501	444	409	367	312	256	220	186	148	24	●

Consulate:
Yorckstr. 19
D-40476 Düsseldorf
tel. (02 11) 9 44 80

Embassies and consulates
of the United Kingdom
in Germany (continued)

Embassy:
35, rue du Faubourg St-Honoré
F-75383 Paris Cedex
tel. (1) 42 66 91 42

in France

Embassy:
Lange Voorhout 10
NL-2514 ED Den Haag
tel. (0 70) 3 64 58 00

in the Netherlands

Embassy:
rue d'Arlon 85
B-1040 Bruxelles
tel. (02) 2 87 62 11

in Belgium

United States of America (U.S.A.)

Embassy:
Jubiläumstrasse 93
CH-3005 Bern
tel. (0 31) 3 57 70 11

in Switzerland

Consulate general:

Zollikerstrasse 141
CH-8008 Zürich
tel. (01) 4 22 25 66

Embassy:
Deichmanns Aue
D-53179 Bonn
tel. (02 28) 33 91

in Germany

Consulate general:

Siesmayerstr. 21
D-60323 Frankfurt/Main
tel. (0 69) 75 35-0

Embassy:
2, avenue Gabriel
F-75382 Paris Cedex 08
tel. (1) 42 96 12 02

in France

Consulate general:

14, avenue d'Alsace
F-67082 Strasbourg
tel. (88) 35 31 04

Embassy:
Lange Voorhout 102
NL-2514 EJ Den Haag
tel. (0 70) 3 10 92 09

in the Netherlands

Practical Information

<table>
<tr><td>Embassies and consulates of the U.S.A. in the Netherlands (continued)</td><td>Consulate general:

Museumplein 19
NL-1071 DJ Amsterdam
tel. (0 20) 5 75 53 09</td></tr>
<tr><td>in Belgium</td><td>Embassy:
27, boulevard du Régent
B-1000 Bruxelles
tel. (02) 5 13 38 30</td></tr>
</table>

Canada

<table>
<tr><td>in Switzerland</td><td>Embassy:
Kirchenfeldstrasse 88
CH-3005 Bern
tel. (0 31) 3 52 63 81</td></tr>
<tr><td>in Germany</td><td>Embassy:
Friedrich-Wilhelm-Str. 18
D-53113 Bonn
tel. (02 28) 9 68-0

Consulate general:

Prinz-Georg-Str. 126
D-40479 Düsseldorf
tel. (02 11) 17 21 70</td></tr>
<tr><td>in France</td><td>Embassy:
av. Montaigne 35
F-70008 Paris
tel. (1) 44 43 29 00

Consulate:
Polysar France,
rue du Ried
F-67110 Strasbourg - La Wantzenau
tel. (88) 96 65 02</td></tr>
<tr><td>in the Netherlands</td><td>Embassy:
Sophialaan 7
NL-2514 JP Den Haag
tel. (0 70) 3 61 41 11</td></tr>
<tr><td>in Belgium</td><td>Embassy:
2 av. de Trevueren
B-1040 Bruxelles
tel. (02) 27 35 60 40</td></tr>
</table>

Emergency calls

There are emergency telephones (SOS) on all Swiss motorways and on major mountain roads.

Switzerland

Police	dial 117
Fire	118
Ambulance	144
Breakdown assistance	140

There are emergency telephones on all motorways and certain federal highways.

Germany

Police	dial 110
Fire	112

These numbers apply throughout almost the whole of Germany

There are emergency telephones on all motorways and some national highways.

France

In the larger towns dial 17 for the Police de Secours; in the country call the local Gendarmerie. In the case of an accident with no injury to persons it is sufficient to call a 'huissier' (notary) to record the damage.

There are emergency telephones on the Dutch motorways.

Netherlands

Emergency number, covering nearly the whole country, for calling police or ambulance services: dial 06 11.

There are emergency telephones on the Belgium motorways. Breakdown assistance is provided by a number of motoring organisations.

Belgium

Police	dial 101
Accident rescue service	100

Where emergency medical attention is required for a passenger on a KD ship it is summoned at once by radio-telephone.

N.B.

Events (selection)

Switzerland
Many places: Dreikönigssingen (Three Magi carol-singing)
Basle: Vogel Gryff (guild festival)

January

Switzerland
Many places: masquerades

Shrovetide

Germany
Many places: *Shrovetide celebrations,
Carnival (particularly in Cologne and Mainz)

France
Colmar, Mulhouse: Shrovetide celebrations

Basle Shrovetide: 'Morgenstraich'

Cologne Carnival: 'Jeck'

Events, Shrovetide (continued)	Belgium Many places: Carnival
After Ash Wednesday	Switzerland Basle: Morgenstraich (Basle Shrovetide celebrations)
Holy Week and Easter	Switzerland Many places: processions
	Germany Frankfurt am Main: Easter Fair
	Belgium Many places: processions
April	Switzerland Zurich: Sechseläuten (Six o'Clock Ringing: guid and spring festival) Basle: Trade Fair, European Watch and Jewellery Fair
	France Strasbourg: Spring Fair
	Belgium Antwerp: Flemish Song Festival
April–May	Germany Kaub: Spring Festival

Switzerland
Many places: May Day celebrations
(first Sunday)
Zurich: Trade Fair

Germany
Iffezheim: Spring Meeting (horse-race)
Koblenz: Blossom Festival (in Güls)
Leutesdorf: Spring Wine Festival
Mainz: Wine Fair
Mannheim: *May Market
Wiesbaden: May Festival

France
Molsheim: Spring Festival, Wine Fair
Neuf-Brisach: Lily of the Valley Festival
Wissembourg: Lily of the Valley Festival

Netherlands
Many places: National Windmill Day

Belgium
Antwerp: Special Market (1 May)

Germany   May–June
Kehl: Messdi (street festival)

Germany   Mai–September
Brühl: palace concerts

Switzerland   June
Basle: Town Festival, Art Fair
Zurich: International Festival, Seenachtsfest (night festival on
lake)

Germany
Many places: Vine-Blossom Festival
Braubach: Rose Festival
Frankfurt am Main: Wäldchestag
Mainz: Midsummer Night (with fireworks) and 'couching' of
printer's apprentices
Neuwied: Heddesdorfer Pfingstritt (Whitsun Ride)
Wiesbaden: International Riding and Jumping Tournament

France
Colmar: Folk performances in front of Old Custom House
Mulhouse: Summer Weeks
Ribeauvillé: Kougelhopf Festival
Strasbourg: Musical Festival

Netherlands
Many places: Holland Festival
Amsterdam: performances in Vondel Park; cruises in traditional
sailing boats

Belgium
Antwerp: Fair

Germany   June–September
Zons: Fairytale plays

Practical Information

Koblenz: "The Rhine Aflame"

Mainz: 'Couching'

Germany
Many places: vintage festivals

Events (continued)
October

France
Molsheim: Wine Festival
Mulhouse: October Days
Obernai: Wine Festival

Germany
Bonn: Federal Press Ball

November

Switzerland
Many places: Lichtkläuse (around 6 December), Silvester-
kläuse, etc.

Dezember

Germany
Many places: Christmas fairs

Netherlands
Everywhere: St. Nicholas's Day (5 December)
Many places: 'Midwinter Blowing' (a traditional custom to pro-
claim the birth of Christ)

Excursions

On cruises run by the KD German Rhine Line (→ Köln-Düsseldorfer) optional excursions are arranged from various ports of
call. The cost of these is not included in the fare.

Apart from the excursions run in connection with the KD Rhine cruises there are also excursions from the following places: Frankfurt am Main, Mainz, Wiesbaden-Biebrich, Eltville, Rüdesheim, Bingen, Assmannshausen, Niederheimbach, Lorch, Bacharach, Kaub, Oberwesel, Sankt Goar, Sankt Goarshausen, Bad Salzig, Kamp-Bornhofen, Boppard, Braubach, Rhens, Oberlahnstein, Niederlahnstein, Koblenz, Engers, Neuwied, Andernach, Bad Hönningen, Bad Breisig, Linz, Remagen, Unkel, Bad Honnef, Königswinter, Bonn-Bad Godesberg, Bonn, Wesseling, Porz, Cologne, Zons and Düsseldorf.

These excursions are run by the largest passenger vessels in service on European inland waters, with accommodation for more than 1000 passengers and excellent restaurant and refreshment facilities. The fastes ships in the fleet are the hydrofoils "Rheinpfeil" ("Rhine Arrow"; 65 km/h) and "Rheinjet" ("Rhine Jet"; 70 km/h).

Food and drink

Switzerland

Swiss restaurants are noted for the excellence of their cuisine, which is as varied as the ethnic composition of the population. The cuisine of the different parts of Switzerland is strongly influenced by that of the neighbouring countries – in the German-speaking cantons by German cooking, in the French-speaking cantons by the 'cuisine française', in the Italian-speaking cantons by the 'cucina italiana'. In addition, however, there are a number of specifically Swiss dishes, mostly using locally produced ingredients such as dairy produce and fish.

Notable among meat dishes is the 'Berner Platte', a very nourishing plateful of ham and sausage with sauerkraut and beans. The Mittelland has another very substantial dish, 'Gnagi' (slightly salted pigs' trotters), so tender that it is said to melt in the mouth. Favourite Zurich dishes are 'Gschnetzeltes' (veal stewed with cream) and 'Leberspiessli' (a kind of noodles made of paste and mashed liver). A specialty of the cantons on the Rhine is 'Mistkratzerli' or 'Giggeli' (young chicken, roasted).

Switzerland has a rich assortment of excellent sausages. Basle has 'Klöpfer' (succulent cervelat sausages), St Gallen 'Schüblige' (a mild sausage of beef, pork and bacon) and 'Bratwürste' (made from pork and/or veal, with onions), Appenzell 'Pantli' and 'Knackerli'.

Among favourite accompaniments to meat are 'Berner Rösti' (sliced potatoes, lightly browned with bacon cubes), gratiné potatoes, aubergines and artichokes. There are also a variety of attractively seasoned salads.

Fish dishes play a large part in the Swiss menu, and the country's many lakes yield a variety of species.

Pasta is eaten mainly in the northern part of Switzerland, where the influence of German cuisine makes itself felt. In addition to 'Spätzli' or 'Knöpfli' there is a Zurich specialty, the 'Zürcher Topf' (macaroni with minced meat and tomato sauce, cooked in the oven).

A selection of Swiss cheeses

The Swiss are particularly good at making cakes and sweets. Among the most tempting are 'Basler Leckerli' (a kind of gingerbread), 'Schaffhauser Zungen' (Schaffhausen tongues), 'Gottlieber Hüppen', the cherry tart of Zug, the cream-filled meringues (from Meiringen) of the Bernese Oberland and the 'bagnolet' cream of the Jura (eaten with raspberries and aniseed biscuits). Swiss chocolate is world-renowned.

Food and drink in Switzerland
(continued)

The excellent dairy products of Switzerland are widely famed, and the Swiss menu includes a range of cheese dishes, varying from region to region. 'Fondue' is made by melting cheese and white wine, flavoured with kirsch and spices, in a special one-handled dish known as a 'caquelon'. The dish is then set in the middle of the table over a flame to keep it hot, and each member of the party helps himself by dipping a piece of white bread on a special fork into the communal bowl. Anyone who lets his bread fall into the dish is required to pay for the next bottle of wine. In 'raclette' (from French 'racler', to scrape) a large cheese is cut in half and heated until it melts, when the melted cheese is scraped off on to the plate and eaten with a potato in its jacket and various savoury accompaniments.

Favourite drinks are beer (best-known brands Feldschlösschen and Cardinal) and wine (→Facts and Figures, Wine). Fruit juices and mineral water can be had in great variety. Swiss fruit brandies are of excellent quality – Kirsch (the best of which comes from Zug), Zwetsch/Prune (made from plums), Enzian (from the roots of the yellow gentian), Birne/Poire (from pears), Grappa and Marc (from the skins of pressed grapes), Bätzi (from apples), etc.; Alpenbitter, Chrüter (a herb liqueur).

German cooking is nourishing and varied, with many local specialties, most easily found in the smaller restaurants. As a general rule more vegetables and potatoes are eaten in North Germany, while in the south there is a preference for soup, pasta and salads.

In Westphalia meat dishes predominate. Smoked meat products are popular, particularly Westphalian ham, accompanied by dark pumpernickel bread. Other substantial dishes are 'Puffbohnen mit Speck' (broad beans and bacon), 'Pfefferpotthast' (highly spiced boiled beef), 'Mettwurst mit Linsen' (pork and beef sausages with lentils) and 'Westfälische Reibekuchen' (made of grated raw potatoes and buckwheat flour). Fresh-water fish add variety to the menu.

In Hesse there is a preference for substantial pork dishes. Frankfurter sausages have of course achieved international fame. Other specialties are 'Speckkuchen' (bacon pie), 'Kasseler Rippchen' (smoked pickled loin of pork), 'Bauernfrühstück' (peasant breakfast – ham, potatoes and egg) and 'Handkäse' (curd cheese). 'Bethmännchen' (marchpane) and 'Frankfurter Brenten' are popular types of biscuit.

Popular dishes in the Rhineland are 'Sauerbraten' (braised pickled beef), 'Himmel und Erde' ('heaven and earth' – a purée of apples and potatoes with blood sausage), 'Hämmchen' (knuckle of pork), 'Hunsrücker Festessen' (sauerkraut and pease pudding with potatoes, horse-radish and ham), 'Schweinepfeffer' (jugged pork) and fish from the tributaries of the Rhine and the volcanic lakes in the Eifel. During the season

Cold buffet on a KD cruise ship

many restaurants serve mussel dishes. A 'Halver Hahn' is a
sandwich of rye bread and cheese, accompanied by beer. There
are a great variety of cakes and biscuits – 'Spekulatius',
'Muzenmandeln', 'Aachener Printen', etc.

The people of south-western Germany like meat dishes and
farinaceous food (dumplings, pasta). In Swabia there is a great
range of soups. 'Spätzle' are a form of pasta made of flour, eggs
and salt, grated and boiled. 'Maultaschen' are also made of
pasta, filled with minced meat, spinach, onions, etc.; they are
eaten either in soup or with onions browned in fat. 'Sauerkraut'
is served with 'Ripple' (pickled rib of pork), blood and liver
sausage or pig's stomach. In the Black Forest there are trout
and the well known Black Forest bacon and ham. A favourite
accompaniment of new wine is an onion pasty.

The predominant German drink is beer (round Cologne and
Düsseldorf the top-fermented 'Kölsch' and 'Altbier'). On the
Rhine and in its tributary valleys, however, the dominant position is occupied by wine (→Facts and Figures, Wine). In the
Black Forest there are excellent fruit brandies – Kirschwasser
(from cherries), Zwetschgenwasser (from plums), Himbeergeist
(from raspberries), etc.; farther north corn brandy and
schnapps (made from juniper berries) predominate.

French cuisine is world-famed both for its quality and its variety. Since the average Frenchman attaches importance to a well
chosen menu and sets aside between one and two hours for his
meals, eating plays an important part in daily life, and cooking
has developed into an essential component of French culture.
Typical features of the highest standard of French cooking –
'haute cuisine' – are the use of fresh ingredients (anything
canned or preserved is anathema) and of plenty of butter and
cream. Herbs are used on a large scale and in a variety of
combinations. French sauces are famous.

France

In recent years there has been much talk of 'nouvelle cuisine',
which avoids over-elaboration but relies on the very best ingredients.

There are also various 'cuisines régionales' which are much
esteemed by discriminating gourmets.

A special position is occupied by the cuisine of Alsace, which
combines the special preferences of the Upper Rhine with the
culinary skill of France to produce results which are of high
quality, distinctive and varied. Many of the dishes are unknown
or rare to the east of the Rhine, and are often known by dialect
names; the menus, however, are always written in French.

The wide range of hors d'œuvres includes 'pâté de foie gras'
(goose liver pâté), a world-famed delicacy the recipe for which
(with truffles, veal, madeira and herbs) was devised in Strasbourg around 1780 by Jean-Pierre Clause, cook to Marshal
Contades; many other types of pâté, made from meat, fish or
game; snails with herb butter, onion pasties, sausage salad
(with cheese), etc. The little rivers and streams of the Vosges
yield excellent fish (mainly trout). Popular main dishes are
'choucroute garnie' (sauerkraut, cooked in white wine, with
sausages); 'coq au riesling' (steamed in white wine with onions

Practical Information

and mushrooms); pheasant (on sauerkraut) and other game dishes in season; and 'baeckaoffa' (a stew of pork, mutton and beef, with potatoes, onions and wine). The meal is rounded off with excellent cheese; two among the many kinds are Munster, an aromatic soft cheese from the Munster valley, and Géromé, a cream cheese flavoured with aniseed, fennel or caraway seed. A popular accompaniment to wine (→Facts and Figures, Wine) is the 'kugelhopf', a ring-shaped cake made from yeast dough, usually with raisins and almonds. Another favourite drink is Alsatian beer, brewed in many local breweries. The fruit brandies of Alsace (quetsch, framboise, mirabelle, etc.) are not so strong as those of Baden and accordingly have a very delicate bouquet and aroma.

Netherlands

The Dutch begin their day with a substantial breakfast; then at some time between 9 o'clock and noon they have another 'kopje koffie' with milk and sugar. Lunch consists of the so-called 'koffietafel', which is mainly bread with cheese, etc., and sometimes a cold or a warm dish.
Between 3 and 5 there is tea and perhaps a biscuit. The main meal of the day is in the evening, between 6 and 8, usually consisting of meat, vegetables and potatoes and often preceded by soup and followed by a sweet.

Fish plays a large part in the Dutch diet. During the first few weeks after the opening of the fishing season in May 'green' or 'new' herrings are on sale. There is also an abundance of crustaceans and shellfish; from May to September there are oysters and mussels from the province of Zealand.

Dutch cuisine includes a great variety of meat dishes. As a rule meat is only lightly grilled or fried on both sides; those who like their meat well done should ask for it to be 'doorbakken'. A 'duitse biefstuk' is a hamburger. Two Dutch specialties are 'rolpens' (brawn in a vinegar marinade, sliced and grilled, served with apple sauce and roast potatoes) and 'huzarensla' (meat salad). Fresh vegetables grown under glass are available throughout the year.

Favourite Dutch drinks are beer and 'genever' (schnapps made from juniper berries). Two well known liqueurs are 'advocaat' (with a raw egg base) and 'curaçao' (made from the skins of bitter oranges).

Belgium

Belgium has long been a land of gourmets, and the Belgians of today still like to make any special event in their life the occasion for a festive meal. The people of Flanders in particular attach great importance to food and drink.

Belgian specialties include the Flemish 'karbonade' (braised beef, cooked in beer), 'heaven and earth' (a dish found also in northern Germany, consisting of a potato and apple purée with blood sausage), smoked ham from the Ardennes and calves' kidneys Liégeoise. Among game dishes there are Flemish jugged hare with onions and prunes and rabbit cooked with prunes and Geuze beer. Brussels chickens, reared in the vicinity of the capital, are particularly tender.

'Waterzooi' is chicken trimmings in stock with a variety of vegetables. Belgian cakes and pastries are much esteemed.

The favourite Belgian drink is beer, of which there are many varieties. A new experience for beer-drinkers is offered by Belgian cherry-flavoured beer.

Wines, which are served on board the KD Rhine ships, may be bought at the following address:

Weingut
Selbach Erben
Hohenzollernstr. 49–51
D-56068 Koblenz
tel. (02 61) 30 43-5 02 or -5 22.

German Rhine Line

→ Köln-Düsseldorfer (KD German Rhine Line)

Hotels (selection)

Some hotels in the towns served by the Rhine cruise ships can be booked direct through the shipping line. For details apply to the KD German Rhine Line (→ Köln-Düsseldorfer).

The following list of hotels at the main ports of call of KD ships is no more than a selection. In Switzerland, France and the Netherlands hotels are officially assigned to categories, and the information given in this Guide is based on the official listing. In Germany and Belgium there is no comparable system of classification, and accordingly the selection of hotels in this list, and the order in which they are listed, is based on general criteria.

	Official categories		Categories
Switzerland	France	Netherlands	in this Guide
*****	L****	L	L (luxury)
****	****	I	A
***	***	II	B
**	**	III	C
*	*	IV	D

In this Guide luxury hotels are marked with an *asterisk.

b = beds; r = rooms

*Hilton International, Hohenbühlstr. 10, L, 550 b.
*Zürich, Neumühlequai 42, L, 400 b.
*Atlantis Sheraton, Döltschiweg 234, L, 320 b.
*Dolder Grand Hotel, Kurhausstr. 65, L, 300 b.
*Baur au Lac, Talstr. 1, L, 225 b.
*Savoy Baur en Ville, Poststr. 12, L, 150 b.
*Eden au Lac, Utoquai 45, L, 75 b.
Nova Park, Badenerstr. 420, A, 1018 b.
International, Marktplatz, A, 700 b.
Mövenpick Hotel Zurich Airport, CH-8152 Glattbrugg, A, 560 b.
Continental, Stampfenbachstr. 60, A, 244 b.
St. Gotthard, Bahnhofstr. 87, A, 195 b.
Glockenhof, Sihlstr. 31, A, 168 b.

Zurich
(CH)

Practical Information

<table>
<tr><td>Hotels in Zurich
(continued)</td><td>Stoller, Badenerstr. 357, A, 156 b.
Schweizerhof, Bahnhofplatz 7, A, 150 b.
Central, Am Central, A, 138 b.
Glärnischhof, Claridenstr. 30, A, 130 b.
Trümpy, Sihlquai 9, A, 130 b.
Atlantis Sheraton Guesthouse, Döltschihalde 49, A, 120 b.
Engematthof, Engemattstr. 14, A, 120 b.
Waldhaus Dolder, Kurhausstr. 20, A, 120 b.
Welcome Inn, Holbergstr. 1, B, 180 b.
Florida, Seefeldstr. 63, B, 150 b.
Seidenhof, Sihlstr. 9, B, 142 b.
Plaza, Goethestr. 18, B, 120 b.
City, Löwenstr. 34, B, 113 b.
Im Park, Kappelistr. 41, B, 110 b.
Rigihof, Universitätsstr. 101, B, 110 b.
Limmathaus, Limmatstr. 118, C, 110 b.
Regina, Hohlstr. 18, C, 102 b.</td></tr>

<tr><td>Basle
(CH)</td><td>*Basel Hilton, Aeschengraben 31, L, 368 b.
*International, Steinentorstr. 25, L, 350 b.
*Drei Könige am Rhein, Blumenrain 8, L, 120 b.
*Euler, Centralbahnplatz 14, L, 100 b.
*Schweizerhof, Centralbahnplatz 1, L, 100 b.
Europe, Clarastr. 43, A, 250 b.
Victoria am Bahnhof, Centralbahnplatz 3–4, A, 170 b.
Basel, Münzgasse 12, A, 105 b.
Alexander, Riehenring 85, A, 100 b.
Admiral, Rosentalstr. 5, B, 200 b.
City-Hotel, Henric-Petri-Str. 12, B, 130 b.
Basilisk, Klingentalstr. 1, B, 100 b.
Jura, Centralbahnplatz 11, B, 100 b.
Rheinfelderhof, Hammerstr. 61, C, 70 b.</td></tr>

<tr><td>Strasbourg
(F)</td><td>*Sofitel, 4, place St-Pierre-le-Jeune, L, 180 r.
*Novotel Centre Halles, quai Kléber, L, 97 r.
*Terminus Gruber, 10, place de la Gare, L, 78 r.
Hilton International Strasbourg, avenue Herrenschmidt, A, 253 r.
Grand Hôtel, place de la Gare, A, 90 r.
France, 20, rue du Jeu-des-Enfants, A, 66 r.
Holiday Inn, 20, place de Bordeaux, B, 165 r.
Nouvel Hôtel Maison Rouge, 4, rue des Francs-Bourgeois, B, 130 r.
Monopole Métropole, 16, rue Kuhn, B, 104 r.
Motel PLM, Parc du Rhin, B, 93 r.
Hannong, 15, rue du 22-Novembre, B, 70 r.
Pax, 24–26, rue du Faubourg National, C, 110 r.
Ibis, 1, rue de Sébastopol, C, 97 r.
National, 13, place de la Gare, C, 87 r.
Paris, 13, rue de la Mésange, C, 78 r.
Carlton, 15, place de la Gare, C, 72 r.
Couronne, 26, faubourg de Saverne, D, 39 r.</td></tr>

<tr><td>Speyer
(D)</td><td>Rheinhotel Luxhof, at Rhine Bridge, 104 b.
Goldener Engel, Mühlturmstr. 27, 66 b.
Kurpfalz (no rest.), Mühlturmstr. 5, 25 b.
Schlosser (no rest.), Maximilianstr. 10, 23 b.</td></tr>

<tr><td>Mannheim
(D)</td><td>*Steigenberger Hotel Mannheimer Hof, Augustaanlage 4, 280 b.</td></tr>
</table>

*Novotel, Friedensplatz 6, 360 b.
Wartburg, F 4, 4–11, 272 b.
Augusta, Augustaanlage 43, 140 b.
Basler Hof, Tattersallstr. 27, 96 b.
Wegener (no rest.), Tattersallstr. 16, 70 b.
Holländer Hof (no rest.), U 1, 11–12, 64 b.
Intercity Hotel, Bahnhofplatz 15, 63 b.

Rüdesheim
(D)

*Waldhotel Jagdschloss Niederwald, 6.5 km NW, 76 b.
Parkhotel Deutscher Hof, Rheinstr. 21, 136 b.
Central-Hotel, Kirchstr. 6, 76 b.
Rheinstein, Rheinstr. 20, 78 b.
Rüdesheimer Hof, Geisenheimer Str. 1, 75 b.
Zum Felsenkeller, Oberstr. 41, 133 b.

In Assmannshausen:
Krone, Rheinuferstr. 10, 132 b.
Anker, Rheinuferstr. 5, 110 b.
Nassauer Hof, Niederwaldstr. 18, 110 b.

Boppard
(D)

*Klostergut Jakobsberg, 13 km N, 207 b.
Bellevue-Rheinhotel, Rheinallee 41, 147 b.
Rheinlust, Rheinallee 29, 166 b.
Rheinhotel Spiegel, Rheinallee 34, 60 b.
Baudobriga Weinhaus Ries, Rheinallee 43, 69 b.
Motel am Ebertor, Heerstrasse, 120 b.

Braubach
(D)

Hammer, Untermarktstr. 15, 21 b.

Koblenz
(D)

City-Hotel Metropol, Münzplatz 54, 90 b.
Brenner (no rest.), Rizzastr. 20, 48 b.
Trierer Hof, Deinhardplatz 1, 57 b.
Diehls Hotel Rheinterrassen, in Ehrenbreitstein, 120 b.
Kleiner Riesen (no rest.), Rheinanlagen 18, 55 b.
Continental – Pfälzer Hof, Bahnhofsplatz 1, 50 b.
Hamm (no rest.), St.-Josef-Str. 32, 50 b.

Cologne
(D)

*Excelsior-Hotel Ernst, Domplatz, 260 b.
*Dom-Hotel, Domkloster 2a, 182 b.
*Inter-Continental, Helenenstr. 14, 580 b.
*Mondial, Bechergasse 10, 300 b.
*Consul, Belfortstr. 9, 235 b.
*Holiday Inn, at Cologne/Bonn Airport,
Waldstr. 255, 160 b.
*Hotel am Wasserturm, Kaylgasse 2, 90 Z.
*Crest Hotel, in Lindenthal, Dürener Str. 287, 210 b.
Senats-Hotel, Unter Goldschmied 9, 100 b.
Königshof (no rest), Richartzstr. 14, 141 b.
Am Augustinerplatz (no rest), Hohe Str. 30, 105 b.
Coellner Hof, Hansaring 100, 100 b.
Haus Lyskirchen, Filzengraben 26, 83 b.
Rheingold (no rest), Engelbertstr. 33, 130 b.
Ludwig (no rest), Brandenburger Str. 24, 100 b.
Kolpinghaus-International, St.-Apern-Str. 32, 85 b.

Düsseldorf
(D)

*Hilton, Georg-Glock-Str. 20, 612 b.
*Breidenbacher Hof, Heinrich-Heine-Allee 36, 220 b.
*Nikko, Immermannstr. 41, 600 b.
*Dorint Kongress-Hotel, Karl-Arnold-Platz 5, 500 b.
*Steigenberger Parkhotel, Corneliusplatz 1, 230 b.

Practical Information

Hotels in Düsseldorf
(continued)

*Ramada Renaissance, in Mörsenbroich, Nördlicher Zubrin-
ger 6, 389 b.
*Ramada, in Oberkassel, Am Seestern 16, 380 b.
*Rheinstern Penta Hotel, in Oberkassel, Emanuel-Leutze-
Str. 17, 352 b
Holiday Inn, Graf-Adolf-Platz 10, 204 b.
Savoy, Oststr. 128, 180 b.
Esplanade, Fürstenplatz 17, 110 b.
Uebachs, Leopoldstr. 3, 110 b.
Excelsior (no rest.), Kapellenstr. 1, 100 b.
Börsenhotel (no rest.), Kreuzstr. 19a, 102 b.
Graf Adolf (no rest.), Stresemannplatz 1, 130 b.

Nijmegen
(NL)

Schaeferhotel (no rest.), Grote Markt 39, A, 33 b.
Sionshof, Nijmeegsebaan 53, C, 50 b.
Rozenhof, Nijmeegsebaan 114, D, 34 b.

Rotterdam
(NL)

*Rotterdam Hilton, Weena 10, L, 487 b.
Parkhotel, Westersingel 70, A, 146 b.
Rijnhotel Rotterdam DMP, Schouwburgplein, A, 240 b.
Central, Kruiskade 12, A, 115 b.
Savoy Golden Tulip Hotel, Aert van Nesstraat 4, A, 250 b.
Wilgenhof, Heemraadsingel 92–94, B, 77 b.
Van Walsum, Mathenesserlaan 199, B, 44 b.
Pax (no rest.), Schierkade 658, C, 90 b.
Baan (no rest.), Rochussenstraat 345, C, 26 b.
Emma (no rest.), Nieuwe Binnenweg 6, D, 50 b.
Scandia, Willemsplein 1, D, 93 b.

Amsterdam
(NL)

*Okura Amsterdam, Ferdinand Bolstraat 175, L, 747 b.
*Amsterdam Sonesta, Kattengat 1, L, 700 b.
*Amsterdam Marriott, Stadhouderskade 19–21, L, 675 b.
*Amsterdam Hilton, Apollolaan 138–140, L, 500 b.
*Apollo, Apollolaan 2, L, 400 b.
*Amstel, Prof. Tulpplein 1, L, 187 b.
*De l'Europe, Nieuwe Doelenstraat 2–4, L, 154 b.
Novotel Amsterdam, Europaboulevard 10, A, 1200 b.
Grand Hotel Krasnapolsky, Dam 9, A, 552 b.
Crest Hotel Amsterdam, De Boelelaan 2, A, 520 b.
Pulitzer, Prinsengracht 315–331, A, 365 b.
Parkhotel, Stadhouderskade 25, A, 350 b.
American, Leidsekade 97, A, 323 b.
Victoria, Damrak 1–5, A, 320 b.
Die Port van Cleve, N. Z. Voorburgwal 178–180, A, 210 b.
Doelen, Nieuwe Doelenstraat 24, A, 160 b.
Memphis, De Lairessestraat 87, A, 139 b.
Alexander, Prinsengracht 444, A, 44 b.
Euromotel Amsterdam, Oude Haagseweg 20, B, 350 b.
Carlton, Vijzelstraat 2–18, B, 272 b.
Golden Tulip Centraal, Stadhouderskade 7, B, 216 b.
Amster Centre, Herengracht 255, B, 213 b.
Schiller, Rembrandtsplein 26–36, B, 193 b.
Arthur Frommer, Noorderstraat 46, B, 185 b.
Caransa, Rembrandtsplein 19, B, 132 b.
Jan Luyken, Jan Luykensstraat 58, B, 130 b.
Casa 400 (June–Oct. only), James Wattstraat 75, C, 700 b.
Museum, P. C. Hoofstraat 2, C, 293 b.
Euromotel E–9, Joan Muyskenweg 10, C, 260 b.
Terminus, Beursstraat 11–19, C, 176 b.
AMS Hotel Terdam, Tesselschadestraat 23, C, 140 b.

Cok Budget Hotel, Koninginneweg 34–36, D, 200 b.
Lancaster, Plantage Middenlaan 48, D, 100 b.

*De Keyser, De Keyserlei 66–70, 117 r.
*Plaza, Charlottalei 43, 78 r.
Crest, Gerard Legrellelaan 10, 306 r.
Waldorf, Belgiëlei 36, 95 r.
Theater, Arenbergstraat 30, 83 r.
Empire, Appelmanstraat 31, 70 r.
Antwerp Tower Hotel, Van Ertbornstraat 10, 51 r.
Eurotel Antwerpen, Copernicuslaan 2, 350 r.
Holiday Inn, Luitenant Lippenslaan 66, 179 r.
Congress, Plantin en Moretuslei 136, 173 r.
Tourist, Pelikansstraat 20–22, 146 r.
Novotel, Luithagenhaven 6, 119 r.

Holidays

→ Public holidays

Information

→ Tourist information

Köln-Düsseldorfer (KD German Rhine Line)

KD German Rhine Line
(Köln-Düsseldorfer Deutsche Rheinschiffahrt AG
Frankenwerft 15   P.O.B. 10 21 52
D-50667 Köln   D-50461 Köln
telephone: (02 21) 20 88-0 (exchange),
20 88-3 18 and -3 19 (information), 20 88-2 88 (bookings)
Telex: 88 82 723, telegraphic address: Rhineline Köln

Headquarters

The KD German Rhine Line is represented in many countries all
over the world, e. g. in the United States of America, Great Britain, Canada, Australia, Japan, Mexico, Brazil, France, Switzerland and Austria. The addresses of the KD agencies are to be
found in the KD brochures available at the representations of the
German National Tourist Office (Deutsche Zentrale für Tourismus; → Tourist Information, Germany) or directly at the KD German Rhine Line headquarters.

Information and
reservations abroad

History of the KD

In 1976 the Köln-Düsseldorfer Deutsche Rheinschiffahrt AG,
the Cologne-Düsseldorf German Rhine Line, could look back
on 150 years of existence, having been founded in 1826 as the
Prussian Rhine Steamship Company of Cologne. In the following
year the company's two steamships, the "Concordia" and the
"Friedrich Wilhelm" – entirely built of wood – made 129 trips
between Cologne and Mainz, carrying not only large quantities
of freight but also 33,352 passengers.

Practical Information

Reproduction of the front page of the time-table for steamship services operated by the Cologne and Düsseldorf shipping companies – today's KD German Rhine Line –, effective as from May 15th, 1889

Köln-Düsseldorfer, History (continued)

During the first third of the 19th century the steamship services on the Rhine were organised on a regional basis. At first their main role lay in the transport of freight, but after the middle of the century passenger excursions became increasingly popular, while in the field of goods transport the railways offered increasingly formidable competition. This led the Cologne and Düsseldorf shipping companies, hitherto rivals, to join forces in 1853, and this association, renewed in 1859, was to be maintained until the complete amalgamation of the two companies in 1967.

In 1867 the first fast double-decker steamers designed solely for passenger transport, the "Friede" and the "Humboldt", were brought into service.

The establishment of the German Empire in 1871 did away with many obstacles to travel like frontiers between petty states, customs barriers and different currency systems, leading to a great expansion of holiday traffic. From 1885 onwards an average of one new steamer a year was brought into service and one older vessel scrapped; and by 1913 the company was carrying some two million passengers a year. In 1927 it acquired a majority holding in the Nederlandsche Stoomboot Reederij (Dutch Steamship Line), and in the same year the first passenger motor ship was brought into service.

During the second world war the company lost almost all its ships, but by November 1945 it was already operating again – at first for the transport of essential freight but from May 1946 for local excursion traffic as well.

In the late 1950s and early 1960s several large motor ships came into service, and these made it possible for the first time to run cruises along the whole length of the river between Basle and Rotterdam which soon became extremely popular. In 1982 regular cruises by vessels equipped with comfortable cabins began on the Mosel (Moselle) between Trier and Koblenz.

In 1967 the Cologne and Düsseldorf companies amalgamated to become the Köln-Düsseldorfer. Nowadays 24 ships run under the KD flag on the rivers of Rhein (Rhine), Main, Mosel (Moselle), Elbe and Donau (Danube); in addition to the eight large cruise ships used for longer lasting excursions and MS "France" for special tours, there are 12 vessels for day excursions and two hydrofoils for fast trips.

KD's large motor ship "Loreley" in front of Burg Rheinfels

The KD Fleet

Name	Length m	Width m	h.p. DIN/kW	Engines	Passenger capacity	Average speed km/h	Built	Max. draught m
Cruise ships								
MS Deutschland	110	11.6	1920/1413	Diesel	184	20.5	1971	1.40
MS Italia	104	11.6	1920/1413	Diesel	184	20.5	1971	1.40
MS Austria	104	11.6	1920/1413	Diesel	184	20.5	1971	1.40
MS Britannia	110	11.6	1920/1413	Diesel	184	20.4	1969	1.40
MS France*	105	11.6	1700/1250	Diesel	200	20.5	1966	1.40
MS Heinrich Heine	106	11.1	2040/1530	Diesel	104	18.0	1991	1.30
MS Clara Schumann	95	11.0	1630/1200	Diesel	124	18.0	1991	0.95
MS Theodor Fontane	95	11.0	1630/1200	Diesel	124	18.0	1991	0.95
MS Europa	89	11.6	1700/1250	Diesel	128	20.6	1960	1.48
* only for special tours								
Excursion ships								
Large motor ships:								
MS Wappen v. Köln	93	15.8	1400/1030	Diesel	2000	21.2	1967	1.55
MS Loreley	92	15.8	1300/955	Diesel	2000	21.7	1963	1.55
MS Wappen v. Mainz	91	15.8	1400/1030	Diesel	2000	21.7	1961	1.60
MS Berlin	89	15.5	1300/955	Diesel	2000	21.6	1959	1.40
Motor ships:								
MS Stolzenfels	77	10.0	900/662	Diesel	1000	21.7	1979	1.40
MS Koblenz	70	11.1	800/589	Diesel	1000	21.0	1940	1.60
MS Rüdesheim	69	8.8	800/588	Diesel	750	21.7	1987	1.25
MS Drachenfels	65	8.6	800/588	Diesel	750	21.7	1985	1.25
MS Jan von Werth	40	7.8	640/468	Diesel	240	21.0	1992	1.60
MS Domplatz	36	6.5	460/338	Diesel	250	21.0	1969	1.70
Paddle steamer:								
D Goethe	83	15.7	700/515	Steam	1660	22.1	1913	1.50
(at the moment not in function)								
Hydrofoils:								
Rheinpfeil (Rhine Arrow)	27	5.0	1100/810	Diesel	64	65.0	1972	1.80
Rheinjet (Rhine Jet)	18	6.0	~ 800	Diesel	60	70.0	1994	1.10
(Catamaran)								
Hydrofoil:								
Rheinpfeil	27	5.00	1100/ 810	Diesel	64	65.0	1972	1.80

Distinguished passengers carried by KD

1845	Queen Victoria, accompanied by the Prince Consort, the King and Queen of the Belgians, King Frederick William IV of Prussia and his queen, sails to Schloss Stolzenfels, near Koblenz, on the steamship "König".
1930	President Hindenburg sails from Ludwigshafen to Koblenz on the steamer "Hindenburg".
1953	Chancellor Konrad Adenauer attends the celebrations of KD's hundredth anniversary on MS "Köln".
1956	The Indian prime minister, Pandit Nehru, sails on MS "Bonn" as a guest of Chancellor Adenauer.

During a state visit to the Federal Republic of Germany King Paul I and Queen Frederica of Greece sail on MS "Köln", accompanied by President Theodor Heuss and Ludwig Erhard, minister of trade and commerce.

Köln-Düsseldorfer,
Distinguished passengers,
1956 (continued)

Chancellor Julius Raab of Austria is a guest on a KD ship.

President Olympio of Togo sails on MS "Berlin". — 1961

During an EEC summit meeting Chancellor Adenauer and President de Gaulle of France sail on MS "Deutschland" (now MS "Drachenfels").

During the formal opening of the canalised Mosel (Moselle) Grand Duchess Charlotte of Luxembourg, President de Gaulle of France and President Heinrich Lübke of the German Federal Republic sail on MS "Trier". — 1964

Queen Elizabeth II sails from Koblenz to Kaub on MS "Loreley". — 1965

President Gustav Heinemann gives a reception on MS "Loreley" during his visit to Rhineland-Palatinate. — 1969

During Franco-German discussions President Pompidou and Chancellor Willy Brandt meet on MS "Loreley". — 1971

Emperor Hirohito of Japan sails from Bingen to Koblenz on MS "Loreley".

NATO ministers of foreign affairs meet on board MS "Loreley" on the invitation of the West German foreign minister, Walter Scheel. — 1972

President Heinemann gives his farewell party on MS "Drachenfels". — 1974

US President Gerald Ford sails on MS "Drachenfels" on the invitation of West German President Scheel. — 1975

Mrs Rosalyn Carter, wife of US President Carter, sails from Bingen to Linz on MS "Köln" with Frau Schmidt, wife of the West German Chancellor. — 1978

King Khalid of Saudi Arabia sails from Bingen to Koblenz on MS "Stolzenfels". — 1980

During the meeting of NATO's Council Mrs Nancy Reagan and Frau Schmidt sail from Bingen to Koblenz on MS "Stolzenfels". On the same day the "Stolzenfels" takes the heads of the NATO states on an evening cruise from Bonn. — 1982

KD Rhine cruises

With its six comfortable cruise ships the KD German Rhine Line offers a variety of cruises, ranging between Switzerland and the Netherlands. Among the cruise destinations are Basle, Strasbourg, Nijmegen, Rotterdam and Amsterdam. The length of the trips is from two to eight days depending on the distance

KD Cruise Ship "Deutschland"

The KD Cruise Ships on the river Rhine

Cabin plan

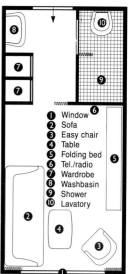

MS DEUTSCHLAND (see above)
MS BRITANNIA
Length: 110 m; width: 11.60 m; height above water-line: 9.30 m; max. draught: 1.40 m; engine power: 1920 h.p. DIN/1413 kW. Three air-conditioned decks, sun deck, covered leisure deck, heated outdoor swimming-pool, sauna. 184 beds in 92 cabins, all with shower and toilet. Dining-saloon, bar, observation lounge, reading-room, veranda. Gift shop.

MS AUSTRIA
MS ITALIA
Length: 104 m; width: 11.60 m; height above water-line: 9.30 m; max. draught: 1.40 m; engine power: 1920 h.p. DIN/1413 kW. Three air-conditioned decks, sun deck, covered leisure deck, sauna. 184 beds in 92 outside cabins, all with shower and toilet. Dining-saloon, bar, observation lounge, reading-room, veranda. Gift shop.

① Window
② Sofa
③ Easy chair
④ Table
⑤ Folding bed
⑥ Tel./radio
⑦ Wardrobe
⑧ Washbasin
⑨ Shower
⑩ Lavatory

MS EUROPA
Length: 89 m; width: 11.60 m; height above water-line: 9.30 m; max. draught: 1.48 m; engine power: 1700 h.p. DIN/1250 kW. Three air-conditioned decks, sun deck, covered leisure deck, heated outdoor swimming-pool. 128 beds in 64 outside cabins, most of them with shower and toilet. Dining-saloon, bar, observation lounge, reading-room, veranda. Gift shop.

MS FRANCE
(only for special tours)
Length: 105 m; width: 11.60 m; height above water-line: 9.30 m; max. draught: 1.40 m; engine power: 1700 h.p. DIN/1250 kW. Three air-conditioned decks, sun deck, covered leisure deck, heated outdoor swimming-pool. 204 passenger capacity in 104 twin bedded cabins, all with shower and toilet. Dining-saloon, bar, observation lounge, reading-room, veranda. Gift shop.

nsegel   Kommandobrücke   Aussichtssalon

a Solarium   Veranda / Bar   Rheinland-Deck

op   Loreley-Deck

A	A	A	A	A	A	A	A	De Luxe	A	A	A			A	A	A	A	A	A	A	A	A	A	A	A	A	
601	603	605	607	609	611	613	615	617/19	621	623	625			629	631	633	635	637	639	641	643	645	647	649	651	653	**Loreley-Deck**
602	604	606	608	610	612	614	616	618/20	622	624	626			628	630	632	634	636	638	640	642	644	646	648	650	652	654
A	A	A	A	A	A	A	A	De Luxe	A	A	A			A	A	A	A	A	A	A	A	A	A	A	A	A	

B	B	B	B	B	B	B	B	B	B	B	B	B	B		B	B	B	B	B	B			
659	661	663	665	667	669	671	673	675	677	679	681	683	685		687	689	691	693	695	697			**Rheinland-Deck**
658	660	662	664	666	668	670	672	674	676	678	680	682	684		686	688	690	692	694	696	698		
B	B	B	B	B	B	B	B	B	B	B	B	B	B		B	B	B	B	B	B	B		

Cabin ▼

KD cruise ship "Britannia", off Burg Ehrenfels

Köln-Düsseldorfer,
KD Rhine Cruises
(continued)

covered. The ships sail only during the day so that the passengers can enjoy the scenery; and the moorings where they tie up at night are so quiet that they can be sure of undisturbed sleep. During the journey up or down stream the ships call in at various towns, offering wide scope for sightseeing trips on land. Various trips are arranged by the KD German Rhine Line, including city tours (e.g. of Cologne and Strasbourg) and excursions to nearby towns (e.g. to Heidelberg).

In addition to the regular cruises run between April and October there are also special-interest cruises, i.e. wine and gourmet cruises, cruises to the "Rhine Aflame" (cf. events), Holland–Flanders–Tours as well as Christmas and New Year cruises.

It stands to reasons that reservations for the entire cruise have priority over reservations for only a section of the cruise.

The fare includes accommodation in a cabin of the type selected, excellent service and a varied cuisine of the highest quality.

Not included are drinks in the restaurant and bar, shore excursions (booked at purser's office) and gratuities (→Tipping).

The KD cruise ships – floating first-class hotels – offer admirable facilities for private parties. Where the numbers are sufficient the ships can be hired for exclusive use, with substantial reductions in price: it is worth while chartering a ship for as few as 100 people. The timing of the trip and the choice of ports of call can be arranged according to personal requirements.

Where the party is not large enough to justify a charter reductions can be arranged for groups on regular cruises.

The cruise ships have four decks, with finely appointed public rooms, restaurants with large windows, an observation lounge completely surrounded by glass, a large sun-deck and a bar. Most ships also have a heated swimming-pool.

All cabins face outwards, with windows overlooking the river. They are roomy and well equipped, almost invariably having a private shower and toilet, radio, telephone and air-conditioning.

The ships are some 100 m long and 12 m wide, and the top deck (the sun-deck) is 7 m above the waterline. They are driven by four diesel engines, using two Voith-Schneider propellers. Navigational aids include radar and echo-sounding equipment. Average speed upstream is about 10 km/h, downstream 16 km/h.

Köln-Düsseldorfer,
KD Rhine Cruises
(continued)

Regular KD passenger services

From 1 April to 30 October there are daily passenger services between Cologne and Koblenz and between Koblenz and Mainz (with continuation to Frankfurt am Main on some services). Calls are made at all places of importance on the route.

On the Rhine

At all KD landing-stages most of the railway tickets can be transferred to ship tickets (or vice versa) against a transition tax. In both ways, tickets can only be transferred at KD landing-stages, never at the railway ticket offices of the German Railway.

Joint KD/German Railway
Services (ship/railway)

There are daily services on the Mosel (Moselle) between Koblenz and Cochem.

On the Mosel
(subject to change)

KD excursion services

Evening trips with music and dancing are usually run on Fridays or Saturdays. Departures from Cologne, Bonn, Wiesbaden and Mainz.

Evening trips

Sightseeing cruises at different times of day, affording a panoramic view of Cologne or Düsseldorf from the river.

Sightseeing cruises from
Cologne and Düsseldorf

A variety of excursions with programmes of entertainments are available: information from KD offices.

Excursions with on-board
entertainments

A number of popular excursions of this kind are run. On twoday trips the fare includes overnight accommodation. Details from KD offices.

Excursions with
land-based programmes

The KD offers various tickets at reduced prices. For detailed information ask travel bureaus, KD agencies or KD headquarters in Cologne:
tel. (02 21) 20 88-3 18 and -3 19 (information),
tel. (02 21) 20 88-2 88 (booking)

Tickets at
reduced prices

Practical Information

Landing points of the KD in the Rhine area

Ports of call	KD landing-stages	KD agencies[1] (p. 275)
Amsterdam	Passagiers Terminal, Oostelijke Handelskade	
Andernach	Rhine bank	
Antwerp	Tavernierkaai, near Loodswezen Building	
Assmannshausen	Rhine bank	
Bacharach	Rhine bank	
Bad Breisig	Rhine bank	
Bad Godesberg (Bonn)	Von-Sandt-Ufer, Bastei	
Bad Honnef	Rhine bank	
Bad Hönningen	Rhine bank	
Bad Salzig (Boppard)	Rhine bank	
Basle	Elsässer Rheinweg, near St.-Johanns-Tor	
Biebrich	see Wiesbaden-Biebrich	
Bingen	Rheinanlagen	
Bonn	opposite Rheingasse and near Bundeshaus	
Boppard	Rhine bank	
Braubach	Rhine bank	
Cologne (Köln)	Frankenwerft (Rheingarten)	Frankenwerft 15 D-50667 Köln (Cologne)
Cologne-Porz	Rhine bank	see Cologne
Düsseldorf	Theodor-Heuss-Bridge, Rheinterrassen and Rathausufer	
Eltville	Rhine bank	
Frankfurt am Main	Eiserner Steg	
Gernsheim	Rhine bank	

KD motor ship "Stolzenfels", off Sankt Goarshausen

Ports of call	KD landing-stages	KD agencies[1] (p. 275)
Höchst (Frankfurt/M.)	Main bank	
Kamp-Bornhofen	Rhine bank	
Kaub	Rhine bank	
Koblenz	Konrad-Adenauer-Ufer (near Deutsches Eck) and Rheinanlagen	
Köln	see Cologne	see Cologne
Köln-Porz	see Cologne-Porz	see Cologne
Königswinter	Rhine bank	
Lahnstein	Oberlahnstein and Niederlahnstein	
Linz	Rhine bank	
Lorch	Rhine bank	
Mainz	Adenauerufer, Town Hall	
Mannheim	Stephanieufer, Rheinpromenade	

Practical Information

KD Hydrofoil "Rheinpfeil" at full speed

Ports of call	KD landing-stages	KD agencies[1] (p. 275)
Neuwied	Rhine bank	
Niederheimbach	Rhine bank	
Niederlahnstein	see Lahnstein	
Nijmegen	Waalkade	
Oberlahnstein	see Lahnstein	
Oberwesel	Rhine bank	
Porz	see Cologne-Porz	see Cologne
Remagen	Rheinpromenade	
Rhens	Rhine bank	
Rotterdam	Maasboulevard	
Rüdesheim	Rheinanlagen and Rhine bank	
Rüsselsheim	Main bank	
Sankt Goar	Rhine bank	

KD paddle steamer "Goethe" on the Rhine (at the moment not in function)

Ports of call	KD landing-stages	KD agencies[1]
Sankt Goarshausen	Rhine bank	
Speyer	Rhine bank (Municipal Bath)	
Strasbourg	Gare Fluviale, Quai des Belges	
Unkel	Rhine bank	
Wesseling	Rhine bank	
Wiesbaden-Biebrich	Rheingaustrasse	

[1] At many KD landing-stages there are KD agencies, where you may obtain any information and can do bookings. You may also call KD headquarters directly under tel. (02 21) 20 88-2 88.

Languages

On the Vorderrhein and Hinterrhein the local language is Romansh, a tongue derived from Vulgar Latin which is spoken in the Grisons in several dialects and was recognised in 1938 as the fourth official language of Switzerland (the others being

Switzerland

Practical Information

German, French and Italian). Farther north the written language is standard German (Schriftdeutsch), but the spoken language is a characteristic form of German, Schwyzerdütsch, which is a descendant of Alemannic, in a variety of local dialects. The use of Schwyzerdütsch is deliberately preserved and promoted, and it is strongly preferred to standard German on radio and television and even in the political and military field.

Germany

Standard German (Hochdeutsch, Schriftdeutsch) is the official language throughout the Federal Republic of Germany. The various dialects spoken in different parts of the country fall into two broad groups, Upper German (Oberdeutsch) to the south and Low German (Niederdeutsch) to the north, separated by the 'Benrath line', which runs from south of Limburg, passes to the north of Aachen, Düsseldorf and Kassel, and continues eastward to pass south of Magdeburg in East Germany.

France

The official language is French, which developed out of the Vulgar Latin spoken by the Gauls after the Roman occupation and preserved its Romance character in spite of the assimilation of many words of Celtic and later of Germanic origin. In Alsace a Germanic dialect, Elsässerditsch, is still spoken; like the Schwyzerdütsch spoken in Switzerland and the dialects of Baden on the right bank of the Rhine, it is a variant of Alemannic.

Netherlands

Dutch is a Germanic language derived from Old Lower Franconian.

Belgium

In the northern (Flemish) part of Belgium Dutch is spoken, and there is also a small German-speaking area. In the southern (Walloon) part of the country French predominates.

Leisure parks

→ Recreation and leisure parks

Maps

For land excursions of any length in the course of a Rhine cruise and for independent tours by car or other means, good maps should be part of the traveller's equipment. The following is a selection.

1 : 600,000

Wasserstrassenkarte Rhein (Bodensee – Nordsee)
(Waterways Map of the Rhine – Lake Constance to North Sea)

1 : 250,000

Shell Autokarte Niederlande
(Shell Motoring Map of the Netherlands)

1 : 200,000

Generalkarte Deutschland
(General Map of Germany)
Sheets 8, 10, 12, 5, 16, 18, 21, 24 and 25

Generalkarte Schweiz (General Map of Switzerland)
Sheets 1 and 3

Generalkarte Vogesen/Elsass
(General Map of the Vosges and Alsace)

Michelin map of France
Sheet 87

Postal, telegraph and telephone services

Mail for passengers on KD ships can be sent to the overnight
stopping-places on a cruise.

The following information must be included in the address:

passenger's name,
name of the ship,
date of departure,
cabin number and
overnight stopping-place.

It is advisable to give the purser a forwarding address for mail
before leaving the ship.

Urgent telegrams should be sent to the KD Line (telegraphic
address: 'Rhineline Köln'), since it can then be passed on by the
company to the ship by telephone. It is also possible to telephone
direct (by means of the C-System of the German Telekom) to a
passenger on board a KD ship:

MS "Deutschland"	tel. 01 61/2 20 75 69
MS "Britannia"	tel. 01 61/2 20 35 77
MS "France"	tel. 01 61/2 20 37 78
MS "Italia"	tel. 01 61/2 20 37 40
MS "Austria"	tel. 01 61/2 20 37 61
MS "Europa"	tel. 01 61/2 20 75 10

The fact that KD ships are equipped with telephones means that
in case of emergency medical assistance can be summoned
right away.

Public holidays

Germany
Switzerland

1 January (New Year's Day)
6 January (Epiphany)
Good Friday
Easter Monday
1 May (Labour Day)
Ascension
Whit Monday
Corpus Christi (in predominantly Catholic areas)
1 August (National Day)
1 November (All Saints)
Day of Repentance and Prayer
25 and 26 December

1 January (New Year's Day)
6 January (Epiphany; only in Baden-Württemberg and Bavaria)

Federal Republic of Germany

Practical Information

<table>
<tr><td>Public holidays in Germany
(continued)</td><td>Good Friday
Easter Monday
1 May (Labour Day)
Ascension
Whit Monday
Corpus Christi (only in
Baden-Württemberg, Bavaria, Hesse, North Rhine-Westphalia,
Rhineland-Palatinate and the Saar)
Assumption (only in
parts of Bavaria and the Saar)
3 October (Day of German Unity)
1 November (All Saints:
only in Baden-Württemberg, Bavaria, North Rhine-Westphalia,
Rhineland-Palatinate and the Saar)
Day of Repentance and Prayer
25 and 26 December</td></tr>
<tr><td>France</td><td>1 January (New Year's Day)
Good Friday (only in Alsace)
Easter Monday
1 May (Labour Day)
Ascension
Whit Monday
14 July (National Day)
Assumption
1 November (All Saints)
11 November (Armistice, 1918)
25 December
26 December (only in Alsace)</td></tr>
<tr><td>Netherlands</td><td>1 January (New Year's Day)
Easter Monday
30 April
Ascension
Whit Monday
25 and 26 December</td></tr>
<tr><td>Belgium</td><td>1 January (New Year's Day)
Easter Monday
1 May (Labour Day)
Ascension
Whit Monday
21 July
15 August
1 November (All Saints)
11 November (Armistice, 1918)
25 December</td></tr>
</table>

Recreation and leisure parks in the Rhine area

<table>
<tr><td>Germany</td><td>Traumland-Park
D-46244 Kirchhellen

Ruhrzoo
D-45889 Gelsenkirchen

Phantasialand
D-50321 Brühl</td></tr>
</table>

Taunus-Wunderland
D-65307 Bad Schwalbach

Kurpfalzpark Wachenheim
D-67157 Wachenheim/Weinstrasse

Holiday-Park Hassloch
D-67454 Hassloch/Pfalz

Europa-Park
D-77977 Rust/Baden

Madurodam
NL-2584 EE Den Haag-Scheveningen

Recreation and leisure parks
in Germany (continued)

Netherlands

Rent-a-bike

→ Bicycle hire

Rent-a-car

→ Car hire

Restaurants (selection)

*Agnes Amberg, Hottingerstr. 5
*Riesbacherhof, Zollikerstr. 157
Kronenhalle, Rämistr. 4
Zunfthaus zur Schmiden, Marktgasse 20
Zunfthaus zur Waag, Münsterhof 8
Zunfthaus zum Saffran, Limmatquai 54
Zunfthaus zur Zimmerleuten, Limmatquai 40
Zunfthaus zum Rüden, Limmatquai 42
Zunfthaus am Neumarkt, Neumarkt 5
Conti, Dufourstr. 1
Widder, Widdergasse 6
Lindenhofkeller, Pfalzgasse 4
Mövenpick Paradeplatz, in Paradeplatz

Zurich
(CH)

*Pfeffermühle, Grünpfahlgasse 4
*Stucki, Bruderholzallee 42
*Safranzunft, Gerbergasse 11
Schützenhaus, Schützenmattstr. 56
Walliser Kanne, Gerbergasse 50

Basle
(CH)

*Le Crocodile, 10, rue de l'Outre
*Buerehiesel, 4, parc de l'Orangerie
Valentin-Sorg, place de l'Homme de Fer
Maison Kammerzell, 16, place de la Cathédrale
Gerwerstub (Maison des Tanneurs), 46, rue du Bain aux Plantes
Gourmet sans Chiqué, 15, rue Ste-Barbe

Strasbourg
(F)

Backmulde, Karmeliterstr. 11
Rôtisserie Weisses Ross, Johannesstr. 2

Speyer
(D)

Practical Information

Restaurants in Speyer (continued)	Domnapf, Domplatz 1 Stadthalle, Obere Langgasse 11
Mannheim (D)	L'Epi d'Or, H 7, 3 Blass, in Friedrichsfeld, Langlachweg 30 Kopenhagen, Friedrichsring 2 a Savarin, Friedrichsplatz
Braubach (D)	Weisser Schwan, Brunnenstr. 4 Weinhaus Wieghardt, Marktplatz 7
Koblenz (D)	Rhein-Mosel-Halle, at Pfaffendorfer Brücke Le Bastion, in Pfaffendorf, Emser Str. 87 Asia, Münzplatz 14 Zum Bitburger, Rizzastr. 36 Weindorf, Julius-Wegeler-Str. 4
Cologne (D)	*Restaurant Bado (La Poêle d'Or), Komödienstr. 52 *Goldener Pflug, in Merheim, Olpener Str. 421 Lüders Bar and Franz Kellers Restaurant, Aachener Str. 21 Chez Alex, Mühlengasse 1 Fontana di Trevi, Ebertplatz 3 St. Georg, Ebertplatz 3 Sigi's Bistro, Kleiner Griechenmarkt 23 Auberge de la Charrue d'Or, Habsburger Ring 18 Weinhaus im Walfisch, Salzgasse 13 Kellers Tomate, Aachener Str. 11
Düsseldorf (D)	*Orangerie, Bilker Str. 30 *Frickhöfer, Stromstr. 47 *Robert's Restaurant, in Oberkassel, Oberkasseler Str. 100 Müllers und Fest KD, Königsallee 12–14 Im Schiffchen, in Kaiserswerth, Kaiserswerther Markt 9 eNTchen, Königsallee 27 The Victorian, Königstr. 3 a Nippon-Kan (Japanese), Immermannstr. 35 Schneider-Wibbel-Stuben, Schneider-Wibbel-Gasse Zum Schiffchen (top-fermented beer), Hafenstr. 5 Zum Uerige (top-fermented beer), Berger Str. 1
Nijmegen (NL)	In d'Oude Laeckenthal, Grote Markt 23 St. Stephens, Oranjesingel 1 Belvédère, Kelfkensbos 57 In de Boterwaag, Grote Markt 26
Rotterdam (NL)	Coq d'Or, Van Vollenhovenstraat 25 Old Dutch, Rochussenstraat 20 Euromast, Parkhaven 20
Amsterdam (NL)	Dikker en Thijs, Prinsengracht 444 Boederij, Korte Leidsedwarsstraat 69 't Swarte Schaep, Korte Leidsedwarsstraat 24 Auberge, Leidseplein 8 Neptunus, Rokin 87 Molen De Dikkert, Amsterdamseweg 104
Antwerp (B)	La Pérouse, on floating bridge at Steenplein La Rade, Ernest van Dijckkaai 8 Critérium, De Keyserlei 25 Cigogne d'Alsace, Wiegstraat 7

Le Relais, Kelderstraat 1
St. Jacob in Galicië, Braderijstraat 12–16
Sir Anthony Van Dijck, Oude Koornmarkt 16
China Garden, De Keyserlei 17

→Hotels

Restaurants in Antwerp
(continued)

Hotel restaurants
Germany

Season

→ When to go

Souvenirs

The best-known Swiss products are watches and jewellery. Other very popular buys are textiles, St Gallen lace and embroidery and the many-bladed Swiss army knives. A good selection of Swiss craft goods can be seen in the showrooms of 'Schweizer Heimatwerk' in Zurich and other towns.
Switzerland offers a wide variety of foodstuffs of excellent quality, notably chocolate, cheese and various spirits (e.g. the kirsch of Zug and the herb liqueur of the Grisons, Chrüter), as well as such specialties as the 'Bündnerfleisch' (air-dried beef) and 'Birnbrot' (pear bread) of the Grinsons.

Switzerland

Among favourite souvenirs from Germany are cuckoo clocks, dolls in traditional local costume, beer mugs (though these, strictly speaking, are not appropriate to the wine-drinking Rhineland) and wine-glasses (particularly the type with a brown or green coiled stem known as a 'Römer'). Records (mainly folk music) are also popular. Baden produces excellent schnapps (Kirschwasser, Himbeergeist, etc.). One celebrated product of the Rhine is genuine eau de Cologne (Kölnisch Wasser; noted brands are Farina and 4711).

Federal Republic of Germany

Alsace is well famed for its pottery; the painted ware is not only decorative but also stands up very well to daily use. A special place is occupied by French culinary specialties, which are available in wide variety, often tinned or otherwise preserved: meat and liver pâtés, honey from the Vosges, fruit brandies, etc. Cognac may not be such a good buy, since prices in France are high because of the heavy excise tax.

France

Typical Dutch clogs are to be found everywhere. Delft pottery (usually blue on a white ground) is world-famous. For those who are prepared to spend rather more there are silverware and diamonds.

Netherlands

Among Belgian products worth looking out for are jewellery, copperware, pottery, crystal, textiles and lace (Brussels lace being particularly renowned).

Belgium

Telegraph and telephone services

→ Postal, telegraph and telephone services

Time

All the countries bordering the Rhine are on Central European Time, one hour ahead of Greenwich Mean Time. Central European Summer Time applies during the summer; this is one hour ahead of British Summer Time, but the starting and finishing dates may not be the same.

Tipping

In hotels and restaurants a service charge is now almost invariably included in the bill. It is usual, however – if satisfied with the service given – to round up the amount of the bill.

No service charge is made on KD ships, but passengers usually leave something for the staff – again, if they are satisfied with the service – at the end of a cruise. An appropriate amount would be 4–5% of the fare, distributed between the cabin stewardess, the steward in the restaurant and any members of the staff who have given the passenger special attention.

Tourist information

KD agencies → Köln-Düsseldorfer (KD German Rhine Line), landing points

Switzerland

Central office

Schweizerische Verkehrszentrale (SVZ)
Bellariastr. 38
CH-8027 Zürich
tel. (01) 2 88 11 11

Basle

Offizielles Verkehrsbüro Basel
Schifflände/Blumenrain 2
CH-4001 Basel
tel. (0 61) 2 61 50 50

Zurich

Verkehrsverein Zürich
Information: Bahnhofplatz 15
CH-8023 Zürich
tel. (01) 2 11 12 56

Germany

Central offices

Deutscher Fremdenverkehrsverband (DFV)
Bertha-von-Suttner-Platz 13
D-53111 Bonn
tel. (02 28) 98 52 20

Deutsche Zentrale für Tourismus (DZT)
Beethovenstr. 69
D-60325 Frankfurt am Main
tel. (0 69) 7 57 20

Austria:
Deutsche Zentrale für Tourismus e.V. (DZT)
Schubertring 12
A-1010 Wien
tel. (01) 5 13 27 92

Belgium:
Office Allemand du Tourisme /
Duitse Nationale Dienst voor Toerisme
rue A. De Boeckstraat 54–56
B-1140 Bruxelles
tel. (02) 2 45 97 00 and 2 45 98 08

Canada:
German National Tourist Office /
Office National Allemand
du Tourisme
175 Bloor Street East
North Tower, 6th floor
Toronto, Ontario M4W 3R8
tel. (4 16) 9 68 15 70

Denmark:
Danmarks Touristråds hovedkontor
Vesterbrogade 6 D III
DK-1620 København V
tel. 33 12 70 95/96

France:
Office National Allemand
du Tourisme
9, Boulevard de la Madeleine
F-75001 Paris
tel. (1) 42 86 02 17

Great Britain:
German National Tourist Office
Nightingale House,
65 Curzon Street
GB-London W1Y 7 PE
tel. (0 71) 4 95 39 90/91

Italy:
Ente Nazionale Germanico
per il Turismo
Via Soperga 36
I-20127 Milano MI
tel. (02) 26 11 17 30

Centro de Turismo
Via Negri 8
I-20123 Milano MI
tel. (02) 87 73 23 and 86 13 83

Japan:
German National Tourist Office
Deutsches Kultur-Zentrum (OAG-House)
7-5-56 Akasaka, Minato-ku
J-Tokio 107
tel. (03) 35 86–03 80

Practical Information

Netherlands:
Duits Verkeersburo
Hoogoorddreef 76
NL-1101 BG Amsterdam Z.O.
tel. (0 20) 6 97 80 66

Slovenia:
Predstavništvo
DZT
Slovenska c. 58
SLO-6100 Ljubljana
tel. (0 61) 31 42 42

Spain:
Oficina Nacional Alemana de Turismo
San Augustín 2
Plaza de las Cortes
E-28014 Madrid
tel. (01) 4 29 35 51 and 4 29 58 77

Sweden:
Tyska Turistbyrån
Birger Jarlsgatan 11
S-10392 Stockholm
tel. (08) 6 79 50 95

Switzerland:
Offizielles
Deutsches Verkehrsbüro
Talstr. 62
CH-8001 Zürich
tel. (01) 2 21 13 87

United States of America:
German National Tourist Office
11766 Wilshire Boulevard
Suite 750
Los Angeles, CA 90025
tel. (2 13) 5 75-97 99

122 East 42nd St.
52nd floor, Chanin Bldg.
New York, NY 100168-0072
tel. (2 12) 3 08-33 00

In other countries ask for information at Lufthansa German
Airlines offices.

Ask for detailed information at the main ports of call of KD ships
in Germany at the following local tourist offices:

Speyer

Städtisches Verkehrsamt
Maximilianstr. 11
D-67346 Speyer
tel. (0 62 32) 1 43 92

Mannheim

Städtischer Verkehrsverein
Bahnhofplatz 1
D-68161 Mannheim
tel. (06 21) 10 10 11

Verkehrsamt
Rheinstr. 16
D-65385 Rüdesheim
tel. (0 67 22) 29 62

Information at Rüdesheim

Tourist Information
Oberstr. 118
D-56154 Boppard
tel. (0 67 42) 38 88

Boppard

Verkehrsamt
Rathausstr. 8
D-56338 Braubach
tel. (0 26 27) 97 60 00

Braubach

Städtisches Verkehrsamt
Pavilion at Main Station
D-56068 Koblenz
tel. (02 61) 3 13 04

Koblenz

Verkehrsamt der Stadt Köln, next to the cathedral
Unter Fettenhennen 19
D-50667 Köln
tel. (02 21) 2 21 33 45

Cologne

Verkehrsverein
Konrad-Adenauer-Platz / Immermannhof
D-40210 Düsseldorf
tel. (02 11) 17 20 20

Düsseldorf

France

Secrétariat d'Etat au Tourisme
8, avenue de l'Opéra
F-75001 Paris
tel. (1) 42 96 10 23

Central offices

Auskunftsbüro Berlin
Keithstr. 2–4
D-10787 Berlin
tel. (0 30) 2 18 20 64

Direktion für die Schweiz
Löwenstr. 59
CH-8023 Zürich
tel. (01) 2 21 35 78

Office du Tourisme de Strasbourg
10, place Gutenberg
F-67000 Strasbourg
tel. (88) 52 28 28

Strasbourg

Netherlands

Nederlands Bureau voor Toerisme (NBT)
Vlietweg 15
NL-2266 KA Leidschendam
tel. (0 70) 3 70 57 05

Central offices

Tourist information, Netherlands (continued)	Niederländisches Büro für Tourismus (NBT) Hohenzolllernring 38–40 D-50672 Köln tel. (02 21) 25 70-3 83
	Niederländisches Büro für Tourismus (NBT) Talstr. 70 CH-8001 Zürich tel. (01) 2 11 94 82
Nijmegen	VVV Rijk van Nijmegen St. Jorisstraat 72 NL-6511 NH Nijmegen tel. (0 80) 22 54 40
Rotterdam	VVV Rotterdam Coolsingel 67/Hoek NL-3012 AC Rotterdam tel. (0 10) 4 02 32 00
Amsterdam	VVV Amsterdam Stationsplein 10 NL-1012 AB Amsterdam tel. (0 20) 5 51 25 12

Belgium

Central offices	Vlaams Commissariaat-Generaal voor Toerisme 61, rue du Marché aux Herbes (Grasmarkt) B-1000 Bruxelles tel. (02) 25 04 03 90
	Belgisches Verkehrsamt Berliner Allee 47 D-40212 Düsseldorf tel. (02 11) 32 60 08
	Tourismuszentrale Mariahilfer Str. 121 A-1060 Wien (Vienna)
	Belgisches Verkehrsamt Aeschenvorstadt 48–50 CH-4051 Basel tel. (0 61) 23 77 95
Antwerp	Dienst voor Toerisme Grote Markt 15 B-2000 Antwerpen tel. (03) 2 32 01 03 Information Office at Central Station Koningin Astridplein tel. (03) 2 33 05 70

Tourist season

→ When to go

Travel documents

Nationals of the United Kingdom, United States and Common-
wealth countries require only a valid passport for a tourist visit
to the countries bordering the Rhine.

Visitors travelling in their own car must carry their driving licence and the car's registration document. Cars must bear the
oval nationality plate. It is advisable (in France obligatory) to
have an international insurance certificate (green card).

Passengers on KD cruises are requested to deposit their pass-   N.B.
ports or identity cards at the purser's office on joining the ship.
All passengers will be issued with a card, written in several
languages, identifying them as passengers on a KD ship.

Travel to the Rhine

International airports

The following airports offer convenient points of access to the
Rhine:

Zurich (Kloten) Airport   Switzerland
11 km north of city centre

Rhein-Main Airport, Frankfurt am Main   Germany
12 km SW of city centre

Cologne-Bonn (Wahn) Airport
17 km SE of Cologne city centre

Düsseldorf Airport
8 km N of city centre

Amsterdam (Schiphol) Airport   Netherlands
10 km SW of city centre

Brussels National Airport   Belgium
12 km NE of city centre

Main ports of call of KD ships

KD agencies → Köln-Düsseldorfer (KD German Rhine Line),
landing points

Airports:	Basle-Mulhouse-Freiburg EuroAirport (8 km NW)	Basle
	Zurich (70 km E; airport bus service)	(CH)
Railway	Badischer Bahnhof (German Railway);	
stations:	Bahnhof SBB (Swiss Federal Railways)	
Motorways:	A 5 (Germany); N 2 (Switzerland); A 35 (France)	
Airport:	Strasbourg-Entzheim (12 km SW)	Strasbourg
Railway station:	Strasbourg	(F)
Motorways:	A 5 (Germany); A 4, A 35 (France)	

Practical Information

Travel to the Rhine, Speyer (D)	Airport:	Frankfurt am Main (80 km N)
	Railway station:	Speyer
	Motorway:	A 61
Mannheim (D)	Airport:	Frankfurt am Main (60 km N)
	Railway station:	Mannheim
	Motorways:	A 5, A 6, A 61, A 65, A 656, A 659
Rüdesheim (D)	Airport:	Frankfurt am Main (50 km E)
	Railway station:	Rüdesheim
	Motorways:	A 60, A 61
Boppard (D)	Airport:	Frankfurt am Main (100 km E)
	Railway station:	Boppard
	Motorway:	A 61
Braubach (D)	Airports:	Frankfurt am Main (90 km E)
		Cologne-Bonn (80 km N)
	Railway station:	Braubach
	Motorways:	A 48, A 61 (to Koblenz)
Koblenz (D)	Airports:	Frankfurt am Main (100 km E)
		Cologne-Bonn (70 km N)
	Railway station:	Koblenz
	Motorway:	A 48, A 61
Cologne (D)	Airport:	Cologne-Bonn (17 km SE)
	Railway station:	Cologne
	Motorways:	A 1, A 3, A 4, A 57, A 59, A 555
Düsseldorf (D)	Airport:	Düsseldorf (8 km N)
	Railway station:	Düsseldorf
	Motorways:	A 3, A 44, A 46, A 52
Nijmegen (NL)	Airport:	Amsterdam (100 km NW; airport bus service)
	Railway station:	Nijmegen
	Motorways:	A 50, A 52
Rotterdam (NL)	Airport:	Amsterdam (60 km N; airport bus service)
	Railway station:	Rotterdam
	Motorways:	A 13, A 15, A 16, A 20, A 29
Amsterdam (NL)	Airport:	Amsterdam (9 km SW)
	Railway station:	Amsterdam
	Motorways:	A 2, A 4, A 6, A 7, A 8, A 9
Antwerp (B)	Airport:	Brussels (40 km S)
	Railway station:	Antwerp
	Motorways:	A 1, A 13, A 14

Water sports

Motor and sailing boats

The Rhine is one of Europe's most important waterways, and the use of the river by craft of all kinds is controlled by the Inland Waterways Regulations (Binnenschiffahrtsstrassenordnung). Skippers of sailing boats with auxiliary motors or motor boats of over 3.68 kW (5 h.p. DIN) must have a licence ('Sportbootführerschein') issued by the German Sailing Club

(Deutscher Segler-Verband) or the German Motor Yacht Club (Deutscher Motoryachtverband). For vessels over 15 tons a special licence ('Sportschifferpatent') is required.

On Lake Constance it is necessary to have a special licence ('Bodenseeschifferpatent') for motor boats over 4.41 kW (6 h.p. DIN) and sailing boats with a sail area over 12 sq.m.

Canoes and kayaks

The beautiful scenery bordering the river and the excellent maintenance of the river bed make the Rhine an attractive stream for canoeing enthusiasts, with facilities for camping on the islands. The German Canoe Club (Deutscher Kanu-Verband) has established many boathouses, hostels, camping sites and canoe stations up and down the river, details of which are given in "Das Deutsche Fluss- und Zeltwanderbuch".

Information and advice on the facilities for water sports on the Rhine can be obtained from the motoring organisation ADAC (Allgemeiner Deutscher Automobilclub). Many maps of the Rhine for the use of navigators are available in bookshops.

Fishing

Fish stocks in the Rhine have been decimated to an alarming degree by heavy pollution of the river. In quite recent years, however, the efforts made to reduce the volume of harmful substances discharged into the Rhine have begun to bear fruit. The most promising waters for the angler are the arms of the Old Rhine. It is necessary to have a fishing licence and also a permit from the owner of the fishing rights.

Weather

→ Facts and Figures, Climate

When to go

The best time for a trip to the Rhine is from mid May to the beginning of October – though it should be borne in mind that there is very heavy tourist and holiday traffic in July and August. In the early spring the banks of the Rhine and most of its tributaries are largely bare, since they lack the enlivening green of the vines. The period of the vintage, towards the end of October, is still attractive, although there may frequently be misty weather at this time of year.

Youth hostels

Accommodation for young people at reasonable prices is provided by youth hostels. As a rule the maximum stay in any hostel is limited to three nights (though it may be possible to stay longer if the hostel is not full). Advance booking is always advisable, and during the main holiday season it is essential. Youth hostellers must have a membership card issued by their national youth hostels association or an international visitor's card.

Index

Index

Index